The Politics of Trade in
Latin American Development

STEVEN E. SANDERSON

The Politics of Trade in
Latin American Development

STANFORD UNIVERSITY PRESS
STANFORD, CALIFORNIA 1992

Stanford University Press
Stanford, California

© 1992 by the Board of Trustees of the
Leland Stanford Junior University

Printed in the United States of America

CIP data are at the end of the book

To Rosalie

Acknowledgments

FOR THE RESEARCH leading to this book, I received support from the Council on Foreign Relations / National Endowment for the Humanities International Affairs Fellowship Program, through which I spent 1984–85 in the Office of Trade Policy Development, Office of the U.S. Trade Representative. Additional support was provided thanks to Senior Assistant Trade Representative Geza Feketekuty and Deputy Assistant Trade Representative Richard Self. Many others in the Office of the U.S. Trade Representative were helpful, including Harvey Bale, Robert Fisher, and especially Bernard Ascher, whose friendship and tremendous professional command of trade policy caused him to suffer endless questions from my corner.

From 1985 to 1987, while I was in Brazil with the Ford Foundation, I had the opportunity to consult with many trade specialists in and out of government. Professors Marcelo de Paiva Abreu, Dionisio Dias Carneiro, and Winston Fritsch of the International Economics Faculty of the Pontificia Universidad Católica of Rio de Janeiro were particularly enjoyable company, and their work on trade policy from various Latin American perspectives helped shape some of the ideas in this book. In the Ford Foundation, my friends Kathryn Burns and Peter Fry were constant inspirations. The office staff of the Foundation deserve special thanks for the informal education about Brazil. Suzana Delgado helped my research admirably and deserves special thanks.

In 1987–88, the Heinz Endowment supported a second phase of my research through its grant program for research in Latin American economic issues. Under that grant, I was able to continue the difficult task of amassing some consistent data on trade and to travel to various Latin American countries for that purpose. Thanks are due especially to preliminary readings and criticism from participants in the Heinz Endowment Latin American Research Seminar at the University of Pittsburgh in April 1988.

Also important were the help and criticism of many individuals who read part or all of the material, suggested additions to the bibliography, and endured periodic howls from my office. First and foremost, William C. Smith, Ana Doris Capistrano, and Charles Wood read the entire manuscript and improved it greatly. Keith Alger, Thomas O. Bayard, and Michael Shifter also read parts and helped me think through various topics. The turn toward resource politics as an angle on trade I owe in part to my association with Professors Kent Redford, Marianne Schmink, and Charles Wood of the University of Florida, and John Robinson, Director of Wildlife Conservation International.

Research assistance from Gamaliel Perruci and Debra Rose was invaluable. Both of them were with this project for at least two years and contributed to its organization and development. They became intellectual colleagues over this period, too, and braved many drafts to offer good criticism and new data. Amelia Álvarez helped push this project through its final stages.

Grant Barnes at Stanford University Press also deserves acknowledgment. He encouraged me to publish with Stanford and showed the patience to wait for it to happen. Since he was also responsible for acquiring and producing my dissertation as a book a decade ago, he has had an especially important role in bringing my writing to public light.

My family was not much help at all this time. April and Robert distracted me from work with regular reminders of the pleasures and horrors of parenthood. Rosalie competed for writing time on the computer, all the while acquainting me with the leading edge of computerized data-base reference and easing the task of keeping up with rapid political change. All three reduced my concentration and pretended not to understand why I would trade the obsessions of family life for more solitary alternatives.

I am privileged to dedicate this book to Rosalie, whose companionship has made the last two decades indescribably richer. Despite her coolness toward Maria Callas, I will invoke Cavaradossi's ode to Tosca:

> Ogni cosa in te mi piace—
> L'ira audace
> E lo spasimo d'amor!

S.E.S.

Contents

Tables and Figures   xi

Introduction   1

1. Trade Power and National Development in Historical Perspective   12

2. Connecting Trade to Development, Tempered by Adjustment   40

3. Natural Resource Politics, Trade, and Development   70

4. National Power and the Structure of Latin American Trade   107

5. National Power, the Multilateral Agenda, and Trade with the United States   139

6. National Goals for Latin American Trade Politics: Issues of Insulation and Autonomy   177

Conclusion   212

Notes   221

Bibliography   255

Index   281

Tables and Figures

Tables

1.1 Latin American Terms of Trade, 1983–88   15

3.1 Natural Resource Production Growth Rates Compared with General Economic Growth and Exports, Selected Countries, 1961–89   96

3.2 General Trade Coefficients Compared with Natural Resource Trade Coefficients, Selected Countries, 1980–87   98

3.3 Agriculture, Fishing, Forestry, and Hunting as a Percent of GDP, Selected Countries, 1980, 1983–87   99

4.1 Ranking Latin American and Caribbean Countries by Openness   117

4.2 Hirschman Indexes of Geographic Trade Concentration by Latin American Country, Selected Years, 1960–88   118–19

5.1. Domestic Production, Imports, Exports, and Consumption of Cereals in Latin America, 1980–88   149–51

5.2. Latin American Trade Balances with the United States and the OECD, Selected Years, 1975–88   158–59

6.1 Room for Maneuver in Trade Politics: Latin American Countries Ranked on the Three Criteria of Size of GDP, Openness, and Value Added in Manufacturing   185

6.2 The Share of Agriculture and Manufacturing in GDP and Exports, Selected Latin American Countries and Years, 1960–88   190

6.3 Growth in Value Added by Sectors, Selected Countries, 1960–89   191

6.4 Coefficients of Exports, Imports, and Total Trade, Latin America, 1970, 1980, and 1988   192

xii   *Tables and Figures*

6.5   Latin American Trade Balances, 1980–89   200
6.6   Value Added by Government, Latin America, 1980–89   204

Figures

2.1   A Hirschman-Lewis Test of Development Thinking   55
4.1   State Presence and Economic Orientation in Latin America   131
4.2   Government Presence and Economic Orientation in Latin
       America   132
6.1   Change in Openness and Public Sector Activity, Selected
       Countries of Latin America, 1970, 1980, 1988   208

The Politics of Trade in
Latin American Development

Introduction

IF THIS WERE A STUDY about trade policy, it would be born outdated. In recent years, the trade system has been constructed by a committee of architects, each representing a different, self-interested opinion about construction materials and techniques and even different hopes for the final edifice. Predictably, rich countries have been set against poor, free traders against protectionists, nationalists against internationalists—all sharing only the conviction that trade is worth fighting over. Trade consensus, which guided the postwar Bretton Woods system, has evaporated. Many have argued that the proliferation of voices on the issue of trade means the end to multilateralism and the evolution of a new order.

In 1990 alone, the global blueprints of trade policymakers were reconfigured by the December collapse of the GATT Uruguay Round, various regional initiatives for free trade in the Western Hemisphere, the Bush administration's Enterprise for the Americas announcement, and the Iraqi invasion of Kuwait. Throughout the year, OECD pretensions to global economic reorganization repeatedly slipped in the wake of the disintegration of Eastern Europe and spirited fights on the Continent over the nature of Europe after 1992. The resignation of Margaret Thatcher alone promises to change the future of the OECD. Latin American nations responded in widely different ways to changes of structure and circumstance, straining stereotypes and shortening the life of regional generalizations.

This book evolved out of a desire to make sense of the shifting sands of inter-American trade while resisting a current events focus that depends on constancy in an environment of change. It also stems from a more permanent disquiet with academic treatments of the relationship between trade and development in the political history of Latin America. For several years, I have approached Latin American trade politics from various angles and have found that the discipline-bound, issue-specific trade literature did not explain some important aspects of trade. Trade is considered to be a matter for international economic theory or for policy prescription, but the literature in neither field does justice to the social and political phenomena behind trade politics. U.S. foreign economic policy literature does not offer much help either, because it has turned to Latin America only in the debt crisis. Before that, chroniclers of the Bretton Woods system shunned the region with a consistency that mirrored the northern focus of the postwar system. There is little in the Latin American field with the sweep of Charles Maier's *Recasting Bourgeois Europe*, Richard Gardner's *Sterling-Dollar Diplomacy*, or the broad historical literature on Bretton Woods and the West. With few exceptions, diplomatic histories also avoided the analytical generalization the subject demands.

The gaps in past research led me to depart from the bulk of the literature that supports this study but to remain within an approach identifiable as historical political economy:[1] the study of the interconnections of politics and economics tinted with the infusion of historical context. That choice of an approach is compelling in its own right, as the monographic literature shows. Historical political economy permits us to cross over disciplinary boundaries and to use a broad range of overlapping literatures to explain the historical progression of events in Latin America. It also allows the use of different national historical narratives and the histories of "economic epochs" to validate theoretical propositions about development. The iterative nature of analyzing national histories in comparative perspective provides an implicit check against historicist fallacy and some of the more egregious pitfalls of case-based analysis.

Here, then, I will "poach" or "trespass" on different turfs, in development economics, international trade theory, and Latin American economic history. I am not a specialist in these areas, and I cannot pretend to convey to the reader the technical or intellectual dynamism of the specialists' literature. Instead, I have opted for a nontechnical elaboration of some of the themes we have in common. Fortunately, I have had much (occasionally bilious) advice from economists and historians.

My point was not to replicate those fields but to provoke new ways of thinking about trade politics in light of the rich literature that borders the field. The economic and political questions treated in this book require a synthesis of theory and historical experience that does not undermine the subtleties of either. The Latin American trade and development literature lacks a single theoretical, historiographical, or methodological center, and that compelled me to stitch a patchwork of pieces that draw from diverse works and traditions important to trade and development. Because the analytical critique that led to this book is important to the selection of those patches and how they were sewn together, it is only proper to lay out the origins of the critique at the beginning. Admittedly, the coherence of the argument that follows was more apparent at the end of the final draft than at the beginning.

One of the central framing questions behind the book is, Why does Latin America as a region consistently yield such a distinct view of "free trade" vis-à-vis trade theorists, partisans of the multilateral trading system, and, especially, the United States? Here, this question is reframed to ask what have been the *political* terms of trade in Latin America, and why have they differed so from the multilateral and national trade politics of the advanced capitalist countries, especially the United States? A conceptually adequate approach to this question helps us understand why, and with what limits, Latin America now (in 1991) seems ready to accept the mantle of free trade.

The quick rhetorical answers—that Latin America is "different" or has been exploited in trade relationships—are built on some obvious anecdotal premises that every student of the region can recite. But the student of trade politics trying to formalize the difference lands in the middle of one of the most interesting debates among postwar academic and development practitioners: whether different premises lie behind the political economy of development, and under what circumstances a "peripheral" country might use politics to advance its own foreign economic relations and domestic development purposes. Never mind for the moment the debate over whether center and periphery make sense as concepts in the new international division of labor.

I began to consider these questions systematically in the early 1980s in Washington, D.C., not because of the richness of the development debate, but because the "hall talk" in the Office of the U.S. Trade Representative (and in embassy offices, the U.S. Departments of Agriculture and Commerce, the International Trade Commission, and elsewhere) differed so radically from trade perspectives heard in Latin America. At the time, the anomalous Latin American attitude toward the Western trading system was engaged in Washington primarily as a political matter. The Reagan administration was paying passing attention to the "Latins" because they threatened to hold up the train of the new GATT round. In interviews and informal conversations from 1980 to 1985, U.S. trade officials showed disturbing zeal for "showing the Latins how to get their trade perspectives right" (that process invariably meaning conformity with U.S. free trade principles). For my part, I felt a regional specialist's natural urge to explain Latin America's reluctance to trade freely with the developed world in terms less biased and ungenerous than did the Reagan administration. My counter usually involved showing the "downside" of trade for Latin America or suggesting that such zeal might be better placed at the service of getting the U.S. trading machine in order.

For me, though, the policy approach soon lost its charm, not only because of the limited Washington perspective, but also because southern trade policymakers provided such poor ammunition. They seemed to show no better feel for what trade should do for their nations than did the cardinals of the GATT or the representatives of the U.S. executive branch. The positions of both North and South seemed too stylized and intransigent to portray the subtleties of trade politics, and the theoretical issues of optimal levels of protection or mechanisms for shifting the terms of trade were too abstract for the movers and shakers of trade policy bureaucracies. They seemed to think of trade for its own sake, and little else. The discussion of the purposes of trade beyond expanding the international system or generating scarce foreign exchange had become secondary. And the policy approach was too "output-oriented" and unconcerned with structure and input.

More importantly, the trade system was not working politically, in the sense that all sides seemed permanently aggrieved by outcomes and critical of the process itself. This was startlingly at odds with the ambitions of the Bretton Woods system, and it became interesting to look for the paths that had led to the abbreviation of trade optimism and the portent of trade conflict.

The key to national trade politics lies with the benefits it brings to the domestic economy, a shorthand notion of development. A logical first step in resolving the connection of trade to economic growth and ostensibly to development was to explore the academic literature on international trade policy, the technical language of which must be second only to that in the international arms and disarmament field. But the mainstream literature of international trade policy treats Latin America only in a derivative way, and treats neither the questions of development nor national sovereignty well.

Latin America's peripheral position in the geopolitical architecture of trade policy attests to the historical evolution of the Bretton Woods system and the North-North blinders of the United States as the "hegemon" of that system. Latin America represents the largest developing country group of trading countries outside the "Four Tigers" of East Asia. It counts among its largest economies Argentina, Brazil, Colombia, and Mexico, whose gross national products are on a rough par with those of Mediterranean Europe, and whose industrial plants are monuments to the most significant Third World industrialization experience outside the postwar occupied territories of Asia. At the same time, smaller countries in Central America and the Caribbean provide theoretically and politically important examples of economic openness, external sector weakness, vulnerability in foreign exchange, dependence on primary commodities, and extremely complicated connections between politics and economic development—all linked to external trade. Whether in those small countries, or in Peru and Chile, with their own models of international exchange and domestic economic growth, Latin America has cases to spare for those committed to understanding the meaning and impact of trade policy, rather than merely its political value in the GATT.

To improve on the trade policy literature requires a treatment not hopelessly wedded to multilateralism and Bretton Woods or to a West-West orientation. It demands that we turn the tables on the policy literature by devoting more attention to Latin American cases and putting politics before policy, instead of the other way around. Theory and structure must inform process. And such a study must make the heretofore missing link between the rich historical experience of postconquest Latin America, the complex trade data, the domestic development problems of the twentieth century, and the politics of North-South relations.

This is nothing short of a social science grail quest, well beyond the scope of one volume. But in partial response to these gaps, I began this study by taking an inventory of useful elements of the otherwise rich trade literature. The hope was to construct Latin America–specific orientations that might be persuasive, at least in argument, to trade analysts who otherwise would look at Latin America only in response to Brazilian informatics protection or U.S. pharmaceutical companies' lobbying against new Mexican drug legislation, the U.S.-Mexican bilateral negotiations, or some other episodic catalyst for U.S. policy. These themes, I thought, could serve as an integrative challenge to Latin Americanists, comparativists, and students of international relations to engage in "open system" comparative politics when thinking of development issues and to fashion a new development optic respectful of the mainly economic analysis of traditional literature, but appropriate to the political dimensions of trade, as the millennium approaches.

Multilateral trade policy currently has little to do with national development concerns, beyond the stylized and by now little-examined conviction that more trade means more national welfare, economic efficiency, capital flows, and other measures of economic progress. This attitude is revealed most clearly in the current U.S.-Mexico bilateral free trade negotiations, in which trade policymakers' concerns that a prospective agreement "not become a legislative Christmas tree" translates into a trade-obsessed agreement not taking into account the long-term problems of adjustment on either side.

This view reveals a lack of consensus on what the relationship between trade and development might be, even after more than a century of expanded trade between the U.S.-European "core" and the Latin American "periphery." Thus recasting trade politics starts with a long process of reconsidering the connection of trade to development. To anticipate the argument a bit, it also means bringing the development debate forward theoretically.

A first task is to take the gains from trade and their relation to policy a step back from the level of religious ejaculation, through which ideological free traders in the U.S. executive branch and international trade economists endorse free trade rather uncritically, and Latin American economic nationalists and *dependentistas* disavow it with equal intensity. Reappropriating trade politics from a prosaic trade policy framework demands a reexamination of the historical evolution of Latin American trade politics, a *reconstruction* of the connection of trade politics to economic growth, and a new regional and country-specific *deconstruction*, which separates the real problems of today's trade from the hoary litanies of foreign policy bureaucracies.

The most appropriate place to begin such a reexamination is the literature of development economics, especially the broad-gauged economic histories that have generated so much of our learning from that field. Paul Streeten has called for a "finer typology of countries and regions," "multidisciplinary work at the deepest level," and a strengthened historical dimension to our analysis of economic development.[2] Although I will leave an evaluation of the fineness, depth, and strength of this study to future critics, the cross-disciplinary diachronic mission is a serious one. Classics such as Albert O. Hirschman's *National Power and the Structure of Foreign Trade*, W. Arthur Lewis's *Growth and Fluctuations*, and Maier's *Recasting Bourgeois Europe* are a fundamental class of source books for such an analysis, as are some of the key regional works, from Paul Drake's *Money Doctor in the Andes* and Richard Graham's *Britain and the Onset of Modernization in Brazil*, or James Scobie's *Revolution on the Pampas*, to Stanley Hilton's *Brazil and the Great Powers*, Lorenzo Meyer's *Mexico and the United States in the Oil Controversy*, and John Wirth's *Politics of Brazilian Development*. Important also are more general works such as Celso Furtado's *Economic Development of Latin America*, Hirschman's *A Bias for Hope*, and a recent series of volumes on the economic history of Latin America in the international context.[3] This aspect of the research coincided nicely with a(nother) reconsideration of development economics, led by the excellent two-volume retrospective *Pioneers in Development*, edited by Meier and Seers.

The development economics literature suffers its own lacunae. This study undertakes a reconsideration of development economics just at the time of its funeral in the United States. Much of the most promising work now comes from Latin America, but in somewhat spotty fashion and with less comparative design.[4] Besides the alleged "poverty of development economics,"[5] other problems appear in the literature that will take a good part of this text to elaborate: the poor connections between international and domestic economic change, the even less robust analytical link between economic change and politics, and the hopelessly remote connection between sectoral change and improvement in people's livelihoods, that is, a connection between the study of development economics and daily life.

As to the former, Lewis will remark parenthetically that a country facing a trade-led transformation to industrialization would have to overcome internal political obstacles to move away from overspecialization in primary products.[6] But as a parsimonious economist, he fails to specify the political processes that might overcome the obstacles or to detail the political texture of the transition experience itself. That parsimony has carried over to some key works of the 1980s, in which politics through even the most politically sophisticated economists' eyes are seen to be a "non-price rationing device."[7]

Hirschman, whose great book *National Power and the Structure of Foreign Trade* deserves periodic rereading, makes some noble attempts to associate political questions with economic ones, but at the international level. In his many other "trespasses" in trade and development politics, the political side is less case-specific than analytically powerful and, for the most part, historically removed from current cases. Succeeding chapters of this book will try to relate his analytical observations to specific empirical circumstances of today's Latin America.

Ultimately, this book focuses on the politics implied by development economics when applied to the trade problems of today's Latin America. In retrospect, the poor connection of the more general trade scholarship to Latin America should have alerted me to the possibility that this focus also would run into shortcomings in the literature. Most importantly, it seems that the weight of the debt crisis has crushed the critical search for "genuine" development that so preoccupied the study of Latin American political economy in the 1960s and 1970s. Concern for the alleviation of poverty as the centerpiece of public responsibility apparently has given way to "getting prices right," subjecting public initiative to the efficiencies of the market, and stabilizing the external accounts. Moreover, the entire tradition of state-led development in Latin America has been dismissed in the new drive toward privatization, partly stimulated by the recognized fiscal insolvency of the Latin American state. From the World Bank and International Monetary Fund to U.S. government and commercial bank "conditionality," the password to debt resolution is reducing the public sector deficit, eliminating "inefficient" public sector enterprises, and "freeing" the forces of the market to "correct" populist distortions in macro-economic policy.

These carefully chosen descriptors of stabilization suggest a far more promising relationship that Latin American countries actually have found in the IMF embrace. They also conveniently forget the historical legacy of U.S. macroeconomic policy itself, at least during the New Deal years. After all, while the Bretton Woods institutions were being laid out on the drawing boards of Washington, D.C., the U.S. government was enthusing over economic planning for the public sector.[8]

But the movement away from broad-spectrum public sector development planning for poverty alleviation and growth is a product of the international system's growing impatience with Latin American skepticism about trade and the surprising vigor with which new Latin American governments embrace free trade. Whereas the economic nationalism of the 1940s to 1960s encouraged the belief that development was a sovereign hedge against the untrammeled power of the international market, now from Chile to Mexico, trade policy reform has moved in a neoliberal direction. What would have been called *entreguista* heresies of the 1960s and 1970s have been converted into policy today. Mexico at the height of oil boom nationalism refused to join the GATT in 1980. In 1985 Mexico reversed its field and the next year joined the GATT. In 1990, Mexico pushed the United States to accelerate bilateral free trade. Chile is trading freely as never before, even signing the most liberal patent protection agreement in Latin America, to the delight of politically conservative free traders the world over. Argentina and Brazil, traditional trade rivals, have embraced the concept of a regional free trade agreement in the Southern Cone. President George Bush's Enterprise for the Americas initiative, connecting debt, development, and free trade, was embraced by virtually every chief executive in the region. The virtues of the market are sung in every corner.[9] Structural adjustment is referred to as "economic revolution." And the erstwhile "black sheep" of economic nationalism—Argentina, Brazil, and Peru—have abandoned their statist apostasy.

The puzzle is not how Latin American governments came to such a conversion. The failures of state-led growth are horrendous; the pressures of the external payments crisis have been crushing; and ideological liberation in the cases of Argentina (1976–78) and Chile (1973 to the present) has sometimes come at the point of a gun. But the internationalists' victory may be short-lived. The balance between "internationalist" and "nationalist" political forces has swung several times over the twentieth century, each gaining ascendance with the momentary exhaustion of the other. A historical perspective is necessary to appreciate that such occasional broad swings in trade and development politics are not unprecedented, and that they are profoundly connected to the health of the international economic system. It is also worth remembering that populist economic nationalism, declared dead in the wake of the bureaucratic-authoritarian juggernaut (itself now mortally ill), is resurging. The momentary victories of neoliberalism in trade and macroeconomic policy do not spell the demise of nationalist political agendas, and the future of trade politics in the hemisphere must take into account the dynamics and relative strengths of both nationalists and internationalists.

Much of the text that follows addresses the interstices among all these concerns. It is an attempt to use some of the most provocative hypotheses from the international trade, development, regional economic history, and resource management literatures to link them to national politics in Latin America. To make those connections requires a tour of the literatures themselves, in this case a somewhat abbreviated one because of the size and complexity of the bibliography. So, even though much attention is paid to diverse intellectual traditions in international relations and Latin American affairs, the reader should expect a representative and not an exhaustive bibliography from each. The individual country literature inevitably has suffered in the cross-national reach of this study.

The sum of this list of *inquietudes* has led to an attempt to refashion old approaches to the politics of trade in Latin American development. What this study does attempt is a new look at old academic acquaintances and a careful criticism of the received knowledge on trade, as well as some new data, documents, and indexes. Many of the bibliographic building blocks used here are familiar to many readers likely to be interested in this book; but the elements are not used in this mix elsewhere, as far as I know. It is not necessarily the literature on Latin American trade that the reader will find to be new; but the other literatures, of resource conservation, poverty alleviation, national development strategies, and so on, are ingredients in a revised look at the political economy of the region, steeping in the broth of trade.

The chapters that follow conceptualize the political terms of trade, to counter the purely economic focus of development policy. Defining the political terms of trade involves evaluating the meaning of development itself and reconnecting it to trade, including a new resource perspective on trade and development. In that context, traditional approaches assessing national interdependence/dependence as a way of evaluating the developmental gains from trade need a new look. Also, the current trend toward looking at constraints and possibilities in the trade system will be reshaped to ask familiar questions in a concrete empirical way. What changes in development design come from external shock, and under what conditions? Does the pressure of the international system actually force Latin

American countries to alter their rates and kinds of natural resource exploitation? With what variations? Can a political course of export promotion address the debt crisis effectively? Are the multilateral trade negotiations a useful format for Latin American trade and development problems? Can we say anything with authority about Latin America as a region?

In offering partial answers to those questions, this book suggests a way of looking at Latin American trade politics that combines trade policy, historical political economy, development economics, and ecological concerns. The main argument follows this sequence: historically, trade relations in Latin America have been a key currency of domination by the developed world, antedating direct foreign investment and surviving the loss of formal empire. The gains from trade under the best conditions in Latin America's past have accrued unevenly, provoking political conflict at the international level over the political terms of North-South trade, and at the domestic level over the distribution of the gains from trade (or no trade) for development. At the international level, trade politics continues to focus on U.S.–Latin American economic relations because the United States dominates Latin American trade and the international trade system embodied in the GATT. Political power or weakness resulting from trade affects Latin America's attempts to escape traditional trade policy conflict; and it cripples the development gains from trade that might accrue in a more equitable trade system. Latin America, in the grip of the debt crisis, is forced to trade more, even though it is mainly incapable of remarkable export improvements. The reallocation of economic resources to trade comes at the cost of domestic development, and often at the cost of nonrenewable natural resources. Those allocative decisions provoke further conflict at the international level and undermine a future of sustainable economic development for the poor. And all options for trade-linked development seem to lead to resource degradation and poverty.

Two further prefatory remarks are necessary. It is essential to recognize that none of these arguments reflects an uncomplicated chain, or a dynamic that can be modeled easily, especially in its political aspects. Latin America as a region is extraordinarily complicated, and even simple observations about trade seem to hide more mysteries than they pretend to explain. Policy mavens may ask for answers that fit, but trade is messy and inconvenient, precluding general answers to fluid, country-specific questions. In fact, the premise of this study is that answers are better fashioned after careful consideration of the questions they address. This is not a policy study; its somewhat dismal conclusions are intended neither to dramatize nor to downplay the difficult conditions facing Latin American trade.

Finally, the study is limited by the lack of precedent and the gross deficiencies in trade data. Even at the end of the project, there seems little reason to place much confidence in cross-national trade data, which sparks a concern that some of the arguments should rest very lightly on the evidence. Behind this final disquiet lie some difficulties in comparative analysis. There is little real effort to produce comparative empirical work on trade and development, except in studies at a meaninglessly aggregate level. Many comparativists, myself included, generally concentrate on case studies, only with extreme caution tiptoeing out of the case materials to make a comparative observation. This study is comparative to its roots. The data, the travel, the historical reading, and the typologies of trade policy all try to cross the difficult open ground between the conceptual quiet of the single case and the many tangles of comparative analysis. Whatever the limitations, it is hoped that future work on hemispheric trade politics will look beyond policy to consider some of the connections offered in these pages.

CHAPTER I

Trade Power and National Development in Historical Perspective

Benjamin Franklin argued that no nation was ever ruined by trade. Contemporary partisans of this left-handed praise for commerce continue the quest for the liberalization and expansion of trade, despite its failure to alleviate the debt crisis and domestic economic turmoil in Latin America.[1] Trade reform is the tonic prescribed by international economists and OECD trade policymakers, who continue to insist that more trade is better and that trade is a proper and even necessary "engine of growth" for most nations of the world. From the vantage point of the Northern Hemisphere, trade is the great revolutionary element in European exploration and conquest of the New World, the modernizing medium for traditional "low-output" societies, the vehicle for small nations' transcending their otherwise meager economic prospects. Trade in the modern world represents the international expansion of the market, the free contest among economic competitors whose shields are comparative advantage, economic efficiency, productivity, and growth.

These classical pillars of international political economy are remarkably durable. But in Latin America, where free trade began as the beacon of new national economies and a liberating force in the transition from colonial domination to independence, the liberal light has dimmed to a doubtful prospect for resolution of the modern debt crisis, even as it brightens as a policy tool for external sector balance and domestic economic growth.

For some time, Latin American scholars have questioned the connection of trade to development in general, and a diverse literature doubts the developmental worth of trade's legacy in Latin America.[2] Particularly important to this skepticism are the intellectual differences between "internationalists" and "developmentalists" in the academic community (and within the latter, those concerned with growth versus those emphasizing distribution).

The virtues of trade for development are not simply the subject of academic debate. Latin American governments have risen and fallen on the waves of international commerce. And because of the political association of expanded international trade with northern domination of the South—whether it be British free trade imperialism[3] or the U.S.-dominated Bretton Woods system—international trade in the Americas has had an uneven reputation. That reputation is subject to varying interpretations, by nationalists suspicious of expanded internationalism or internationalists suspicious of nationalist populism.[4] Perennially, political opportunism offers a new chance to reinterpret Latin America's trade history, whether it justifies a liberal economic foundation to Brazilian independence from Portugal or Mario Vargas Llosa's misfounded allegation that Peru has never had a free trade experience.[5]

For much of the post–World War II period, a consensus built on economic expansion overshadowed the debate between opposing camps. Particularly among politicians, it was rare to find internationalist ideologues as eloquent and uncompromising as the nineteenth-century Brazilian Anglophiles who lauded the conquest of free trade "over the wreckage of artificial obstacles created by governments,"[6] or nationalists so convinced of the potential of "delinking" their economies as to recommend closing their nations to trade completely. A reluctant pragmatism regarding trade replaced ideological rigor in Latin America. Trade policymakers sought to minimize vulnerability to external trade shocks, maximize the gains from trade, and simultaneously promote "infant industries" and "industries of transformation" that otherwise would not compete in open international markets. That pragmatism was the default option in a world of trade expansion. Whether or not it served the national economies of Latin America well, it prevailed. In its wake, the meaning of the longer-term historical legacy of Latin American trade politics appears to have been misplaced or forgotten.

Particularly among academic analysts of the role of trade in national development, contentious arguments have dissolved into "received ideas" largely unrelated to actual political choices. To the free trader, the efficiencies of international exchange in agricultural commodities make food security arguments nonsensical, even though food security was the agricultural development watchword of the 1970s. Many assume also that Latin American economies can "export their way out of debt," even though the export performance of the high-debt countries has not been steady, much less spectacular. And international economic sages still exhort the international system to maximize global production, irrespective of the environmental ravages of the late twentieth century. Virtually without exception, these positions display an unqualified aversion to the role of the state, which is considered to be a force against trade.

Among the critics of free trade, by contrast, international competition is assumed to threaten local artisan industry in Latin America, despite contradictory evidence from case studies. Likewise, critics of trade often continue to cite a secular decline in the terms of trade, even after a generation of criticism and qualification of the original Prebisch thesis.[7] Some authors caution that expanded exports are accelerating the depletion of nonrenewable natural resources, but studies that confront the extremely complex data and theoretical problems of demonstrating such a case are in short supply. Others advocate food security programs to reduce national vulnerability to world cereal markets, but they rarely model the trade-offs between cheap urban food policies and rural development, much less the trade-off between import substitution in agriculture and externalities such as deforestation. Opponents of the postwar trade system equate trade for debt relief with selling the national patrimony and often advocate an expanded role for the national state as a buffer against the forces of dependence and a stimulus to national development.

For all their familiarity, on closer examination none of these positions stands up without controversy. Artisan crafts, for example, may have suffered from increased competition but benefited from expanded economic activity that created new markets. At least some artisan industry in Colombia and Ecuador thrived despite (or because of) the nineteenth-century expansion of trade in manufactures. Markets, after all, are based partly on discriminating consumers who know the difference between superior Ecuadorean cacao, panama hats, and Colombian saddles and their competitors. Yet textile imports severely damaged the artisan weaving industry in Guatemala, and rising tariffs were unable to save it. In Peru, well-organized artisans stood for high tariffs, suggesting threats from both imports and import substitution. Only the rise of the working class tempered protectionist trade policy there.[8]

Evidence on the declining terms of trade is mixed, especially in the periods most central to the critique of neoimperialism it is usually trotted out to support. The terms of trade between Latin American exports and OECD exports to the region have varied by country and period and have been outrageously unstable during the past decade, as Table 1.1 shows. That at least raises questions about the validity of the terms-of-trade argument as a primary foundation for national development strategies. The common reduction of the terms-of-trade argument—that bilateral dependence is built on exploitative terms of trade—is not borne out in Latin America. Although the terms of trade for primary commodities have been generally negative for much of the last century, it is perfectly reason-

TABLE 1.1
Latin American Terms of Trade, 1983–88
(1980 = 100)

Country	1983	1984	1985	1986	1987	1988
Argentina	86	99	81	71	72	79
Bolivia	97	102	104	95	92	89
Brazil	78	86	84	91	82	86
Chile	84	78	73	79	83	101
Colombia	94	101	92	120	92	90
Costa Rica	86	90	88	106	94	100
Dominican Rep.	77	97	82	95	86	95
Ecuador	82	95	97	73	72	67
El Salvador	83	73	69	89	61	69
Haiti	66	83	88	99	91	96
Honduras	93	96	82	101	90	100
Mexico	77	76	72	52	57	52
Nicaragua	83	105	98	104	101	112
Paraguay	90	144	121	127	132	143
Panama	95	99	101	125	117	132
Peru	96	94	90	87	94	108
Uruguay	94	98	89	103	106	116
Venezuela	104	116	111	54	66	55

SOURCE: IDB, *Economic and Social Progress in Latin America: Savings, Investment, and Growth.*

able to argue that the stronger power in the bilateral relationship might be willing to suffer concessional terms of trade with the weaker partner so as to gain influence over the long term.[9] In fact, this assertion is validated historically in nineteenth-century Latin America, during the expansion of British free trade imperialism,[10] as well as in our own time with the Reagan administration's Caribbean Basin Initiative. In any event, the theoretical and empirical literature on the terms of trade, as with most of the other areas touched on above, is complex, case-specific, and inconclusive, where it does not clarify the political priorities that accompany the economic evidence. Unfortunately, because so little interdisciplinary work is conducted in the area of trade, the gap between empirical evidence and theoretical conviction is often filled with ideological disposition, not specific political alternatives.

Much of this material will receive attention in subsequent chapters. The point is that the Latin American historical record is important to making the case for trade. Sorting out the political terms of Latin American trade involves creating an interpretive historical, as well as theoretical, framework. That task is inherently controversial because it requires making political judgments about the effects of colonialism on postindependence Latin America; the evolution of British and then North American hegemony through trade; and economic nationalism as a set of political strategies by which Latin America could wrest itself from northern control. For the purposes of this study, the important threads to follow trace the problematic legacy of trade as a liberating and constraining influence on Latin American political history.

From Colonialism to Dependent Integration in the Nineteenth Century

The colonial system hangs over the modern trade system as part of the political culture of Latin American elites. It is no more likely that Latin Americans will forget the colonial legacy than it is that the United States will forget the Revolutionary War. Whatever the overall merits of colonial trade—and they vary widely by period and country—its political legacy is inescapably negative. Colonialism and its decline triggered the complex nineteenth-century international economic dynamics that dictated Latin American nations' roles in the trade system. Without exception, those countries have used trade politics as a development tool to rise above their condition. Trade politics stimulated the wars for independence from Spain, the national consolidation of fragmented Latin American societies, and the international projection of strong states in Latin America through international economic institutions. Trade politics was not always the first order of public dispute and not always decisive, but it was always part of the blueprints of Latin America's architects of independence. Today, as then, trade has helped shape national politics by separating the political platforms of nationalists and internationalists on a variety of macro-economic policy issues.

When the nineteenth century began, the colonial trade system was in the midst of Bourbon mercantilist reforms and stood witness to France's invasion of Spain and Portugal to isolate Britain from Continental trade. Britain, in response, looked to the New World, where it had asserted its trade power by treaty and competitive strength for a century. In late colonial Latin America, the conjuncture of these events meant the opportunity to season political and economic rebellion with a liberal flavor. Latin American nativists saw new opportunities to escape the constraints of the colonial system and to bypass Spain and Portugal in the expanding trade with Europe. Economic liberalism coincided to a certain extent with political liberalism, secular modernization, revolutionary constitutionalism, and the other progressive banners of the day.

Though it apparently would surprise such neoliberal politicians as Vargas Llosa, and even less historically inclined trade analysts in Washington, Latin America from 1800 to the Great Depression has been described as "the purest and most tenacious pole of liberal orthodoxy of the modern world economy."[11] The merchants and traders of the Latin American independence period were eager to join the free trade economy emerging outside the Spanish and Portuguese empires. As early as 1811, in Chile, laws were passed opening major ports to all trading nations, in direct challenge to the old order.[12] Free traders dominated much of the ideological discourse of the nineteenth century, even though national development objectives such as fiscal solvency and protection of traditional industries caused them to qualify their total dependence on the marketplace to create economic change.

The overall commitment of Latin America to liberal trade emancipation did not dissipate strong ideological tension and debate, however. All too quickly, liberal internationalism and nationalism became opponents in the battle over economic priorities facing the young nations of the hemisphere, an antagonism that continued in politics through the century.[13] As Richard Graham has pointed out, economic liberalism was at first a means by which the erstwhile colonies could free themselves from colonial dependence.[14] Later, as economic nationalists began to see the prospect of industrialization and the limits of free trade imperialism/dependence, free trade became inimical to nationalist development projects.

As early as the 1820s, opposition between economic liberals and nationalists began to appear, though it would not take full form until the close of the century in most countries.[15] In Argentina, tariff policy in 1835 turned on President Juan Manuel de Rosas's attempt to protect provincial interests without sacrificing the *estancia* economy. It gave the federalist cause credibility and satisfied a protectionist lobby that had already formed in opposition to *porteño* liberalism.[16] Later in the century, protectionism became more general, in the form of high tariffs. Colombia was divided over the meaning and the level of tariffs, resulting in divisions among "radical" and "moderate" liberals, as well as between exporters and the petit bourgeoisie.[17] Brazil and Mexico both eventually moved in the direction of high tariffs on manufactures at the very time they benefited most from the export advantages of the free trade system.[18] Even liberal Peru invoked high tariffs briefly at the end of the nineteenth century, which enhanced the returned value of foreign exchange and stimulated import substitution.[19]

In the longer term, international trade under the postcolonial international division of labor met with suspicion among Latin American nationalists and internationalists alike. Though postindependence trade became an integral part of twentieth-century Latin American economic life, it cast the shadow of an inconsistent and fickle contributor to national well-being and sovereignty. The boom-bust cycles of the nineteenth-century mining and tropical agricultural export enclaves distorted political processes and goals for economic growth of countries from Chile to Colombia to Mexico. And the political involvements of the hegemonic powers in Latin American affairs validated a permanent nationalist political legacy.

From the viewpoint of newly independent Latin American nations, nineteenth-century economic and political liberalism appeared as a continuous evolution of trade politics, rather than a revolutionary rupture. Presaged by late colonial economic reforms, independence liberalism traded Spanish monopoly for British market domination.[20] Though Latin American liberalism was viewed as the progressive standard opposing premodern society, that reputation depended to a great extent on the bankruptcy of its opponents.[21] Liberalism advocated the emancipation of private property from the clutches of the colonial corporations, the military, the church, and the Indians; the rationalization of government administration; the creation of a competent state apparatus to govern national territory; and the adaptation of national development to a new international economic order, led by foreign companies sculpting Latin America's role in international trade. Once free of the fetters of colonialism, the day-to-day political meaning of liberalism became murky, beyond the content infused by charismatic personalities operating under liberal flags.[22]

As far as Latin America was concerned, the two masters of that postcolonial trade system were the British and the Americans. Both embraced singular visions of free trade empire. Predictably, both were treated well by liberal economic history. "Free trade imperialism" under the British flag and the emerging hegemony of the United States in the Western Hemisphere were cloaked in relative peace and prosperity, in which the expansion of trade played the dominant role in the overall economic growth of the West.

In the British-dominated "old international division of labor," from 1870 to 1914, Latin America was seen to have fared well, at least on international dimensions.[23] The boost of trade helped national states become realities after the prolonged, miserable conflicts of the immediate postindependence period. Excepting Lima, many of the great cities of South America "arrived" on the crest of that trade boom. Buenos Aires, which started as a backwater to provision the viceroyalty of Peru and then eclipsed Lima after being declared a viceroyalty in 1776, became in the nineteenth century a metropolitan host to Mediterranean immigration, foreign capital investment, and European high culture, all from the staple wealth of the pampas.[24] Santiago, which had suffered along with Lima and Mexico City in the wake of the destruction of colonial mining, was resurrected by the nitrate and copper trade, creating fortunes that rivaled the largest in the hemisphere. São Paulo, a frontier outpost that boasted 31,000 inhabitants as late as 1872, became the coffee boomtown and financial heart of Brazil, growing to rival, then eclipse, Rio de Janeiro in economic importance. Bogotá sported opera, public spectacles, and fine fashions well before Manaus constructed its famous Opera House following the rubber boom. Even Guayaquil outstripped the growth of trade-isolated Quito, entering the unsteady Pacific trade in cacao and hats.[25]

Whatever the internal battles stirred by trade, there is little doubt that Latin American economic expansion in the late nineteenth century made trade the region's addiction until the 1930s. Even in the large economies, commodity exports were not only the backbone of growth but invariably constituted the skeleton of the fiscal system.[26] In Chile, taxes on the nitrate industry amounted to an average of 41.6 percent of total ordinary fiscal revenues over the period 1880–1924. In Peru, at the height of the guano trade in 1873, revenues from the guano monopoly totaled more than six times customs revenues. Together, customs receipts and guano amounted to more than 85 percent of total government revenue that year. In 1882, Buenos Aires customshouse receipts alone constituted 82 percent of total government revenues. In Brazil, the domination of coffee was complete, the momentary promise of rubber notwithstanding. Coffee was estimated to contribute 60 percent of foreign exchange and a similar proportion of fiscal revenue for the Brazilian government between 1870 and 1910. In Colombia, customs receipts in the 1860s accounted for over two-thirds of government revenue. In Mexico, as early as the 1820s customs revenues represented half of total government revenue, fifty years before the takeoff of the Porfirian trade boom.[27]

The meaning of this trade expansion for government was manifold. First, the governments of many Latin American countries—even Colombia, until its retreat from trade over the last quarter of the nineteenth century—were fiscally dependent on trade. Government expenditure became a direct function of the health of the international system, over which the individual Latin American countries had no control. Second, the public sector's involvement in trade, either through state commodity monopolies such as guano, tobacco, and sugar, or through export promotion designed to expand the fiscal base, ratified the interventionist tradition of the state in market activities, a tradition that already had been sustained for three centuries under colonial rule. Consequently, the state was held responsible for the economic well-being of the trading economy, and its values were reflected in such diverse areas as exchange rate and fiscal policies, or such novelties as the Brazilian valorization scheme in coffee. To the extent that state policy affected profit rates in the key commodities, it became a surrogate for modern income and economic development policies, as was particularly evident in the Chilean management of the northern nitrate and copper labor force.

The large economies managed state-market–international relations in more robust fashion than did the smaller countries, which were buffeted by the international market and interventionist powers. The Brazilian coffee boom laid the foundation for republican government, a more or less peaceful shift in the geographic center of gravity, and the growing role of the national state in the future of the economy. The Nicaraguan coffee expansion of the 1890s provided the political and fiscal wherewithal for political intrigue against Central American neighbors, ultimately contributing to the overthrow of the Zelaya government in 1909. The customshouse was seized by the United States for debt repayment, and a "national bank" was created under U.S. control.[28] At about the same time, both the Dominican and Haitian governments suffered U.S. customs receivership under the "dollar diplomacy" of bilateral debt agreements with the United States.[29] Those agreements were backed up with military force in the form of U.S. occupation for significant periods from 1915 to 1934.[30]

In the evolution of the notorious banana trade in Central America in the 1920s, managed prices stabilized the external accounts of Costa Rica, Guatemala, and Honduras, but also constituted a political surrogate to the national state in the corporate presence of United Fruit and its competitors. The isolated banana plantations were enclaves in the most profound sense, their banking, transport, and corporate decision-making all foreign-controlled. United Fruit as the symbol of imperialist domination in Central American "banana republics" stems partly from the incapacity of the Central American states to control export-dominated economic activity within their borders, as well as the fabled machinations of the banana barons.[31]

Other characteristics of pre–World War I trade expansion included the concentration of transportation in Latin America, in which British-led shipping conferences dominated the high seas. In 1890, British tonnage represented half the world's ocean freight and undercut competition through rate fixing, exclusive contracts, and collusion among major shippers.[32] Domestic railroad networks sprang up, but their purpose was to integrate the export sector in agriculture or mining to the ports shipping goods to Europe and the United States, not to complete a national system of infrastructure for national development. Railroads in Porfirian Mexico were intended to ship goods to the northern border and served other centers of population only as an afterthought.[33] In Honduras and Guatemala, track was laid from banana plantations to seaport, with little general spin-off to the host nation.[34] In Argentina, north-south rail networks were ignored in favor of linking the humid pampas to the entrepôt of Buenos Aires.[35]

Perhaps more galling than the foreign control of transportation was the fact that railroad networks—and regions—succeeded or failed on the international demand for the commodities they carried. São Paulo railroads succeeded because of the growing importance of coffee but failed to stimulate regional economies based on cotton. Northeastern railroads in the sugar zone failed because of unfavorable international market conditions. In Mexico and Argentina, the laying of rails paralleled the conquest of indigenous populations. And in Colombia, the coffee railroads, in the evocative prose of the time, either called the people to "well-being and liberty" or crushed them beneath their wheels. Nevertheless, politicians embracing economic liberalism and its demands for domestic development equated railroads with the mission of civilization, exulting over the material progress that would provide "the masses with prosperity and [eliminate] their misery and ignorance."[36]

Such enthusiasm over foreign influence was tempered by the growing power of foreign merchants in Latin America, who in the words of a Chilean observer, "suppressed our expanding commercial enterprise abroad, and in our own backyard eliminated us from international traffic, largely replacing us in every respect."[37] In fact, from 1882 to the Great Depression, foreign control over the export sector increased remarkably in Chile. (Chilean nitrate firms accounted for only 13.6 percent of sales in 1925.)[38] Likewise, in Brazil, foreign control lingered long after simple trade relations might indicate. After Brazil had shifted its coffee trade overwhelmingly to the United States in the 1910s, British merchants continued to dominate the trade. U.S. Steel dumped exports on the Mexican market to wreck Mexican domestic competition and concentrated the control of oil in northern Mexico under British and American flags. In Argentina on the eve of World War I, foreign capital represented half of all fixed capital stock, and 60 percent of railroad capital was Britain's alone.[39]

Nationalists, who, admittedly with some trepidation, had embraced British expansion at independence, now called upon the state to intervene for the sake of the national economy. Aggravating this nationalist tension were the attitudes of foreign entrepreneurs, who noisily suffered what has been described in the Peruvian case as "guano-weariness," complaining about the presence of the Latin American state and its power over trade.[40] This seems quite disingenuous, in light of the tendency by foreign entrepreneurs to create monopolies, cartels, and other combines to dominate the leading export sectors of Latin American economies and the relative helplessness of governments to stand in their way.

In any event, Latin American government grew in the late nineteenth century, mainly in the service of foreign expansion but also in response to new nationalist critiques of internationalist *entreguismo*. It was not surprising that government monopolies and regulatory agencies, with their modest capacities and broader political agendas, clashed with foreign merchants, who conspired on their own to create the great combines of the Western Hemisphere, whether they be the famous Meat Trusts of Argentina or lesser-known industrial associations, such as the United Alkali Company.[41]

The Nationalist Alternative to International Economic Crisis

As if nineteenth-century trade expansion were not problematic enough for Latin America, the collapse of international commerce in the Great Depression led to profound crises of legitimacy that changed the face of Latin American politics forever. The Depression for Latin America meant the end of confidence in primary commodity export markets, a rising and systematic skepticism about the durability of the international capitalist system, the consolidation of radical labor organizations throughout the hemisphere, the obsolescence of pre-Keynesian approaches to national monetary and fiscal policy, and a rift between North and South that would not be healed until well after World War II. In the process, the old order in Latin America, dominated by an old oligarchy linked to export-led growth, was swept away by new political forces.

The depth of the crisis that led to such upheaval cannot be overestimated, though national variation was tremendous.[42] Chile, as a small exporting country dependent on the well-being of international agriculture and industry, was particularly hard hit; the real value of its exports in 1932 was less than one-fifth that of 1929.[43] Victor Bulmer-Thomas argues that Central America rebounded relatively well, given the world economy and the region's traditional vulnerability to external shock. Even so, the lessons for Central America were typical of the region: recovery was a function of the ability to turn inward, which was dampened by the heavy penetration by foreign banana interests.[44] Import substitution (mainly in agriculture) supplanted export promotion, and domestically controlled crops outperformed those produced by foreign enclaves.

The large countries were different, as usual, though hardly exempt from hard times. Mexico was less affected because of the intensity of its revolutionary economic reorganization and the economic dislocation resulting from the revolution. Its turn inward was made more effective by a radical redistribution program in both incomes and property, as well as the nationalization of key economic assets. Argentina and Brazil benefited greatly from the special favor of Great Power competition for their trade in the mid-1930s.

National variation and episodic recovery in the late 1930s cannot dispel the images of trauma everywhere. Cordell Hull describes his arrival at the port of Santos, Brazil, in December 1933, commenting on "huge columns of smoke rising into the sky . . . [from] surplus coffee. . . . Tens of millions of dollars worth of coffee was changing into useless heat and smoke. It was a graphic commentary on the world's economic dislocation."[45] Throughout the region, exports fell by at least one-quarter between 1929 and 1932 and did not recover until World War II. Import capacity for Latin America as a whole dropped by 45 percent in three years. In extreme cases, such as Chile, the real value of exports fell by over 80 percent in the same three years. Governments were destabilized by the apparent failure of the old order, and radical opposition of various stripes appeared, enhanced by the evaporating legitimacy of the old international division of labor based on the success of externally generated growth.

The 1930s were a period of economic reordering and domestic retrenchment, reminiscent of Colombia's severe political changes in the late nineteenth century, as a product of the failure of trade to provide sustainable growth and development. The consequences of the changes of the 1930s did not become evident until the latter days of World War II, however, when domestic political upheaval throughout Latin America combined with a reconstruction of the international economic system under the new hegemony of the United States.

As World War II came to a close, Latin America was still reeling from the Depression, convinced of the poverty of the old international economic order and facing a new political agenda. This time, at least in the large economies, Latin America offered a broader, more complex array of social classes opposing the limits of the old order and a more ambitious state apparatus with which to treat national economic problems. In the 1930s, Chile had created an impressive public sector, led by the Corporación del Fomento (CORFO). Brazil had created the Estado Nôvo, whose fundament was state-led economic growth.[46] Argentina had overthrown the internationalists of the "infamous decade" and created the underpinnings of the Peronist economic "model." And Mexico, finally after more than two decades of economic upheaval, had reconstituted the national economy under *cardenismo*, led by public sector agrarian reform, the nationalization of foreign industries, and the inauguration of import-substitution industrialization led by infant industries.[47] In all of these countries, the new political realities reflected a fundamental transformation in social class composition in Latin America.

Equally important, these countries had broadened the political base to which the state responded. Populism, born in the 1920s in Uruguay and Peru, had swept its leaders into power in the Depression and war years: Lázaro Cárdenas in Mexico, Juan Domingo Perón in Argentina, and Getúlio Vargas in Brazil. The macroeconomic policies of Latin American populism were not so coherent as to justify lumping them together, but they did offer common ground: the consolidation of a multiclass political program to forward a design for national development.[48] Leaders of that design were the "new class"[49] of nationalist businessmen, who pushed for protection and state-led development; new labor unions that transcended the traditional craft base of union elitism; and, at least in Mexico and Central America, well-organized rural social organizations militating on behalf of redistribution of income and assets. Latin American populism was nationalist and import-substituting, either in agriculture or industry. It was built on the ruins of the international trade system and informed by the evolution of economic nationalist thinking in the wake of World War II.

The post–World War II period was colored by a combination of growing state intervention on behalf of populist class coalitions and decreasing confidence in the role of trade in national development politics. The proximate reason for Latin American "trade pessimism," which most notably generated the U.N. Economic Commission for Latin America "Prebisch thesis" on post–World War II development prospects, stemmed from the collapse of the trade system in the 1930s and the physical and economic devastation of the core trading nations of Europe in World War II. But in Latin America its roots are historically far deeper than the twentieth century. Several times during the nineteenth century, Latin American countries suffered from adverse terms of trade or external shocks to their trade systems. The debt crises of the nineteenth century, now more clearly understood in light of the stimulus to scholarship from present-day debt problems, made clear the dependence of Latin American trading nations on the stability of the international system for general economic well-being and even fiscal survival.[50]

Free trade liberalism had also come to represent a fetter on domestic industrialization in Latin America. Even though in Argentina, Brazil, and Chile industrialization began in the nineteenth century, British free trade imperialism worked against its success.[51] In the end, the old international division of labor did not operate purely on grounds of comparative advantage but on such familiar tools of empire as restraint of trade and investment, monopoly power, and the like. Latin American politicians for some time had been pursuing protection against imports through high tariff walls, and the credibility of free trade opposition to protectionism had continued to diminish in the Depression years. Similarly, Britain, through its Imperial Preference System, inaugurated in 1931, and the United States, with its traditional protectionism underscored by the 1930 Smoot-Hawley Tariff, showed their own skepticism of free trade, which certainly added fuel to nationalist fires in Latin America.

Accordingly, the virtual collapse of the international system in the Great Depression not only validated the more episodic pessimism of the nineteenth-century crashes but strengthened new economic forces on the Latin American political scene. In the first decades of the twentieth century, several economies, led by Argentina, Brazil, and Chile, had progressed industrially so that by the turn of the century São Paulo was described as "a forest of chimneys."[52] The forward linkages of primary commodity exports, particularly in temperate zone agricultural commodities,[53] not only stimulated immigration to Argentina and Brazil but offered an economic base for advocates of industrialization. In turn, agroindustries and other light manufactures helped create the structural base for the organization of labor and the evolution of working-class politics in the 1920s and 1930s.[54]

A leading study of the export sector and its domestic social impact argues that trade was especially relevant to the development of working-class politics in late nineteenth-century Latin America, though the cases treated are not confined to temperate zone agricultural economies and generally avoid the question of linkages.[55] This analysis converges well with the most serious empirical studies of such countries as Peru,[56] as well as Latin American structuralist interpretations of the role of trade, as evidenced in the work of such scholars as Celso Furtado.

The Furtado thesis discriminates among tropical, temperate, and mining economies. But the view is somewhat problematic, given the virtual absence of data on Central America,[57] the important additions of Charles Bergquist's work on Chile, the monographic work on industry integration in mining,[58] and the role of mining industry unions in the development of the Mexican Revolution. Nevertheless, the trade economy played a substantial role in developing the national bases for populism and import substitution in the 1930s and 1940s.

World war also strengthened the political influence of economic nationalists, despite the price boom the war represented for the primary commodity exporters. The war impelled import substitution in Latin America, both because of foreign exchange surpluses from war commodities and weakness on the import side from the reallocation of First World resources to the war effort. In both world wars, Latin America found its normal trade patterns somewhat abandoned. European markets were closed to normal traffic, and credits were strained to the maximum. As would later be true in the 1980s, the world wars meant a combination of import substitution and a reorientation of trade in favor of exports to the United States. Faced with global upheaval and endowed with trade-generated current account surpluses, Latin American nations institutionalized the turn inward that had begun with the shock of the Great Depression.

The use of domestic resources for industrialization most certainly would have lagged without the wars, and the post–World War II public philosophy of import substitution has its origins in the war boom. Domestically, the political ambitions of bourgeois parvenus, as well as the popular forces of displaced peasants and militant new unions, forced a shift in the political center of gravity away from the old oligarchy and its defenders in the traditional political system, toward the more "modern," urban political forces of populism. As in Brazil and Cuba, those shifts often implied at least a nominal commitment to bourgeois democratic values and a retreat from the previously fashionable corporatist authoritarianism that typified the Vargas Estado Nôvo or the traditional corporatist personalism of Jorge Ubico in Guatemala.

The Limited Menu of Political Choice

Today, Latin America is forced to favor growth and liberalization of trade, regardless of its political predispositions, because of the conditions of the debt crisis and the mechanisms of external stabilization and adjustment. We shall see in subsequent chapters that Latin American leaders approach trade with great suspicion. Constantly forced to resist a temptation to restrict trade, but often succumbing anyway, the Latin American leader is not simply unable or unwilling to understand the superior virtues of trade for the nation's well-being. Wrong is the argument often heard in Washington that Third World leaders are not up to the mark on matters of international trade, or that they are willing to sacrifice their countries' futures in free trade in order to oppose the United States out of some misbegotten notion of nationalism or *tercermundismo*. An alternative explanation is that trade with the OECD countries is so enormously complicated and difficult in its implications that two reactions ensue: to restrict trade per se, or, more commonly, to manage (often poorly) its extent and control its mechanisms. Never mind for the moment the possibility that Latin American nations pursue self-interested short-term strategies that do not embrace the ideology of free trade, while the OECD pursues similar strategies whose flavor is altered by a light dusting of the sugar of free trade.

By the time Franklin Roosevelt became president in 1933, the United States had, through overbearing policies, cultivated an atmosphere of resentment and ill will against itself. As Cordell Hull observed with typical acuity,

> The high tariffs of preceding administrations, coupled with the panic of 1929, had brought grave economic distress to the Latin American countries. . . . [From 1929 to 1933] our total trade with Latin America in four years had dropped to just one-fourth of what it had been. In 1932, certain Latin American countries, stung by our high tariffs, actually conferred with one another to form a customs union for defensive action against us.[59]

The customs union idea died, but the sentiment favoring insulation against the United States lived on.

After World War II, the lamentable condition of regional trade, combined with a general ideological predisposition against the beggar-thy-neighbor trade policies of the 1930s, made the United States emphasize free trade as a central part of the architecture of its multilateral commitments. The resulting Bretton Woods system was not only a product of U.S. hegemony acting in its own interests but a logical and empirically valid consequence of the regional animosities against which the Good Neighbor policy had inveighed. In the end, the free trade system still gravitated toward the Great Powers and away from southern concerns. The General Agreement on Tariffs and Trade failed to follow through on the proposed Havana Charter for a fuller International Trade Organization. Multilateralism was simply free trade without preference, built on reciprocity and the most-favored-nation principle, without even the Good Neighbor's inconstant attentions to the Latin American region's special problems. And even though the GATT system eventually created preferential trade arrangements for the Third World, the specter of open markets and borders continued to elicit defensive responses in the most liberal economic systems of Latin America. As we shall see in the next chapter, the Bretton Woods system hardly has received the willing embrace of Latin America, despite the pressures of the OECD countries and the Bretton Woods institutions.

The disappointing results of the multilateral system for Latin America are at one with a general historiographical argument of dependency literature: that trade liberalization was first and foremost an attempt by a declining colonial power to ensure Spain a place among ascendant northern European countries and had little to do with colonial development per se. After independence, the overweaning commitment of Latin America to free trade ultimately crippled chances for national development and tethered the newly freed nations to an empire even more pernicious for its efficiency and power, embodied in Great Britain and the United States. Using the nineteenth-century transition between colonialism and independence as evidence, *dependentistas* argue that the powers of the center dominated those of the periphery and precluded authentic and autonomous national development.[60]

The counterposition has argued that poor endowments of capital, labor, materials, and technology "must have made the alternatives to a foreign connection as uninviting to Latin Americans at the time as they seem speculative to the historian today."[61] Traditional case histories have emphasized the isolated, fragmented, and technologically primitive condition of Latin American societies as trade expansion began and the "modernizing" role of British capital in Latin American change. Latin American scholarship tends to concentrate on the substantial compromises to national autonomy implied by foreign capitalist domination. Revisionist scholarship tends to emphasize the inequities in the division of labor as a problem of international inequality, described variously as unequal exchange, dependency, neocolonialism, business imperialism, and free trade imperialism. Northern liberal scholarship tends to point to the internal Latin American maldistribution of income and concentration of resources, as well as the sybaritic life-styles of the Latin American elite.[62]

Current analysts of the North-South system are equally divided on both the origins of and the solutions to the system's shortcomings. A politically conservative and distinctly northern perspective on the international trade system points to the shortcomings of an international approach to inequities in the international system, preferring to point out the gross inequalities both among the nations of the South and within individual countries' societies. Reforms in the international system, it is argued, would come to little without a reappropriation of the benefits of those reforms for the sake of the disadvantaged.[63] Conversely, the now-dormant North-South literature from the late 1970s emphasized the importance of concessions from the North to provide the possibilities for change in the world's division of wealth.[64]

From the standpoint of this study, both of these architectonic statements miss the point in the same fashion as do latter-day "de-linkers." The question is not whether there was an alternative to the system in place— an argument that elevates political choice to extreme heights. The more important issue today concerns the legacy of the successive insertions of Latin America into the international trade orbits of the Great Powers, especially when considering the role of trade in national political strategies of the 1990s. The integration of Latin America into the international trade system limits the range of choices available to the nations of the region but still demands that political leaders stand against unqualified liberalization of the kind prescribed by putative hegemons and their international institutions. The question for Latin American trade strategists in the 1990s is not whether to integrate but how to change and qualify the role of Latin America in the international trade system to enhance national power, to improve prospects for domestic development, and to sustain national resources.

Latin American Exceptionalism

It is important that Latin America not appear so exceptional in its reluctant participation in the trade system. Latin American skepticism about trade is understandable in light of the development experience of the United States. If Benjamin Franklin had looked westward, he either would have had to ignore the litter of Indian nations ruined by the fur trade or revise the clever saying that began this chapter. By the time of the American Revolution, the tributary commerce of Russia and the expansion of European frontiersmen into the North American Indian domains had changed the culture and future survival prospects of Iroquois, Midewiwin, Cree, Sioux, and Blackfoot, among others. What began as an ecologically sustainable extractive industry dependent on the use of traditional Amerindian intermediaries gradually pushed the indigenous peoples to the margin. As Eric Wolf has documented, subsistence hunting gave way to early forms of extractive "putting out," which forever transformed the ethnic identities, social organization, and cultural purposes of Amerindians.[65] Under different political circumstances, the cultural destruction of the North American Indian might have had durable influences on the U.S. political culture of trade. As it was, Ben Franklin was able to forget the wide swath cut by trade even as it was happening, a convenient amnesia revisionists attribute to opportunism.[66]

In the 1850s, Henry Thoreau lamented the "maimed and imperfect nature" left to him in New England, where over half a million acres of woodlands had been cleared for farming before Ben Franklin's birth and where in Thoreau's time only 40 percent of Massachusetts was still wooded land. As a contemporary commented, "The cunning foresight of the Yankee seems to desert him when he takes the axe in hand."[67] Such critiques are common in today's indictments of the Amazon countries opting for untrammeled growth over resource conservation. They are unfortunately less common in the literature describing U.S. and Canadian destruction of old-growth forests in the Northwest.

Latin America and the United States had similar political reactions to the Great Depression, turning inward for development. Import protectionism, combined with demands that other countries open their markets and abandon their preferences, were not the purview solely of Latin American nations of the 1930s. And in the fiscal, trade, and debt troubles of the 1980s, the United States shared with Latin America the problems of structural adjustment, exchange-rate management, foreign debt, and populist pressures against free trade.

If Latin America and the United States have in common certain negative attributes of trade expansion and trade crisis, the case for Latin American exceptionalism strengthens when we add political power to the equation. Latin American nations have never been prime movers in the political organization of international trade. At Bretton Woods, no less a figure than John Maynard Keynes wrote, "Twenty-one countries have been invited which clearly have nothing to contribute and will merely encumber the ground. . . . The most monstrous monkey-house assembled for years."[68] Among the twenty-one countries crowding the "monkey-house," Keynes listed fourteen from Latin America and the Caribbean, mercifully excepting Argentina, Bolivia, Brazil, and Cuba. The agenda of those countries was ignored or defeated. As Chapter 5 will show, the Bretton Woods system that emerged from World War II did not give the Latin American countries the voice they had hoped for. Few were charter members of the GATT. None had great influence at the Bretton Woods Conference itself. The Charter of Havana, which was to create the International Trade Organization, failed. The multilateral trade system went along as it always had, based on the club of elite northern nations, now enveloped in their postwar recovery by U.S. hegemony.

In addition to the power disparities in international institutions, commercial power is unequal, to the disadvantage of the Latin American nations. With the exception of momentary successes owing to the Arab oil boycott in 1973, Latin American exporters have never enjoyed appreciable commercial power vis-à-vis the United States. The failure of cartels organized in the 1970s bears witness to the globalization of commodity markets and the inability of single providers of bananas, bauxite, copper, and most other commodities to influence OECD consumers or international prices.

Certainly some of Latin America's resentment of the powers of international trade resides in the fragile basis of the region's economic growth and development under the old international division of labor. The many historical vignettes familiar to Latin American historians and political analysts of this century cannot be dismissed as aberrations in the development of the New World. Nor can Latin America be considered oversensitive compared with other Third World areas under colonial rule. Latin America held an exceptional place in the international division of labor because it was the first region to be free of European colonialism and to have its sovereignty tested through the marketplace and not through formal dominion.

From the standpoint of nation building, the early independence of Latin America clearly had advantages. But those did not include freedom from the same traders that dominated the formal empires of the nineteenth century. The political power that accompanied free trade as an ideology made its influence deeply felt among the countries of the New World. From a Latin American perspective, Spanish and Portuguese colonial mercantilism, British free trade imperialism, and the post–World War II free trade hegemony of the United States all shared one fatal political flaw: they were trade systems built on North-North axes, without regard to Latin America's growth and development per se, and certainly without the region's full-fledged participation in the formation of the global trade system. Stated otherwise, Latin America was forced to join an international division of labor, which encourages specialization based on comparative advantage and maximizes the exploitation of world resources at a given level of technology.[69]

The desultory political and economic aspects of this unequal diplomatic exchange are found at every level. Notwithstanding the systemwide benefits of a nation's integration into a given international division of labor, there is no guarantee that any single member of the system will benefit from trade. In fact, based on the unequal circumstances of Latin American insertion into the international trade system, there is little reason to expect that the region will benefit broadly from trade without a redistribution of the benefits from trade (both between North and South and within the South itself). This is one of the themes of Chapter 2 and the focus of Chapter 5, which begins with a reanalysis of Hirschman, considers the role of trade concentration, and examines the Latin American trade profile in the current international economic setting.

It is equally important to realize that the impact of the trade system on domestic power is critical to modern Latin American history. Under mercantilism, trade was considered to be a means of enhancing national power.[70] Enhancing one nation's trade enhanced its power and deprived the trade partner of power by capturing more wealth. Wars against Amerindians, or between Chile, Peru, and Bolivia, or between Argentina and Brazil, or the United States and Mexico can be seen in light of one nation's enhancing national power by capturing wealth, this time through violent confrontation, not trade.

Latin America is different not only because of its early independence but because of the long involvement of the state in national development, the early industrialization of some key trading countries relative to the rest of the Third World, and the evolution of a distinct set of policy principles underpinning a nationalist development strategy.[71] The famous U.N. Economic Commission for Latin America (ECLA) nationalism of the Prebisch thesis was predicated on greater self-reliance for Latin American countries, if primarily of benefit to the large economies. The import substitution of the postwar period was not just a product of trade pessimism but was padded by large foreign exchange reserves, new national political coalitions, charismatic leaders in new civilian political arrangements, and a certain postwar internationalism in which the Third World might find a forum.

The much-cited weaknesses in Latin American economic development strategies of the period are only partially a product of national errors, only marginally susceptible to "good policies." The economic development strategies of Latin America, seen from the trade angle, responded to a "trade pessimism" that questioned the constancy and the virtue of the international economic system itself, and a "policy optimism" that placed great faith in the ability of governments to guide economic development in progressive ways. The Latin American state was not considered at the time to be a constraint on growth or capital formation, but rather as a facilitator.[72]

As Latin America staggers out of the 1980s, trade pessimism is again in place, challenged only by the questionable and regionally not very applicable trade optimism that generated policies in favor of export-oriented industrialization.[73] Gone, however, is the policy optimism, replaced by funereal pronouncements over the mission of the public sector. Today's policy pessimism about the region's development stems from a critique of the public sector that questions Latin American exceptionalism and advocates a "market minimalism" founded on belief in the importance of privatizing economic activities. With the disappearance of policy optimism goes the confidence in innovative approaches of development pioneers. "State bashing" is the order of the day, by which free trade and private sector liberals led by Britain and the United States assault "*dirigiste* dogma" and reject the role of the state in development.[74] So, in the temper of the late 1980s and early 1990s, trade politics strikes at what Latin American politicians have viewed as the guardian of national economic autonomy: the state.

The diminution of Latin America's special role in the Third World accompanies more global skepticism than is revealed by simple attacks on the state. The international trade system is built on the virtue of maximizing global production and efficiency to produce more goods and services for a growing world. As Chapter 3 will show, however, maximizing use of resources is far from a boon, particularly from the standpoint of development. That is not to disregard Ragnar Nurkse's warning that "the world is not rich enough to despise efficiency."[75] But even in economics, which generated the term, efficiency is a short-term concept measured by production functions, which themselves vary according to resource endowments.[76] And international economics has not made a convincing connection between trade theory and economic development, still leaving the field open to Gunnar Myrdal's criticism of its "strange isolation . . . from the facts of economic life."[77] The overall isolation of economics from political life is still stranger, especially in light of broad-brush recommendations to abandon the public sector's role in the economy.

The overall creation of wealth in the world is a necessary but insufficient precondition for economic growth, which itself is not necessarily the same as development. The linkage between international economic welfare through trade expansion and national economic welfare through growth in underdeveloped countries is a political concern. The connection of overall economic growth within underdeveloped countries to genuine broad-based development is also a political question. If short-term efficiency creates "surplus populations," development may be prejudiced. If surplus populations degrade trade-related resources, short-term efficiencies may create long-term diseconomies. Those diseconomies can be counted in the rough and violent currency of political disquiet, international resource depredation, and underdevelopment.

Because of its special place in the international system, Latin America offers an excellent angle from which to examine trade: a domestic Latin American political angle. But an outsider's view of the inside is not enough, though it has its charms. To examine the frustrating limits and elusive benefits of Latin America's insertion in the present trade system would not be so new, nor would it achieve the purposes of this study. More than a simple domestic orientation to international economic exchange, the next chapters will try to introduce several other planes along which the trade phenomenon can be viewed. They are three: political power, social and economic development, and resource exploitation. Within the weave of these three themes can be analyzed the social consequences of economic liberalism; the relationship of various trade regimes and external pressures to the human ecology of critical zones of Latin America; the political range of motion available to Latin American leaders vis-à-vis trade, international investment, and domestic development; and the dynamic, multi-leveled impacts of trade on local life in Latin American countries.

So, for example, the creation of a labor market in export-oriented economies in transformation may mean employment for some at a higher wage, but at the cost of concomitant dispossession of peasants, the destruction of corporate communities, and the impoverishment of subsistence landholders.[78] Such is current inattention to these "downside costs" of economic development that despite the human and resource costs of trade-impelled economic growth, ideologues can still pronounce that the impoverishment thesis of Karl Marx has been refuted convincingly.[79] These ex cathedra imprecations against those who continue to question the association of the expansion of capitalism with the improvement of material life for all are unsupported by the data (which, appropriately, are rarely examined). Conventional models of the impact of economic growth on income inequality, such as the Kuznets curve, must be examined in light of the external impacts of trade on such dynamic elements as savings, consumption, and resource husbandry. And the goal of this treatment is to take hold of these development principles not as ideological weapons but as criteria by which we examine the politics of trade and the balance of external stabilization and adjustments against domestic growth and distribution.

Another usually undertreated aspect I will examine has to do with development politics during trade collapse, as well as trade expansion, and development politics during durable trade imbalance, as well as relative equilibrium in external accounts. As to the first, it is important to treat the trade options available to a government in times of relative abundance and scarcity of foreign exchange; the policies a government might employ to create either condition, and their domestic causes and effects; and how those choices are affected by the country's overall insertion into the international trade system. Mexico's food security options under different trade and development regimes are worth examining, for example, especially because food policy has been such a high priority in recent years and because Mexico has passed through a number of external sector and exchange rate scenarios in a relatively short period of time, from oil boom and dollar abundance to devaluation and import collapse. Whereas traditional food policy analysis has focused on domestic politics as a relatively closed system, the treatment offered herein "opens" the system to focus on the trade aspect. As Chapters 3 and 6 will show, the question of food security has a marked impact on domestic use of natural resources, especially deforestation.

Historically, of course, trade collapse has been one of the most influential arbiters of political and social change in Latin America. The impulse to import-substitute came in the wake of a collapse of the free trade system in the Great Depression, in which the export value of Latin American commodities was virtually erased (or, in the case of bananas, production was managed and prices administered, to similar domestic effect). Domestic production was stimulated by the familiar foreign exchange bottleneck, not by industrial capital formed through a successful trade system. In World War II, the import-substitution-industrialization stimulus was not trade collapse but trade imbalance, as commodity prices rose, offering Latin American economies foreign exchange bonanzas with little in the way of imports available for purchase. Big countries, and even some of the smaller ones such as Guatemala, import substituted throughout the 1940s, spending the war surplus on economic and labor force transformation. But even after successful import substitution in the big economies of Latin America, import demand was not reduced, external balance was not guaranteed, and "balanced" growth continued elusive. The politics of import-substitution industrialization continues to hang over Latin American development in the 1980s, whether it be in the charge by U.S. trade policymakers that Latin America is "hiding behind its debt skirts to begin a new wave of ISI," or in the race to become competitive in an increasingly desperate move to integrate high-debt economies into the international economic system for the sake of economic survival.

To avoid red herrings, this book concedes three basic premises of trade economics: (1) that trade is beneficial to growth, certainly more beneficial than no trade; (2) that politically unencumbered trade grows faster than managed trade; and (3) that trade governed by markets is more efficient in the aggregate sense than other, more "political" regimes commonly employed.

Does this mean that the following chapters will argue the case of U.S. free trade ideologues, who regularly lambast Latin American (along with European and Japanese) *dirigiste* trade policies? Not at all. We can understand Latin American trade exceptionalism by reshaping a notion offered by Richard Rosecrance[80] to show that the axis of international exchange is denominated by trade for external balance versus trade for internal development and by arguing that a variety of points along that axis offer reasonable state responses to the forces of trade. Viewed this way, the condition of the United States and Latin America is the same, but the optic may be different. In the axis of external balance versus development, the United States traditionally favors trade; Latin America favors development. Part of what makes this study historically interesting is that in the early 1990s, it seems that the United States has retreated from its unqualified endorsement of free trade, while Latin America seems to be embracing free trade more heartily than at any time since independence.

Entries on the Historiographical Balance Sheet

Trade has transformed Latin American society so as to affect the political and development questions Latin Americans will face as this century closes. Without the nineteenth-century commodity trade booms led by bananas, cacao, coffee, cotton, copper, nitrates, rubber, and sugar, frontiers would have been settled later, capital would have formed more slowly, infrastructure would have been more limited, and technology would not have been transferred so quickly. The transformation of sugar technology certainly changed the face of Cuba after 1830, not just in its trade profile, but in the fashion business was done and sugar was produced. The vulcanization of rubber, the competition between American and Asian rubber in international markets, and the threat of synthetic substitutes for natural latex all stimulated Brazilian development in special, durable ways still felt today. Peru was transformed by the guano trade, then nitrates, oil, fish meal, cotton, and other commodities dependent on markets created by the technological modernization of agriculture in nineteenth-century Europe and the twentieth-century United States. The history of the southern Andes would be written quite differently without consideration of the wars among Bolivia, Peru, and Chile over the nitrate and copper territories of the region—commodities that found their markets in Europe and the United States and dictated the fiscal future of the Chilean government, not to mention its military deployments. And who can doubt the role of trade in the settlement of the north Mexican frontier, where filibusters and speculators rode the "copper skyrocket" or wiped out Indians to secure part of the growing Pacific Coast trade with San Francisco?

Likewise, the historical political economy of Latin America would not be complete without struggle among the Great Powers. Almost with the cry of independence, the Great Powers of Europe competed with the United States for rights to an Isthmian canal that would give the victor a critical edge in the Pacific trade.[81] Contemporaneously, the United States was involving itself in the southwestern consolidation of what had been half of Mexico's territory. In the end, the victory of the United States in the Isthmian competition meant the permanent involvement of an expanding hegemon in the political economy of Central America. In the Southwest, it meant war with Mexico, domination of the Gila and Monterrey trails, and the finishing touches to the continental United States.

Similarly, U.S. annexationist and, later, expansionist urges helped weave together concerns of national security and international economic expansion in Cuba and Puerto Rico. As one enthusiast of annexation put it in the Cuban case, the task of the United States was to "carry the present conditions or any decent conditions along . . . [so that] commercial interests . . . can dictate the final policy of the whole people."[82]

Another variable in historic Great Power competition over Latin American trade has been periodic upheaval in the metropolis itself. Consider that after two centuries of colonial rule, Portugal and Spain gave way to economic liberalism with Britain and the United States ascendant. Then the balance and direction of trade shifted gradually toward the United States as the British-dominated growth period 1870–1914 lurched from crisis to crisis: the Panic of 1873, the Baring Crisis of 1890, the rubber boom and bust, the copper skyrocket, and so on. World War I changed the structure of Western Hemisphere economic relations, as well as the structure of power in the developed countries, away from Britain in favor of the United States. Without the stimuli and constraints of two world wars, Latin American commodity prices certainly would have behaved differently.

Again, only a decade later, the entire international trade system collapsed with the Great Depression, throwing previous financial and trade relationships open to question and forcing much of Latin America back onto its own resources. The collapse of the international system in the interwar period already had reduced Latin American trade in Europe, but the Great Depression crippled Latin America's economies for at least a decade. Even as the Depression set in, though, Great Power competition sought to bring Latin American countries into the orbit of future Axis and Allied powers.[83] Germany, Japan, the United States, and the United Kingdom competed over Latin American trade as a part of Great Power diplomacy, each seeking to deny the others access to commodity-rich and occasionally strategic countries in Latin America.

The Great Depression led to the death of the old order throughout the region, whether its executioner took the form of Vargas and the Liberal Alliance in Brazil, the nationalist recoil from the "Infamous Decade" in Argentina, or the many national uprisings in Central America that led to the overthrow of Ubico in Guatemala or the displacement of lesser authoritarians such as Calderón in Costa Rica. The outbreak of World War II stimulated import substitution in such a way as to permit the nascent economic nationalism of the Depression years to find its fiscal center of gravity and to seek a restructuring of North-South relations in the postwar period.

These general lines of argument are all more or less familiar. In some ways their familiarity to students of Latin America masks the liveliness and creativity of historiographical disputes over the benefits of trade. The question of the secular decline in Latin American terms of trade is far from settled, though its subtlety is often lost in polemics. Likewise, the question of British free trade imperialism is still debated by the most established British historians of Latin America. The relationship between debt and trade is not established with great specificity, though rhetorically the assumption reigns that more debt forces more trade. The trade role of the public sector (and the reasons for its particular evolution) is likewise difficult to trace with a theoretical framework that satisfies the historical record.

More central to our concerns here, the *political* history of Latin American trade is still untreated for its own sake, especially by political science. It is a job apparently outside the purview of development and international economics.[84] But for the politics of the region, it is crucial. If the economic history of Latin America is built on a trade foundation, its political history is ruefully anchored to that same base. If the silver trade of Alto Peru (Bolivia) was the wellspring of Andean colonization, it was also the economic catalyst for ecological change and cultural undoing among the Indians of the region. If the old oligarchy of the colonial hacienda gave way to burghers newly created by nineteenth-century trade liberalism, those liberals were certainly not overburdened by notions of broadening the political base beyond their own inclusion. If agricultural and mineral commodity enclaves boosted overall economic output throughout the colonial period and again in the late nineteenth century, they did not generally develop infrastructure to spin off benefits to the economies at large.[85] In fact, as Colombia showed, domestic development passed through phases of export-led growth that gradually gave way to economic crisis and retrenchment, in which shifting international competitiveness ended booms in cacao, cinchona, coffee, cotton, hides, indigo, rubber, sugar, and tobacco.[86] At the same time, however, even the most classic enclave economy, Peruvian guano, has been seen to vary importantly from the limits of the concept.[87]

Politically, trade is too conveniently dismissed or its impacts assumed. Generally, *dependentistas* argue that a weak national state in the nineteenth century offered free trade imperialism an open opportunity to exploit Latin America. But even that conclusion has been questioned, in Peru, for example. Likewise, it is commonly assumed that terms of trade for primary-commodity-producing economies of Latin America were adverse and that the metropolis "bought cheap and sold dear," exploiting the hewers of wood and drawers of water of the periphery. In fact, the terms of trade were favorable to Latin America for much of the first half of the nineteenth century and several times thereafter, for a variety of reasons.[88]

In a similar vein, popular treatments of Central America conjure up a *comprador* class allied with bourgeois *entreguistas*[89] paving the way for imperialist interests in their countries. But the tradition of Latin American nationalism comes in part from liberalism—in Colombia, or in Central America, especially in the case of Nicaragua, where liberal José Santos Zelaya became synonymous with anti-Yankee defiance at the turn of the twentieth century.[90] The rise of economic nationalism is associated with the collapse of the free trade empire in the Great Depression of the 1930s; but import substitution in some countries (notably Chile and Colombia) was present as early as the 1890s, whereas Argentina attempted to resuscitate the old free trade regime throughout the Concordancia of the 1930s. In a new study of the growth of the Brazilian state, one historian even argues that the rise of the state did not follow 1930 but preceded it in the policies and institutions of the Old Republic.[91]

Similarly, there are controversies over the importance of foreign influence and its effects on national development. As Warren Dean has pointed out in the case of Brazilian rubber, the resentment of Brazilians over the "theft" of rubber seeds overlooks the benefits to Brazil of the British transfer of Liberian coffee to Brazil and foreign collaboration in the introduction of such familiar cultivars as eucalyptus, mango, and Asian rubber itself.[92] Concentration on foreign ownership in Argentine beef tends to underemphasize the gradual transfer of equity to national capital. And though trade history may correctly disavow British privateers on the Mosquito Coast, ne'er-do-wells were responsible for the transnational dissemination of pepper, nutmeg, cloves, and cinnamon from Cayenne.

It is not that traditional arguments about trade are simply wrong. But Latin America is a more diverse and subtle region in matters of trade than is generally thought. Among the key trading nations of the hemisphere, a variety of political forces with different ideas about trade have contended for power throughout the twentieth century. Useful interpretations of trade politics must portray both the diversity of the cases and the subtlety of national trade politics. The chapters that follow are devoted to sketching out some of the general lines of that diversity and subtlety and offering an analytical framework for characterizing Latin American national responses. The emphasis is on the political foundations and limits created by the trade system under which Latin America has labored.

CHAPTER 2

Connecting Trade to Development, Tempered by Adjustment

There is a real danger of the macro-models of economic development "running on their own steam" without any reference to the fundamental human problems of backwardness.
—Hla Myint, "An Interpretation of Economic Backwardness."

[Sustainable development] is development that meets the needs of the present without compromising the ability of future generations to meet their own needs.
—World Commission on Environment and Development, 1987.

DEVELOPMENT IS AS ELUSIVE conceptually as it is politically. Makers of development theory and policy spend a great deal of time and money wedging broad development objectives into narrow political alleys, frustrating devotees of Latin American development politics and widening the gap between development ambitions and politically viable goals. In the end, theoreticians may disdain small countries' modest steps in the direction of development as insufficient. But in a tightly constrained international economic environment, development politics often involves small change, not written in the broad strokes of an underlying dependency versus autonomy. Development in Latin America is defined more by the struggle than the outcome.

Development is a process infused with historical and politically specific meaning. For a monocrop exporter tied to the United States for 90 percent of its trade, commodity and geographic diversification of exports may be an important development goal. For the newly industrialized country, increases in steel production may be a central purpose of development politics. And for the foreign-exchange-constrained country, reducing dependence on imported foodstuffs may be an important development index. For measuring development, secular movement is much more important than reaching targets in arbitrary time frames. In practice, development has been defined by its connection to moving a country away from, rather than closer to, some impending crisis or durable problem in its economy and society.

Economic development literature has dominated the conceptualization of development. But in this and subsequent chapters, development will be denominated by a variety of factors, not all of which are production-determined. On the domestic side, economists have defined development by its connection to "growth with change," which links economic growth to sectoral balance, increased national productivity, attention to social needs, and enhanced aggregate national welfare. Turning domestic macroeconomic policy in Latin America in progressive social directions has been extraordinarily difficult, however. There is little in Latin America to show capitalist growth combining successfully with a redistribution of existing income or a radically different distribution of future increments of growth to achieve development outcomes consistent with basic needs or other reform literatures.

On the external side, development has traditionally involved diversification of agricultural exports and reduction of imports, as well as movement from traditional to nontraditional exports. It has mandated a variety of goals, including commodity and geographic trade diversification, to achieve balance-of-payments equilibrium. Sometimes it has meant the industrial transformation of an economy, rather than its reliance on more orthodox ideas of comparative advantage under free trade liberalism. This is partly because comparative advantage and free trade suggest the continued prospect of geographic and commodity specialization. Few politicians in Latin America are willing to embrace the status quo antedating economic nationalism.

External sector politics, however, does not offer a satisfactory broad-gauge definition of development, or even trade's connection to it. Some literature pretends to offer more in this regard, most notably studies of the scope and empirical craft of Geoffrey Bertram and Rosemary Thorp's volume on the history of Peruvian economic development. In general, though, little reward awaits the reader in search of a definition of the relationship between trade and development. Work on economic stabilization sometimes focuses on the impact on domestic investment of policies directed toward equilibrium in external payments but rarely on questions of domestic development priorities per se. Recent literature on development, however, strangely has avoided defining development altogether, assuming apparently that economic progress writ large is sufficient concern.[1]

This shortcoming in the literature apparently results from theoretical lack of interest in explicitly political aspects of economic development and well-founded aversion to writing general recipes for recovery from the current crisis. Economists are particularly shy about the political aspects of their work, though the political implications of economic stabilization and structural adjustment do not inspire similar caution.

Adding to economists' disciplinary disinclinations, Latin America offers plenty of its own obstacles to a full definition of development. Despite the convenience of considering Latin America a homogeneous region, there are few uniform linkages between trade and debt politics. The possibilities of a uniform regional policy toward trade and debt crises are slim, and even ambitious policy recommendations are pointed at country-specific short-term crises.

Nevertheless, if trade in today's international system is to be considered from the development standpoint, the relationship between debt and adjustment, on the one hand, and trade and domestic politics, on the other, must invite a characterization of various national strategies for trade, which will be subdivided into general camps here and taken up again in Chapter 6. In this chapter, we will concern ourselves with two great dividing elements: the historical division between Latin American countries undergoing industrialization versus export expansion in primary commodities, and the current division among countries according to the politics of their external adjustment policies. Before turning to the specific sequences and alternative paths in Latin America, though, we must establish some theoretical and empirical connections between trade and development, then between trade and adjustment.

Trade as an Engine of Growth for Development

Trade as an engine, handmaiden, or lubricant of growth has received much attention in the traditional literature on economic development. Trade may generate domestic growth, be a product of domestic growth, or prevent domestic growth from suffering balance-of-payments problems.[2] It does not necessarily conflict with goals for industrialization, but that depends on specific factors in each country. As has been observed elsewhere, the engine of growth is worthless until it is harnessed.[3]

Largely ignoring the origins of trade and debt crises, a new policy literature on stimulating growth in Latin America uses the rich tradition of trade for growth to make a case for trade and exchange liberalization, debt concessions, and new capital inflows to the region.[4] To some extent, this line of thinking has shifted the emphasis of adjustment toward trade liberalization plus "destatization" or privatization.[5] The apparent intellectual foundations of these recommendations appear in traditional economic theory and in the ideologies of authors of "policy-relevant" proposals for Latin America's economic future. The core of their thinking lies in theories about the role of trade in overall economic growth.

Those who argue for trade as an engine of growth for Latin America's future are supported by the historical record of regional dependence on trade for growth and by the truism that development cannot occur without economic growth. But the policy reductionism of current literature makes assumptions that are questioned in this study and in the most careful casework on foreign trade and economic development in Latin America.[6] It assumes that trade as an engine of growth can build on the growth that has shaped Latin America in the postwar era; that room exists for substantial, balanced export growth in Latin America; that trade liberalization will enhance such growth; and that trade-impelled growth will benefit Latin American countries.

The simple recommendation that Latin America liberalize, the theme of virtually all of the policy literature on Latin American economic growth in the 1980s and 1990s, apparently assumes both that trade barriers are a primary constraint on growth and that, if liberated, trade-generated growth will benefit development. Remarkably, these assumptions are often disingenuously hidden and left undefended by empirical evidence. Here, their consequences require a deconstruction of the premises of trade liberalization, which will be held to the empirical test of case literature drawn from earlier, more circumspect examinations of economic liberalization.

Trade Constraints on Growth

First, it is necessary to distinguish between import and export constraints and to point out a badly hidden agenda in the otherwise reasonable policy logic of the trade liberalization for growth literature. Latin American constraints on trade are identified with public sector distortions, which prohibit the setting of market-clearing prices. By definition, liberalization policies involve reducing the role of the state in trade, allowing the market to clear at the "right prices," and enhancing economic efficiency in the external sector. Liberalization in the policy literature is discussed as if it were a simple matter of removing artificial obstacles to the efficient exchange of commodities among nations.

Behind this ideologically appealing liberal banner, however, is a mandate for a structural transformation of Latin American economic development, governed by the forces of the international market, valuing above all the maximization of production, and disregarding some of the most important domestic political and economic consequences. In addition to its inappropriateness to the region's historical record and its inattention to the political means of accomplishing this structural transformation, the policy prescription of trade liberalization for growth reduces the economic development problems of the region to their external connection.

The state is not simply charged with acting as a force against an efficient import policy. It is also criticized for subsidizing exports unfairly to generate the foreign exchange that presumably financed imports in the past, even without liberal trade regimes.[7] The policy-based lending of the World Bank,[8] particularly in the agricultural sector, has emphasized reducing public subsidies that impel the (over)production of agricultural commodities, in favor of trading under liberal regimes based on international prices and comparative advantage. The emphasis of policy-based structural adjustment lending has been to move a borrower country toward market-based pricing and toward tradables to maximize the effect on external payments problems. Through these emphases, the World Bank and the International Monetary Fund have turned domestic Latin American economic priorities around, to emphasize growth as "the stamina needed for adjustment."[9]

It is generally recognized that the multilateral development assistance system has failed to supply the levels of financing required to achieve such goals. The result has been the displacement of the public sector, neglect of the state's fiscal anemia, suppression of domestic demand, and a foreign-exchange-constrained economy.[10]

Trade liberalization thus has two sides. Economic internationalists argue that removing protection against imports, which has sustained Latin American industry under the "infant industry" and "industry of transformation" concepts, will enhance overall economic welfare. Data from studies of subsidization indicate, however, that the costs of subsidies and protection are extremely high, even in less intrusive economies than those of Latin America.[11] It is even argued that through adjustments in the labor force jobs lost in industry will be replaced by jobs in the trade sector, an argument that avoids conceiving of such adjustment as specific workers' losing (or winning) jobs versus aggregate job creation in the economy.

On the export side, reducing state subsidization of exports is purported to allow "the playing field of trade to be leveled," by bulldozing away unfair trade practices. Exporters and importers playing on that field will win or lose on the basis of their buoyancy in international markets. This, of course, is the central conflict in the agricultural negotiations in the GATT Uruguay Round, in which all of the key Latin American players have been arrayed on the side of reducing subsidies. The failure of that argument lies in the intransigence of EEC farm policy, not Latin American *dirigisme*.

The Problem of Elasticity Pessimism

Celso Furtado argues that historically the tropical and mineral export economies were doomed to severely limited growth and development because of the declining terms of trade and the limited linkages and spread of benefits they offered to the economy at large. Furtado suggests that the most propitious conditions for genuine economic development in Latin America were to be found in the temperate zone countries that exported agricultural commodities, such as Argentina, Uruguay, and some areas of Chile.[12]

The commodity terms of trade for agricultural exports during the period of trade expansion in the nineteenth century do not bear out Furtado's argument consistently.[13] As Carlos Diaz-Alejandro has pointed out in a different connection, the role and performance of commodity prices are a sort of lottery.[14] The factoral terms of trade suggest, however, that the tropical economies did suffer disadvantages in the old international division of labor.[15] The prices of tropical products over the 1870–1913 period did not perform as well as temperate zone products.[16] In the long run, the factoral terms of trade were biased against the tropical economies, where market forces and extreme stratification conspired to push down prices and wages.

But to divide Latin American economies as tropical or temperate is too simple. The large countries, Brazil and Mexico, have temperate and tropical zones, as well as upland and lowland tropics that vary greatly in the composition of labor and commodities. Evidence from Central America shows great disparity in terms of trade and price behavior in the 1920s and 1930s, requiring a much more carefully defined thesis than Furtado offers. And economies such as Guatemala's in the nineteenth century showed strong linkages between labor markets in the tropical and highland zones. The distinction between temperate and tropical economies is more robust when applied to northern versus southern nations, where barriers to labor flows showed the differences in factoral terms of trade between the two.[17]

More generally, the premise that Latin American exports can increase under the right trade policies has severe limitations. As was shown in the National Bureau of Economic Research studies on foreign trade regimes and Latin American development, the connection between policy initiative, trade results, and domestic development is extraordinarily complicated. In Colombia during the 1950s, for example, the collapse of international coffee prices caused a balance-of-payments crisis that was ultimately reflected in the country's ability to transform savings into capital investment. Coffee prices, hardly susceptible to short-term policy initiatives, resulted in a loss of productivity in heavy industries. A similar connection between commodity prices and productivity occurred in Argentina as well.[18] In Chile, the dilemmas of policy initiatives were stark, and each of several liberalization efforts in the 1950s and 1960s failed because of domestic political reasons, falling copper prices, and intractable domestic economic difficulties.[19]

Likewise, it is clear that many of Latin America's exports have highly inelastic supply curves so that exporters cannot easily increase the amount of a commodity exported in response to an improvement in price. This was not the case in the tropical export economies of the nineteenth century, in which, Lewis argues, supply elasticities were practically limitless because of the huge quantities of unused labor and land.[20] It was and is true in the case of rare commodities, though, and in commodities with fixed technologies and inputs that cannot be changed quickly, such as cochineal in the nineteenth century. In the cochineal trade, output was based on traditional technologies, active community cooperation, and, above all, the ability of the community to increase the supply of insects for dye. The prospect of building the trade invited abuses that would destroy the cultural context of cochineal extraction itself, a well-known problem in common-property-based extractive regimes.[21]

Inelasticities of supply also plague many other tropical products because of a lag between the price stimulus and the supply response, which is further complicated in the twentieth century by government intervention and international commodity regimes. A lag in supply response is characteristic of virtually all plantation crops that depend on perennials requiring years to mature before they yield fruit. Coffee is perhaps the most appropriate example, in view of our consideration of Latin America and public sector support schemes. It is also true, however, for bananas, cacao, rubber, chicle, and other plantation crops, as well as for livestock, especially beef cattle, which have a slow reproductive cycle. The beef cycle, which is an analytical representation of supply responding to movements in price, is eight to twelve years long.[22]

In the 1970s, Latin America provided ample evidence of the inelasticities of exports in bananas, bauxite, coffee, and copper, among other commodities, as key producers tried to form cartels with the hope of restricting supply so as to raise prices in the developed world. The International Bauxite Association, the Union of Banana Exporting Countries (UPEB), the International Coffee Organization, and the international copper cartel, CIPEC (Conseil Intergouvernemental des Pays Exportateurs de Cuivre), all tried to increase prices of commodities by restricting supply, in a fashion similar to that of the Organization of Petroleum Exporting Countries (OPEC).[23] Ecuador and Venezuela were members of OPEC, of course, in which Venezuela had played a founding role.[24] Since the turn of the century, Brazil had been engaging in monopoly pricing of coffee on a unilateral basis through the domestic valorization scheme. And from tobacco to guano to cochineal, Latin American countries had created public sector monopolies to manage supplies, and to some extent prices, in the international economy. Major private banana producers such as United Fruit managed prices in Central America, based on demand and profitability. Their monopoly pricing in the private sector was analogous to public sector activities in other commodities, except that the public sector has broader imperatives than simple profitability.

The limitations of cartels and monopoly pricing schemes are now well-known. As the banana producers learned, a commodity that is held back must not be perishable, nor should it be substitutable, and demand for it should be inelastic. It helps if the number of suppliers is small and relatively homogeneous, but this refers more to the social organization of cartels than to the economics of monopoly pricing. In any event, an extremely limited number of commodities fit these criteria. During the oil crisis of the 1970s, petroleum was considered to be the "great exception." Now, even that is under question, in the wake of developed countries' responses and the impact of higher prices on the behavior of the cartel. Certainly the copper cartel was unable to continue to raise prices and withhold supplies, because consumers in developed countries substituted and recycled and found new suppliers. Bauxite producers were in even worse straits, as was shown when the International Bauxite Association attempted to raise prices unilaterally in the wake of the first oil shock. Jamaica, Guyana, Suriname, and the others faced a powerful handful of foreign companies dominating the processing of bauxite to alumina and aluminum, and their efforts to break that control failed.[25]

The inelasticity of supply can also mean an irregular response of supplies to demand. In modern markets, buyers have little patience with inefficient or irregular suppliers, in systems that may mask potential output with corrupt or excessive bureaucracy. In his study of the Colombian apparel industry, David Morawetz showed that, despite its potential to supply U.S. imports, Colombian clothes manufacturers were undone by import and export licensing requirements, corruption, and long delays. Even in the special U.S. 807 tariff category exempting in-bond exports from all tariffs except on value added in production (this is one of the rules under which the well-known Mexican *maquiladora* industry operates), Colombia was not able to exploit its competitive advantage.[26]

Inelasticities of demand in the consuming countries also may constrain the expansion of exports. For countries that are important to a market and for whose products demand is inelastic, increasing output may prejudice their own development. Even if they are not important to the world's trade but demand is inelastic, national gains are zero-sum victories over other exporters, often Third World neighbors. This was the case with coffee, according to Lewis. After 1910 Brazil produced the bulk of the coffee in world trade, but the international price would not sustain planters' costs because of adverse regional labor costs. Other Latin American countries picked up coffee as a primary export, and their low labor costs continued to work against Brazil and world prices.[27]

Raul Prebisch raised the question, What is to be done when the further expansion of exports would bring a fall in prices?[28] Furtado's answer, and Charles Kindleberger's, is that exports continue to expand unless change occurs in one of the critical factors (exhaustion of the agricultural frontier, for example, or labor shortages). So, for example, expansion of coffee production in Brazil slows because of the adverse costs of labor, the frost line limiting the expansion of agricultural land devoted to coffee, and a variety of public incentives that drive former coffee lands into alternative crops. Once again, the possibilities for insulating the national economy from the vicissitudes of the international system lie mainly in diversification. Prebisch and others offered a different answer to this dilemma: inward-looking industrialization (export promotion in manufactures was not yet a possibility).

Specialization versus Transformation

Another argument against trade liberalization in Latin America, which does not require acceptance of the elasticity pessimists' argument, is that, irrespective of the barter terms of trade, the gains from trade are limited because the Latin American economy is unable to transform under free trade regimes.[29] Exports of primary products expand because of the factoral terms of trade; imports of manufactures foreshorten the process of industrial diversification both because of the increase in imports from expanded exports and the uncompetitive nature of infant industries. The extreme version of this is the "Dutch Disease," one of the distressing symptoms of which involves an abundance of foreign exchange driving high import demand and suppressing domestic industrialization.[30] The gains from trade limit the transformation of the national economy. Trade expands even when the result will be no development for the economy. Specialization is the mandate of the international system; economic transformation is not.

The problem of supply and demand elasticities may evaporate somewhat as the trading nation moves up the value-added ladder and trades more manufactures or diversifies its commodity export bill. The wage share of national income may be improved by shifts in the share of income to workers moving out of traditional occupations into higher-paying jobs.[31] These are empirical questions; but a regime of free trade raises questions about the possibility of industrial transformation, which is a prerequisite to the Latin American trader's adding more value to exports.

Even Lewis, who argues eloquently that there was no inherent conflict between free trade in primary commodities and domestic industrialization, qualifies that argument severely. He recognizes the elasticity problem as fundamental, limiting the export prospects of many tropical countries. And he admits that the possibility of industrial transformation through trade was restricted mainly to those countries that already had a substantial industrial sector in the late nineteenth century—that is, the large economies of Latin America.[32] For the rest, the only hope for growth lay with export of primary commodities, and economic transformation would face extreme difficulties.

If this thesis is correct, the argument against trade liberalization would include the prospect of forgoing industrialization in favor of export expansion in the small countries. Where initial industrialization succeeds—in the large economies—the liberal prospect still threatens "deindustrialization by competition," unless import barriers on competition are raised and new technologies are aggressively pursued.

In the big countries, liberalization can occur only by the defeat of the entrepreneurial classes who made import substitution possible in the 1930s and 1940s. Because import substitution has prevailed in the region for forty years or more, liberalization must be a product of pressure from external sectors and the ascendance of internationalist entrepreneurs tied to trade and international integration, not domestic capital formation and import substitution. The result—which may be defined in the first decade of the twenty-first century if free trade continues to ascend in Latin America—would seem to favor an industrial regression (the domestic process of winnowing out firms and sectors by competition) in a new international division of labor, combined with competitive industrial reintegration into the international system on the basis of comparative advantage. Mexico and Chile are the furthest along on this path. Brazil, Peru, and Argentina have only begun. The smaller countries, as usual, have few options.

Latin American economic history seems to support Lewis's theories and to qualify the limits on transformation dictated by free trade. In Latin America, even at the height of free trade imperialism before World War I, several countries already had begun industrial transformation. The linkages between Argentine exports and domestic manufacturing are well established. In Chile, manufacturing expanded impressively in the aftermath of World War I. And in Brazil and Mexico, important signs of industrial transformation antedated the Great Depression by decades. Some of the most impressive gains in industrial transformation came in response to external shock (e.g., World War I) or to protectionist changes in tariff policy. Though the collapse of the trade system in the Great

Depression convinced Latin American economic theorists that trade and industrial transformation were leading in opposite directions, the distinction is probably overdrawn in reality.

Even if these obstacles are overcome and industrial transformation progresses, Latin America still faces a major obstacle: the early experience with import substitution showed industrialization to be permanently import-dependent in most countries of Latin America. Trade as the "lubricant" of growth was insufficient to the task. The "exhaustion of the easy phase" of import substitution was based on the saturation of the local market for first-phase industries and the permanent dependence of industrialization on imported inputs. Rather than fulfilling the hope of insulating Latin American industrializers from the old import dependence, import-substitution industrialization ran into the problem of increasing import requirements for "deepening" the industrial sector and new requirements for imports of raw materials. Transnational corporations found trade protectionism and internal incentives the perfect culture for growth, as foreign firms became "national companies." The Latin American newly industrialized countries continued to be subject to chronic balance-of-payments deficits, and the foreign exchange constraint on the economy endured.

Appropriating the Gains from Trade

Both the theoretical and the historical record resist a categorical answer to the assumption that trade benefits development. I conceded the case of trade for growth in Chapter 1 and remarked on various aspects of the terms-of-trade debate. Two further considerations are important, though: the appropriation of the gains from trade, and the related matter of turning externally generated growth into development. The next section defines the concept of development and its connections to the external sector. In regard to appropriating the gains from trade, it is important to question whether trade benefits are used for consumption or investment and whether that process is guided by the private or the public sector. The questions of optimal trade mix and protection will be considered in Chapter 6.

The general point is that even if export expansion provides the foreign exchange that might be used for industrial transformation, a country's ability to turn the gains from trade to industrial use depends on the "returned value" of the export activity for the domestic economy. As Bertram and Thorp have shown convincingly in the case of Peru, this is why a successful liberal model of trade has failed to develop domestic linkages adequate to the challenges of national development. The ability of a nation to guarantee more returned value from the external sector is a function of appropriate public sector interventions.

Trade Liberalization and the Resource Question

The trade for growth literature suggests that Latin America can trade its way out of the debt crisis. This argument is weak on three fronts: the problems of inelasticity in Latin American exports, the import dependence of increased exports (especially in a manufacture-based export-substitution strategy), and the considerable resource cost of such trade, if it were possible. The entire foundation of free trade exalts the growth of global output, which leads to the maximization of global welfare. The means by which that output and welfare should be allocated are left untreated. More importantly, in the past decade, Latin America and the Western industrialized nations have become increasingly concerned about the resource costs of increased trade. It is commonly asserted that trade should be conducted on the basis of dynamic comparative advantage, but the consequences for such trade from a resource perspective are not studied with equal vigor.

The Identity of Growth and Development

Finally, the argument assumes that economic growth and economic development are identical, apparently discarding the bulk of the theoretical literature on trade and development, as well as the argument made by Dudley Seers when he wrote that "for very few [countries] would an acceleration of growth *per se* be a solution to social problems."[33] Seers's questioning of the role of (in this case trade-based) growth for development is one of the main guiding beacons of my research, helping lead to the conclusion that trade and economic growth are sometimes destructive of sustainable development directed at the Latin American poor. Though this argument is relatively well developed in the theoretical literature and sprinkled throughout case-specific studies of economic growth, it is rarely addressed in policy prescriptions for economic growth in Latin America.[34]

From the Latin American side, but certainly applicable to the United States as well, a developmental agenda for the politics of inter-American trade must imply new understandings of the purposes of trade. A recent monograph on the new GATT round referred to the central theme of the negotiations as "trade for growth," in the tradition of the Kennedy Round's concentration on tariffs and the Tokyo Round's preoccupation with nontariff barriers.[35] Trade for growth in well-articulated economies of the West and in poorer, more open and vulnerable economies suffering foreign exchange constraints on growth is directly beneficial to employment and general economic activity. But it is not sufficient for the development problems of the 1980s and 1990s. A more appropriate theme for trade in the South is "trade for growth for what?" That is, trade in Latin America, though linked to growth, is not directly linked to economic well-being, especially among the 40 to 60 percent of the population of the region who are seriously deprived of regular work, adequate housing, and most of the other basic amenities of life.

Although the international institutions guiding development and balance-of-payments finance are required by their charters to concentrate on the positive benefits of trade for growth, the connection of such growth to development does not follow in an unqualified way in the economies of Latin America. One recent treatment of trade and development prospects argues that in early stages of development, protrade and antitrade policies really amount to a Hobson's choice between gross inequalities delivered by one trade regime or another.[36] Particularly in rural areas, where Latin American poverty is most intractable, the relationship between trade and development is complicated and difficult to manage. The positive effects of trade are restricted to general overall economic health with presumed benefits to the general population relative to antitrade regimes.

The Relationship Between Trade and Development

The best bridge between the international economics of trade, debt, and growth, on the one hand, and national development, on the other, may be found in the traditional literature of development economics, especially in the creative cross-disciplinary "trespassing" or "poaching" that has made the work of Albert Hirschman and Charles Maier so valuable. As the next chapters will show, the political terms of trade are bounded by some of the concepts first argued in Hirschman's classic *National Power and the Structure of Foreign Trade*. The broader development literature that appeared following World War II has been recaptured in a variety of treatments, from David Morawetz's *Twenty-Five Years of Economic Development* and John Sheahan's *Patterns of Development in Latin America*, to the retrospective *Pioneers in Development*.

All of these works rely on traditional notions of economic development: per capita income, employment, and various socioeconomic indicators. With slight variation, they maintain the limited and rather slippery definitions of development put forth by development economics, or they provide no definition at all. Sheahan, for example, admits that development economics has no "commonly accepted core meaning of its own,"[37] but he does not offer a definition of development that goes beyond that tradition. In the single chapter on trade, he does not define the connection between trade and development except to discuss the strategies of import substitution and export promotion.[38]

Morawetz defines his development concerns as growth, alleviation of poverty, and national independence or self-reliance, a definition consistent with the tradition of growth for change. But though the politics of the postcolonial and post–World War II economic environment demanded great institutional change, development economics did not interfere in the political realm except through the prescriptive norms of its leading advocates. As Meier observes, "The pedigree of Development Economics reads 'by Colonial Economics out of Political Expediency.'"[39]

The political implications of development economics sometimes contrasted starkly with the traditions of neoclassical economics. Economic growth with change, especially in the new nations emerging from European empires in retreat, meant profound political and institutional changes, the growth of the state as an intermediary in development, and a modification of some of the dicta of economics for the sake of equity, balance, modernization, and a variety of noneconomic concerns. The Bretton Woods system that framed northern leadership of the postwar international system, however, was infused with a set of Cold War concerns about the political leanings of the Third World, a skeptical approach to the state as a vehicle for trade or development policy, and a disdainful attitude toward deviations from the principles of economics for the sake of development. In the course of the 1950s and 1960s, a broad ideological and strategic gulf appeared in the approach of the United States and the Bretton Woods institutions toward development versus the state-led, developmentalist strategies of Latin America.

Not surprisingly, current trade politics stem from radically different visions of the gains from trade, depending on whether trade is viewed from the U.S. or Latin American perspectives, or, indeed, from those of different countries within Latin America.[40] Trade policymakers in the United States generally assume that expanding trade for Latin America is beneficial for growth and development; Latin American policymakers do not share that assumption. To sort out some of those differences, it is useful to analyze briefly the evolution of Latin American economic development thought as it applies to trade in the postwar era. Whatever the differences, it must be kept in mind that in all countries of the region, linking domestic development policy goals with trade policies and debt payment has become more important in the 1980s.

A Hirschman-Lewis Guide to the Trade-Development Connection

As Paul Streeten has wryly observed, the world consists of two kinds of people: those who divide the world in two and those who don't.[41] Using this mandate, Streeten describes two tests that can help sort out the literature on inter-American trade politics: a "Lewis test" and a "Hirschman test."[42] The Lewis test divides the world into those who think the South would be better off if the North disappeared, versus those who would lament such a disappearance.[43] The Hirschman test divides the world into those who make the "monoeconomics claim" and those who think that development economics has merit as a field and (more importantly from our standpoint here) that less developed countries (LDCs) have special problems not governed by economic theory.[44]

Perhaps unintentionally, these two clever tests divide political thinking on trade in corresponding ways. There are those who think that more North-South trade is better, and those who do not (among them those who think that more South-South trade is better, and those who see no virtue in any trade). Likewise, there are those who think that trade theory itself is a justification for LDCs to trade and those who think that trade is justified only if it has a connection to development. The former seem to have little patience with the idea of separating economic growth from development, except to the extent that allowances are made for industrial "deepening," investments in human capital, infrastructure, and other growth-related development expenditures. Among the latter, development is altogether more elaborate than growth. Confusing all this is a somewhat precious argument contending that the numbered conceptual achievements of development economics have been integrated into neoclassical economics, and those that have not fit have proven false.

My concern here is with the argument not among economists but among advocates of certain paths of economic growth and their relation to questions of development. The various theoretical positions about the link between trade and development are shown in Figure 2.1.

In this construction, the bulk of academic work and policy-making is done by actors in cells I, II, and IV. Cell III is reserved for special cases, which Diaz-Alejandro has shown convincingly are usually the products of forced circumstances imposed by a hostile international environment (the USSR in the 1920s, Cuba in the 1960s, China in the 1950s), or perhaps are viable on a selective sectoral basis. Nevertheless, thinking on imperialism, shifts in modes of production, the internationalization of capital, and other important themes of Marxist political economy fit more easily into cell III than elsewhere.[45]

This artifice offers the convenience of separating out real intellectual and political differences that show why trade is conceived of and treated differently in Latin America than in the United States and to some extent differently in Latin America and the United States than in such development assistance institutions as the World Bank or Inter-American De-

Hirschman Test: Monoeconomics?

Yes	No	
(I)	(II)	
Neo-classical international economists U.S. trade policymakers	Neo-classical development economists Marxists economists Development internationalists	No Lewis Test: Delink?
Orthodox Marxist economists Closed development nationalists	Neo-Marxist economists Structuralists Development nationalists	Yes
(III)	(IV)	

Figure 2.1. A Hirschman-Lewis Test of Development Thinking.

velopment Bank. If one were to describe the flow of Latin American sentiment across these cells in the period 1985–90, it would clearly show sharp movement upward and to the left, to cell I. How permanent that movement will prove to be is a central question for the 1990s.

One way of discriminating among these various positions is by emphasizing the *historical* development of trade in Latin America versus the United States, which differs from the theoretical case. As Lewis has observed, referring to terms of trade, the historical argument is very different from the theoretical argument.[46] Grand historical and power differences between Latin America and the developed world have generated very different conceptions of trade and its role in development, which then have been married to economic principles in some fashion. Those conceptions are a product of the impact of the Great Depression on Latin American trade, the bitter national battles between economic nationalists and internationalists in the 1930s, the differential role of import-substitution industrialization in Latin American economies, the prevalence of export enclave economies in the Caribbean and Central America, and the impact of the Bretton Woods system (especially the GATT) on Latin American trade politics since 1945. Briefly, Latin American development theorists approached the postwar order as trade pessimists, supposing that prospects for commodity trade were limited and that the gains from that trade would be inadequate to the development needs of the region. Because import substitution was already under way in the larger economies, the path to a trade-pessimist–policy-optimist alternative to the old international division of labor was relatively smooth. Some of the thorny questions they faced included these:

□ How could trade be managed by Latin American nations to avoid the inevitable power imbalances that result from inequalities in economic power?

□ How could the gains from trade be internalized? This question includes broad subthemes, from questions of the purposes of trade per se, to the means of targeting trade for domestic development.

□ At what level must trade be "intervened" by the public sector to mold comparative advantage, to select priority sectors for development, to meet external obligations, and to avoid unacceptable negative internal effects from trade?

□ To what extent could development policy change Latin America's perception that trade had been historically a siphon through which the natural resources and factor endowments of Latin America were drained off in favor of the dominant countries in the international system?

Although such characterizations are somewhat oversimplified, Latin America viewed global trade through a development lens, whereas the United States viewed global development through a trade lens. U.S. perspectives on development focused on the market; the Latin American focus was state-centered, though it must be emphasized that the state in Latin America rarely goes beyond recognized market-based approaches to planning.[47] The political question today revolves around the degree to which the historical experience and political positions of the key trading nations in the hemisphere are valid in the conditions of the 1990s. Lurking behind that policy question is the more profound doubt about whether Latin America is being lured by circumstances into a new dependence on trade, with perhaps even greater consequences for national recovery and development strategies in the future. For Latin America, of course, the question is whether anything in the political realm can be done to ameliorate its new insertion into the international system.

To define development, then, presents political, economic, and historical problems in addition to the analytical one. Three broad approaches may be taken. The first focuses on traditional concepts of economic development, which can be broadened to include noneconomic aspects associated with the social question and long-term prospects associated with sustainability. The second has to do with the historical responses that shape the current political economy of development. And the third, linked intimately to the first two, has to do with the realm of political possibility, building on the constraints and potential of recent political conditions in Latin America. What is most important to recognize is that in this step-level approach to defining development, each of these aspects is inherently political. They call for political decisions on the public allocation of economic resources in society; they involve the relationship between economic change and the formation of political coalitions in Latin American countries (i.e., the relationship between rapid economic change and changing economic interests represented in politics); and they concern the international diplomacy of trade and development, which lies within the exclusive purview of government.

Selected Economic Aspects of Development

The development pioneers of the 1940s and 1950s fixed on the world as they saw it empirically. Their connection to economics was practical and empirical, and their various departures from traditional economic theory were based on real-world assumptions and historical political economy. Hirschman developed his thoughts on Latin American development in Colombia, based on modest previous development economics training. Raul Prebisch confessed to being a neoclassical economist before the trade collapse of the 1930s led him to reconsider the position of the periphery in the international trade system. Gunnar Myrdal, Hans Singer, and others served in the international bureaucratic apparatus responsible for the reconstruction of the war-ravaged world and the economic progress of the newly liberated Third World nations.

Thus, despite its theoretical originality and its distinction in the use of language, development economics involved an agglomeration of diverse intellectuals operating out of a set of loosely connected heresies from classical theory.[48] They offered a refreshingly straightforward set of arguments about the prospects for economic growth, which were empirically well-founded and generally attentive to traditional methodologies for evaluating growth policy.

The developmentalists' concerns were with sectoral balance, problems of external payments, terms of trade, monetary policy, and the like. Yet development economics added some broader concerns to the universal concern with economic growth. In addition to maximizing growth, which soon included population considerations, development specialists concerned themselves with poverty alleviation, income distribution, employment, and basic needs.[49] Unfortunately, these issues all proved to be equally controversial. Income distribution is an inadequate measure of development because it fails to capture economic and social values other than income. Its measure is difficult and disputatious, and changes in its structure are elusive. The assumptions behind employment in Latin America have also proved difficult to sustain, and no consensus has been produced. Unemployment, underemployment, productivity, marginal productivity of rural labor, the informal sector, and other concepts have produced deep and durable debates in the field, without guiding policy-makers forward in their quest for more viable forms of economic growth.

Basic needs, which became the subject of a body of literature in the late 1970s and continues in somewhat different form today, is somewhat arbitrary and generally avoids the question of economic assets and poverty.[50] It takes a welfare approach to the matter of development, giving equity first attention, but through entitlements rather than control over economic assets. In more recent versions, the emphasis is on reacting to domestic adjustment difficulties and the tendency of the shrinking state to shut out the dispossessed first. It has been some time since a positive development agenda has been the first focus of the basic needs literature.

In the early 1970s, a small literature on economic growth and equity grew up, led by the landmark *Economic Growth and Social Equity in Developing Countries,* by Irma Adelman and Cynthia Taft Morris. This volume had the virtue of emphasizing the inadequate connection between economic growth and benefits accruing to the poor, especially in the form of income distribution. It offered an attempt, however initial, to analyze the connections between domestic economic growth priorities, the delivery of equitable shares of that growth to the least endowed, and the level and nature of political participation in society.

Because of the character of the study and the complexity of those connections, this volume did not address the radical political changes required to effect even modest changes in income shares, much less a distribution of future increments of growth.[51] Studies that followed this track in the 1970s never addressed this central question, remaining well inside the boundaries of mainstream development economics and trusting that though old solutions to development had failed to address the question of distributive equity, perhaps new renditions would succeed.[52] That faith in repeated iterations of the development formula was never explained, and the question gradually disappeared from the literature. Perhaps the leading successor of this literature in the Latin American field does not even include the original study in its bibliography.[53]

In the mid-1980s, the question of sustainability came to the fore and was soon embraced by virtually everyone in the development field. The idea that economic growth and development should be environmentally sustainable over the long term appears to have originated in the late 1960s or early 1970s.[54] Advocates of sustainability range in their affiliation with earlier developmentalists from Michael Redclift, whose research clearly indicates greater grass-roots political organization for the sake of equity as well as environmental protection, to a basic needs approach associated with Frances Stewart and the International Labour Organization.

Whatever the controversies in each of these subfields and emphases, together they make up a relatively complete mosaic of the development economics approach to the matter of development. Development economics may have been heretical, but it was not politically revolutionary.

Industrialization for Development

Much of the literature on economic development makes an argument for industrialization. The roots of this argument are clear: the concern for increasing the marginal productivity of labor; the need to avoid the tendency of an economy trading in a primary commodity to overspecialize and tilt away from industrial transformation; the prospect of increasing the wage share of national income through industry (and thereby, the domestic market for import-competing industries); and so on. Historically, industrialization was also a product of the specific course of growth in agricultural exports in such economies as Argentina. Industrial growth became possible in the trade-based expansion of the late nineteenth century, necessary in the trade collapse of the Depression, and virtuous in the postwar recommendations of development economists.

In Latin America, economies either used trade to industrialize in response to European and American industrialization or exported primary commodities to the rich countries, hoping to industrialize later. The former option was open only to the larger economies of the region; the deferred hope has yet to be realized. The small countries faced the daunting problems of substantially expanding their exports to the center and the additional task of restricting imports to make the most of export gains through domestic economic circulation.

The Nonindustrial Development Track

Import-substitution industrialization took on a progressive patina that did not extend to import substitution in agriculture; and small wonder. Imports in agriculture tended to be agroindustrial inputs and other commercial crops that fell outside the production frontier of traditional agriculture. Particularly in Central America, import substitution during the Great Depression and World War II focused on agriculture and not industry, in keeping with the problems of size and economic tradition of the region. Agricultural modernization for import substitution in agriculture meant the concentration of land and agricultural capital, however, and the dispossession of traditional communities in favor of expanding the labor market. Agricultural modernization was accused of focusing excessively on upscale domestic agricultural goods and eventually substituting agricultural export crops for those for domestic use.

A literature quickly emerged to criticize the connection between agricultural modernization and political instability in Central America.[55]

As closer examination shows, however, the disjuncture between export agriculture and domestic-use agriculture is far from complete; agricultural modernization for trade is hardly a zero-sum game, and food self-sufficiency is a tricky business for development. Whatever the shortcomings of the primary sector, it is the mainstay of the small economy, and progressive models of development will have to emphasize resource-based economic activities in most economies of Latin America.

Selected Political Aspects
of Economic Development

The economic development literature at its best leaves political science very little room on the economic side, other than to reiterate concerns for equitable development, meaning political measures that move in the direction of more sustainable growth that benefits the disadvantaged population without entirely compromising the need for growth. As Maier has pointed out, political economy can have either a political or an economic emphasis.[56] Political science can reappropriate economic notions from the market and its advocates into a new political economy. To a limited extent, this has been happening of late.[57] The concerns of political science rest lightly on the tradition of development economics but differ in addressing the questions of economic development from a political perspective, perhaps with greater skepticism about the prospects for development in Latin America's future under any plausible scenario. Political science's pedigree, in this regard, might read "by public economy out of dependency."[58]

In any event, two key areas are still within the purview of political science and of enormous importance to trade and development: international power and the proper role of the public sector. Power defines North-South economic relations in important ways, and the state has an enormously important role in the contest among visions of trade, growth, and development. Considering historical political economy and development economics affords an entry point into the debate over the role of politics in economic development strategy and the role of trade in the political economy of development. It will be particularly useful to recapture the trade debate from international economics, which has a different focus and is not as concerned to understand the dilemmas of development from Latin American perspectives.

Small nations presumably can address the complications of trade through macroeconomic policies, including barriers to trade such as tariffs, and monetary policies that direct the gains from trade into priority development activities. The stylized free trade argument is that trade liberalization promotes more economic activity; maximizes global production, consumption, exchange, and distribution; and enhances the welfare of the trading system. The critic of free trade asserts that maximizing global output may not benefit national development and that policy instruments such as tariffs, licenses, and multiple exchange rates enhance development by tailoring the extent of trade's impact.

The impact of these differences could not be greater for development politics. In one, free traders argue for a reduction in the role of the public sector in the trade system because public policy distorts market dynamics, gets prices wrong, allocates labor inefficiently, and makes political decisions about economic phenomena. The opposition claims that only the public sector can guide development so it will respond to broader development and welfare imperatives not attended by the market. Those imperatives include protecting infant industries (and, by extension, infant economies) from destructive trade competition, limiting the control of foreign investors over the complexion of trade, and so on.[59]

Obviously, this is hardly an argument for blanket protectionism. But three brief points are worth making. First, if governments are to achieve something more than trade for growth (and that only episodically), they must develop careful strategies for managing the side effects of different trade regimes so as to glean the most benefit for development from trade. Trade policy must be linked organically to a refined understanding of national economic development goals, a solid fiscal system, a socially conscious government, and a competent administrative structure. And the export multiplier must be increased especially in countries that count on exports of agricultural commodities if they are to undergo industrial transformation.[60]

Second, the weakness (or indirectness) of the connection between trade and development is not in itself an argument against trade. Although the vicissitudes of some trade regimes are obvious and the benefits of others elusive, policies that work against trade are politically dangerous in the current international system and certainly unproven as vehicles to enhance development, especially in smaller and more open economies. The caution is against ideological embrace of more trade, favoring instead a flexible "trade realism," defined by clear domestic economic and political goals.

Third, in regard to the relationship between open trade and economic efficiencies, it is well to observe that efficiencies are to trade what realism is to diplomacy. That is, Latin American countries as well as the United States are not inclined to govern their trade systems solely on the basis of efficiencies, though the term is often equated with virtue and used as a rhetorical hammer to bludgeon trade enemies. Because of its association with an uncontrolled market and the U.S.-led free trade system, economic efficiency has unfortunately become equated in Latin America with selling out to the United States.

Protectionism has additional flaws. Because of the historical difficulties of trade in Latin America, economic nationalism defines itself by its aversion to trade. Populism defines its agenda in reference to economic nationalism and import substitution. Economic development raises the standard of industrial deepening, which sometimes means an attempt to innovate without foreign trade, or in the case of steel, for example, an attempt to innovate in the most ambitious heavy industries with little regard for global supplies and conditions for competition. State expansion defines itself as a colleague of development; state contraction as the partner of underdevelopment and surrender. Fiscal expansion is seen as a goal in itself; fiscal contraction and fiscal crisis are to be avoided. Export expansion, or at least the generation of a trade surplus, is often the concern of the state but is not always accompanied by the proper mix of imports for development or for consumption.

The question of how to remove protectionism when it is in place is equally difficult. If a government protects an industry to generate rents from innovation in a new industry, what is to prevent these innovation rents from turning into protection rents, as apparently has happened in the Brazilian computer industry?[61]

Rudiger Dornbusch, who has done pioneering work on debt, open macroeconomic modeling, and national economic policy reforms in Latin America, has argued that the debt resolution question is primarily political, not economic.[62] That is true of trade and development questions as well. The political economics of development is, from the standpoint of political science, the political matter of public allocation of scarce resources for the sake of growth, equity, welfare, and other objectives. Aside from the historical record of trade and development in the region, the best approach to the trade-development question is through a definition of development. Because of the earlier contention that development is contextual and time-bound, a proper focus for its definition involves adjustment in the wake of the debt crisis.

The Impact of Debt and Adjustment

The debt literature includes some uneven treatments of the role of the external sector in development. Undoubtedly, this is in part because of the rapidly changing international debt picture and the desire of some scholarship to associate itself with one or another solution to it. The bibliography runs the gamut from traditional concerns for economic adjustment in the international system,[63] to more sympathetic development-oriented adjustment policies,[64] to a new sort of basic needs literature,[65] as well as more descriptive treatments of the past and present debt crises.

The most recent addition to the latter category is Carlos Marichal's *A Century of Debt Crises in Latin America*, which was preceded by Pedro-Pablo Kuczynski's *Latin American Debt*, Barbara Stallings's *Banker to the Third World* (a more substantive global view focusing on capital flows), and a handful of important edited volumes on debt and stabilization.[66] Much of this literature focuses on the international regimes and economic orthodoxies (or, in the case of Brazil and Argentina, the heterodoxies) implied by external stabilization and debt renegotiation.[67]

The importance of external debt as an inducement to trade cannot be denied. It is clearly the principal reason for the tremendous turnaround in Latin American policy circles concerning the virtue of trade. But with the exception of the Stallings volume, this literature is either silent or inconclusive on two principal concerns of the present study: the historical role of trade in the generation of debt crises, and the domestic development consequences of debt repayment and trade promotion schemes. To the extent that domestic development receives attention, it is defined as adjustment to external crisis, measured by domestic economic performance.[68] Recent work on the impact of stabilization in developing countries and the relationship of stabilization and debt to democracy links more directly to the issues under consideration here.[69]

Marichal proposes to tie trade cycles to debt cycles in Latin American history. He hypothesizes that the cyclical trajectory of the international economic system was the prime mover of debt crisis in Latin America between 1820 and 1930. One of the consequences of Latin American trade for domestic development was the dependence of the fiscal system on the customshouse, especially after postindependence tax reform. Marichal contends that the inadequacy of the revenue base generated by trade necessitated foreign borrowing.[70] But necessity did not automatically generate willing foreign creditors. In the cases of Venezuela and Ecuador, the postindependence defaults of the 1820s made foreign borrowing impossible for half a century, and the domestic financial burden fell on customs taxes, the limits of which led to various inventive means of dunning domestic elites.[71]

Marichal and many other analysts of various debt crises demur in trying to establish whether the debt crisis or the trade crisis came first and the particular ways in which one responded to the other. His otherwise excellent analysis of the coincidence of trade and debt crises does not venture a guess as to the primacy of one or the other. Trade crisis could precede debt crisis, and vice versa. Depending on the specifics of its trade bill, the country may have more or less maneuvering room against trade or debt problems.[72]

Historically, the question is of extraordinary importance. If trade crisis is a product of reduced facilities for financing trade among the lending countries, short-term credits may be the solution. Alternatively, if the debt crisis is a product of a generalized recession in the importing countries of Europe, remedies from the center are not likely. If the trade crisis is generated artificially by protectionist influences in the principal markets for Latin American goods, diplomatic solutions are suggested. If deterioration in the external balance is the result of declining terms of trade with the developed countries, a change in export mix or volume seems indicated.[73]

In any case, the implications for Latin American politics are unclear. When facing external shocks, Latin American countries often have limited alternatives. If the shock is the product of worldwide recession, the foreign economic policy options of Latin American nations are minimal. Expanding exports and reducing imports to generate a trade surplus is more difficult when the problems of recession in importing countries compound the usual obstacles of inadequate supply incentives, inflation in exporting countries, and the like. If, however, trade finance problems or selective protection are the sources of trade crisis, the options are presumably greater. Adjustment can be derived from bilateral or multilateral negotiations, assuming that default is not part of the problem. If the terms of trade are deteriorating, a turn inward or a trade diversification strategy might be appropriate, but the feasibility and effectiveness of such strategies are not clear. In any event, the first goal of trade policy is to insulate against external shocks, and the best first step may be through trade and financial diversification.[74]

The prospect of trading to get the country out of debt depends not only on the gross external balance sheet, which is a function of the allocation of trade gains to consumption, savings, and investment, as well as artificial state interventions in trade, but also on the specific trade balances of key industries counted on to finance the debt. Gerald K. Helleiner, among others, argues that contraction of imports in less developed countries has more impact on industrial investment than on consumption—investment which, in the case of Latin American industrial countries, is linked inextricably to export performance, as well as to domestic growth.[75]

Stallings is more theoretically interesting on the relationship between trade and capital flows. She notes that one of the principal arguments in the literature on international capital flows stipulates that capital is exported from the North following a deterioration in the terms of trade in the lending country. Improvement in the terms of trade makes the climate for foreign lending less favorable. The empirical materials to back this line of argument come from nineteenth-century exports of capital to Latin America and other debtors.[76] Stallings criticizes this argument as a general model for short-run capital flows, especially in times of crisis, so its policy relevance for much of the period 1880 to 1930 must come into question. After 1980, the terms of trade turned against much of Latin America, as they did in the 1930s, and capital flows dried up after 1982, as they did after 1929. But the trade response of the United States has been much more robust and the Latin American recovery slower. The international division of labor is much different, and capital export is actually going from South to North, helping finance the U.S. debt.[77]

One of the more interesting and politically relevant theoretical arguments is that both trade and capital flows are functions of national income movements. A model most appropriate to Latin America involves a highly concentrated relationship of trade and capital flows between lender and debtor, in which both the value of the borrower's exports and the availability of credit for domestic investment in Latin America deepen the links between North and South.[78] Several cases in nineteenth-century Latin America seem to fit this mold, including Chile during the nitrate boom, Peru during the guano boom, and Argentina before World War I.[79] Though the paucity of the data makes an empirical test of this relationship extremely difficult, it can be hypothesized that there is a strong positive relationship among domestic investment, trade flows, and debt, and that the relationship is stronger in a concentrated bilateral model. It would seem that the relationship between trade and development is much stronger when the balance-of-payments situation is undemanding. That is, when the benefits of trade are available for domestic investment, economic development (at least in its most narrow definition) is more likely. By contrast, where capital and trade flows are used to face external payments crises, the availability of credit to stimulate imports is reduced and the foreign capital market is leaner. Foreign investments are less likely because of the deterioration in the investment climate. The multiplier effect of easy credit is reduced, and fewer of the gains from trade are reinvested in domestic projects.

That does not mean that trade and development can occur only under conditions of balance-of-payments surpluses. In fact, many Latin American economies have expanded exports and domestic economic investment while running balance-of-payments deficits for years on end. It is not a payments deficit that is in question; it is the significance of an external payments crisis for trade and development.

Discriminating further between external commitments and domestic development, we can stipulate that in the face of balance-of-payments difficulties, Latin American nations traditionally have had a choice either to finance payments deficits or to undertake adjustment. The former is the typical choice for short-term balance-of-payments problems and was the remedy conceived under the original charter of the International Monetary Fund. The IMF offered an international financial facility through which member nations could finance their balance-of-payments shortfalls in the short term. The GATT also provided short-term escape from the international trade regime for countries suffering balance-of-payments problems. It goes without saying that financing external payments problems also involved adjustment because borrower countries were, at a minimum, required to squeeze enough liquidity out of the domestic economy to service the debt.

Chronic balance-of-payments problems, particularly those that veer into crisis, mandate structural adjustment. Although the definition of adjustment has varied over time, it has two interactive components: adjusting to correct external balances, and undertaking domestic adjustment to implement overall changes in the composition of production, consumption, exchange, and distribution in the Latin American economy. Both sides of adjustment are governed by international and national political decisions, which directly affect the prospects for domestic development.

Traditionally, stabilization and adjustment have been associated with orthodox macroeconomic austerity programs to shock the economy back into external equilibrium. Those typically include devaluation of the exchange rate to bring the prices of traded goods into line with underlying economic fundamentals. Devaluation makes imports more expensive, thereby suppressing some demand for unnecessary luxuries. Exports are correspondingly less expensive and presumably more competitive. Other elements of orthodox austerity programs include tightening credit, reducing the public sector deficit, moving to market-based prices and away from subsidies (called "allowing prices to seek their own level"), and engaging in wage restraint. Each of these policies may vary in style and mix, but they all have the common goal of correcting external payments problems via exchange rates, trade liberalization, and other macroeconomic adjustments.

Orthodox stabilization has been criticized for its insensitivity to the social role of the public sector and the huge impact of austerity on the poor. Large contractions in the public sector mean unemployment, because the state is often the employer of last resort (and the politician's patronage system of first resort). Tightening credit and diverting it to the export sector often means the collapse of small domestic industries in favor of large internationally oriented companies.[80] "Realistic exchange rates" mean short-term contractions in imports often necessary for production. Domestic recession, a reduction in the wage share of national income, even deindustrialization are the consequences. Small wonder that in Brazil the 1953 campaign slogan of the "penny against the million" (*o tostão contra o milhão*) becomes, in the debt crisis of the 1980s, "not a penny for the IMF" (*nem um tostão para o FMI*).[81]

Even on its own terms, IMF stabilization has been criticized for failing to achieve its goals. Empirical work in the 1970s and 1980s has shown that each country of Latin America responds differently to the orthodoxy of economic stabilization, choosing wage restraint, fiscal austerity, and the like.[82] Particularly in the side effects of domestic recession, past orthodox treatments have sacrificed domestic growth in favor of external stabilization over the short term. When the state is a willing accomplice, as opposed to an additional victim, such programs can result in a fundamental reordering of the economy through the external sector, with or without a coherent adjustment program.[83] This argument, though historically valuable in understanding the progression of stabilization and adjustment policies in Latin America, is somewhat precious because it merely distinguishes between whether external stabilization leads to a de facto adjustment process under certain circumstances, or whether adjustment itself is part of the initial "package" to combine growth, policy reform, and external stabilization.

By and large, the IMF over the years has come to accept the criticism that domestic recession as a side effect of stabilization is undesirable. That does not mean the disappearance of tough rhetoric about "obeying nurse"[84] or "making hard choices" in Latin American debt and development matters. But it has meant more apparent concern for the domestic consequences of stabilization and adjustment, even though that concern often seems little more than lip service in actual practice. Privileged readers of confidential IMF documents analyzing recent economic events in countries with IMF agreements find that the IMF is sometimes more sympathetic to the social question than either the commercial banks or the World Bank, and certainly more so than the U.S. Treasury Department.[85]

Furthermore, in recent years, especially since the debt crisis began, the emphasis has shifted from short-term stabilization programs to long-term structural adjustment, recognizing the existence of durable structural obstacles to external equilibrium in Latin America. Stabilization and adjustment have begun to emphasize the longer term because short-term strategies often sacrificed long-term sustainability in adjustment programs, and because the terms of external payments problems are stretched out much longer now than in previous decades.

This approach has many problems. Here it is useful to trace the political affinity between certain structural adjustment measures and trade-related policies and to connect them to likely development consequences. In nineteenth-century Latin America, and to a more limited extent today, the alternatives for trade have been very limited, and for development-connected trade even more so. Intraregional trade depends on the regional foreign exchange constraint, the complementarity of national economies, relative peace among likely trade partners, and a relatively sophisticated trade finance system. In nineteenth-century Latin America, the future countries of the kingdom of Guatemala, or the three principals of Gran Colombia, or even the provinces of Argentina and Brazil all existed in relative economic isolation from one another. The demands of intraregional integration were simply too much for the state of the system at that time. Some case evidence suggests that intraregional trade as a proportion of total foreign commerce may have peaked in the independence period, before the nineteenth-century export expansion began.[86]

Intraregional trade has provided only an occasional respite from the reality of dependence on great powers. Since independence, the meaningful long-term trade alternatives for Latin America have come in the form of trading one hegemon for another, turning away from Portugal or Spain toward Britain, or later away from Britain toward the United States. Ironically, externally dependent Latin American countries are protected from external shock only if they can be handed off from one hegemon to another. If the hegemons' economic cycles move together so that both are in financial crisis or recession or protectionist disposition at the same time (as the historical evidence suggests was the case in many of the nineteenth-century financial panics), Latin America is both chronically dependent on the Great Powers and poorly insulated from systemic shocks that affect the international economic system writ large.

In contemporary domestic adjustment to external payments crisis, the costs of adjustment are often socially and politically distributed in regressive ways. For example, in the case of Mexico, the disinclination of the government to import food grains in a time of declining reserves and an external stabilization drive ultimately meant the suppression of demand in Mexico. With demand suppressed, fewer imports were required, and Mexico even managed to declare more than a million tons of wheat to be surplus in 1986, thereupon freeing the wheat for use as cattle feed although previous consumers were going hungry.[87] Similar suppression of demand has taken place elsewhere. Also in Mexico, a central principle of stabilization and adjustment has been wage suppression, lowering wage share of national income and contributing to depressed demand. Some recent scholarship has questioned the economic and social validity of such a strategy for Mexico, with interesting critical implications for other similar cases.[88]

In Central America, the adjustment crisis of the 1980s meant that real per capita consumption fell an estimated 39 to 78 percent in Nicaragua; in Costa Rica, the decline was from 26 to 52 percent.[89] It is significant for the Central American crisis that Guatemala suffered least, partly because of its lesser dependence on external factors. Such partial autonomy suggests the possibility that the domestic impact of adjustment can be reduced by increasing the insulation of the national economy from external influence. Alternatively, political elites may let the burden of adjustment fall directly on the poor, as occurred in Mexico despite its closed economy and high capacity for import substitution in agriculture. Insulation from external shock, then, is only one precondition for a broad development policy at home. But further analysis and qualification of these contentions will be postponed until Chapter 6.

CHAPTER 3

Natural Resource Politics, Trade, and Development

The reasonable man adapts himself to the world: the
unreasonable one persists in trying to adapt the world to
himself. Therefore all progress depends on the
unreasonable man.
—George Bernard Shaw, "Reason"

To conquer the earth, dominate the water, subjugate the
forest, those have been our tasks. And in this struggle,
which now extends over centuries, we are securing victory
after victory. Many other [victories] await the constancy
of our effort and the persistent courage to realize them.
—Getúlio Vargas, "Speech on the Amazon," 1942

THE RECENT 'DISCOVERY' of natural resource issues in Latin America
does not do justice to their historical importance to the region's development experience.[1] From the time of the first conquerors' steps into the
New World, dominion over the natural resources of Latin America shaped
colonial economic policy. The progress of Latin American national economies after independence likewise was framed by natural resource endowments: the resurgence of mining, the settlement of new lands for export
agriculture, and, in the first decades of this century, the pursuit of oil.
Now, as the century closes, Latin America is in the second decade of debt
crisis, and natural resources reappear on center stage as *materia prima* for
politicians and international economic experts seeking to reform Latin
America and "trade away" the debt.

The single most striking difference in the region's environmental politics
at the start of the 1990s is a concern for the conservation of resources as a
first-order political priority. Critics of past development have successfully
indicted the sacrifice of biological diversity, environmental public goods,
and rural welfare as unacceptable costs of exploiting nature for trade and
development. They focus on the effect of external pressure on exploitation
of natural resources, as well as the deficiencies of national development
strategies vis-à-vis the long-term sustainability of a country's natural
resource base.

As the 1990s begin, virtually every institution with an international mandate claims a role in "correcting" environmental abuses in Latin America and other parts of the Third World. The World Bank puts environmental limits on the economic development projects its supports, trying to strike a balance between environment and development.[2] The U.N. Conference on Trade and Development has developed an International Tropical Timber Agreement, a 44-nation International Tropical Timber Organization (ITTO), and a putative commitment to sustainable forest use. The European Parliament has declared its intention to tax timber exports from tropical countries that do not exploit their forest resources in "sustainable ways."[3] The heads of the United Nations, the IMF, and the World Bank have met with the World Commission on Environment and Development in Norway in the first summit of transnational actors concerned with the environment.[4] To great fanfare, the Paris Economic Summit of 1989 was declared "green." The 1972 Stockholm conference will be commemorated with a 1992 global conference on environment and development in Brazil. Each of the governments involved is monitored by nongovernmental organizations whose principal activity is to militate throughout political systems at the international, national, and local levels.

The environmental bandwagon is extraordinarily crowded, but its focus is hazy and its politics deficient. The institutions claiming responsibility for environment, development, and international economic stability emit confusing and contradictory signals. World Bank President Barber Conable (along with much of the OECD community) encourages Latin America to trade more to relieve poverty and to protect the environment, though many argue that increased trade based on specialization is irrelevant (or damaging) to poverty alleviation and that more trade would further exploit resources.[5] Despite its newfound environmental virtue, the World Bank's policy-based lending is inattentive to such a prospect and favors (indeed, mandates) economic development through privatization and specialization through comparative advantage.

The GATT has given mixed signals on trade in tropical products by seeking an accord liberalizing imports by developed countries in the Uruguay Round,[6] the European Community threatens to tax virtually all tropical timber imports, and the United States insists on linking trade in tropical products to the general agricultural trade agenda. Meanwhile, the OECD countries that threaten to engage in punitive sanctions continue their own wasteful subsidies to agriculture and energy, at an estimated cost of $300 billion per year.[7] Those subsidies were considered so inviolate to the Europeans, Japanese, and Koreans that the entire GATT round was undermined to save them.

The World Commission on Environment and Development (Brundt-land Commission) considered the debt crisis to be the most critical international pressure point forcing overexploitation of natural resources in high-debt countries and suggested debt reduction as the first priority of the international system. In Latin American domestic politics, governments are divided over the priority of external stabilization, domestic structural adjustment, and poverty alleviation. Politicians from Mexico to Brazil profess their interest in sustainable development and the conservation of nature, but not at the expense of economic growth. They grouse publicly about the hypocrisy of the OECD and voice concern that international pressure will force them to become hothouses for rich ecotourists.

The critique of overexploitation of natural resources and resulting environmental degradation focuses on two of the principal topics of this book but ignores a third. Criticism focuses on the effect of pressure from the external sector on rates and kinds of natural resource exploitation, as well as the deficiencies of national development strategies vis-à-vis the long-term sustainability of a country's natural resource base. But the description and critique of external sector and national development strategies do not focus on the political structures and processes that generate different political outcomes. This chapter examines the relationship between natural resource politics, national development, and the external sector, with special attention to the role of the current international debt and payments crisis in the rate and nature of resource degradation, and the contradictory role of the public sector in treating the exploitation of Latin America's resource base. Rather than ignoring the political side, this chapter focuses on the political attributes of international trade and national development as they affect natural resource conservation.[8]

For all its historical familiarity, exploitation of natural resources in Latin America has not generated data or analysis adequate to the complexity and variability of the relationship between biological conservation and economic growth and development. Particularly weak is the often asserted but empirically undefended connection between the international trade system, domestic development, and pressure on resources. The literature addressing these connections is mainly outside political science, but it can offer some beginning clues to political relationships that underlie natural resource policies. The purpose in exploring those clues is to give a political interpretation of the integral importance of trade to development and ecological well-being, as well as the relationship between sustainable management, ecological awareness, and the international trade system.

The general criticisms of natural resource use in Latin America fall into two areas of concern: that there is a direct relationship between trade (especially under conditions of debt pressure) and resource depletion;[9] and that incentives to domestic development are perverse insofar as they produce negative long-term consequences for natural resources.[10] Both of these critiques include varying degrees of concern about the policies of multilateral development assistance institutions in depletion of natural resources, especially, but not exclusively, the World Bank. Two of the most commonly defended remedies for misuse of environmental resources involve progressive social policy to alleviate poverty and debt relief that lessens pressures from the external sector on resource use.

The potential consequences of environmental politics for Latin American and international trade and development politics are great. If there is a direct relationship between the debt crisis, external stabilization, and accelerated resource depletion, or among resource depletion and the privatization of natural resource industries and the removal of subsidies from agriculture, forestry, and fishing, they constitute a direct indictment of the World Bank's policy-based lending to less developed countries, the IMF stabilization agreements with high-debt countries, and the entire trade policy architecture of the United States. Worse yet, it would question the validity of the World Bank's newly found environmental virtue, which is the calling card of the bank's policy reform in the late 1980s. This chapter will qualify those stereotyped relationships between the external sector and resource degradation to question environmental policy recommendations focusing on the external sector, while detailing a more complex set of hypotheses about the relationship of trade, development, and environment.

International actors and policy analysts have ignored the role of political structure and process in the environmental debate, in favor of a policy approach.[11] Because global environmental policies have failed to link policy recommendations to the structure and limits of politics at the international level, and because those policies have been guided by disturbing fallacies, the prospect for the 1990s is a continuation of the legacy of unintended consequences that have already degraded so much of the region's biota.

Specifically, environmental policies proposed for Latin America have searched for a nonexistent "smoking gun," a straightforward cause of environmental deterioration that is susceptible to cure through good policy. Naturally, attention focuses on the forces that usually receive blame for Latin America's ills: the state, the debt crisis, "the tyranny of external trade,"[12] and poverty. Reformists assume that environmental dividends will accrue from debt relief, trade reform, progressive incomes policies, agrarian reform, and privatization.

The critique of trade, debt, and development that provides the fundament for proposed international remedies for environmental abuse is based on durable stereotype and unsubstantiated surmise about the relationship of the international system to environmental and economic sustainability. The clichés and assumptions may be valid, but none of these assumptions is based on adequate data or critical examination of the relationship between policy and the political structures and coalitions required to effect them. Nor do these questions receive attention that is methodologically adequate to include the complex interrelationship among OECD development and trade policy and the future of resource conservation and use in Latin America. Policymakers proceed with programs in the absence of convincing evidence that what they are proposing either makes sense or makes a difference, or, in fact, is based on a convincing set of assumptions about human behavior. The prescriptions offered are often laced with policy platitudes that hide the revolutionary political changes required to meet the requirements of a politics of sustainability. The result is a useless and often harmful policy mishmash that shortchanges the global dimensions of environmental politics.

This does not mean simply that "the whole world suffers," but that the policy approach to environmental politics in the 1990s is ineffectual because of its apolitical aspirations. For reasons of efficacy as well as normative concern, a global analysis would be a more appropriate focus of Latin American environmental politics. The main concern would be to create political conditions that might change the styles of development and trade that are currently causing environmental degradation. To the extent that poverty alleviation and other social policies are involved, some decision-making at the national level is important. But the clear implication of this argument is that radically different approaches to environmental politics in the 1990s must go beyond Latin American national systems and U.S.–Latin American relations to include the entire OECD and the international political system. The conclusions are extreme, but certainly less so than the prospect of continued complicity in the environmentally destructive dynamics of past decades.

Trade and Natural Resources in Latin American History

The historical antecedents of current depredations are well-known in the study of ecology. For centuries, conservation and human dominion have been counterposed, and the ravages of human destruction of biological resources have inspired polemicists and poets alike.[13] In Latin America, certainly, the historical relationship between external shock or, more generously, external incentive and domestic resource use is clear. In Argentina, the modern economy was built on expanding the agricultural frontier for sheep and maximizing the use of land resources through specialization. Indeed, Argentina's settlement was delayed by the failure of conquerors to find silver in the basin of the Rio de la Plata. Its role as an entrepôt in the first part of the colonial period itself was dictated by the resource importance of the Viceroyalty of Peru.

The connection between resource depredation and conquest was perhaps even clearer in Brazil and along the littoral of Central America. From the Yucatán Peninsula of Mexico, to Hispaniola, Central America, Cuba, and Brazil, early conquistadors were introduced to brazilwood. Soon the Europeans cleared forest for agriculture, dyewood, and fuel; in the Age of Wood in Latin America civilization carved up the biomass of the New World's primeval forests. Even the name of Belize is said to derive from the first dyewood cutter to land on its shores in 1640.[14]

In Belize, on the fringes of the British incursions into the Western Hemisphere, the mahogany and logwood trade combined with privateering, smuggling, and territorial disputes across the Bay of Honduras and down the Mosquito Coast. Mosquito Indian communities were expected to provision buccaneering ships with game from manatee to sea turtle as the adventurers made commercial runs from Belize to Jamaica. Following Elizabethan tradition, British and Spanish crowns fought over the territories from Yucatán to Nicaragua. Logwood and Indian endowments were among the riches disputed in the courts of Europe.[15] From Haiti to Honduras, Europeans sought to exploit mahogany for the European cabinetmaking industry. By the 1820s, traditional mahogany oligarchs in Belize faced threatening competition because of depleted local mahogany resources and the advent of foreign traders taking advantage of British free trade politics. Smuggling from Guatemala, Mexico, and Honduras was the short-term result, followed by British expansionism, opportunistic land grants, and concessions wheedled from the Indians of the Mosquito Shore.[16] Later, after independence, the kingdom of Guatemala and its heirs in Central America would view trade with suspicion precisely because of the imperialistic design of the British in the Central American Atlantic region.[17]

Logwood, mahogany, and brazilwood were hardly the only lures of Central America. Colonial authorities built on centuries-old traditions of resource extraction in cochineal, forcing overproduction, which in the short term would make the value of cochineal farming in the Spanish Indies second only to precious metals at the end of the sixteenth century.[18] Consideration of the unique political economy and culture of cochineal extraction was far from the conquerors' minds when they permanently undermined an artisan dye industry possessed of fabled technology and lore.

Connected to the egregious ecological abuses of the colonial period was the annihilation of Indian communities throughout Latin America or their subordination as a labor force for the colonial economy. As can be seen in different resource-scarce traditional settings under threat today, externally impelled transformation of traditional resource exploitation carries with it a much different and more exploitive logic.[19] The colonial trade legacy for the Indians and the woodlands of Latin America was extinction, paralleling in some respects that of the United States in its transformation of traditional populations. Portuguese conquerors, once recovered from the charms of Amerindian utopia, drove Brazilian coastal tribes into *aldeias*[20] and sent out the storied *bandeirante* to capture prospective workers for brazilwood extraction or later for sugar production, transforming idyllic pre-Columbian Brazil into a death camp for natives. The Indian population of Brazil now numbers something like 200,000, in contrast to the 3.5 million or more at the time of conquest.

The exploitation of Brazil became the driving force behind the Portuguese slave and sugar trade as well. Africans proved inhospitable to Portuguese imperial plans, so the sugar industry shifted to Brazil, defense of Portuguese commerce in Africa was left to the Brazilians, and "in the seventeenth and eighteenth centuries Angola was a Portuguese province of Brazil."[21] As Brazil grew to eclipse its parent Portugal, the twin pillars of sugar and slaves fed Afro-Brazilian economic growth until the nineteenth century.

In the Spanish viceroyalties of Peru and New Spain, the story of trade-based decimation of the Amerindian population was similar. In the New World, the Spanish crown destroyed a population of perhaps 50 million indigenous subjects in its colonization efforts.[22] Traditional institutions of forced labor such as the *mita* in Peru were adapted and "hostile" Indians committed to outright slavery in central Chile and Bolivia (Upper Peru) to man the mercury and silver mines of Huancavelica and Potosí by New World populations apparently not considered by those who later associated the progress of the human race with expanded commerce and civilization with Christianization. As a result, the entire pre-Columbian "vertical archipelago" system analyzed by economic and ecological anthropologists was undermined, and ritual crops coca and maize took on new significance, to the detriment of local communities.[23]

Amerindians in Chile and Argentina were also decimated, though somewhat later. Argentina's destruction of the Indians of the pampas was a direct consequence of changing trade relations with Europe, as well as the violence and economic adjustments of the early national period. In Chile, the elimination of the Mapuche was a tortured outcome of a national frontier settlement policy that began with the first efforts of Pedro de Valdivia.[24]

Modern conceit allows us to dismiss these depredations of the Old World—after proper lament—by saying that the twentieth-century world (or the postabolition world) employs a different system: secular, wealth expanding, modernizing, and progressive. As one leading analyst of international relations has argued, the British free trade empire and the post–World War II American free trade hegemony have in common the prospect of peaceful and expanding trade that enhances the welfare of all nations under a growing web of interdependence.[25]

But a look at Guatemalan Maya in the coffee and banana booms from 1890 to 1930 dispels that rosy notion, as indigenous communities were dispossessed and shuttled to tropical plantations to work for United Fruit. Yaqui, Mayo, Seri, and other Indian nations were rounded up by Porfirian slavers and sold off to the henequen aristocracy of the Yucatán peninsula. In Colombia, the cost of labor in coffee was managed through a complex system of *enganchamiento*, or "hooking" labor recruits. International competition among the United States, Canada, Argentina, and Chile was partly responsible for Chile's pursuing its comparative advantage in rural labor, thereby preserving an antiquated and exploitative rural social system for the sake of price competition.[26] To bring the horrors forward to our own time, *empreiteiros* or *gatos* hunt laborers for the Amazon gold mines, and *coyotes* contract labor for the export tomato industry in Mexico, often under abysmal conditions. Resource-impelled destruction of Indian communities continues, whether against the Yanomami in the Brazilian frontier of Roraima, or the Waorani in the eastern extremes of Amazonian Ecuador.

Ample evidence exists that in the nineteenth and twentieth centuries the accelerated depletion of natural forest throughout Latin America paralleled that of North America. Forest in Brazil had been cleared since aboriginal times, but after the conquest the southeastern Atlantic forest was subjected to repeated devastations, either by frontiersmen, swidden farmers, cane growers, or coffee planters. Warren Dean estimates that as much as 30,000 square kilometers in the southeast of Brazil was cleared to plant coffee in the nineteenth century. The coniferous forests of southern Brazil have virtually disappeared since the 1920s. This deforestation in the economic center of the country contrasted with the almost negligible rates in the Amazon, where until the 1960s something like three-fifths of the region's labor force was still dedicated to extractive industries.[27]

In Mexico, forestry concessions during the Porfiriato (1876–1910) accompanied mining and railroad booms to contribute to massive deforestation throughout the *mesa central*. In the mining areas of Michoacán, especially, the devastation of the high forests is still apparent. Throughout Latin America, the requirements of the mining industry and the development of rail transportation, along with such energy-intensive agroindustries as sugar, resulted in the accelerated depletion of forest resources after 1870. The imperative of deforestation then, as today, was development, impelled to a great extent by external demand and pressure.

External Pressures, National Imperatives, and Natural Resource Use

Despite historical experience and the recent appearance of two important volumes on the historical origins of resource exploitation and transformation in the New World,[28] resource degradation has been connected to the international system mainly through narrative, not tied to the theoretical or empirical work on development. In particular, it is strange that the impact of debt-related export promotion and import constraint on resource management in Latin America has not received much scholarly attention, except in the interesting preliminary analysis undertaken by the U.N. Economic Commission on Latin America and the Caribbean in cooperation with the U.N. Environmental Program.[29] To a great extent, resource issues have become a matter of social science interest only recently, and then mainly emphasizing the development side, with only occasional, fragmentary connections to the external sector.

This has not deterred policymakers from arguing mightily about alternatives to deforestation and land degradation in international fora, but generally without benefit of adequate formal research. Admittedly, policymakers are not accountable for research findings that do not exist, but neither are they known for their patience with the formal canons of scholarship or the parsimony of their findings. In this event, they are particularly hard-pressed to await the long research horizons of rain forest or arid lands ecology. Were they to wait, they might well be disappointed with the political naïveté of conservationists, as well as the continuing ignorance of developmentalists.

The dangers of proceeding with policy packages without such research are generally understated, compared with the risks of doing nothing. The political and ecological blunders made in the name of expeditious policy should inspire caution.[30] To modernize seminomadic herdsmen, for example, development specialists have recommended herd-building strategies, consistent with the goal of maximizing output from a given resource base. But the goal of steady herd growth often conflicts with the sustainable management of fragile lands, and overgrazing, desertification, and starvation ensue.[31] In similar fashion, developers in Brazil assumed the eucalyptus plantations in the Amazon would provide charcoal for the pig iron plants associated with the gigantic Carajás iron ore project. Yet, after several years of effort, dissembling, and failure in cultivating eucalyptus, authorities in the late 1980's issued plans to cut natural forest to provide the estimated 2.4 million metric tons of charcoal needed each year for Grande Carajás. This would mean the use of an estimated 10.4 million metric tons of dry wood annually, or an equivalent of a 620-story building with a base 100 meters square.[32] Now the Japanese, under the International Tropical Timber Organization, are proposing a "sustainable" forest production program in the western Amazon, without having undertaken necessary research to determine the meaning of sustainability in that fragile and contested area.

Connecting the Phenomena to Theory

Paradoxically, the general inadequacy of academic work on the relationship between trade, development, and environmental conservation has not slowed theoretical or policy generalizations about the nature of the process. Commonly, analysts connect the external sector directly to domestic resource allocation under the stress of debt and external payments problems. This permits the categorical assertion that macroeconomic changes induced by the debt crisis cause intensification of trade in Latin America and that such trade accelerates exploitation of natural resources there. Perhaps the most popular case cited is the "hamburger rain forest," in which Central American deforestation is seen to be a direct function of export cattle production for the institutional beef industry in the United States.

The environmental and resource allocation questions facing high-debt countries are powerful and potentially devastating, as are related consequences of theoretical and policy arguments. There is thus great value in learning more about the intellectual background and empirical reality of Latin American resource connections to the exterior. At first blush, there is strong intuitive ground to suppose that deforestation, poaching, animal smuggling, and high-impact frontier settlement all respond to external economic shock. The anecdotal evidence seems endless. The collapse of the mining industry in Bolivia forces the government to develop new human settlement policies affecting fragile watersheds and biosphere reserves in the tropical lowlands.[33] Foreign exchange bottlenecks result in more exploitation of coastal lowlands in Peru, accompanied by a halt in agrarian reform, the destruction of cooperatives, and the presumed intensification of marginal, steep-slope agriculture as the labor market changes on the coast.[34] Promotion of agricultural exports changes the cropping, credit, and microecological management strategies of smallholders and *ejidatarios* in rainfed Mexico, as does the removal of agricultural subsidies as a part of economic stabilization. Export promotion may also extend to the overexploitation of game animals and aggravated abuse of species covered under the Convention on International Trade in Endangered Species (CITES), ignoble for its own sake, but also threatening traditional communities where commercial incursions change lives that are built around natural resources. The debt crisis in Ecuador is associated with greater incentives to expand shrimp cultivation for export, resulting in the degradation of mangrove nurseries along the coast. And population pressures combined with regressive incomes policies and limited industrial development in the center-south of Brazil provoke the federal government to intensify settlement of the Amazon frontier, resulting in the accelerated deforestation of the western rain forests of Rondônia and Acre.[35]

The assumption that trade is both the cause and the reflection of these intensified uses of natural resources has some foundation in economic theory, though it is not usually treated explicitly. In recent years, efforts have focused on the allocated impact of the overvaluation of foreign exchange attributed to natural resource-based growth, particularly oil in the "Dutch Disease" literature. Another subject receiving attention is the comparative advantage and related attractiveness of foreign investment resulting from differential stringency of environmental regulations. And the connection between trade and derived demand for resource inputs has been examined. Despite these efforts, though, the literatures on international trade, natural resources, and development remain unintegrated.[36] Here I will lay out some of the traditional theoretical arguments behind each of those fields, which can guide subsequent analysis connecting trade and development to the politics of natural resource management. Again, this overly simple exposition is useful mainly for its heuristic value in locating the empirical work and political analysis that follow.

International trade theory provides the rationale for increased production and export of natural resources. The factor-abundance hypothesis argues that a country will specialize in producing goods that take advantage of its relatively abundant factors of production. The relative abundance of a factor of production suggests a relatively low opportunity cost associated with its use, manifested through a low relative price vis-à-vis other factors. Since the price of the final product depends to a large extent on prices of resources important to its production, abundant resources, including natural resources, are more likely to be exploited to reduce costs and enhance competitiveness.[37]

Further, if land (or forests or fisheries) is generally abundant in Latin

America, we would expect its growing exploitation through the expansion of the agricultural frontier, linked both to external performance and domestic development. In fact, this has been the essence of agricultural modernization, food security, and import substitution in agriculture policies since the Great Depression. The most flexible of these is agriculture; many countries of Latin America do not figure large in the forest or fish trade for lack of endowments or tradition (or because they have already destroyed their forests).

From resource economics, the Hotelling rule contends that natural resource conservation makes economic sense according to the net rate of return over time, as well as rates of return on alternative investments. Hence the rationality of "banking" oil (or some other exhaustible resource) in the ground, as opposed to extracting it for sale, depends on the expectation of future net rates of return on oil and rates of return on alternative investments to which oil revenues might be put.[38] In renewable resource management, the argument is similar, except for the possibility of increasing the gross value of the resource in the market through regrowth and regeneration. In general, the intensity of use or harvesting responds both to the cost of extraction and the price of the final output. Resource harvesting leading to depletion can result from both low extraction cost and high final output value.[39]

Combining the Hotelling rule and the trade-offs of international trade versus domestic production according to factor (and resource) abundance, it becomes clear that one easy path toward equilibrium in external payments can be found in the expansion of agriculture, forestry, and other natural resource industries. As the factor (land or labor) becomes scarcer and/or increases in price, the rate of exploitation of exhaustible natural resources goes up. The value of land is determined to some degree by external demand for agricultural commodities, which changes the opportunity costs of conservation for the landholder. Depending on world agricultural prices, technology, and investments, marginal lands are brought into agricultural use, forests are cleared for planting, and groundwater is tapped to make semiarid lands arable.

The social results will be that agrarian redistribution and the price of land or, more generally, the welfare of the rural poor and the price of land will vary inversely.[40] As land values increase, the landowners' marginal propensity to dispossess low-output tenants also increases. As the value of land goes up, so does speculative investment in land and the interests of landowners in protecting their lands against redistribution. Other things being equal, resource-based exploitation for either the external or the domestic sector may well result in a redistribution of land upward, even in cases when expanding the agricultural frontier has an explicitly reformist political goal. So, through a variety of economic mechanisms, the Brazilian politics of *fixando o homem no campo* (keeping people in the countryside) through agrarian reform, or joining "men without land to land without men" through Amazonian colonization experiments, may have contrary redistributive effects. Though little examined by careful research, the overall social costs of rain-forest conversion are also quite different from the private costs.[41]

Macroeconomic realities have contributed to this tendency to exploit rather than to conserve natural resources. In times of high inflation, the nominal value of land has increased rapidly, and agricultural land speculation has become part of the economic scene in Latin America. Orthodox domestic adjustment to the debt crisis has meant high rates of unemployment, lower wage rates over the 1980s, depressed domestic demand for agricultural commodities, and greater pressure on the rural poor to intensify their use of local resources. It is well-known that in hard times *campesinos* sacrifice conservation of assets in favor of consumption, slaughtering cattle, cutting trees for fuelwood and other domestic needs, taking off more game, and depleting their natural resource "savings accounts." Official agricultural credit and subsidies that might orient intensified exploitation to better lands are reduced by the general fiscal crisis, further marginalizing poor farmers from the land they hold and undermining the precarious condition of occasional day laborers who depend on the small farm labor market.

Public policies in such countries as Brazil give fiscal incentives to resource exploiters who clear land for agricultural or cattle enterprises.[42] When combined with agrarian reform that targets idle land first, such public policies mean an incentive to clear land to show that it is productive. Quite often, those displays of productivity are simply short-term demonstrations of resource exploitation—clearing land or grazing cattle—that have little to do with long-term productivity or resource conservation. General Philip Sheridan once observed that cattle are the harbinger of civilization; from Brazil to the Mexican gulf, they are the harbinger of erosion and degradation.

On the trade side, governments have devalued local currencies competitively over the 1980s to stimulate exports and address balance-of-payments problems. This not only makes the exploitation of tradables in resources more likely but encourages foreign direct investment in enterprises that produce those goods. Devaluation also makes foreign imports more expensive relative to domestic products. This provokes a tendency to import-substitute in resource-based products, often reinforced by domestic import restrictions imposed with uneven regard for real costs. The trade cost of import restrictions is passed along to the domestic consumer, who pays for the government's policy of creating a rent for domestic producers.[43]

Unfortunately, efforts to increase trade along lines of comparative advantage can result not only in the socially undesirable redistribution of land upward but in negative environmental externalities. That is, increased trade following the lines of comparative advantage can result in environmental degradation. Efforts to protect the environment from such externalities can change a country's comparative advantage in a given commodity.[44] Thus Ecuador's exploitation of Amazonian oil reserves results in destruction of rain forest, a negative domestic externality. An attempt to impose a conservation tax on the exploitation of that oil changes Ecuador's comparative advantage in the crude petroleum trade. Brazil's decision to use native forest to fuel pig iron mills lowers the cost of steel production by shunting the economic burden of energy to a "non-economic" resource, the forest. Similar energy subsidies in Mexican petroleum make agricultural products and manufactures more competitive internationally, leading U.S. competitors to call for countervailing duties against natural resource subsidies in those countries.[45]

The most novel critique of natural resource exploitation policies involves the degree to which international trade and domestic development dynamics affect the sustainability of the resource. Sustainability itself is a slippery concept; some definitions essentially mandate conservation to the exclusion of human use, and others simply call for a production system that is stable over a relatively short period of time.[46] The definition of the Brundtland Commission in the epigraph to Chapter 2 is a reasonable rough concept.[47] It associates sustainability with development and stipulates its criteria to include "development that meets the needs of the present without compromising the ability of future generations to meet their own needs." Obviously, there are some difficult assumptions behind that simple definition, including those that outline the needs of the present and future generations in the abstract. Nevertheless, for our purposes here, whether one conceives of sustainability as a rate of extraction that guarantees that the stock of the resource does not decline, or simply a concept that allows production over more than one generation, it serves to underline the central economic point for resource use: the minimization of domestic resource externalities that result from trade and development.[48]

These propositions lead to five summary hypotheses that help define the connection between the external sector and resource use: (1) that external pressures force increased resource exploitation directly in ways observable in a nation's trade; (2) that domestic adjustment to the pressure of the external sector will intensify the exploitation of natural resources; (3) that the marketplace is an unlikely mechanism to govern environmental externalities, especially intertemporal externalities; (4) that the privatization of Latin American economies offers in the abstract a greater prospect of environmental degradation than does the continuation of public involvement; and (5) that the public sector in Latin America as presently constituted cannot be expected to challenge environmental degradation unless substantial political reform occurs.

The Role of the Public Sector

These last two propositions point up two further complications in combining the economic goals of development and trade: that the social welfare aspects of the development gains from trade, especially in natural-resource-based trade, are different from private comparative advantage; and that for either development or sustainability issues to be addressed, public policy has to concern itself with what economists call "intertemporal externalities," in this case, the survivability of the resource over generations.

If trade based on increased exploitation is the proposed answer to external payments problems, unwanted side effects include the import of international environmental problems and the loss of control over the resource costs of production. For example, the intensification of agriculture for export via the use of pesticides imports pesticide contamination problems from the developed world. To the extent that specialization in trade involves substituting Latin American agricultural production for OECD production (in soya, for example), the environmental costs of that production are imported to the producing country. In this connection, the United States has been criticized by environmentalists for "exporting topsoil" through its productionist farm policies. It may be, if trade were freed in agricultural products, that Latin America would have to bear the burden of world topsoil experts, which would be displaced on a competitive basis from the heavily subsidized OECD agricultural systems. Although the current economic crisis makes predictions the domain of the foolhardy, at least one study indicates that coming decades may find Brazil sawing down its tropical forests to fuel domestic pig iron production, while becoming a large exporter of eucalyptus to the developed world.[49]

If the consumers of goods produced at high environmental cost are outside the country, there is no way to tax consumption to pay for such costs (as happens with domestic gasoline taxes, for example). Consumer taxes such as those proposed by environmentalists against EEC imports of tropical timber are simple tariffs, whose fiscal benefits do not accrue to the exporting environmental abuser and whose economic impact is not guaranteed to increase environmental protection.[50] If the producer country is competing with others and desperate for private sector investment, taxing production runs the risk of losing investment or diminishing competitiveness by altering comparative advantage. Advocates of privatization often point to distorting subsidies in the domestic price system, but the short-term subsidy to developed-world consumers in the form of environmental degradation in Latin America causes less public worry.

Social Policy and Environmental Degradation

It is also reasonable to contend that the social costs and benefits of natural resource exploitation will reflect the distribution of wealth in the national economy and the architecture of political power in government. It would be extraordinary to think that all publics would be served equally by the preservation of public goods, or that gains from conservation benefit society in just ways. An intuitively more realistic, albeit less appealing, proposition is that the benefits from natural resource exploitation or conservation will reflect the structure of power in society, and that the political strength of the poor will determine to a great extent whether the state acts in their interests. As Fernando Henrique Cardoso has argued, if the state is itself an entrepreneur and defender of entrepreneurial interests, there is little prospect that the state will turn its power to the advantage of the voiceless, absent radical change.[51] If the base of political power in a Latin American society reflects the tremendous economic and social inequality pervading the region, there is little reason to expect the state to act progressively.

Given the unequal distribution of wealth and power in the marketplace and the absence of a market-based mandate to guard the commonweal, it seems utopian to expect the market to attend to the social consequences of environmental degradation or to prevent them through its own actions. The objective of national economic growth is the maximization of production, just as the purpose of free trade is the global maximization of production. The private sector in Latin America has steadfastly militated against state intervention for social redistribution, counting instead on the virtues of the marketplace to allocate economic resources most efficiently. There is little evidence of concern in this logic for the long-term externalities of economic growth, whether it be in Brazilian export agriculture, Mexican chemicals, or Ecuadorian oil. Defenders of the market would be hard-pressed to show examples where this is not true, and the bankruptcy of the state *qua* entrepreneur does not offer absolution to the private sector.

These points, when matched with the historical responsibility of the public economy for natural resources and resource-based industries, lead to the central political point of the trade-development–resource-exploitation nexus: that the public sector, not the marketplace, is uniquely endowed to treat questions of intertemporal sustainability on behalf of society in general, but that the public sector, reflecting as it does the skewed (and generally unaccountable) outcome of political conflict and negotiation, is poorly constituted to represent the interests of the poor or to challenge the logic of maximizing natural resource exploitation in the short term.

The role of government in determining the appropriate rates of natural resource exploitation is most obvious, even in the developing world, in the case of petroleum. Its conservation has waned in the wake of lower consumer prices and growing world reserves. The concerns that over-consumption poses for resource exhaustion, pollution, and long-term economic harm are clearly in the purview of government. It is manifest that the marketplace does not have a mechanism to preserve long-term sustainability. But governments have responded with varying successes to this challenge. To the extent that Latin American governments try to restrain petroleum production, they are countered by deals offered by developed countries to ensure low-cost opportunities to buy oil and to assure steady supplies.[52]

In Latin America, the guardian role of the state is evident mainly in the abstract. In reality, its performance has been lamentable—even worse, at times, than that of the private sector itself, which has fewer long-term concerns and a narrower mandate of profitability. It is difficult to conceive of less environmentally sensitive policies than took place under the aegis of the Mexican oil monopoly PEMEX or the state-led CAPEMI enterprise in the Amazon. If it is arguably more utopian to expect the private sector to treat the environment with sustainability in mind than it is the state,[53] we must divine the reasons behind public sector failures in the resource area and evaluate the degree to which they are structurally imposed. Those reasons are largely political.

Neither the private sector's calculus of short-term gain nor the state's imperative for social change and economic growth has included full-fledged consideration of the question of resource sustainability. Indeed, because the Latin American state embraces short-term economic growth and development goals, because the public economy is responsible for much of the resource base of the nation, and because external shocks exert extraordinary pressure on vulnerable Latin American governments, the logic of government policy toward natural resources conflicts with the fiduciary responsibility of the public sector over the nation's public goods.

In view of the immanent political character of these questions, the absence of political analysis in conservation and development literature is inexplicable. The scholarly bibliography on resource management questions is almost completely without reference to politics. Jeffrey A. McNeely's

Economics and Biological Diversity offers recommendations for policy incentives but does not treat the political process at all. In a series of monographs on environmental questions sponsored by the World Bank Environment Department, authors addressed such explicitly political topics as resource sustainability, discounting, frontier colonization, deforestation, and property rights. One even proposed future research priorities to contain deforestation.[54] None of them focused on the intrinsically political character of the issues at hand. None brought the tools of political science to bear on the questions of the environment. The research and political recommendations were framed in terms of policy, not politics, evincing a conspicuous reluctance on the part of economists and ecologists to treat the question of political mission in the relationship between social and environmental change. In fact, if theory follows historical experience, the politics of sustainability is central to the creative implementation of social change necessary to avoid the disastrous environmental consequences foreseen by virtually all who write in this field.

Unfortunately, a full-fledged treatment of the unique role of the public sector cannot fit in this book, and even a partial look is undermined by the poor quality of data on public involvement in the Latin American economy. The argument will be necessary at least at a superficial level, however, precisely because the public sector will continue to be involved in the control of public goods and because the public sector is by definition the locus of the politics of sustainability.

Resource Politics and the Development Agenda

Latin American resource exploitation in the twentieth century is fashioned by designers of primary sector modernization, as is true of the developed countries (especially the United States) that provide the models for Latin America. In Latin America, however, productive modernization and exploitation of rural resources have been wrapped in the cloak of "the social question." The logic of resource-based exploitation in modern Latin America, as contrasted with the colonial epoch, is that high rates of exploitation are necessary to effect the modernization and development of the country and its poor residents. In the quest for economic transformation, primary sector modernization for export is key.

In its most spectacular manifestations, this quest leads Latin American nations to behave as Brazil did in the 1972 Stockholm conference, in which it declared environmental consciousness to be a luxury of the developed nations, far removed from the harsh necessities of Brazilian economic progress. Again in 1989, at a meeting considering the prospect of debt-for-nature swaps as a way of combining tropical conservation with external adjustment, the Brazilian minister of interior suggested that the problem of deforestation and resource degradation was a product of debt pressure, and in any event was more the responsibility of the rich, consuming nations than of Brazil.[55] But Brazil's resistance to the idea of becoming a "developed world nature park" is less a result of hubris than of a logic of development that emphasizes economic modernization to maximize the national product. To use a favorite metaphor of trade negotiators, economic progress in Latin America is like riding a bicycle: forward momentum is essential, lest the rider fall off. Questions are seldom asked about the direction of the bicycle and its relation to the long-term survival of the rider.

Because in Latin America economic progress is measured in the currency of per capita income, gross domestic product, and other traditional economic indicators, little regard has been given to intertemporal externalities such as sustainability. The rigors of current survival are such that little attention is afforded future generations. Because the mandate of Latin American economic growth is tied to a certain extent to exploiting "abundant factors," it is hardly surprising that a first impulse of development agents is to expand the usable resource frontier. Because the state is both the (inadequate) regulatory guardian of those resources *and* the likely enterprise for their exploitation, the short-term economic interests of the state conflict with its long-term mandate. The long-term costs of economic growth under current technologies and social systems may mean that for the sake of staying on the bicycle, the cyclist pedals over a cliff.

On the other side, international economists, looking on a Latin American scene characterized by long years of high inflation, huge public sector deficits, warped exchange rates, domestic price distortions, balance-of-payments deficits, and high debt, recommend economic stabilization[56] and adjustment, followed by trade liberalization to remove the state from center stage and bring the national economy back into equilibrium. Argentina, Chile, and Uruguay are typically cited as examples, with Chile the main "success story."[57] Its success is in finding through structural adjustment a free economic base for the efficient exploitation of natural resources in a trade-based economy.

Development and resource economists are less immediately concerned with the external sector, but still argue against perverse government incentives favoring overexploitation of resources, though long-term resource conservation goals often run up against the exigencies of short-term exploitation in an inflationary economy. Multilateral developmentalists often recommend a sectoral approach, which cleans out the distortions of subsidized agriculture or energy to increase productivity and to "get prices right."[58] Technological optimists argue on behalf of using more trade to streamline technology transfer to the Third World, which would purportedly make Third World agriculture and industry less wasteful.[59]

Both the stabilization and economic development approaches to resource use, tied as they are to production and markets, miss a particularly horrifying—and likely—possibility: that, however great the direct exploitation of resources for production, significantly greater deforestation, erosion, water contamination, and other practices are taking place without any measurable reflection in output. This is the real political point behind José Márcio Ayres's connection of debt to deforestation. If the full impact on domestic resources of external debt is so great and deep as to escape reflection in the market, then both macropolitical strategies to enhance the wage share of national income and market approaches to getting prices right are woefully inadequate to the role of the poor in resource degradation.

To date, whether demand is managed by government and market working together to get prices right, or through effective import substitution in agriculture, more pressure is placed on the agricultural frontier, and the social question in the countryside is aggravated rather than addressed. As has been shown throughout the world, there is a consistent and devastating relationship between deteriorating incomes among the poorest and resource degradation. To the extent that the rural poor no longer can sustain basic consumption needs through traditional low-output farming, they are pressed to intensify production for survival. Expansion of the agricultural frontier for import substitution tends to dispossess small and even medium-sized farmers and certainly displaces landless workers in the short term. Pushed off their lands, small farmers retreat to farm hillsides.[60] Forced out of their regular labor markets by agricultural modernization, the growing numbers of rural poor become "informal sector" workers in the countryside, farming ditches, squatting, taking off game and fuelwood, "mining" the margins of the rural economy. If the prospect of debt-induced overproduction of natural resources is grim, how much grimmer is the idea that much resource degradation goes on with no productive dividend other than the social reproduction of utter misery.

To the extent that Latin American growth and economic development are tied to the external sector, there is a direct relationship between biological resource use and external shocks. The future of resource politics is thus to some degree a function of external debt and payments, the trade balance, foreign direct investment, and the like. It may be hypothesized that the greater the economic insulation from the external sector, the less is the tendency to overexploit the natural resource base of the country. If so, the putative role of industrial transformation in insulating Latin American countries from international shocks is indirectly put to the test.

One would expect that if the international trade system is the source of increased rates of resource exploitation, those countries more open (and vulnerable) to trade are more likely to show increases in resource exploitation in times of increased pressure from the external sector. The higher the level of industrialization, the lower is the expected level of trade vulnerability (a variant of the law of declining trade) and the greater the resistance to externally imposed resource overuse.

This hypothesis is undone somewhat by the indirect environmental effects of industrialization. Apart from the pollution associated with industry, the energy requirements of industrial transformation lead to higher rates of resource exploitation than would be the case in simple agricultural production. There is often sharp competition between agricultural and agroindustrial water users, for example. Agroindustrial integration in such simple areas as packaging may lead to direct competition for resources, especially in such water-intensive, polluting industries as the manufacture of recycled paper cartons. So while the insulation of a country from external pressures may be some complex function of industrial transformation, that should not lead us to assume that industrialization somehow answers the resource question; it simply shifts its ground.

The question of resource exploitation cannot be confined to the producing country, however. Relatively unnoticed in official developed country critiques of natural resource exploitation in the Third World is the role of consuming nations in the rate and character of exploitation. While the community of nongovernmental organizations has shown convincingly that Japanese and European wood consumption is responsible for great devastation in the Philippines and Brazil, governmental critiques from the United States, Japan, and Europe are not as self-critical. A recent survey of forest products trade in Latin America remarks on overcutting and "mining" of commercial timber in Latin America but says nothing about the consumers' responsibility for such devastation.[61] It is more likely, for obvious reasons, for a developed country's critique of global warming trends to point to burning of rain forest in Brazil than to hydrocarbon consumption in the United States. Similarly, the Japanese find it more convenient to invest huge sums in "sustainable forest production" in fragile areas than to question the extraction of wood from those areas via long-term investigation.[62] In analogous fashion, the all too tragically convenient image of backwoods landlords killing poor peasant organizers is easier for the Brazilian government to condemn than its own policies for the consumption of millions of tons of charcoal in the development of pig iron facilities on the eastern Amazon margins of Maranhão state.

In fact, one of the most persuasive connections among trade, development, and environmental degradation is the historical link between export enclaves, industrial transformation, and demand from developed countries. From the colonial system to the new international division of labor, the shape of trade and industrialization has been guided by the mold of developed country trade partners, then multinational corporations and their local counterparts. In general, the environmental performance of Latin American economies cannot be expected to outstrip parent production systems in the developed world. Paper mills and lumber industries have all of the deficiencies of their developed world partners (and forebears), often with few of the environmental safeguards imposed lately by developed country governments. From commercial fishing to mechanized agriculture, the technologies of production come largely from research and development in the developed world, where their environmental record is poor. Set as they are in fragile lands and tropical settings, such industrial models as the great Ford and Jari experiments in the Amazon show the disastrous ecological and economic limits of cross-national economic transplants.

This connection to the external consumption requirements of the developed world is a dangerous one, though, mainly for the excesses and stereotypes it creates. One of the most oversimplified is the argument that the rain forest is being carved up for hamburger meat production exported to fast-food purveyors in the United States. The argument contends that McDonald's, Burger King, Wendy's, and others are supporting deforestation to provide low-quality lean beef for American consumers. It undoubtedly helps that fast food is vulnerable to cultural criticism on several other grounds. In any event, the contention needs to be qualified greatly, in light of its frank irrelevance to deforestation in Brazil and its marginal connection to Central America and Mexico.[63] One indication of the inadequacy of the data supporting the argument is that the U.S. Department of Agriculture does not even keep data for ground meat production and consumption in the United States. Such dramatic images as the "hamburger rain forest" fail to make the role of Latin American development itself clear.

Such images of OECD country gluttony also foster another false generalization: that if developed countries' consumption of ecologically sensitive products were to diminish, the problem of resource overuse in Latin America would diminish correspondingly. This logic leads in two directions: constraints on trade from Latin America, and debt relief to alleviate pressures on Latin America's external sector, thereby reducing resource exploitation.

Other than the demand for rare resources in consuming countries, from fine hardwood veneers and wood chips in Europe or Japan, to monkeys for experimentation in the United States,[64] to skins and hides in all three areas, external pressures exist for greater exploitation of the region's resources through the external sector. First, it is obvious that the debt crisis creates a general imbalance in the external sector, in which short-term external payments problems combine with the need to adjust domestic production to comparative advantage. Consistent with the argument of Chapter 2 and the theoretical arguments of this chapter, increased debt pressure opens the economy, relative to previous periods; pressure on the trade balance would tend to lead a trading nation to favor production of goods in which it has relative factor abundance. In much of Latin America, this means land and natural resources.[65] Returning to the first two orienting propositions of this chapter, that external pressures force increased resource exploitation directly, and that domestic adjustment to the pressure of the external sector will intensify the exploitation of natural resources, the first would lead us to expect that natural resource exploitation would be directly observable in trade, as resource-based commodities are exported to meet external obligations.

Under the second possibility, trade data would not necessarily reflect changes in rates of exploitation, but domestic production and consumption would. This would occur either because national economic growth requires import substitution in resource-based commodities for direct consumption, or because external pressures cause more exploitation to "source" domestic manufactures domestically. Thus the foreign exchange constraint can operate either directly through the external sector or through a domestic shift caused by import constraints.

As for the role of industrial transformation in externally stimulated resource exploitation, we would expect an inverse relationship between rates of exploitation and degrees of industrial transformation. One would expect to see those countries depending on primary sector exports to exploit resources more than those exporting manufactures. This must be qualified by the extent to which exports in manufactures are dependent on domestic natural resources. To the extent that Latin American growth and economic development are tied to the external sector, there is a direct relationship between use of biological resources and external shocks. The future of resource politics is, then, to some degree a function of external debt and payments, the trade balance, foreign direct investment, and the like.

Advocates of debt relief aver that the greater the economic insulation from the external sector, the less is the tendency to overexploit the natural resource base of the country. They argue that the international trade system is the main culprit in the growing rates of resource exploitation, and that the weaker, more open countries of the Third World are clearly destined to show accelerated resource degradation under increased external pressure. The greater the economic turn inward, the greater the resistance to externally imposed overuse of resources. These hypotheses are consistent politically with the history of post–World War II Latin American developmentalism.

The quality and specificity of the data do not permit a test of this proposition, and its complications are daunting. Intervening variables include such difficult to measure considerations as government incomes policies, which may be led by cheap food programs that overexploit agricultural resources; the energy cost of industries; the share of agriculture and industry in investment and credit; and so on. What is clear without an empirical test is the political dimension of industrial and resource development policies.

Problems with Testing These Hypotheses

In theory, the general hypotheses posed above are attractive; they present the basic architecture that is often assumed in arguments about resources, debt, and the external sector. But as the complications of industrial development dynamics suggest, they suffer from deficiencies. First, there is too much intervening between the external sector and resource output to make tests of these hypotheses either very obvious or robust, given the data available. For example, one would expect in this construction that Mexican shrimp production for export would increase dramatically. In fact, sharp swings in Mexican public policy toward the ownership and management of the shrimping industry over the 1980s undermined domestic production and certainly did not provide the economic or political climate that would satisfy the argument. In that period, the Mexican government went from a mixed system to one based entirely on public sector producer cooperatives; it is now privatizing the sector again. Modeling those dramatic shifts and their impact on resource exploitation is extremely difficult; comparing them with equally complicated cases in other countries of the region over the same period is next to impossible.

Second, the duration of the recent current economic crises in Latin America is too short to provide data that would test the hypotheses adequately. Between 1973 and 1979, there were two major oil shocks, with recession and recovery wedged in between. Between 1980 and 1988, there were sharp commodity price swings and shifts in interest rates; two extremely severe contractions in Latin America as a whole (1982 and 1986); radical changes in domestic macroeconomic policy in the most important trading economies (Brazil's Cruzado Plan upended the entire performance of the external sector in 1986, for example); and the collapse of regionally important commodity groups, from coffee to tin to sugar. In the case of the breakdown of the International Sugar Agreement or the International Coffee Agreement, the consequences for production are still unclear. The general climate of instability since about 1975 has been compounded because the nature of output in Latin America changed in that period through secular shifts in the international division of labor, which include the industrialization of the large economies and the reorientation of the OECD economies. The data available do not permit the separation of these secular trends from the impact of shocks.

The danger is great that by assigning too much significance to the data and the trajectory of Latin American trade performance, the analysis will fall into the typical historicist trap: anointing today's events as historical trends. In the late 1980s, for example, Chile's government received much attention for its successful shift away from copper as a leading export, but in 1988, copper was prominent again, accounting for 48 percent of the export bill.[66] One hypothesis for future research is that the period 1982–85 was a time of "test cuts," in which Latin American policymakers reacted only partially to the crisis in the external sector. Data for the 1985–90 period might provide a more instructive look at the depth of environmental wounds from external crisis.

There are other weaknesses in straightforward data analysis, including the variable quality of the data and problems assigning economic value to exports in complicated periods of instability in the exchange rate and currency. Most troublesome is the realization that the shortcomings of current analysis caused by international instability and the shifting economic sands are not likely to improve. The external sector problems of Latin America are not a single crisis but a cascade of difficulties that emerge from the complicated politics of international finance, national development, and OECD economic policies. The nature of economic growth under the external conditions of 1989 depends on the political convictions of bankers, government leaders, individual investors, and other "variables" not captured in the too-convenient postures of "policy analysis." If the current climate is severe, it is also changing. It is difficult in the extreme for the hypothetical relationships proposed here to take into account the impact of European unification in 1992, the future trade restrictions of the U.S. Congress, or the use of discretionary avenues to trade protection afforded the U.S. president.

Nevertheless, the concern here is not with policy prescription but with structure and process. The propositions above are worth examining for the leads they might give to more long-term and micro-level research into these questions in the future. The next section looks at some regional data that are inadequate but heuristically valuable.

Elements of Evidence

If resource exploitation is driven directly by external pressure, we would expect to see increasing openness in Latin American countries during periods of external shock such as 1974–79 and 1982–88, and increases in the resource component of exports during the same periods. Given the disproportionate Latin American share of Third World debt, it is also reasonable to expect an increased share in resource trade in Latin America over the period 1973–88, as reflected in a table offered in a recent article, in which the log of external debt and the log of mean annual deforestation were graphed, showing Brazil, naturally, at the top of the curve.[67]

The relationship is not so simple as the association might suggest, though. First, association is not the same as causality. Second, the correlation between external debt and deforestation would presumably be reflected in increases in forestry consumption or export figures, which is not the case.[68] Research has shown that the rate of extraction of natural resources by Latin American countries does not differ in the early debt crisis years compared with 1975–81.[69] The real rates of growth in agriculture, fishery, forestry, and mining do not relate statistically to openness, rate of change in real exchange rate, or debt service. If forest-based products including those processed domestically are included, the result is the same. Latin America has not increased its output of forest-based wood products in a secular way over the period of the debt crisis.

Moreover, for the region as a whole, agricultural, forest, and fisheries exports have exceeded 1980 levels only once during the years since. For the principal exporting countries of Latin America, aggregate exports in each of these natural-resource-based activities did not increase consistently in the years since the onset of the debt crisis. In general, Latin American primary sector exports have declined in importance over the past two decades, even during the period of the debt crisis (see Table 3.3 below). Particularly interesting in that decline is the reduction in the importance of agricultural exports in Brazil and Mexico, which together represent about half of the region's agricultural GDP.[70] Also interesting is the drastic move away from copper in Chile and tin in Bolivia, subject to the above qualifications.

The assumption that Latin American countries can trade their way out of external crisis by pumping up primary sector exports ignores the traditional problem of such export expansion in the region: the inelasticity of demand. The developed world's consumption suggests that resource-based industries also have their international limits, which are

TABLE 3.1
Natural Resource Production Growth Rates
Compared with General Economic Growth and Exports,
Selected Countries, 1961–89
(Percent)

| | Agriculture, fish, and forest products | | | |
	Production growth	Export growth	Growth in GDP	Overall export growth
Argentina				
1961–70	2.4%	n.a.	4.4%	5.8%
1971–80	2.1	n.a.	2.5	4.8
1981–89	1.0	−3.4	−1.9	4.9
1981	n.a.	0.15	−0.08	0.06
1982	n.a.	−0.22	−0.06	0.03
1983	n.a.	0.20	0.03	0.08
1984	0.04	0.03	0.01	−0.01
1985	−0.02	−0.06	−0.05	0.13
1986	−0.03	−0.19	0.06	−0.07
1987	0.02	−0.15	0.02	−0.01
Brazil				
1961–70	4.2	n.a.	5.4	6.6
1971–80	4.7	n.a.	8.7	9.9
1981–89	3.0	0.12	2.1	8.5
1981	0.08	0.00	−0.03	0.21
1982	−0.00	−0.18	0.01	−0.09
1983	−0.01	0.10	−0.03	0.14
1984	0.03	0.17	0.05	0.22
1985	0.10	−0.11	0.08	0.07
1986	−0.08	−0.16	0.06	−0.11
1987	0.15	0.11	0.02	0.19
Chile				
1961–70	1.9	n.a.	3.8	3.6
1971–80	2.2	n.a.	1.8	10.2
1981–89	3.9	−0.14	1.9	5.5
1981	0.04	−0.02	0.05	−0.09
1982	−0.01	−0.36	−0.14	0.05
1983	−0.03	0.07	−0.01	0.01
1984	0.08	−0.08	0.06	0.07
1985	0.06	−0.42	0.02	0.07
1986	0.09	−0.25	0.06	0.10
1987	0.03	0.09	0.06	0.09
Ecuador				
1961–70	3.3	n.a.	5.2	2.9
1971–80	3.0	n.a.	9.1	14.0
1981–89	3.9	7.0	2.0	4.6
1981	0.07	−0.12	0.04	0.05
1982	0.02	0.03	0.01	−0.05
1983	−0.14	−0.20	−0.04	0.02
1984	0.11	0.22	0.04	0.12
1985	0.10	0.16	0.04	0.12
1986	0.10	0.40	0.03	0.08
1987	0.04	−0.01	−0.04	−0.17

TABLE 3.1 *(continued)*

	Agriculture, fish, and forest products		Growth in GDP	Overall export growth
	Production growth	Export growth		
Mexico				
1961–70	3.9%	n.a.	7.1%	6.1%
1971–80	3.4	n.a.	6.7	8.3
1981–89	0.5	3.4%	1.2	7.2
1981	0.06	−0.11	0.09	0.12
1982	−0.02	−0.04	−0.01	0.22
1983	0.02	−0.17	−0.05	0.14
1984	0.03	0.33	0.04	0.06
1985	0.04	−0.02	0.03	−0.04
1986	−0.02	0.37	−0.04	0.03
1987	0.01	−0.12	0.02	0.09
Peru				
1961–70	4.3	n.a.	5.5	5.6
1971–80	−0.6	n.a.	3.5	3.0
1981–89	3.5	1.4	−0.6	−0.2
1981	0.09	−0.23	0.05	−0.03
1982	0.03	0.10	0.00	0.06
1983	−0.11	−0.31	−0.13	−0.10
1984	0.12	0.25	0.04	0.09
1985	0.04	0.12	0.02	0.04
1986	0.06	0.23	0.12	−0.10
1987	0.05	−0.27	0.09	−0.07

SOURCES: IDB, *Economic and Social Progress in Latin America: Working Women* (Washington, D.C.: IDB, 1990); FAO *Trade Yearbook*, various years.

aggravated further by the recent development of regional trading blocs and the pessimism about future trade opportunities for Latin America in Europe and Asia. The market is most easily expanded by pressuring the United States to open its markets, based on its free trade ideology and its historic involvement in Latin American trade.

At a more general level, expected increases in Latin American openness did occur over the period of the debt crisis (Tables 3.1 and 3.2). Such increases occurred despite reductions in imports, which suffered throughout most of the region. Likewise, the role of agriculture, forestry, hunting, and fishing declined in regional GDP (see Table 3.3) but increased in countries with the most active public sectors. Hypothesizing that the countries traditionally most dependent on agriculture, forestry, hunting, and fishing would be most likely to turn to increased exports in those sectors under external debt pressure, we see that none of them is a significant trader in the region (the first large trader is Colombia, at ninth place). Even among the most dependent, there is no secular evidence of

TABLE 3.2

General Trade Coefficients
Compared with Natural Resource Trade Coefficients,
Selected Countries, 1980–87

	1980	1981	1982	1983	1984	1985	1986	1987
Argentina								
Resources	0.11	0.05	0.09	0.09	0.08	0.09	0.06	0.05
Petroleum	neg.	neg.	0.00	0.00	0.00	0.01	0.00	neg.
Overall	0.11	0.13	0.14	0.14	0.14	0.17	0.15	0.14
Bolivia								
Resources	0.02	0.01	0.01	0.01	0.00	0.01	0.01	0.01
Petroleum	0.00	0.00	0.00	0.01	0.00	0.00	0.00	0.00
Overall	0.19	0.14	0.13	0.12	0.11	0.10	0.10	0.08
Brazil								
Resources	0.04	0.04	0.03	0.05	0.06	0.05	0.03	0.03
Overall	0.08	0.09	0.08	0.11	0.13	0.11	0.08	0.08
Chile								
Resources	0.03	0.03	0.02	0.03	0.03	0.02	0.01	0.01
Overall	0.17	0.12	0.15	0.19	0.19	0.24	0.25	0.28
Colombia								
Resources	0.02	0.02	0.01	0.02	0.02	0.02	0.01	0.01
Petroleum	neg.	neg.	neg.	neg.	0.00	0.00	0.01	0.04
Overall	0.12	0.09	0.08	0.08	0.11	0.10	0.14	0.16
Costa Rica								
Resources	0.04	0.07	0.06	0.05	0.05	0.04	0.03	0.04
Overall	0.21	0.38	0.33	0.27	0.27	0.24	0.24	0.25
Ecuador								
Resources	0.07	0.05	0.06	0.05	0.06	0.05	0.11	0.13
Petroleum	0.13	0.09	0.08	0.13	0.14	0.11	0.07	0.06
Overall	0.22	0.18	0.17	0.18	0.20	0.18	0.20	0.21
Guatemala								
Resources	0.14	0.09	0.09	0.09	0.09	0.07	0.11	0.08
Overall	0.19	0.15	0.13	0.12	0.12	0.10	0.12	0.11
Honduras								
Resources	0.27	0.23	0.20	0.18	0.18	0.18	0.19	0.17
Overall	0.33	0.28	0.24	0.23	0.23	0.23	0.24	0.22
Mexico								
Resources	0.01	0.01	0.01	0.01	0.01	0.01	0.02	0.02
Petroleum	0.06	0.06	0.09	0.11	0.09	0.08	0.05	0.06
Overall	0.09	0.08	0.13	0.16	0.14	0.12	0.13	0.14
Peru								
Resources	0.03	0.02	0.03	0.02	0.03	0.04	0.04	0.02
Petroleum	0.04	0.03	0.03	0.03	0.04	0.05	0.01	0.01
Overall	0.20	0.14	0.15	0.17	0.18	0.21	0.15	0.13
Venezuela								
Resources	0.00	0.00	0.00	0.00	0.00	0.01	0.01	0.00
Petroleum	0.30	0.29	0.23	0.21	0.30	0.26	0.14	0.19
Overall	0.33	0.30	0.24	0.22	0.32	0.30	0.18	0.22

SOURCES: Same as for Table 3.1.

TABLE 3.3
*Agriculture, Fishing, Forestry, and Hunting as a Percent of GDP,
Selected Countries, 1980, 1983–87*

	1980	1983	1984	1985	1986	1987
Argentina	6.4%	17.0%	14.6%	17.1%	13.8%	15.0%
Bolivia	20.0	13.6	15.9	18.8	20.6	18.1
Brazil	11.6	14.4	14.4	14.4	10.8	10.6
Chile	7.6	10.6	11.7	14.8	15.3	14.5
Colombia	25.9	23.3	23.9	26.8	25.7	27.9
Costa Rica	18.9	30.3	28.6	25.2	23.3	21.9
Ecuador	14.6	12.6	13.7	12.2	18.8	23.3
Guatemala	37.4	31.7	30.8	25.9	34.5	32.1
Honduras	31.7	27.3	25.9	24.7	23.4	23.3
Mexico	8.3	11.5	9.8	9.8	13.4	12.1
Peru	14.9	16.4	18.7	23.1	20.9	18.2
Venezuela	5.9	5.2	7.2	7.8	8.4	9.1

SOURCES: Same as for Table 3.1.

increasing importance in the production of these primary goods for export in the period of the debt crisis. For the large traders (Argentina, Brazil, Chile, Colombia, Peru, and Mexico), the evidence is mixed. In Chile, the increase was pronounced, thanks to the growth in agriculture. In Brazil, 1987 was a critical year because it followed on the domestic overconsumption of the Cruzado Plan. In Argentina and Mexico, there was a modest increase in the nonmineral primary sector's output; in Colombia there was a modest decline. In Ecuador, along with Bolivia, the most open, primary-commodity-dependent countries of South America, output from these activities went up, even as oil exploitation increased.

The pressure of the debt crisis is reflected in the general trend toward trade surpluses after 1982, when most countries had lived with trade deficits for much of the postwar period. In economies with the fewest alternatives (i.e., those that did not benefit from early industrialization), the crisis must favor exports of primary-resource-based tradables: either traditional or new primary commodities. Thus in Ecuador, oil exports increased even in the face of declining prices. In Bolivia, until 1985, tin was mined for export, even at a loss. And in the Caribbean, sugar exports remain the backbone of the region's economy, even as many nations try to diversify their export bill in agriculture. Because export receipts typically depend on a few key commodities and prices are set elsewhere, there is no price elasticity of supply effect in these economies. When prices go up, output must increase to acquire foreign exchange. When prices decline, production must go up as well to make up for poor prices. Unfortunately, this extraordinary vulnerability is compounded by the relative inflexibility of domestic production, so that output does not respond well to increased demand.

But the supposition that resource degradation accelerates during the debt crisis because of the external pressure of the debt may be wrong. The fragmentary evidence suggests an alternative explanation. If we look at the resource-based production and trade from Latin America over the past two decades, and not merely over the period of the debt crisis, we see that there were substantial increases in production and export of agricultural, forest, and fishery commodities in the 1970s, after the first oil shock. In the period following 1982, in contrast, resource exploitation reflected in production and exports was reduced or stayed constant.

There are several possible reasons for this apparent dynamic, including the limited ability of Latin American countries to respond in production to pressures from the outside; the lack of expanding markets in consuming countries; and the poor price performance of the goods in which Latin American countries traditionally trade. Another answer to this apparent anomaly may be found in the character of the domestic adjustment process in the 1970s, compared with the 1980s. In the period following the oil crisis of 1973, Latin American governments had available large, attractive loans for infrastructure development and subsidized investment. The domestic economic adjustment process in oil importing countries involved increasing exports to balance trade and generate the foreign exchange necessary to absorb increasing energy import costs. In the case of Brazil, this adjustment was complicated by massive investments in the domestic sugar, nuclear, and hydroelectric development plans, which were direct responses to the national energy crisis. Moreover, Brazil accelerated agricultural modernization and development in the center-south to compete more effectively in international markets in feed grains, poultry, citrus, and other exports.

Data from the period show another interesting trend that did not continue in the post-1982 period. Gross investment continued strong, as did apparent domestic consumption. During the 1970s the external debt afforded Argentina, Brazil, Mexico, and other countries the possibility of undertaking domestic adjustment without the horrendous recessions, economic hardships, and disinvestment that stalked the 1980s. Whereas during the 1970s Latin American borrowers were able to weather economic difficulties and attract new money, no new capital for investment was generated in the 1980s. Domestic consumption declined, even to the point that some of the countries with the fastest growing populations in the region are expecting declines in food requirements. This argument would presumably be revealed more clearly in the second half of the 1980s, according to the "test cuts" hypothesis mentioned above.

The evidence shows that resource-based output increases are a product of the 1970s and not the 1980s. The suggestion here is that domestic adjustment in favor of domestic resource industries provokes growth; decreases in consumption and investment in the 1980s means that similar growth in this decade did not recur.[71] In any event, output evidence supports a hypothesis that external pressure results in increased exploitation of natural resources, but mostly as a product of domestic adjustment, rather than as a simple response to external pressure.

On the import side, there is more interesting evidence, some of which does support a direct relationship between debt and resource exploitation. Regionally, there has been a decline in both volume and value of agricultural imports since 1980, and particularly since 1984. This contraction of imports is not justified by economic performance in the importing countries but is part of the artificially high barriers to imports imposed by governments adjusting externally to the debt crisis. Measured by value, which is a more revealing indicator of the foreign exchange constraint on imports, the decline has been marked, dropping from $143.7 million in 1980 to $97.7 million in 1987.

If imports have declined and exports have not shown a parallel increase, either domestic production is substituting for previous imports (import substitution in agriculture) or demand is being suppressed through the price and distribution mechanisms. It is significant, then, that the regional decline in imports is matched by increases in the agricultural production index. The level of the index of agricultural production has been higher during the debt crisis than before, in spite of general declines in agricultural commodity prices during the same period. This suggests that Latin American countries were engaged in "mining" their land's productivity in the debt crisis years, either through import substitution in agriculture or through promotion of agricultural exports or export substitution.

Preliminary results from research now under way indicates that agricultural production does not vary consistently with government intervention, though as a whole the Latin American agricultural production index is associated with lower levels of government intervention. Such confounding variables as devaluation of real currency make this a difficult phenomenon to measure.

These increases notwithstanding, per capita consumption of agricultural commodities has declined, as would be expected from the impact of stabilization programs on incomes. In the case of Mexico, the drop in consumption is radical, reflecting the "demand management" side of former President Miguel de la Madrid's misnamed *Programa Nacional de Alimentación* and the further contraction of wages under the new administration of Carlos Salinas de Gortari.[72]

Whether demand is managed by the government and market's "getting prices right" to the exclusion of the low-income consumer of imports, or through effective import substitution in agriculture, the result is to put more pressure on resources in the agricultural frontier. As has been shown throughout the world, there is a consistent and devastating relationship between deteriorating incomes and resource degradation. To the extent that the rural poor are no longer able to fill basic consumption needs through traditional subsistence, there is resource substitution in the countryside. Pressed to intensify production on marginal subsistence holdings, small farmers overstress their land.[73]

On the other side, import substitution in agriculture has also proven devastating to forest and fragile lands in general. Robert Repetto and Malcolm Gillis, Jeffrey McNeely, Hans Binswanger, Dennis Mahar, and others argue that perverse incentives for domestic agricultural development relate directly to deforestation and overexploitation of natural resources.[74] Those authors, along with the World Bank, argue that the removal of such perverse incentives would enhance the environment, an argument that is unsupported by evidence and not well grounded in what is known about the market and development. Susanna Hecht and Alexander Cockburn criticize that position by offering a graph that ostensibly shows little association between public rural credit and deforestation. Their analysis is partial, however, and does not account for the possibility of time lags in the impact of credit on deforestation.[75]

There are two points of argument that connect import substitution in agriculture to environmental degradation. First, other things being equal, agricultural import substitution requires either an expansion of the agricultural frontier or an intensification and modernization of agricultural methods. The agricultural frontier is often expanded artificially to include lands previously thought to be unfit for agricultural use. Classic examples include the semiarid north of Mexico, where agricultural modernization and the Green Revolution were driven by overuse of groundwater; the high plains of Texas, a frontier whose exploitation in the 1960s and 1970s revolutionized cattle feeding in the United States and now has been shown to have depleted the Ogallala aquifer; and, of course, the Amazon forest, which has been called "the breadbasket of Latin America" by academics and policymakers devoted to import substitution in agriculture.[76]

Regarding the change in technology required for the substitution of agricultural imports, two remarks are appropriate. First, as Clifford Geertz observed a generation ago, agricultural modernization is much more viable in good land than in bad. The prospect of intensifying swidden agriculture offers mainly environmental degradation. One might add now that the modernization of agriculture even on good lands has been undertaken using energy-intensive, ecologically irresponsible practices that bring into question the long-term value of production increases altogether, regardless of the quality of the land.

It is also important to note that agricultural import-substitution and trade policies are linked profoundly to U.S. agriculture and the politics that govern it. Most notably, the ability of the Mexican government to sustain domestic agricultural production of food grains depends, in part, on the subsidy required to make prices compete with the international market price. To the extent that the U.S. price for key grains determines the international price, U.S. agricultural policy sets the terms of Mexican subsidy policy in the countryside. To a lesser degree, U.S. agriculture also affects commodity pricing and subsidy policy in other key agricultural producers such as Brazil and Argentina.

In the early 1980s, it was often remarked that the artificially strong dollar was the best medicine available for the Common Market Common Agricultural Policy (CAP) because the cost to the EEC for export subsidies was reduced by the lack of competition from U.S. agricultural exports. In somewhat similar fashion, the production, price, and exchange rate policies of the United States have a strong influence on the real cost and alternatives to agricultural import substitution in Latin America. Once again, an open-system approach to agricultural production, and thereby resource degradation, is indicated.

In sum, the rate and character of natural resource exploitation in Latin America are functions of state capacity, international factors (price elasticities, demand, substitutability, growth rates, and the like), international conventions (CITES, International Coffee Agreement, International Sugar Agreement), and national strategies. It is not evident in most cases that exploitation of natural resources is a direct response to the debt crisis. The more likely summary premise is that resource exploitation responds to external shocks, but only if those shocks are accompanied by a domestic adjustment that permits increases in consumption, investment, and economic growth. In the case of Latin America as a region, those conditions were fulfilled much more clearly in the 1970s than in the 1980s.

Nevertheless, even without successful domestic adjustment such as was experienced in the 1970s, resource exploitation in Latin America can continue to increase as a result of lagged effects of the 1970s; the indirect pressures on the poor of the debt shock, irrespective of investment and economic growth; and reduced state capacity.

Returning to the question of the public sector, a number of thorny questions remain. External shock in the 1980s has meant reduced state capacity. What does this imply? If we assign the state the role of developmentalist enemy of the environment, clearly the reduced role of the state has some positive aspects. The lower the capacity of Brazilian or Peruvian development agencies to build huge infrastructure projects, the less degradation results. Presumably, the energy and other subsidies generated by such large projects for the benefit of the private sector also disappear, further lowering the rate of natural resource exploitation, at least to the extent that subsidies increase resource exploitation in irrational ways. Combined with lower investment rates in general, economic slowing and the reduction of the role of the state may be an environmental plus. But at what social cost?

There is a contradictory tendency: lower state capacity means lower levels of environmental monitoring as well. That may lead to increased exploitation by lowering even the modest enforcement gates that exist. Domestic adjustment and reduced state involvement in the economy also put pressure on the agricultural frontier, much of which is focused on public lands. The state begins with a disadvantage in its inability to resist invasions of these lands with impunity. With lower levels of monitoring and enforcement, existing pressures on public lands may accelerate resource degradation. If economic growth continues in such a way as to reduce or ameliorate pressures on public lands, there is no reason to expect greater rates of degradation of those lands. But in the 1980s, when lower levels of state monitoring and enforcement were matched by poor economic performance that put additional pressures on the poor, one could expect the realm of public lands to be invaded. Tragically, in the case of Brazil and Mexico in the 1970s, the government reaction to the oil shocks resulted in increased public incentives to occupy and "mine" public lands. And the domestic economic development designs of the time did nothing to distribute economic growth in such a way as to soften pressure on fragile resources.

To the extent that external shock may mean structural adjustment, some countries may shift away from resource-based exports to nontraditional ones. Hence Chile does not emphasize increases in copper exploitation but shifts economic activity in favor of agricultural exports. The long-term environmental and development consequences of such strategies are still unclear. Chile is not a particularly good case to test possible trends that counter the propositions presented above, both because of the authoritarian and extremely regressive social policies of the government and because Chile does not suffer the population pressures that characterize Brazil, Mexico, and other countries. Bolivia is a better example, but the government's shift away from tin is more recent, and the social and political consequences are only beginning to be felt.

Political Preference and Resource Politics

Because of the impact of external shock and domestic adjustment on resource politics, it is proper to try to distinguish among the preferred values of political options in Latin America and their consequences for resource politics. Faced with external shock, Latin American economies have tried a wide variety of policy packages with mixes of exchange rate, fiscal, and monetary goals. From the standpoint of resource politics, however, there are some reductions that can clarify the most important issues. First, does a government impose an economic package that stimulates or reduces overall economic growth? Second, does the national economic plan include a redistributive element, or at least some attempt to address issues of poverty alleviation? And third, is the general orientation of government internationalist or nationalist?

Regarding the first two questions, it is generally conceded that reduced rates of economic growth, especially where the poor are affected most directly, mean increased pressure on natural resources. In Mexico, the vast bulk of the poorest population is still in the countryside, where there is a direct link between economic growth and government presence. The orthodox stabilization and adjustment program undertaken in 1982, which amazingly continues today, involves the privatization of the economy, the abandonment of traditional incomes policies for the rural poor, and the combined pressures of inflation and unemployment in the countryside. All these mean that rural people must fall back on short-term resource exploitation to survive. The environmental cost of their unemployment and misery, however, is not comparable to the consequences of commercial and state-led resource degradation under favorable conditions of economic growth.

In Brazil, in contrast, the government has undertaken heterodox approaches to stabilization and adjustment, with similarly disastrous results for the environment. Domestic economic growth under environmentally inappropriate conditions is worse in its aggregate effects than the no-growth option adopted in Mexico. In neither country, however, are the fundamental questions being addressed: to what extent are the conditions of economic growth attending to technological requirements for environmental sustainability, on the one hand, and the social requirements of sustainable growth for the poor, on the other? In Brazil and Mexico, the answer is categorical: neither is being attended. In both countries, the sectoral and policy-based adjustment lending of the multilateral development assistance system is reproducing the conditions for environmental degradation, at the same time insisting that environmental concerns enjoy the highest priority in development lending.

There are two messages in this provisional conclusion: first, that slowed growth and deeper misery for the rural poor generate more resource degradation; but second, that economic growth under current models of agricultural modernization, forest production, and fishery exploitation neither address the income and social needs of the poor nor satisfy the requirements of environmental sustainability.

Chapters 5 and 6 will treat the last question, whether a country is nationalist or internationalist in its economic orientation, more concretely. At this point, it is well to raise several questions, to be answered as the text proceeds. First, does a nationalist perspective offer a better prospect for sustainable development than does internationalism? Second, does the redistributive content of nationalism make a difference to sustainability?[77]

One important way to cut across the nationalist-internationalist frontier is by asking the question differently: to what extent does either an internationalist or a nationalist perspective affect the way resources are being exploited? It is likely, given historical experience and current policies, that either nationalist or internationalist perspectives on trade and development will be founded on a common technology, which is day by day more internationally standardized and energy- and resource-intensive. To the extent that any government avoids breaking the tie to uncritical technology transfer from the North, in fishing, forestry, or agriculture, its trade preferences make no difference. National control over resource exploitation is not technology-neutral.

Liberalism fails a second test, however, which nationalism at least sometimes may pass. Any government that embraces a policy of privatization and trade liberalization in resources abandons in the first instance its *potential* national control over the kinds of resource externalities that have occupied so much of our attention in this chapter.

The most important question deriving from this chapter is, Under what circumstances would trade-generated growth in Latin America enhance the environmental prospects of the region and also satisfy the needs of the poor? In the next two chapters, we will examine the international setting that establishes much of the institutional and structural limits of future growth. Chapter 6 will return to the national level.

CHAPTER 4

National Power and the Structure of Latin American Trade

The internationalism of the oligarchs threatens to make us the last prey of world capitalism.
—Rodolfo and Julio Irazusta, *La Argentina y el imperialismo británico*

FOREIGN TRADE has dominated everything, even our morals, which for this reason are so low and confused.
—Leopoldo Lugones, *El estado equitativo*

LATIN AMERICA AS A REGION operates in an international trading system over which it has little governing influence. Beyond that generalization, though, it would be misleading to consider the trade power and prospects of Latin America as a region. Its national economies range from "African" to "Mediterranean" in size and distribution. Within the Latin American region are countries designated MSA (most seriously affected) poverty cases or LICs (low-income countries) by the international development assistance community, as well as MICs and NICs (middle-income countries and newly industrialized countries, respectively).[1]

The trade power of Latin American countries in the international system varies enormously, according to size, openness, commodity, and geographic concentration of trade, level of industrialization, resource base, and the like. Honduras, which generates 69 percent of its GDP from trade,[2] 60 percent of which is in bananas and coffee,[3] has little pricing power or variation in its trade partners. With a population of nearly 5 million and an income distribution among the worst in Latin America, it has little prospect for import-substitution industrialization. And for much of the past two decades, even the modest gains from intraregional trade in Central America have been shattered by war.

Brazil, in contrast, is a price maker in a variety of commodities, most prominently coffee and frozen orange juice concentrate. It not only influences the world sugar market but adds value through refining to set the standard for "new sugar" producers who have made the transition from traditional production of unrefined or partially refined sugar for developed world customers. Since the 1960s Brazil has become so competitive in refined sugar and alcohol that a free international market in either is a threat not only to small Caribbean nations but to producers in the United States and Europe as well. Brazil also competes effectively in oilseeds, poultry, some coarse grains, steel, small commercial aircraft, footwear, and a variety of other products that make it more resistant to external trade shocks than much of the rest of Latin America.[4]

Despite its stature in the world economy, however, Brazil still suffers from the fundamental weaknesses that have plagued Latin American economies in their relations with the developed world. Brazil does not sit at the head table of GATT. It is a supplicant before the multilateral development assistance institutions and the international monetary system. The new cruzeiro is no more an international currency or even a more robust regional currency than is the Argentine austral or the Mexican peso. *Structural adjustment* and *conditionality* are key words in the Brazilian development dictionary, just as they are in Chile or the Dominican Republic. Direct foreign investment, technology transfer, and intellectual property rights are issues as important for Brazil as they are for any country in the Third World. And because of its power and size, trading partners are not inclined to treat it preferentially, as indicated by the American rules for trade graduation.

The general architecture of the international system, then, may be a given, but individual Latin American countries vary in their position in it and in their national political strategies in the world trade system. The degree to which an individual country can operate freely in the international trade system depends on its "market power," its institutional influence in the international system, the geographic and commodity concentration of its trade, its openness, its ability to substitute imports and exports to advantage, and so on. Thus it is stunning that much trade literature—especially critiques of the concept of "informal imperialism"—does not recognize the importance of the political influence immanent in trade relationships, especially those between Great Powers and small.[5] It seems that, when considering the international influence of one country over another, the political power of the marketplace and its institutions finds little place, much less the constraints such power imposes on the powerless. In the main, postcolonial imperialism is based on economic theory, with trade and financial flows as its motor forces.[6]

The definition of imperialism, informal or otherwise, is not our concern here, but it does help force a conceptual reconsideration of politics in the economic history of international trade relations. It also encourages a recognition of the structural inequalities of trade, which have been recognized by students of imperialism but remain mired in the complicated debates about imperialism and underdevelopment. Those historical legacies and political inequalities have not been integrated seriously into the literature on development politics or trade negotiations.

This chapter begins with a simple set of theoretical propositions: that the structure of international trade does influence political power; that trade not only begets economic influence but historically has been used to increase political influence; and that the political power of trade constrains the "policy space" within which the nations of Latin America can respond to the international economic system. This chain of propositions comes close to the most commonly accepted notions of dependency, the politics of which are virtually untreated in the mainstream economic literature on international trade and understated even in the literature of free trade imperialism.

National power, the structure of trade, and their correlate national strategies respond to economic rules, political contingencies, and historical imperatives. Accordingly, part of the analysis here has been historical and data-driven, relying on what Latin American countries have done to confront their external imbalances—the international components of their domestic development plans. That part is intended as empirical synthesis, reviewing a broad and disparate economics literature to make political sense out of different past experiments and their political conditions, and perhaps to offer a new framework for understanding how trade intersects international structure and domestic political life.

Another part of the analysis is driven by theory, inspired in great part by two traditions in the literature. The first tradition was led by Hirschman's analysis, continuing with the provocative implications of *National Power and the Structure of Foreign Trade*, this time adapted to the Latin American context. That analysis is also guided to some extent by recent works on regimes and bargaining[7] and by the recent analyses of Latin American national responses to external stabilization problems treated in Chapter 2. To that work will be added considerations from the Latin American literature on dependency and autonomy, which converges to some extent with the international relations literature on small powers in the international system. This approach will permit a more explicitly political definition of development and its relation to national power, and demands that the analysis take the perspective of the Latin American country as its critical point of departure.

Finally, some of the analysis must rely on the influence of historical legacy on the political moves of Latin American countries confronting the international trade system. Their trade strategies are based on the political ideology of their governments, the scope and autonomy of their public sectors, and the economic background to current political competition.[8]

To some degree those strategies are limited by the force of theoretical propositions about economic growth and international trade power and by the ability of national leaders to mobilize national resources and to create political dynamics that transcend short-term economic rules.[9] Naturally, political successors to those who violate short-term rules often face catastrophic consequences, so the question of the sequence of policies is also important to understanding national strategies.

This chapter, like Chapter 2, offers some framework for the argument that follows. The importance of national power and the structure of foreign trade for national development strategies in Latin America is fundamental. The recrudescence of the United States in Latin American trade is equally important to the way Latin American politics faces the future and the way the trade issues of the hemisphere are considered.

Chapter 5 will specify the bilateral aspect of U.S.–Latin American partner-country trade, as well as the multilateral setting for Latin American trade politics. Chapter 6 analyzes Latin American trade strategies, beginning with the old saw that trade politics is domestic politics exported, which suggests that the different political configurations of Latin American governments generate distinctive trade postures, just as the international economic environment conditions national trade politics. The argument to be followed there also builds on the power relationships of the international trade system, to which we now turn.

The Implications of Power Inequality for Latin American Trade

Hirschman, in the preface to the expanded edition of *National Power and the Structure of Foreign Trade*, argues that the foundations of dependency analysis can be extracted from his 1944 book. He stipulates those to be:

(1) that the structure of international relations facilitates the pursuit of political power by strong countries;

(2) that the asymmetries of trade cause the dependence of small country traders on large;

(3) that asymmetries of national power permit the stronger nation to influence the composition and direction of the weaker country's trade;

(4) that the influence of trade on the dependent country is a function of its willingness to do *anything* to retain trade with the dominant partner, which in turn is a function of its (in)ability to substitute trade away from the dominant partner via other partners or less trade;

(5) that large countries pay less attention to bilateral trade with small

countries, which favors the small country's efforts to escape the bilateral web;

(6) that the small country strategy is to diversify trade rather than to trade too much with one country, especially a larger country;

(7) that the large country strategy is to trade with smaller partners, because of both the marginal income and marginal influence to be gained;

(8) that the optimal large country situation is one in which trade dependence of small countries is great, the large country's imports from the small are too great to be sold elsewhere, and the large country's exports are equally necessary.

The novelty of Hirschman's analysis, and its importance here, is that it rejects the classical economists' view that the principles of free trade economics precluded imperialism and that impartial economic law governing trade relations need not concern itself with imperialist power.[10] The argument here is that the power of trade is implicitly political and that Latin American foreign economic policy is predicated on a recognition of the political consequences of trade. The national politics of trade in Latin America is dictated to a great extent by this description of trade power.

Hirschman's first hypothesis is, by now, a summary proposition in international relations, and it receives attention here only indirectly. The power relationships of the international system in general are beyond the scope of this analysis. Likewise, the second proposition is to be examined indirectly because the notions of dependency have become far too diverse and problematic since Hirschman. But items (3)–(8) are of great relevance to the inter-American trade system and deserve systematic attention here. They can be summarized in two general statements: first, that power asymmetry influences small country trade and that the interests of the powerful are in the dependence of the weak, in both exports and imports; and second, that such power is undermined by differential attention to trade and by small country diversification.

Current circumstances involving the United States are a good deal more ambiguous than those facing an expansionist Germany in pre–World War II Europe, the concern of Hirschman's original analysis. First, the foreign economic policy ambitions of the United States are much more ambiguous. Although the United States would like to maintain influence over Latin American affairs, especially in the area of trade reform and liberalization, it is not clear that maximum Latin American economic dependence is the optimal situation for the United States. The United States is suffering its own trade deficit, and Chapter 2 introduced the problems of its accepting the trade burden of Latin American adjustment to the debt crisis.

It also seems that the current economic crisis and the reconstruction of international economic relations among important OECD trading areas make the formal obstacles to Latin American trade diversification more daunting than at any time in the post–World War II era. Thus the preferences of Latin American small countries vis-à-vis the power of the United States may not be revealed, for lack of alternatives.[11] The best test of the Hirschman theses would involve an unambivalent Great Power, with open competition among other contenders for that Great Power status—perhaps like the pre–World War II Great Power competition for commercial influence in Latin America. These concerns aside, the central question deriving from these two statements involves the degree to which the small country can actually do anything to alleviate its weakness.

Historically, the colonial model of strong-weak country trade created the situation described in point no. 3, in which the colonial power influences the composition and direction of the weaker partner's trade. The Spanish and Portuguese colonial systems in Latin America were built on mercantilist restrictions that determined bilateral dependency. Independence, to some great extent, was measured by colonies' abilities to subvert those trade restrictions through privateering, tax evasion, corruption, and the like. This bilateral domination, with the British as partner, continued through the national period and into the epoch of free trade imperialism, when Britain and gradually the United States dictated the terms (sometimes to their own short-term disadvantage) and composition of trade in Latin America.

The archetype of this situation is Argentina under British influence.[12] Argentina is a particularly strong case to analyze because it may have benefited more than any other Latin American country from international trade in the period 1875 to 1930. Land was Argentina's main asset, and its value was enhanced by rising European demand, technological change in transportation, and successful national strategies for exporting a variety of rural products, among them hides, wool, wheat, and beef. By the time of the Great Depression, Argentina had industrialized to such an extent that agriculture had fallen into third place (behind commerce and manufacturing, respectively) in the composition of the nation's gross domestic product.[13] The diversity of its export bill must have been the envy of the rest of Latin America.

Modern theory on the developmental gains from trade stipulates that exports are the element of national trade that enhances employment and national development, with imports representing a generally necessary "leakage" against that development.[14] Argentina in the national period had only its tradition as an entrepôt to work with, which was built strictly on its importation of goods from the metropole for transshipment, not on the export of its own products.[15] Argentina thus suffered a double liability, because the only advantage of such a transit trade was its uniqueness to the importing and exporting countries. After independence, Argentina lost its unique position in the colonial empire, and free trade opened such services to the marketplace, at least to a limited extent. Local producers lost to British imports, some capital investment turned inward, and the British took over the role of merchants at the expense of local forces.

Even as the cattle industry expanded on the basis of exports of jerked beef to Brazil and Cuba and of hides to Europe, Argentina was forced to import grain because of its low technology, the absence of capital in agriculture, and the resulting high costs of domestic grain output. Conflict in the national period partly involved free trade versus protectionism, with the protectionists led, ironically, by those threatened with competition in subtropical products from Brazil and Paraguay, not Europe.[16] Imports of competing goods left domestic producers marginal to the national economy. A resulting concentration of income among the *estancieros* diminished the amount of capital available for savings and investment and made the conspicuous consumption of imported luxuries *de rigueur* among the denizens of *porteño* high society.[17]

The weakness of an essentially import-dependent entrepôt economy is further evident when Argentina's later "merinization" is considered. In the second half of the nineteenth century, Argentina began to "take off" because of its wool exports to Britain, which aided the expansion of British textile manufactures.[18] The wool and mutton industries, staples which also developed in Canada and Australia, enhanced the market for land, raised the demand for labor, and forced a certain technological modernization in the rural economy, extending not only to breeding but to land management. Under the old international division of labor, however, Argentina was limited to the export of raw materials and to the expanding import of manufactures, including fine textiles made of Argentine wool and hides. This economic dynamic was inflexible on both the export and import sides.

Despite the marked success in achieving a staple-product export base and industrializing at least in export-related industries, Argentina suffered a number of critical shortcomings. It was not able to industrialize beyond some light industries connected to export expansion. Meat packing, meat extract, dairy products, and wool washing were the mainstays of industrial growth; Argentina's first wave of industrialization was primarily export-based, not import substituting.[19] With the exception of textiles, which grew slowly before the post–World War II expansion, foreigners (overwhelmingly British) owned a majority of Argentine industries; two-thirds of industrial establishments were foreign-owned in 1914. Three-fifths of the stock of foreign capital in Argentina at the outbreak of World War I was British.[20]

Trade was geographically concentrated as well, though not so starkly as investment. Britain was the largest foreign partner and bought more than 99 percent of chilled beef exports.[21] But Argentina successfully diversified its commodity trade in such a way as to diversify its geographic trade concentration. The largest market overall remained Great Britain, but the lead market for wool was Germany, for wheat the United Kingdom, for corn Belgium, and for linseed the United States.

As interdependent as Argentina looks by Latin American standards of the time, by the 1930s its continued bilateral dependence became painfully obvious at home, as the liberal internationalist government that suceeded Hipólito Yrigoyen in 1930 tried to force reintegration with Britain on grounds humiliating to economic nationalists. The 1930s were called the "infamous decade" by both fascist and socialist contemporaries for the failed subordination to Britain in the Roca-Runciman pact, as well as the endemic political corruption of the period. Argentina's post-Depression recovery strategy was politically well behind the national capacity to import-substitute and to undertake the kind of turn inward that the other large economies of Latin America were trying at the time. In Argentina, the successful economics of export-led growth between 1875 and 1929 also retarded the national politics of import substitution. Before 1930, no government was interested in industrialization unless it served the export sector. The political leadership of the period of British free trade expansion was unabashedly internationalist and did not cultivate a national industrial policy. Argentina met the Great Depression not with economic nationalism but with the anachronistic forces of political reaction.

This is not to say that other forces were not incubating at the same time. As William C. Smith points out, Argentina was not immune to the emergence of new classes and state managers interested in promoting a different orientation in the economy, a different "style of development."[22] Like Brazil before 1930, Argentina had precociously set the stage for the emergence of Keynesianism with the creation of a more ambitious state apparatus, especially in national finance.

In addition to the pressures of these emerging forces at the national level, Argentina was forced to change its trade orientation by two macro-historical influences: the collapse of the British trade empire over the course of the two world wars and the Great Depression, and the evolution of a politically ascendant nationalist populism that turned its development model inward in the 1940s and early 1950s. Three questions arise:

first, whether Argentina enhanced its national autonomy by diversifying the commodity composition and geographic destination of its exports; second, whether there were forgone development gains to be had on the import side; and third, whether Argentina's vulnerability in the international system has changed accordingly.

Argentina, along with Brazil, Chile, and to some extent Mexico, used early industrial transformation and a broad international market for its output to secure the benefits of increased domestic economic diversity and lower levels of bilateral dependence. Whether or not this makes any difference is a subsidiary question. If Argentina (or Brazil) is used as a standard because of the capacity to move away from dependence on a single partner or to turn inward, it must be recognized immediately that such an approach excludes almost all of the rest of Latin America. Because of its early industrialization, Argentina, along with the other large economies, had the opportunity over time to reduce geographic and commodity concentration in trade and to impel industrial transformation, either through export or import substitution.

Openness, or its lack, as well as size further reinforce the exceptional status of Argentina, Brazil, and Mexico. From Hirschman's hypotheses and from the analysis in Chapter 2, we see that Latin American national power and development prospects revolve around openness and bilateral dependence, measured most simply (and somewhat inadequately) by geographic concentration of trade. The openness of the economy refers generally to its reliance on the international system for economic health. A commonsense hypothesis is that the greater a country's openness, the greater its vulnerability to external shock. Here, openness is measured as the proportion of overall economic activity generated by trade.[23] But this simple proposition does not take into account the importance of the terms of trade on vulnerability. The terms-of-trade argument is so prominent in the history of Latin American trade politics that ignoring it would be to ignore the historical dimension insisted on throughout this study. A rough indicator to measure the impact of external shock on domestic economic performance is thus a function of the terms of trade weighted by the degree of openness.[24]

This analysis leads to several suggestive possibilities. First, it is somewhat counterintuitive that the high-trade countries (Argentina, Brazil, and Mexico) are also the most closed economies in the region. A common notion is that trade and openness are correlates in Latin American trade: the more a country trades, the more open is its economy. And the more open the economy, the more vulnerable it is to external shock. Likewise, the more geographically- and commodity-concentrated the trade of the open economy is, the greater its vulnerability. Latin American countries vary by economic size, geographic concentration, commodity concentration, and relationship of exports to import trade. So it can be hypothesized that in Latin America, first, the openness of a country's economy is more problematic for national policy if trade is highly concentrated, either by trading partner (geographic) or by commodity; second, the impact of trade on national politics (the real political significance of openness) varies inversely with the size of the economy; and third, export and import vulnerability are related and vary in their impact according to the industrial development of the country.

This third point leads to two corollaries, that export vulnerability is partially a function of the terms of trade and commodity concentration, and that import vulnerability is less a function of volume than the proportion of key inputs in the import bill. The first means that the mono-exporter suffers more than the exporter of a variety of goods. By the same token, the exporter of a commodity with volatile or poor terms of trade is also more vulnerable. The second means that the greater the volume of luxury imports, the lower the vulnerability.

As a fourth point, we can hypothesize that vulnerability is also dependent on the relationship of exports to necessary imports. That is, a country that depends on necessary inputs to produce export goods (e.g., Mexico's or Peru's dependence on imports of mercury to export silver in the colonial period, or Brazil's dependence on RAM chips for aircraft exports) is more vulnerable than the country whose import and export sectors are more independent.

The problem with ranking countries by their openness is the horrendous turnabouts in the past two decades. As Table 4.1 shows, using a classification borrowed from the Inter-American Development Bank in 1982, Latin American countries have changed the degree of their external "exposure" over the 1970–88 period. Several countries have changed their place in the table dramatically, and the region's level of trade as a proportion of GDP has declined. National experiences vary widely, but the region has been marked by significant increases in trade over the 1970s, with imports generally outstripping exports. Imports were reduced sharply in the 1980s following the onset of the debt crisis in 1982, and the role of exports in Latin American GDP increased significantly.

Other things being equal, one would expect openness and trade concentration to be correlated. If the strong country is taking advantage of its trade power to advance its political agenda and to increase its influence over its weaker trading partners, we would expect the most open countries to move toward greater concentration in trade with the Great Power. Table 4.2 shows this to be a weak proposition, though again the different historical traditions and peculiar economic circumstances of each of the

TABLE 4.1

Ranking Latin American and Caribbean Countries by Openness
(Numbers in parentheses indicate regional ranking)

Degree of openness	1988		1980		1970	
Extremely dependent						
Trinidad and Tobago	61	(6)	201	(1)	91	(2)
Panama	68	(5)	196	(2)	71	(5)
Guyana	109	(2)	154	(4)	115	(1)
Highly dependent						
Venezuela	40	(16)	108	(5)	45	(9)
Jamaica	118	(1)	107	(6)	96	(4)
Honduras	69	(4)	96	(7)	59	(7)
Costa Rica	87	(3)	90	(8)	63	(6)
Relatively dependent						
Chile	52	(8)	80	(9)	39	(13)
Ecuador	46	(11)	78	(10)	33	(15)
El Salvador	42	(14)	74	(11)	42	(12)
Nicaragua	46	(11)	74	(12)	52	(8)
Bolivia	51	(9)	72	(13)	43	(11)
Dominican Republic	43	(13)	60	(14)	43	(10)
Uruguay	42	(14)	59	(15)	27	(19)
Moderately dependent						
Haiti	54	(7)	27	(16)	27	(18)
Argentina	27	(19)	51	(17)	21	(21)
Colombia	35	(17)	47	(18)	34	(14)
Guatemala	25	(21)	47	(19)	29	(17)
Peru	33	(18)	46	(20)	30	(16)
Paraguay	47	(10)	46	(21)	25	(20)
Mexico	27	(19)	44	(22)	20	(22)
Lesser dependent						
Brazil	20	(22)	30	(23)	16	(23)
Average for region	30		50		26	

SOURCE: Inter-American Development Bank, *Economic and Social Progress in Latin America*, 1982, 1989.

NOTE: Openness is measured here as the ratio between the combined value of exports and imports of goods and services and the GDP.

countries in question make simple correlation analysis meaningless. And the period in which we are most interested—the 1980s—was so unstable as to resist characterization.

If, for example, we were to stipulate that Great Power influence reflected in trade concentration is a function of (a) size (the smaller the country, the more likely the influence of the Great Power); (b) historical tradition (the greater the historical depth of the trade relationship, the greater the influence of the Great Power); or (c) openness (the more open the economy, the greater the influence of the Great Power), we see that any generalization is too broad. The smallest economies do seem to have moved toward greater concentration in the wake of the oil and debt crises (e.g., Bolivia, Costa Rica, and Paraguay, but with the significant excep-

TABLE 4.2
Hirschman Indexes of Geographic Trade Concentration by Latin American Country, Selected Years, 1960–88

	Argentina	Bolivia	Brazil	Chile	Colombia	Costa Rica	Dom. Rep.	Ecuador	El Salvador
1960	31.2	60.1	23.9	45.5	66.7	60.1	64.9	64.5	50.8
1970	26.7	53.1	30.5	31.7	42.7	45.0	85.0	47.7	40.3
1975	23.3	42.8	23.5	27.3	37.6	45.6	71.2	52.1	37.9
1976	23.2	43.2	25.8	29.1	37.4	43.6	72.0	43.0	42.1
1977	21.8	43.5	25.2	29.8	37.7	37.0	75.4	42.0	42.1
1978	23.2	40.9	28.0	29.6	38.9	38.9	62.9	49.4	39.6
1979	23.3	36.4	25.4	29.2	37.3	41.1	61.8	48.6	42.3
1980	28.1	36.3	23.9	27.3	36.1	39.7	54.9	45.7	46.1
1981	36.4	47.4	23.6	27.3	34.2	37.7	68.1	54.9	44.3
1982	28.8	53.7	25.7	31.7	33.8	38.8	56.6	62.8	50.4
1983	28.2	51.6	27.6	35.7	36.6	37.5	68.4	67.8	47.6
1984	24.9	53.8	31.7	34.0	37.9	42.1	77.1	78.5	49.3
1985	25.0	58.8	31.1	30.9	38.7	43.0	77.1	72.4	54.6
1986	22.4	56.6	31.7	30.6	38.3	46.8	79.6	71.9	56.5
1987	24.9	50.7	31.4	31.2	44.0	49.7	84.6	65.6	49.7
1988	24.0	52.3	30.7	30.4	43.4	47.8	80.8	61.2	48.6

TABLE 4.2 (*continued*)

	Guatemala	Honduras	Mexico	Nicaragua	Panama	Paraguay	Peru	Uruguay	Venezuela
1960	60.2	59.1	73.2	50.8	97.4	48.5	41.9	35.2	50.8
1970	36.9	56.2	72.0	40.4	67.0	40.4	40.7	25.7	45.0
1975	32.3	54.0	61.9	36.1	60.8	37.0	31.5	27.0	47.9
1976	41.9	58.5	63.5	38.9	52.2	30.5	32.0	25.9	47.9
1977	39.8	56.4	67.8	33.0	49.6	31.4	35.1	28.1	50.1
1978	38.1	60.0	70.3	35.3	48.5	30.1	43.6	31.4	47.8
1979	37.3	55.0	71.6	40.2	58.4	33.7	41.8	34.2	45.7
1980	35.6	52.9	66.7	43.7	59.5	34.8	37.2	29.4	41.9
1981	32.0	56.7	57.2	35.5	57.3	34.7	42.1	24.7	37.3
1982	36.6	54.5	55.1	32.6	53.4	35.6	41.3	25.0	39.2
1983	41.5	56.9	60.9	32.5	62.2	34.1	43.6	25.6	40.4
1984	43.0	55.3	61.2	32.1	62.6	30.8	44.6	25.5	52.8
1985	40.1	52.5	62.9	30.3	65.3	33.2	37.7	28.2	50.5
1986	48.3	51.7	69.2	26.5	69.4	45.8	34.6	34.1	54.8
1987	48.7	55.0	70.6	25.0	69.4	38.5	32.4	29.0	58.7
1988	42.9	52.0	74.2	29.4	53.2	39.6	29.2	27.2	59.3

SOURCE: Calculated from data found in the International Monetary Fund, *Direction of Trade Yearbook* (various years); see Hirschman, *National Power and the Structure of Foreign Trade*, for methodology on concentration index.

tions of Honduras, Panama, and Uruguay). The more open economies also tended to move in the predicted direction, though two of the perennially most open economies, Panama and Honduras, both defy the trend. And on the other end of the scale, both Mexico and Brazil moved toward greater concentration despite their relatively closed character.

One observation that stands out is that the oil economies—Ecuador, Mexico, and Venezuela—all moved away from trade concentration during the oil boom and toward it again in the debt crisis. This is not consistently true of the other primary-commodity-producing countries during the same period (Peru, Uruguay, and Honduras). It may be that other primary commodities were not as promising as oil in the 1970s and therefore did not admit more aggressive diversification strategies.

In any event, the Hirschman indexes are instructive, but each country must be analyzed individually to tease out the political changes in trade that might explain changes in concentration. For example, it may be that in the late 1980s, Brazil's and Mexico's changes in the direction of trade liberalization are reflected in the concentration indexes, but without qualitative analysis of their trade policies we cannot know.

In general, the trade patterns of most of the countries of Latin America were more concentrated at the end of the 1980s than at the beginning, and much of that is a result of the U.S. acceptance of Latin American trade adjustment in the debt crisis. It is unclear, however, from the regional data that the United States is behaving in the way described by Hirschman for a hegemonic partner.

The region as a whole became more open over the 1970 to 1988 period. Virtually all countries followed that trend, mainly on the export side. In the period 1970 to 1988, most countries of the region stifled imports as a response to the external shock of the 1980s but did not do so in the 1970s. Throughout Latin America, imports as a proportion of GDP rose over the 1970s, despite the two oil shocks. This response is consistent with the arguments about investment and growth outlined in Chapter 3. In the wake of the debt crisis, however, deep cuts in imports occurred throughout the region, which for most countries brought the role of imports as a proportion of GDP more or less back in line with 1970 levels. Striking are some small Caribbean economies (notably Haiti and Jamaica) and Paraguay, which have been unable to bring down imports in keeping with the rest of the region or their own past. Otherwise, the depth of the region's import reduction is also reflected by the increase in exports; export value goes increasingly to service the debt, returning little value to domestic growth.

Once again, the industrialized economies of Latin America are generally less concentrated than their non-industrial counterparts, by both partner and type of export, and presumably less vulnerable to the vicissitudes of the international trade system. Mexico is exceptional in this regard because of its historical concentration of trade with the United States and the singular role of devaluation and liberalization in investment that explains its recent success as an exporter of manufactures.[25] But it is necessary still to qualify these initial observations and to place them in context.

Bilateral Dependence Versus Diversification of Trade

A maxim of Latin American economic thinking is that bilateral trade concentration is dangerous and that trade diversification is a precondition of sustained development and economic stability.[26] These arguments are based on the reasonable premises that excessive dependence on one trade partner makes a country more vulnerable to external economic shocks caused, for example, by economic recession in the partner country, changes in the investment climate affecting capital flows, or a wave of protectionism. There is also a literature in international economics arguing that bilateral trade concentration is inimical to economic development and that trade diversification is necessary to maximize national welfare. The traditional hypothesis is that both commodity and geographic concentration of trade correlate strongly with country size. The smaller the country, the more likely it is to be dependent on a small set of commodities and a small set of partner countries for trade.[27] In the abstract, this association of size with concentration is overly simple. Small countries of Europe and Asia have traded broadly, and resource endowments are not the only consideration in the dynamics of trade. Likewise, a great deal of partner country concentration depends on factors other than size, such as the importance and substitutability of the goods traded, the location of the small country, and the structure of demand. The historical record vitiates this defense to some extent because of the influence of the colonial powers, the United States and Europe, and the association of political power with trade influence.

Bilateral economic dependence correlates strongly in Latin America with political dependency because the almost universal "other" in the Latin American trade dyad is the United States, the regional hegemon. Familiar exemplars of bilateral dependency in Latin America, Mexico, and most of the Caribbean Basin countries, including Cuba before 1959, constantly try to wriggle free of U.S. influence. Because of the enormous power and historical influence of the United States in the region, the opposite of dependency in these scenarios is something like distance from U.S. domination, or at least greater autonomy over economic decision making.[28]

The empirical evidence for this proposition is generally built around notions of disadvantage or exploitation, in which the Latin American country finds itself in a bilateral trade orbit that represents the embodiment of the international system of economic power. As Stallings has shown, bilateral dependence can extend both historically and theoretically to flows of finance capital, as well as trade and direct foreign investment. The weakness in the historical record comes from the lack of cases in which partner concentration in trade has *not* been the durable condition of a Latin American country, or in which a Latin American country has, at least, dissociated itself from the Western system of trade. The literature on that kind of "delinking" as an economic alternative to bilateral dependence has already received comment.

Whatever the limits of alternative models, it is difficult to dispute that bilateral trade dependence can restrict development options, based on exogenous factors such as the trade partner's rate of growth, the terms of trade in partner country (and general developed country) exports, or the political whims of major trade partners. When the large power in the bilateral dyad is also the regional (or global) hegemon, a small country's problems become greater. In the case of U.S.–Latin American trade relations, there is a direct association with the hegemonic power and trade liberalization, including the pressure to remove obstacles to further bilateral dependence. Neither political nor theoretical grounds can be found for the idea that the United States might promote liberalization in favor of greater Latin American trade diversification. The arguments of Hirschman inveigh against such a possibility. The current-day rigors of trade liberalization in the Western Hemisphere, matched by bloc consolidation in Europe and Asia, hardly encourage diversification under liberal rules.

The small, less-endowed dependent country's success in addressing a restricted number of political choices is a direct function of its ability to sidle up to power in the dominant country and to negotiate the terms of its bilateral dependence. A surrogate measure of progress in the external sector in Latin America is its ability to shake free of the U.S. trade orbit; a measure of weakness is the degree of bilateral dependence based on preferential trade arrangements. Accordingly, Latin American nations have striven over the entire post–World War II period to diversify their trade to include other OECD countries (mainly Europe and lately Japan) and selected Third World markets, especially within the Latin American region. One of the key prescriptions of trade policymakers in the U.N. Economic Commission for Latin America and the Inter-American Development Bank from the late 1940s until today has emphasized regional integration based on expanded trade, customs unions, and experimental common market arrangements, exemplified by the Andean Pact and the Caribbean and Central American Common Markets.[29]

A common alternative "open system" argument is that preferential trade arrangements with dominant trade partners offer benefits that cannot be won in the marketplace. So if a small country can gain preferential treatment by the hegemon, it can exceed the limits of its economic possibilities. (This is one, rather unsatisfying, way in which aggressive political leadership can move against economic rules limiting the small economy.) This is particularly persuasive in the cases of small countries (the African, Caribbean, and Pacific countries of the Lomé Convention, for example, or the Caribbean Basin Initiative beneficiaries) benefiting from regional or subregional agreements, as it was with the benefits derived by Cuba and Puerto Rico during the last decades of Spanish colonial rule.

Currently, some participants in the U.S. sugar quota, though protesting the protectionist disposition of the quota itself, realize that in a declining international market for sugar, in which prices have been subject historically to wild fluctuations and have been quite low and unstable over much of the post-Depression period, the U.S. sugar quota offers a certain protection against the uncompromising marketplace. This situation has in common with bilateral dependence without a preference system the necessity for the smaller country to negotiate from weakness better treatment by the greater power. From the standpoint of national pride and the autonomy of economic decision-making, this is an unattractive condition. Cuba before 1959, for example, maintained center stage in the U.S. quota system but watched its overall share decline, while the United States insisted on reciprocal agreements for U.S. exports of manufactures.[30]

Critics of this position contend that the small country should seek liberation from bilateral dependence. This critique fails to address the chief constraint of the small country exporter of primary commodities, which is dependent on preference systems to survive in a market that would sweep it away under rules of free competition. Whatever the limits of small country bilateral preference schemes (or those that offer preference in a multilateral context), they may offer the only trade alternative.

The 1960s and 1970s represented a convergence of two important economic phenomena in Latin America: the expansion of international trade, and the perceived "exhaustion of the easy phase" of import-substitution industrialization.[31] The expansion of trade took place in an unusual climate of trade pessimism. Nevertheless, the expansionary climate of the period allowed large Latin American economies the opportunity to import-substitute and to diversify their trade bills so that single-partner dependence was reduced. At least it can be said that no other climate in the twentieth century has offered both the broad-based international growth impulse facilitating import substitution, and the political philosophy that permitted an essentially nationalist turn inward in Latin America.

Despite this favorable climate, the realities of Latin American trade in the period reveal that only a handful of countries managed to shift their commodity concentration, to diversify their trade partners, or to reduce their openness over time. The sad conclusion for advocates of economic diversification and a closed economy approach is that even under the best circumstances in this century, very few Latin American economies managed a significant turn away from the United States as a dominant trade partner and few indeed managed to change their export bill significantly in favor of manufactures or to close their economies over previous periods. Even those small economies trying to diversify agricultural exports achieved very limited gains.

Some of the large trading countries of Latin America did reduce the concentration of their trade with the United States significantly during the period 1960 to 1980. Most remarkably, Brazil reduced its export dependence on the United States from 44 percent in 1960 to a low of 15 percent in 1975. Even in the years surrounding the oil shocks of 1973–74 and 1979–80, Brazil reduced exports to the United States to about one-fifth of overall exports. The other country to experience such significant changes was Chile, which moved substantially away from its dependence on the U.S. import market in the Alliance for Progress years. Not surprisingly, this move was most striking during the Allende years, when the Unidad Popular government tried to reduce international vulnerability and U.S. policymakers tried to make the Chilean economy "scream," partly through a reduction in trade.

Most disheartening to advocates of diversification are the cases of Peru and Mexico. Because of Peru's long tradition of economic liberalism and trade openness, along with foreign exchange pressures, it hardly wavered from its long-standing dependence on the United States for export trade. Its modest successes in reducing this dependence have come amid the chaos and economic disorganization of the García years (the United States bought 26 percent of Peru's exports in 1988).[32] And in Mexico, even during the nationalist resurgence of the Echeverría years (1970–76) and the oil boom of the López Portillo government (1976–82), the government found it impossible to reduce its trade dependence on the United States. The worldwide value of both countries' export commodities (minerals and fish meal in Peru, oil in Mexico) failed to divert their trade compass from a U.S. polarity.

Several observations are warranted from the U.S.–Latin American trade bill in the 1980s. First, it is apparent that the United States accepted, and continues to accept, the burden of Latin American trade adjustment in the wake of the debt crisis. This is owing to two overwhelming influences: the relative openness of the U.S. trade system, and the robustness of the U.S. economy in the early 1980s, after the Reagan recession of 1981–82. As to the first, Chapter 5 will detail the United States's relative openness to Latin American exports, when compared to Japan or the Common Market, the two most obvious alternatives for Latin American commerce. In the debt-induced collapse of intraregional trade in Latin America during the first half of the 1980s, the United States became the default partner in Latin American trade, which, coupled with historical ties, meant that the United States was saddled with Latin American exports in an extraordinary way in the early 1980s.

Second, it is important to recognize that the majority of Latin American countries have not enjoyed the import-substitution industrialization option, despite the experience of the larger economies for all or part of the twentieth century. Those who have not must rely on import substitution in agriculture and develop different export-promotion schemes. Mainly, they have failed to move away from dependence on a small set of primary commodities. With the notable exception of Chile, which in the years of the Pinochet dictatorship tried to change the course of its history (with mixed success) by reducing export dependence on copper (in 1972–76, copper represented 66 percent of Chilean exports; in 1983–87, 38.9 percent; but in 1988, it rose to 48 percent),[33] small Latin American economies continued to labor under the burden of sugar, coffee, cotton, cattle, petroleum, and other traditional exports. Even in the case of Chile, there exists great skepticism about the virtue of its structural adjustment for trade, particularly in view of the low value-added content of the new exports[34] and the resurging importance of copper.

Countries substituting other nontraditional exports have not moved significantly away from primary commodities. If, for example, Ecuador moves away from cacao and hats, the nineteenth-century export base, to petroleum in the third quarter of the twentieth century, and then prospectively to gold, it does not affect the fundamental commodity dependence of the country, with the limited prospects for backward and forward linkages for development. These realities constrain national strategies in fundamental ways, greatly limiting the prospects for development.

The Open Versus the Closed Economy

The counterargument is that basing national development on trade is a poor choice, especially in a system of free trade based on reciprocity.[35]

Reciprocity is seen as unfair, operating to the disadvantage of Third World traders. In fact, the history of northern preference systems for southern trade partners is based on concessional access and conditional openness, not reciprocity. That is, from the British Imperial Preference System to the global generalized system of preferences designed in the 1960s (to which the United States responded with its Generalized System of Preferences [GSP] program in 1974),[36] the rich countries have recognized that poor countries should be conceded special conditions of trade that are not as rigorous (i.e., imbued with reciprocal responsibilities) as the global trade system as a whole.[37]

Throughout the post-Depression period, many countries have considered a turn inward for substitution of imports in agriculture or manufactures, or of traditional exports, to be a better alternative. Two elements generally defend this position: first, that the peripheral country must be absolved of its trade obligation to reciprocate in order to defend its infant industries (or, by extension, its infant economy) from ruthless competition that would ruin its development aspirations. Second, developmentalists argue that because of the high income elasticities of demand in the periphery, any increase in exports to the center countries will result in an element of reciprocity.[38] This point may be correct on grounds of historical experience but depends on a variety of policies that affect savings, consumption, and investment.

A third, relatively rare, position is unpopular, difficult to prove, and intriguing: that preference operates to the disadvantage of Third World countries in the multilateral trading system, and that national power would be enhanced by their rejecting preferences in favor of equal standing in the GATT with higher levels of national discretion in short-term barriers to trade.[39] In other words, preference is a trap that keeps the Third World in its place. Behaving like a "normal" protectionist within the GATT requires less apology and gives up little. The virtue of this position for the OECD countries is a presumed movement in the GSP country toward more transparent trade barriers, that is, away from nontariff barriers toward tariff barriers, which are easier to govern and reduce. From the LDC perspective, it is argued that the South will never be able to win in negotiations in the GATT until it is able to claim equal status, and that status will never be granted until preference (and graduation) disappear. There is also a fiscal argument on behalf of tariff barriers replacing nontariff barriers: that revenues from tariffs accrue to the importing government, rather than nontariff barriers' creating rents for the producer.

This is consistent in principle, if not degree, with the most rudimentary "closed system" position regarding national power and international trade. It advocates using national development strategy to rid the system of Great Power dependence and to turn inward. This strategy was followed to some degree in the import-substitution years after World War II, but it has its roots among the nationalists of the first half of the nineteenth century as well. At that time, even in liberal Peru, Limeño protectionists "aimed to eliminate the North American presence altogether, through complete import prohibitions or their galvanizing alternative of a closed market system with Chile."[40] Even in Brazil, where colonial trade was not interrupted by violent internal war and where various commodity booms made externally stimulated growth a reality for much of the nineteenth century, nationalists resisted Emperor D. João IV's characterization as the "milch cow" of Portugal.[41] That evocative tradition has continued to figure in the arsenal of nationalist politics.

Theoretically, one reason for turning inward is based on pessimism vis-à-vis the elasticity of Latin American exports. The argument is that market signals favor investment in primary products for export, undercutting alternative domestic investment in industrialization (and precipitating periodic crises of overproduction). If public intervention does not reorient economic incentives, development, defined in this context largely as industrialization to change the country's position in the international division of labor, is undermined.[42]

The most elaborate closed system position has been to dissociate from the entire Western trade system, not just from the hegemonic influence. Recalling the Hirschman-Lewis test from Chapter 3, an argument exists among those interested in economic development in the Third World stipulating that the South would be better off without a connection to the North. Neo-Marxist analysts derive this conclusion from the different theoretical basis of development from neoclassical economics, and from the conviction that southern poverty and underdevelopment are products of exploitative integration into the international system, dominated by monopoly power, transnational corporations, and unequal exchange.

The "exit option" implied by such analysis is appealing, particularly given the historical woes associated with Third World participation in the international capitalist trade system. Several problems burden this analysis, however, both at the theoretical and practical levels. First is the absence of historical cases in which a small, poor country has dissociated itself from the Western trade system voluntarily and successfully. Second, it is questionable whether small socialist countries such as Cuba can operate internally without being vulnerable to the law of value at the international level.[43] Third, in the epoch of the transnationalization of labor processes, such a delinking would seem to relegate the small economy to a position of permanent backwardness in regard to the progress and transfer of technology. Such weaknesses in the countercase to openness define trade as a Hobson's choice for the small economy.

As Chapter 6 will treat in more detail, a variety of considerations are involved in constituting a nationalist position vis-à-vis the international trade system. They range from the unsullied nationalism of Cuba's turn away from sugar and the economic laws of international commerce after 1959,[44] to alternatives that question the terms of trade more than the virtue of commerce itself.

Another aspect important to the politics of trade concentration involves the role of the dominant trading partner in domestic politics. For most of Latin America in the late twentieth century, the United States is the overwhelming economic presence in their trade bill and the dominant figure in trade-related matters of direct foreign investment, trade finance, and debt negotiations. In addition, the political and ideological predispositions of the United States, which differ significantly from those of other OECD countries and Latin American trade partners, are reflected in the institutions of the Bretton Woods system, adding a further U.S. flavor to external influences on Latin American trade. The United States, in contrast to Europe and Japan, is ideologically hostile to state subventions to industry, opposed to the presence of parastate enterprises, and steadfastly against state control of the "commanding heights" of the national economy.

To the extent that Latin American countries are committed to a strong state presence in the economy and to general control over trade relations, diversification of partners might converge with national goals more than adherence to the hegemon, with its presumably greater U.S. influence. Parenthetically, this would suggest that there is a political affinity between the new regional free trade initiatives and the enthusiastic Latin American embrace of the Bush initiatives and the domestic ideological turnaround (toward free trade and the market, away from the strong state) that has followed the debt crisis and structural adjustment.

Returning to the main argument, the association between economic development and the closed economy is not completely untreated in neoclassical theory, as indicated by the "law of declining trade." It stipulates that after initial economic expansion, foreign trade declines in importance in relation to total economic activity.[45] But the role of foreign trade in the national economy rises as a nation integrates more fully into the international trade system. That integration can come as a result of trade expansion, as in the nineteenth century and the period 1945–70, or it can be the result of response to an external payments crisis, as is the case today.

As Kindleberger recognizes, the law of declining trade applies, and even there weakly, to the developed world. Whether the association between increased economic activity and the declining importance of trade is strong or consistent in the Third World depends on the degree to which a country is able to exploit its internal market and the result of the various policy instruments affecting trade and domestic economic development.

Latin American integration, either regional or global, also depends on variables that have not provided much stability over the past century: the elasticities of demand for Latin American exports, rates of growth in consumer countries, stability of the international monetary system, and a consonance of capital flows with the demands of the trade system. It may be, especially in the case of Latin American countries over the past century, that the law of declining trade applies "under normal circumstances," and those circumstances rarely occur.

In the main, it may be hypothesized that the law of declining trade applies to the larger economies of Latin America, in direct function of their "success" in insulating their national economies from the international system, measured mainly by the success of their turn inward.[46] A given country might have turned away from trade in the 1930s in favor of the first wave of import substitution, then reintegrated into the international trade system in the postwar expansion, first through export expansion, then through the linkage of industrial development to the import of intermediate inputs, capital goods, and industrial raw materials. From the standpoint of multilateral trade policy, short-term protectionism in Latin America may be beneficial by generating greater international integration over the long term.

This insulating potential would exclude, for all practical purposes, the small economies, which remain open and dependent on trade for so much of their economic activities. It also says nothing about the political conditions for the law of declining trade to prevail, to which we shall turn shortly. Historically, this is also consistent, as the small, open economies of Latin America were more "passive" in their response to the Great Depression and limited in their ability to undertake industrial transformation, that is, to turn inward successfully.

Perhaps more importantly from the longer view, this thesis suggests that degrees of insulation are themselves dependent variables, subject to movements in the international economic system, as well as to national policy. To the extent that changes in the international economy allow Latin American nations to extricate themselves from dependent conditions, nationalist politics may succeed or fail for exogenous reasons. This is not to say that intelligent policies are irrelevant, only that the international system may govern in great measure the political space in which nationalism operates.

The Role of the Public Sector

It is evident from the economic history of Latin America over the past two centuries that one of the critical axes along which national trade strategies vary contrasts economic nationalism with international integration. As Chapter 1 suggested, this cut is not so convenient because economic liberals in the nineteenth century were often political nationalists, and liberalism often has been wrapped in the cloak of national sovereignty and progress. As with most broad concepts, these characterizations are too sharply defined for the subtleties of national political debate at any one time. They are mainly conceptual conveniences to portray the "lean" of individual political positions regarding Latin American foreign economic relations. Nevertheless, whether characterized as nationalism versus integration or sovereignty versus surrender, Latin American nations have battled for their entire histories over the question of the proper alliance with the international system.

A nation's approach along this track is obviously related to its position in the Hirschman-Lewis table in Chapter 2 and the characterization of power benefits from trade above. In the 1960s and 1970s, the notion of dependency guided Latin American intellectual, and to some extent political, thinking in regard to foreign economic policy. Once again, this chapter skirts the dependency debate, for the same reasons of parsimony that dictated avoiding the gains from trade literature per se. It is not so much the fine distinctions among *dependentistas* that interest us as the specifics of trade-impelled dependence and the resulting domestic political consequences.

The general dependency argument does stipulate that the international capitalist system is a fundamental obstacle to the development of peripheral nations, and that a radical dissociation of the South from the North would facilitate development. One question arising from dependency writing that is difficult to ignore, however, is What is the opposite of dependency? That is, What would a nation's condition and dynamics look like if dependency were overcome? Obviously, that is a matter for historical and empirical evidence to determine fully. But some suggestions can be made, summarizing the above theoretical arguments about Latin American trade and development and the historical predicament in which Latin America has found itself in the past century of trade.

First, as the last chapter argued, the trade aspect of dependency is a product of power inequalities among nations. Lessening dependency involves reducing those power inequalities to the extent possible and in-

	High state	Low state	
	(I) STATIST INTERNATIONALISM Chile 1964–73 Nicaragua 1979–present Peru 1968–75 Ecuador	**(II)** LIBERAL INTERNATIONALISM Argentina 1989–present Chile 1973–present Costa Rica Colombia Venezuela El Salvador	Open economy
	(III) STATIST NATIONALISM Argentina until 1989 Mexico before 1982 Brazil until 1990	**(IV)** LIBERAL NATIONALISM Mexico 1982–present United States	Closed economy

Figure 4.1. State Presence and Economic Orientation in Latin America.

sulating the dependent country from the inequalities it cannot resolve. Second, the flip side of dependency is autonomy, not as a condition but as a matter of degree. Moving away from dependency involves increasing the national autonomy of decision-making that is essential to development planning.

Considering domestic alternatives, there is an important substantive matter that divides economic nationalist versus internationalist trade and development policies in the postwar period: the presence and activity of the public sector. Accordingly, another hypothesis may be added to the four above that treat openness and vulnerability: external sector vulnerability is a function of public sector involvement in the economy.

Diaz-Alejandro's distinction between "reactive" and "passive" economies during the Depression correlates with our conception of high and low state, though one could conceive of a high-state, passive case in the abstract.[47] This brings us to the association of "high stateness" with a closed economy, with only the United States filling the cell reserved for a low-state closed economy. Figure 4.1 arrays countries according to the presence of the public sector in the economy: a "high-state" country would have a high level of public investment in the economy and, likely, a large array of public and parastate enterprises. In Figure 4.1, the state refers not only to government but especially to the public and parastate enterprises that generate economic activity and are responsible for a share of investment in the national economy. Figure 4.2 takes the same di-

High government	Low government	
(I) DIRECTED INTERNATIONALISM Argentina 1976–78 Chile after 1973 Peru since 1968	(II) LIBERAL INTERNATIONALISM Peru before 1968 Ecuador Costa Rica Venezuela Mexico since 1988	Open economy
(III) DIRECTED NATIONALISM Mexico before 1988 Brazil	(IV) LIBERAL NATIONALISM United States	Closed economy

Figure 4.2. Government Presence and Economic Orientation in Latin America.

mensions and defines "high government" according to the government's trade and development politics. It distinguishes "high state" from "high government."[48]

In this scheme, Chile and Argentina in the 1970s are considered "high government," even though their policy orientation is internationalist and their economic identification is neoliberal. Ecuador is considered "low government" but "high state" in Figure 4.1 because of the preponderant role of the state in extractive industries and the low government capacity to control them. The reason for this distinction is that the presence of government in the national economy may have more to do with historical tradition and national strategies of employment and incomes than with short-term international trade orientation. Thus the governments of Chile and Argentina in the years following the military takeovers (1973 and 1976, respectively) appear to be internationalist and liberal. But the political mechanisms under which that internationalism was effected were authoritarian and "high government." The attempted "deindustrialization"[49] of Argentina after the fall of Isabel Perón was an authoritarian policy designed to rid the public sector of power over the national economy. It was undertaken at the point of a gun. Likewise, in Chile, the so-called "Chicago boys" reoriented the national economy in radical internationalist ways, but under a ruthless and personalistic dictatorship that did not feel obligated to respect institutions that had been built over decades. Accordingly, the "structural adjustment" of the Chilean economy under Augusto Pinochet has been symbolized, somewhat unfortunately, as Milton Friedman with a gun.[50]

John Sheahan usefully categorizes some of these regimes as "market authoritarian."[51] He groups Brazil under the military dictatorship of 1964–85 together with Chile under Pinochet and Argentina under Juan Carlos Onganía (1966–69) and the dictatorship of 1976–82. Other analysts[52] would discriminate more clearly between Onganía, on the one hand, and Jorge Videla and Roberto Viola, on the other, in Argentina, and would eliminate the Brazilian dictatorship altogether from this group.[53]

Conversely, two radically different governments in Nicaragua before and after the revolution of 1979 have had a similar "high state" and "open" orientation, despite their totally opposite approaches to national development policy. This also attests to the limits of a small, open economy in the face of external constraints to national policy—in the Nicaraguan case, the forced constraints of the U.S. trade embargo and the strained relations with traditional Central American trading partners. One can hypothesize, on the basis of historical experience as well as programmatic statements from power contenders, that Chile in its ongoing transition to civilian rule will not undo the economy's intimate link with the international system. It is clear, however, that the democratic forces of President Patricio Aylwin in Chile have a very different domestic political orientation about the gains from trade than do the retiring Pinochet government and its civilian alter egos.[54]

There thus seems to be a set of countries with modest state and government capacity (which is not necessarily identical to low stateness, as one can easily imagine a high government/low capacity or high state/low capacity scenario, such as in Ecuador and Nicaragua) and high openness: the classically vulnerable small economies of Central America and the Caribbean, the currently desperate case of Peru, and the "successful" case of Chile.

Empirically and theoretically, the government's capacity is reflected in its power over trade politics and its disposition to exercise the power it has. Government orientation toward the trade system in general (its position on the Lewis test) is politically a function of the formation of coalitions at the national level and structurally somewhat determined by the apparent empirical demands of its national situation. Theoretically, for example, small countries are limited by the classic economic proposition of tariff theory, that "a small, open, price-taking economy gains no advantage from a protective tariff and bears the cost of its own trade protection with no significant impact on trading partners."[55] This proposition does not vary by state or government disposition but by economic power and international structure. It is important to recognize that this limit to the welfare benefit of tariffs hardly restrains politicians, who are not necessarily persuaded by trade theory. Often, it is not a question of who bears the cost at the international level but of who bears the consequences of inefficient tariffs at the national level.[56]

It is easy to assume—as U.S. trade policymakers, development assistance institutions, and private sector actors often do—that state and government are forces against trade, and that low stateness in the economy and low levels of government intervention in trade mean that the market dictates an appropriate level of trade for economic growth and development. As we shall see in Chapter 6, this means favoring privatization for ideological as well as fiscal reasons. For whatever purpose, the prospect of privatization affects the capacity of a Latin American country to insulate itself from negative influences in the international system and foreshortens prospective national strategies for trade and development. The result is to throw trade's role in national development back onto the economic efficiencies that have proven so unsatisfactory in the past.

Still, the virtues and limits of the public sector in mediating national power in international trade tell little about the ability of a state to steer toward or away from the international system based on national policy versus the impact of external variables on internal political change. At the same time, the abruptness and complexity of regime changes in Latin America constitute persuasive obstacles to proposing a complex political model to explain those swings in openness and state presence. At its best, the public sector can be held up as the only buffer against the brute forces of the international trade system, always with the crippling stipulation that it has performed poorly on this score throughout this century.

The Dynamics of National Power in the Current Crisis

To say that Brazil is a high-state, closed economy with a geographically concentrated but commodity-diverse trade bill is to take a snapshot of the country at a particular moment in time. It says nothing about the dynamics of these variables and what those dynamics tell us about national trade power. Sadly, it is difficult in the extreme to measure these dynamics with any precision, but there are a few clues to current vectors.

First, in response to pressure from the World Bank, the Inter-American Development Bank, and the International Monetary Fund, along with the U.S. government, Latin American countries are reducing the size of their public sectors. Some of the impact of that pressure is slow to be felt and certainly difficult to see in the public sector deficits of the high-debt countries. Adjustment policies indicate the certainty of those retreats, which imply eventual changes in the composition of production and trade. Mexico reduced the number of its public sector firms from 1,200 to 300 from 1986 to 1989. The effects of such privatization are wide-ranging. For example, the privatization of sugar production or shrimp cooperatives in Mexico has grave implications for national production and trade in those commodities. The removal of "upstream" natural resource subsidies likewise affects production in Brazil, Mexico, Peru, and many other countries. In keeping with the general argument so far, the most likely hypotheses are that (1) the role of the public sector has deteriorated over the 1980s; and given the lean of state involvement, (2) public sector presence varies directly with export openness, meaning that (3) reduced public sector presence means lower export performance but increased import vulnerability; so, (4) public sector presence varies directly with trade surpluses. The fragmentary evidence that does exist supports these arguments. In Brazil, the role of public enterprises declined over the 1980s from 5.3 percent of GDP in 1982 to 3.9 percent in 1987.[57] Over the first years of the debt crisis, subsidies and transfers also declined, giving a rough indicator of fiscal adjustment to the debt crisis.

The crucial cases are Brazil and Mexico, which are making serious efforts to privatize agriculture and fishing. In Brazil, the long tradition of agricultural subsidies is being dismantled as a combined effect of economic turmoil, conscious government privatization for deficit reduction, and external pressure to reduce the role of the public sector. Likewise, in Mexico, the government has turned a full 180 degrees since the height of public sector involvement in the economy at the peak of the oil boom in 1978–81.[58] In both economies, the highly intervened sugar economies (including Brazilian alcohol and ethanol) are being privatized. Mexico planned to dispose of its last state-owned sugar refineries before the end of 1990. Both Brazil and Mexico are reducing credit subsidies, crop support prices, subsidized storage facilities, and a variety of other protections against the vicissitudes of agricultural commodity markets.[59]

Returning to Hirschman's theories, we see that the onset of the debt crisis has had unpleasant side effects for U.S.–Latin American trade relations. First, it has been stipulated that it is in the interests of the United States to keep Latin America highly trade dependent. This view must be qualified because of growing protectionist sentiment in the United States, which fractures the free trade consensus of the Bretton Woods years. Likewise, the global political decline of the hegemon means that the United States has to face labor force adjustment, chronic trade deficits, an insecure dollar, and other problems of "ordinary countries" that militate against a Great Power posture vis-à-vis Latin American trade.

Because of its traditional national security concerns in Latin America, however, the United States finds itself in even deeper trade paradoxes. It must remain open to Latin American exports to guarantee that Latin

America can "trade its way out of the debt crisis." In that respect, the regional trade deficit of the United States is held hostage to the needs (i.e., high Latin American trade surpluses) of the international banking system. The putative U.S. interest extends beyond the commercial, generally being spoken of as part of the quest for economic conditions that lead to political stability.[60] Trade policy plays a large part in this drama, extending now even to concerns that the U.S. "war against drugs" is being undermined by international trade conflict over the International Coffee Agreement.[61]

National power in Latin America is reduced not only by U.S. power but by the increasing fragility of public sector influence in the region. Returning to the traditional argument that imports are a sort of "leakage" against development gains from growth in the external sector, we find that the greater the openness the greater the impact of that leakage. The great hedge against such leakage has been state control over imports. The great fear is that import openness is the result of privatization and that development opportunities will dissolve with openness. On the development side, the public sector's control over trade policy and markets has defined social policy to a great extent. In Mexico, subsidies to producers of cereals are a sort of rural incomes policy, given the structure of production in corn and beans. In all highly intervened agricultural economies of the region, the level of state involvement in agriculture determines a large part of the rural labor market, the organic composition of capital in agriculture, the rate and kind of technology transfer, and the prices of land assets. Devolution of primary sector production to the forces of the market, it is feared, will mean that there is no public mediator to allocate shares of the burden of externally imposed domestic structural adjustment.

Social Policy, Resource Sustainability, and Openness

Irrespective of the empirical truth of this fear, the state is losing even its extremely limited control over the external sector; whatever the consequences, national trade power, embodied in the state and expressed through trade policy, is diminished by the ascendance of the market.

Three particularly devastating possibilities exist: that export openness will result in greater exploitation of the natural resource base of Latin America; that opening the economy to more trade will mean that the rural poor will be buffeted about by the waves of international commerce; and that the abandonment of activist public sector trade policies will mean that export performance deteriorates.

The first prospect is particularly important, because it orients the domestic environmental sustainability of Latin American nations along the axis of nationalism-internationalism. This argument implies that resource degradation is less likely under nationalist strategies of development, a proposition that will be examined more carefully in Chapter 6. Here suffice it to say that, in the first instance, national power over domestic resource use is an inverse function of openness. Whether or not domestic development designs are appropriate to resource sustainability, without national power to govern resource use, domestic development design is irrelevant.

The evidence that the state actually "protects" the poor from international competition is weak and varied, and there is a strong argument among advocates of adjustment that the long-term price of not adjusting is more damaging to the poor than the short-term burdens of adjustment. If the Latin American state is the only safety net between the poor and the ditch, the prospects for alleviation of poverty are grim.

It is evident, however, that the market has no mandate whatsoever to ameliorate the abysmal conditions of the poor in Latin America. Structural adjustment is "economic revolution" to the bankers but economic disaster to those who bear the burden. To the extent that opening the external sector to international competition involves removing the public sector, the question is, What will protect weaker elements in the market from being pushed to the margin? The United States and the international banking community—including the development banks—welcome privatization as a matter of doctrine, convinced of perceived efficiencies in the marketplace that have eluded otherwise perceptive Latin Americans. The rate of change resulting from privatization is difficult to measure. But there is precious little in the adjustment literature that addresses the social questions of development.[62]

The important point for this chapter is that the conditions of the late 1980s mean that national power over international trade in Latin America is diminished. The geographic reconcentration of trade in the 1980s has meant, in Hirschman's terms, that the potential influence of the United States increased. The failure of earlier diversification efforts in the wake of the debt crisis meant a reorientation of Latin American trade either to traditional commodities or to "nontraditionals" that really do not solve the problems of primary commodity exporters. And the role of the public sector, which was fundamental to the relative success of integrating trade into national development design in the 1940s and 1950s, now has received a durable and relatively unchallenged attack from the advocates of adjustment.[63] There appears to be little prospect that the orientation of

Latin American trade will change in the near future, or that the public sector will recoup its real power (as opposed to the shadow power of rhetoric among neopopulists). Those two realities, along with the increased power of the United States in the Latin American trade scene, are the landmark influences on Latin American national trade and development strategies, to which we now turn.

CHAPTER 5

National Power, the Multilateral Agenda, and Trade with the United States

It is the nature of all greatness not to be exact, and great
trade will always be attended with considerable abuses.
—Edmund Burke, "Speech on Conciliation with America,"
    March 22, 1775

THERE IS NO CLEARER testament to the unpredictability of trade in Latin America than the 1980s. In 1982, the Inter-American Development Bank focused on the external sector as the theme of its annual publication *Economic and Social Progress in Latin America*. Even though publication of the volume coincided with a two-year global recession and the first wave of the debt crisis, the bank predicted that relatively constant petroleum prices would contribute to a more positive climate for Latin American growth in coming years. Beyond that, the international economic system offered little but uncertainty. Exchange rates, fiscal and monetary policies, the growth rates of OECD countries, the uncertainty of capital markets, and the worrisome prospect of increasing debt burden were all imponderables in the early 1980s.

Sharp changes in Latin American trade in the 1980s confirmed these worries, dizzying regional analysts with a roller-coaster ride of export promotion, import restriction, crippled diversification efforts, and foreign exchange constraints. The heralded trade expansion of the 1960s and 1970s gave way to a trade system in disrepair, driven to a great extent by debt and suppression of domestic demand, with politicians swinging wildly in their schemes to stabilize the external sector in its relation to development. In the end, the 1980s were labeled the "lost decade" in Latin America.[1] It has now become common to talk of a "new dark age" in the high-debt countries.

The 1980s divide roughly into two periods: 1980 to 1984, when recovery from the 1979 oil shock was smothered by the first wave of the debt crisis; and 1985 to 1989, when political adjustments in the trade system changed the inter-American trade picture, not necessarily reducing unpredictability in trade but qualifying the expectations created during the first period.

Despite the historiographical dangers of looking at such recent data, some trade trends are evident.

1. Prospects for trade growth outside the hemisphere are declining, both because of the fiscal and monetary policies of OECD countries during the recession of the early 1980s and because of the trend toward regionalism in international trade led by European integration in 1992 and the failure of the GATT talks in 1990.

2. Intraregional trade collapsed in the first half of the decade, followed by only modest, irregular recovery for some countries in the second half.

3. The importance of the United States to Latin American trade grew, surpassing the expectations of the 1970s and reaching a level of uncomfortable closeness for all trade partners.

4. Commodity traders, who began the 1980s on the crest of high prices in petroleum and copper, are again in the most disadvantaged position of all. Some, most notably Bolivia and Chile, have restructured domestic production radically. Other economies still open and exporting primary commodities are the least advantaged of the traders in Latin America.

5. Latin American trade adjustment concentrated on the import side, with a few significant examples of countries that were successful in export promotion.

6. The most closed economies of the region appeared to open to the exterior in ways that will be difficult to reverse.

The 1980s brought a crisis-impelled realignment of the regional trade system, unhappily wed to a global realignment, based on historical and regional preferences, and the decline of the Bretton Woods trading system under American hegemony. The most important consequences of that realignment, as this chapter shows, include increasing dependence on the United States, renewed emphasis on bilateralism, and a growing influence of trade power in the hemisphere. Ironically, the increase in potential U.S. influence occurred at a time when the United States showed itself increasingly reluctant to exercise its hegemonic prerogatives.

In recent international relations literature, the suggestion is made that the declining hegemony of the United States may offer other countries in the international system more opportunity to avoid the kind of power dependence inherent in a bilateral trade dynamic or an international monetary system dominated by the dollar.[2] The "hegemonic stability" thesis avers (at its simplest) that international regimes are most stable under conditions of Great Power hegemony. The "surplus capacity" thesis argues that an economic sector's productive overcapacity and its spread among several important producer countries diminish the coherence of stable regimes. International structural adjustment results, and it is reasonable to hypothesize, based on the work of Hirschman and Susan

Strange, that political power influences the nature of that adjustment. These hypotheses are a central concern of this book, and they depend on a reading of the postwar Latin American trade compass.

Hirschman argued in *National Power and the Structure of Foreign Trade* that (1) the qualitative gains from trade are unequal, depending on the importance of the trade and the "subjective gains" accruing to each partner; (2) the differential importance of trade to each partner generates differential attention to trade so that the more important the trade relationship, the higher the level of attention; and (3) trade concentration is a source of influence or power. We can stipulate further that (4) the gains from trade are subjective in at least one more dimension, depending on their assignment to strategic uses internally and their cost to domestic resource management; (5) differential attention by the more powerful partner does not mean inattention but rather may mean inattention to the development aspect of trade in favor of the raw bilateral power relationship, in which attention focuses on narrow self-interest; and (6) higher levels of Great Power attention to Latin American trade may mean more "progressive" trade relations, not the reverse, as has been suggested in the dependency literature. Ironically, the prospect that Great Power attention means more progressive trade politics probably depends directly on the degree of domination by the hegemon.

Gross changes in the international system since Hirschman's book appeared require some modifications in his observations about power. In the wake of the debt crisis and the reorientation of Latin American trade toward the United States, the marginal gains from trade in the bilateral U.S.–Latin American country context increase. That is, because of the lack of alternatives for trade in the region and the crisis of the external sector, each increment of trade gained with the United States is more important than in "normal times." But since the United States is now a trade deficit country and perceptibly weakening as an economic power in the international system relative to its postwar position, U.S. policymakers infuse those increments of additional trade with Latin America with a political meaning far beyond their real economic importance to the United States. Hirschman's hegemon might well be willing to concede broad preferences in trade for the sake of political influence. The United States is less willing to make such concessions, or to suffer chronic trade deficits with the region, because of its desperation to address the trade deficit in general and to forward the 1980s liberalization agenda. Export gains in Latin America are not concessions to development but distortions in the system. Subsidized competitiveness becomes chronic unfair trade practice, in the context of the neoprotectionist U.S. Congress. Thus because of the defensive quality of U.S. trade policy globally, increased U.S.

trade power in the region is not likely to result in progressive trade politics over the long term.

The United States has a renewed interest in pursuing a regional trade agenda, partly because of its own ideological commitment to free trade and to structural economic reforms in Latin America, and partly because of the importance of regional blocs in the wake of the weakening of the multilateral system in the Uruguay Round. The 1990s are expected to be a decade of contradiction and irony, with the United States concerned about increasing regional trade and preference while the U.S. Congress continues to shy away from free trade arrangements that might harm constituents.[3] Latin American leaders, by contrast, embrace free trade uniformly for the first time since the Depression, even though the short-term domestic consequences for their populations are more severe than ever.

The focus of this chapter is the international trade system, with special emphasis on inter-American trade. Following on the treatment of national power and the structure of foreign trade in Chapter 4, this part of the study will argue that the political terms of inter-American trade frame the general constraints and possibilities facing trade policies in today's Latin America. Earlier, it was stipulated that the political terms of trade are denominated by the connection of trade to domestic development, to resource sustainability, and to external stabilization and adjustment. Here I will also consider the insertion of Latin American countries into the international trade system, denominated by the degree of concentration of trade with the United States and alternative sources of potential trade expansion.

This chapter argues that the relevance of the multilateral trade system to Latin America varies inversely with the concentration of particular countries' trade with the United States or Europe. The central point is that Hirschman's arguments about the trade-based influence of Great Powers on their lesser neighbors are still vitally true today, but that the implications of power must be qualified because of the complicated role of the United States as a "declining hegemon."

All of the countries of Latin America find themselves in some kind of Great Power trade orbit or enveloped by the increasing OECD tendency toward regionalism. That regionalism is dominated primarily by the United States, and its logic is the familiar realism that described power politics in the postwar period. For most of Latin America, the GATT and the U.N. Conference on Trade and Development (UNCTAD) are less important "side games" than are bilateral consultations with the United States and to a lesser degree with Europe and Japan. Global regionalism— in this case led by the new U.S. bilateralism—supplants the multilateral agenda in favor of a novel but limited hemispheric trade debate. This situation is certainly unattractive from the standpoint of Latin American autonomy. It is also undesirable in the context of U.S. trade politics in the 1990s.

Trade has always placed high on the Latin American economic development agenda, despite its uneven history. Trade has been touted as the engine of growth for modern industrialization and the avenue for more equitable integration into the Western economic community. More recently, trade expansion has been offered weakly as the only escape route from the debt crisis. Now, in more pessimistic times, it is at least a means of financing the debt service burden and rationalizing distorted Latin American economic systems.

To understand the political power that stems from U.S.–Latin American trade, we must understand the relative importance of North to South America and South to North America. Both history and current political dynamics shape Latin American and U.S. understanding of hemispheric trade. Moreover, noneconomic values such as national security enter into the trade equation; they are particularly relevant to the weakening U.S. "hegemon" and to countries with aspirations to project their influence into the international system, such as Brazil and Mexico.

Multilateralism and U.S.–Latin American Trade

Latin America accurately views the post–World War II multilateral system as a foreign institutional circumstance beyond its control. The Bretton Woods system evolved out of the turmoil of that period and was conceived to address failures to construct a viable multilateral trading and monetary system after World War I.[4] One of its fundamental goals was to institutionalize the development of the international system under a coherent, Western-led (i.e., U.S.-led) international division of labor. As Richard Gardner has put it in his classic *Sterling-Dollar Diplomacy in Current Perspective*, "The economic case for multilateralism is essentially the same as the familiar case for free trade." The premise behind Bretton Woods was to create a postwar order that would stipulate an

> international division of labour and [encourage] each country to specialize in the production of those things in which it enjoys the greatest comparative advantage. Two important advantages may be claimed for this régime. First, the most is made at any given time of the world's existing stock of productive resources. Second, that stock of resources will be likely to increase over time more rapidly than under any alternative system. The latter result will occur because capital will be induced to flow to those parts of the world economy where it can make the greatest net contribution to productivity. At the same time, productivity will be stimulated by competitive forces acting through the

operation of the market mechanism. In this way multilateralism will tend to maximize the real income of the world as a whole.[5]

As Gardner points out, however, this international division of labor did not address the inter- or intranational division of the gains in international welfare. It did not stipulate how the international system would regulate the distribution of income to guarantee development of the poorest segments of the world economy. Nor did it say anything about national development strategies that might prejudice or advance the individual country's share in the proceeds of the postwar system or the just distribution of those gains internally. The Bretton Woods system was plainly designed for the winners in the international system, without much design for the losers in the allocation of economic values in the system.

Another deficiency not remarked upon by Gardner is the central question of the 1980s and 1990s in Latin America: the degree to which maximizing the use of resources through trade corresponds to development. Since the early 1970s, the question of limits to economic growth has been raised, from a variety of standpoints. Chapter 3 treated much of this material, and Chapter 6 will return to it. What is clear now in the multilateral system is that none of the institutions with a putative claim to authority over the international economic order is treating the issues of trade, debt, and growth—much less development—from a resource perspective. Even the rhetorical commitments of the Bretton Woods institutions to environmental and development goals are internally contradictory and not founded on resource-based criteria.

The multilateral system has given way to regional trading blocs, long-term bilateral agreements, voluntary restraint agreements, and other North-South deals that have attested to an overall weakening in the multilateral system. In the period following the 1970s oil crisis, debt-induced reconcentration of trade between Latin American countries and the United States has made the multilateral agenda less important to most of the region. Even the effects of the Generalized System of Preferences program of the United States and the Lomé concessions of the EEC on some Latin American and Caribbean countries were reduced in the late 1980s. Latin America faces a possible return to dependence on the United States with the mixed benefit of "posthegemonic" U.S. economic weakness and reduced political ambition.

The gloomy regional trade picture was framed throughout the 1980s by a new round of multilateral trade negotiations, which have become part of the regular agenda of the General Agreement on Tariffs and Trade and the banner event showing off U.S. commitment to the multilateral trade system surviving from Bretton Woods. The new round, christened the

Uruguay Round after its 1986 convening host, was more ambitious in its scope than any previous round, more limited in its prospects for success, and more important in symbolic value to the multilateral system. The new round came at a time when much of the original work of the GATT, which concentrated on tariff reduction, had been accomplished. Tariff rates among the OECD countries are relatively low, and many key less developed countries have agreed to undertake programs of trade liberalization, subsidy reduction, and transparency in trade regulations. The Uruguay Round concentrated on new and extremely difficult areas, such as trade in services and the traditional sacred cow, trade in agricultural products. There was little consensus on the agenda of the new round when it was being planned in the mid-1980s. There was even less consensus on the final agenda, which closed—at least temporarily—in Brussels at the end of 1990.[6]

The GATT round was complicated even further by the changing alignment of the international economic system in the 1980s. The most obvious example is the increasing focus on the creation of a single internal European market in 1992.[7] As plans for 1992 proceed, the EEC will become the largest single trading entity in the world, and the reorchestration of its trade policy may mean a new "Fortress Europe," to which access by outside traders may be even more difficult than it is today.[8] Compounding the dangers of this prospect for Latin America are similar bilateral or regional trading agreements that suggest the abandonment of multilateral commodity agreements and the creation of regional trading blocs in which less developed countries will have to negotiate from weakness to gain limited access to a Great Power market.[9] The recent disintegration of Eastern Europe's political economy does not appear to lessen that prospect.[10]

For less developed GATT member countries, the Uruguay Round began at a time of particular hardship and was built on a foundation of discontent with the extremely modest achievements of the Tokyo Round vis-à-vis less developed countries' special problems, as well as concern over the "new regionalism" of the OECD countries. When the Tokyo Round concluded in 1979, it was apparent that the most difficult matters of the GATT's new agenda—nontariff barriers, dispute settlement, agricultural trade, trade in services, and services-related investment—did not meet with the enthusiasm of the contracting parties. The result has been a widening gap between the OECD and less developed countries on trade agendas. In great part, the Uruguay Round was burdened from the beginning by the need to define realistic goals that would push the GATT agenda forward in an environment not conducive to trade optimism.

For Latin American agricultural exporters, the litmus test of the new

GATT round was the elimination of subsidies in agricultural trade. Argentina and Brazil, along with Uruguay, are members of the Cairns Group, which began the push to include free trade in agriculture in the Uruguay Round. For Brazil and Argentina, the issues are crucial, and they involve more than simple competition. As both have pointed out, U.S. export bonuses to soya producers force Latin American competitors out of markets. Restricted access to EEC and Asian markets affects the response of agricultural trade to economic crisis in Latin America. And in commodities for which developed countries heavily influence world prices, domestic subventions distort the international market. The dimensions of these trade issues are dramatic. In 1988, Brazil estimated its trade losses in soya alone at U.S.$600 million.[11]

For agricultural importers such as Mexico, the trade issue per se is less clear because the effects of economic liberalization on price are not obvious. It may be, for example, that removal of subsidies to U.S. farmers would drive land values down and ultimately result in short-term price reductions for some grains. Or it may be that market signals will allocate economic values so much more efficiently throughout the world's grain-producing countries that prices will stabilize at "reasonable" levels and national producers will become more productive. In the short term, however, the central issue for importers revolves around the connection of agricultural trade to the social question, both through the allocation of domestic economic effort to grain production and through the management of internal demand for basic foods.

In any event, it seems that the OECD in general, and the United States specifically, will continue to pursue long-term bilateral agreements in agriculture, at least to set the framework for major grain trade in cereals. Such agreements are criticized even within the OECD for distorting the market by "hampering market transparency." Although long-term bilateral agreements do not bind the countries to fulfill the limits of their purchase obligations, they are intended to stabilize international trade among major partners in ways that are not strictly governed by the market itself.[12] Latin American agricultural exports are also governed by such agreements, so they are less a North-South than an exporter versus importer issue. Whatever the case, long-term bilateral agreements are not generally seen as contributing to the strength of the multilateral trade system.

The real crux of agricultural trade negotiations in the inter-American system involves trade in cereals, food security, and domestic development allocations to agriculture. Much of the region is in food deficit, and the United States is the principal provider of cereal imports. In the 1970s, food security (first advertised more optimistically as food self-sufficiency) was a high priority in many Third World countries, in part because of political interest in increasing national economic sovereignty, but also as a pragmatic response to high grain prices and worldwide food shortfalls. Mexico was the most obvious food-deficit country in the hemisphere, and its food self-sufficiency campaign (Sistema Alimentario Mexicano), bloated by oil dollars, was the most ambitious in scope.[13]

Sadly, Latin American food production systems were unable for a variety of reasons to become self-sufficient, even with constrained demand among the poor. The demands of the international trade system pushed small countries to continue to emphasize export commodities over domestic staples and larger farm units over low-output producers.[14] The result has been that Latin America was pushed back onto the international market for grains, and the campaigns for food self-sufficiency have withered before the growing ideology of free markets in agriculture.

For this reason above all, Latin American food-deficit countries are dependent on the reordering of the international agricultural system, a process in which they have little say. Argentina, Brazil, and Mexico (more as a huge market than as an international competitor) are the principals on the Latin American side, and the OECD countries set the agenda in multilateral agricultural trade negotiations. So far, the high-profile negotiations of the GATT round have not addressed the enormous impact of any agreement in agriculture on the international production, consumption, exchange, and distribution of agricultural commodities.

As Table 5.1 shows, estimates of Latin American import demand for cereals suggest two main strategies in the region: stimulating domestic production through import substitution in agriculture, and suppressing domestic demand through the price and import mechanism, as reflected in import requirements and total apparent consumption per capita. An illustration of the importance of these two alternative strategies will be detailed in the next chapter.

If the GATT Uruguay Round had embraced trade liberalization in agriculture, it would have meant an abandonment of the rural incomes policies that have addressed the social question in the countryside. That is, Latin American countries subsidizing basic food production for domestic consumption would have been encouraged by the price mechanism and the politics of the GATT negotiations to move away from state subventions in favor of international markets. For all of their limits and liabilities, these policies have been the only buffer protecting the low-output poor producer from complete neglect by the state. Because the politics of GATT agricultural liberalization marry so well with the general fiscal crisis of the Latin American state, there is little prospect of turning to other public policies for the rural poor once subsidies are gone. Instead, as has already been seen in countries favoring an export-oriented agricultural policy subsidizing cash crops for international markets (such as Brazil or, for that matter, the United States), more of the limited resources of the state go to the exporting agriculturalist and less to the rural poor. We will return to this question in the next chapter.

The prospect of regional integration as an alternative to trade with the OECD and especially the United States—which had been the hope of postwar integration efforts—has also failed. The region is in dire economic straits, and intraregional trade has been shaky throughout the 1980s. Positive economic integration on a regional basis, in which small economies would gain both through trade preference with larger neighbors and in technology and experience, suggests an expansionary climate in Latin America, which is far from the case as the 1990s begin. Instead, the prospect of regional integration is undone by a combination of the trade preferences of the United States and the increasingly ruthless competition among Latin American states for national shares of trade in key commodities. As will be shown in this chapter, countries dependent on primary commodities and small economies are especially driven by the need to compete for Great Power attention.

In the Caribbean, solidarity among the small agricultural exporters falls prey to competition for access to the European market after 1992. The Caribbean is pitted directly against Central American producers in bananas and other tropical products.[15] The sugar quota is also a zero-sum competition for Latin American exporters, as are the benefits of the U.S. Generalized System of Preferences. More and more, it appears that each of these "plums" goes to the country that behaves itself in accordance with EEC, U.S., or other regional system objectives. In the case of sugar, U.S. behavior was so striking that Australia successfully petitioned the GATT in 1989 to cite the United States for arbitrarily assigning quota amounts to countries exporting under the U.S. quota program. By far the largest Latin American exporters under the quota system are Brazil and the Dominican Republic, which are generally considered to be the most competitive producers as well. The United States agreed to abide by the GATT finding and in September 1989 expanded its quota allocations by nearly a million metric tons.[16]

The region has also broken into conflicting blocs over the International Coffee Agreement, again with the United States playing a pivotal role.[17] In 1989, the coffee agreement collapsed when the United States tried to negotiate more favorable terms and to resist the tendency of the coffee-producing countries to sell outside the agreement to nonparty importers at lower prices. Latin American and other Third World producers quickly broke into three groups: one, the *robusta* producers, led by Brazil; a

TABLE 5.1

Domestic Production, Imports, Exports, and Consumption of Cereals in Latin America, 1980–88

(Millions of tons)

	Domestic production	Imports	Exports	Consumption
Argentina				
1980	18,473	8	9,932	8,549
1981	29,998	6	18,378	11,626
1982	34,277	1	14,676	19,602
1983	30,916	–	22,389	8,527
1984	31,307	–	17,374	13,933
1985	28,076	1	20,437	7,640
1986	26,158	19	13,618	12,559
1987	22,888	1	9,377	13,512
1988	21,597	3	9,933	11,667
Bolivia				
1980	613	283	–	896
1981	766	280	–	1,046
1982	701	303	7	997
1983	492	374	1	865
1984	824	244	6	1,062
1985	973	316	–	1,289
1986	839	275	–	1,114
1987	785	408	–	1,193
1988	801	328	–	1,129
Brazil				
1980	33,217	6,740	29	39,928
1981	32,050	5,570	102	37,518
1982	33,838	4,491	646	37,683
1983	29,198	4,918	807	33,309
1984	32,711	5,300	220	37,791
1985	36,011	4,857	18	40,850
1986	37,314	6,246	20	43,540
1987	44,168	3,871	13	48,026
1988	42,540	1,387	11	43,916
Chile				
1980	1,755	1,362	15	3,102
1981	1,535	1,381	1	2,915
1982	1,448	1,426	9	2,865
1983	1,437	1,370	6	2,801
1984	2,116	1,036	22	3,130
1985	2,360	486	5	2,841
1986	2,675	264	19	2,920
1987	2,819	249	7	3,061
1988	2,800	339	12	3,127
Colombia				
1980	3,242	1,068	41	4,269
1981	3,334	505	23	3,816
1982	3,615	797	1	4,412
1983	3,348	1,094	7	4,435
1984	3,239	840	37	4,042
1985	3,201	860	33	4,028

TABLE 5.1 (*continued*)

	Domestic production	Imports	Exports	Consumption
Colombia (*cont.*)				
1986	3,067	898	3	3,962
1987	3,598	822	–	4,420
1988	3,554	8,614	–	4,418
Costa Rica				
1980	285	180	39	426
1981	331	176	47	460
1982	259	174	13	415
1983	426	194	31	589
1984	363	158	60	461
1985	381	138	–	519
1986	342	144	21	465
1987	284	187	–	471
1988	310	318	–	628
Ecuador				
1980	682	361	–	1,043
1981	786	307	1	1,092
1982	787	386	16	1,157
1983	558	293	–	936
1984	846	288	–	1,139
1985	816	278	–	1,104
1986	1,075	410	–	1,353
1987	935	563	25	1,320
1988	891	204	–	1,454
Guatemala				
1980	1,068	204	16	1,256
1981	1,163	167	–	1,330
1982	1,275	101	–	1,376
1983	1,224	122	–	1,345
1984	1,281	131	3	1,409
1985	1,260	140	5	1,395
1986	1,402	215	2	1,615
1987	1,376	315	2	1,689
1988	1,423	166	–	1,589
Honduras				
1980	410	139	1	548
1981	576	91	1	666
1982	462	89	6	545
1983	552	83	3	632
1984	538	107	9	636
1985	483	112	21	574
1986	552	133	–	685
1987	522	144	–	666
1988	604	144	–	748
Mexico				
1980	21,119	7,091	26	28,184
1981	25,536	7,198	–	32,734
1982	20,201	3,153	8	23,346
1983	22,424	8,484	28	30,880
1984	23,721	5,848	5	29,564
1985	27,163	4,780	5	31,938

TABLE 5.1 (*continued*)

	Domestic production	Imports	Exports	Consumption
Mexico (*cont.*)				
1986	22,491	2,710	–	25,201
1987	23,576	4,794	–	28,370
1988	21,992	5,650	113	27,529
Peru				
1980	1,137	1,309	11	2,435
1981	1,631	1,266	4	2,893
1982	1,659	1,464	2	3,121
1983	1,548	1,295	1	2,842
1984	2,169	1,019	1	3,187
1985	1,810	1,227	3	3,034
1987	2,367	1,574	2	3,939
1988	2,285	1,857	2	4,140
Venezuela				
1980	1,634	2,484	17	4,101
1981	1,480	2,675	1	4,154
1982	1,487	2,444	26	3,905
1983	1,302	2,554	8	3,848
1984	1,428	2,655	–	4,083
1985	1,822	2,795	–	4,617
1986	2,250	1,694	7	3,937
1987	2,418	2,003	3	4,418
1988	2,386	3,054	–	5,440

SOURCES: *FAO Production Yearbook, FAO Trade Yearbook,* various years.
NOTE: Consumption is computed by adding imports to domestic production and subtracting exports.

second, called the "other mild" group, aligned with the United States; and a third, led by Colombia.[18] Brazil has refused to renegotiate the agreement, confident of its overwhelming power as a producer, its relative insulation from dependency on a primary commodity (coffee represents an average of only about 8 percent of exports in Brazil, compared with 49 percent for Colombia), and its ideological virtue in opting for free markets over commodity agreements.[19]

The political byplay in the coffee negotiations is fascinating. The "other mild" countries, including Mexico and Costa Rica, produce a mild arabica coffee attractive to the U.S. market and are politically important to the United States for other reasons. Brazil initially expressed interest in renegotiating the agreement, but balked after the agreement collapsed and more desperate countries flooded the market with their product, forcing prices down and hurting Brazilian producers. Now it appears that Brazil is willing to allow the market to shake out inefficient producers, which it assumes will favor a retrenched Brazilian industry. Meanwhile, African coffee producers, some of whom are already reeling from the collapse of the cocoa market, are thrown onto the European scheme for compensatory financing, threatening to bankrupt one of the pillars of the Lomé agreement. All the while, smaller producers blame the United States for its increasing intransigence against commodity agreements.

These examples of intraregional commodity competition reflect the weakness of intraregional trade as a result of foreign exchange shortages. Intraregional trade collapsed after 1982, after already having suffered from the two oil shocks of 1973 and 1979. Between 1979 and 1982, intraregional exports dropped 8.2 percent annually, in contrast to a growth rate of 12.5 percent per year from 1972 to 1979.[20] Even the fragmentary evidence that suggests a recovery of intraregional trade by the end of the 1980s varies widely by country. For example, nominal imports to Bolivia from other Andean Pact countries in 1988 were less than one-fourth 1984 levels, whereas Venezuela's imports from the regional group nearly doubled from 1986 to 1988.[21]

The virtue of intraregional trade is not pure. It integrates small nations into larger markets and often provides large countries with training for later extraregional exports. But it also directs trade toward the large economic poles of growth and around resource booms (viz., the magnetic effect of the Venezuelan oil boom on Colombian trade in the 1970s). Such pull from strong economies reinforces the dependency of the weak on the strong, increases trade instability, and emphasizes an unequal regional division of labor with unequal benefits from trade. One need only spend a short time in Bolivia to see that country's regional dependence on Brazil, the trade aspect of which is reflected in Brazil's U.S.$186.4 million in exports to Bolivia and Bolivia's puny $13.9 million in exports to Brazil in 1988.[22]

In pale reflection of the global system, the large countries of Latin America dominate trade. Mexico and Brazil now run regular trade surpluses with the region, though Mexico maintains the surplus by cutting import growth radically, and Brazil does so by increasing its share of regional exports and reducing its share of imports. Argentina and Brazil alone accounted for 56 percent of 1988 exports in the Latin American Integration Association (LAIA). Their dynamism masks the poor performance of regional trade, which still has not regained 1981 levels and which represents less of overall trade than it did at the beginning of the decade.[23]

These mixed blessings have created problems that have perplexed regional organizations in Latin America (e.g., the Andean Pact, the LAIA, and the Central American Common Market) for the entire post–World War II period of trade expansion. Now, in the late stages of the Uruguay Round, faced with the consolidation of Europe in 1992 and the increasing integration of the United States with Mexico, South America is proposing a new effort at regional integration. Called "South America's Benelux" by Argentina's subsecretary for Latin American affairs, the new effort would begin with a trilateral agreement among Chile, Brazil, and Argentina, which would then open to other nations of South America but would exclude Mexico.[24] This proposal has just begun, and its future is as uncertain as the economies of the trilateral countries. It is interesting at this point mainly for the political and strategic thinking it reveals.

In a similar South-South vein, in 1988, the U.N. Conference on Trade and Development agreed to a completely separate trade preference system to govern trade in developing countries. This initiative was declared to be an expression of the dissatisfaction on the part of less developed countries with the GATT Generalized System of Preferences, in place since 1975. UNCTAD confessed, however, that its trade preference system would not make a large impact on international trade, because the total amount of exports from less developed countries in 1987 amounted to only about one-fifth of total world exports, and its system would cover only about U.S.$10 billion in trade, about one-fifth of U.S.-Mexican bilateral trade.[25]

Despite these interesting new conversations, the limits and possibilities of regional trade are relative, and its collapse probably damages small, open economies more than the big countries of the region. Its demise has been a direct function of liquidity and other problems associated with the debt crisis. The significance of its slump is found in the desperation with which traders in the region must look mainly to other possibilities for their export programs. This once again underlines the growing importance of the United States.

The Importance of the United States for Latin America

As the history of the region shows, the twentieth-century hegemony of the United States has conditioned the economic growth of Latin America and mandated escape from U.S. influence as a primary political goal in the region. From 1945 to 1960, Latin America traded overwhelmingly with the United States. The orientation of trade northward in the hemisphere was a product of the United States's long-standing increase in economic power and political influence, which meant that U.S. companies and investors determined a greater part of international capital movements and merchandise trade in Latin America. Before World War II, that secular trend had gone under various banners: the gunboat diplomacy of the Roosevelt-Taft years, in which customshouses throughout the Caribbean were put into U.S. receivership; Wilsonian idealism, which wanted to make Latin America safe for U.S. business; "dollar diplomacy" in the

1920s, when such luminaries as Dwight Morrow and Edwin Walter Kemmerer went to Colombia, Mexico, and Peru; and the private flags of the robber barons of the Mexican and Peruvian oil fields or Chilean copper mines.[26] In every event, the image of the attracting hegemon was singularly unattractive.

World War II made that magnetic attraction northward much stronger. Because of the destruction of the war and the commitment of the United States to destroying the British Imperial Preference System as part of a new multilateral system under U.S. leadership, the pound sterling became inconvertible. Argentina, among other traders in the British trade system, was left with worthless piles of sterling, part of the "sterling pool" agreements by which war goods were traded to Britain in return for inconvertible pounds to be redeemed at war's end. The import capacity of Latin America's European trade partners was reduced, dependent on U.S. capital exports and affected by Marshall Plan rules.

In addition, as Chapter 2 showed, the postwar period was one of trade pessimism, a belief that trade was not a likely engine of growth, particularly trade infused by bilateral dependence on a Great Power of such dubious reputation as the United States. From 1945 to 1960, then, Latin American nations concentrated on *desarrollo hacia adentro*, or inward development, in which trade became a residual of general development policy. To the extent that trade policy went in a consistent direction, it was away from dependence on the United States and toward regional trade initiatives that have come and gone since the 1950s. Ignoring the evanescence of their success, Latin American countries continued to petition the GATT and the United States for exemption from multilateral trade rules, in favor of attempts at regional integration.[27]

The political tension created by U.S. hegemony has been aggravated because few countries have commanded a "legitimate" claim on U.S. trade policy attention, if trade value is used as an indicator. Those big country cases, which are also now high-debt cases, include Mexico, Brazil, Argentina, Peru, Colombia, and perhaps Chile. Brazil and Mexico are relatively closed by Latin American standards, so trade is not as important to overall economic activity as it is to many other economies in the region (including Chile, Peru, and Argentina). Over the entire period, Mexico is the only country in Latin America that has consistently traded the bulk of its goods with the United States *and* maintained its status as one of the United States's largest trade partners. The rest of the region is of little importance in the architecture of U.S. foreign economic policy.

Moreover, countries that receive the most foreign policy attention in the United States are not important traders, with the exception of Mexico. Nevertheless, the United States is a trade partner of overwhelming importance to those countries, and trade is extremely important to their overall economic activity and development prospects. The economies of Central America and the Caribbean are open, vulnerable, and geographically close to the United States, and they have suffered from the intervention of U.S. policy throughout the twentieth century. For example, El Salvador is still overwhelmingly dependent on exports of primary commodities and has no strategic minerals. Over 90 percent of El Salvador's export bill is agricultural commodities, the bulk of which are sent to the United States, and it dominates no market enough to influence price. It is the embodiment of a worst-case scenario of economic vulnerability. Honduras is in similar straits, and Costa Rica, Guatemala, and Nicaragua have suffered comparable bilateral dependence for much of this century.[28]

In the expansive mood of the 1960s and early 1970s, the successful Latin American exporters optimistically hoped to diversify their trade bills, gradually weaning themselves away from dependence on the U.S. economy. Brazil was certainly the most successful, but traditional bilateral traders such as Mexico and the Central American countries were unable to move to diversify their markets decisively. Europe remained relatively closed to Latin American exports, except for accepting more trade from traditional partners such as Chile and Argentina. Japan became the darling of Latin American trade promoters, but Latin American countries had little more success than the United States in gaining an increased share of the Japanese market.

Although diversification was only occasionally successful, Latin American traders did challenge the United States in several areas. Argentina, Brazil, and Mexico successfully began producing sorghum, soya, wheat, and other agricultural commodities in which the United States had previously enjoyed virtual dominance. Brazil competed effectively with the United States in European and Middle Eastern poultry markets and completely outdid the U.S. frozen concentrated orange juice market. Automobiles, small aircraft, apple juice, ethanol, steel, small electronic appliances, apparel, shoes—the list of goods in which Latin America became competitive with U.S. producers grew, as did the inability of the United States to continue its postwar trade position globally. By the mid-1980s, when the U.S. trade deficit had grown to embarrassing heights and the only consistent producers of a trade surplus were services and agriculture, the United States cried foul against Latin American trade practices. The success of the new Mexican export miracle in manufactures further irritated U.S. lawmakers.

By that time, the economic shocks of the 1970s, particularly the second oil shock in 1979 and the debt crisis that began in 1982, had spun the Latin American trade compass northward again. Slow growth in Europe, combined with new waves of protection in primary commodities, meant that the United States accepted the burden of Latin American adjustment in its own trade accounts. The strong dollar from 1980 to 1985 and the long U.S. expansion under the Reagan administration have sucked trade from Latin America to the United States; at the same time Latin American nations were shutting down their imports to force a surplus in external accounts. U.S. trade deficits with Latin America peaked at U.S.$16.6 billion in 1985 (see Table 5.1). In contrast, U.S. trade with Latin America ran an overall surplus of U.S.$2.8 billion as late as 1981.

This trade deficit made the United States more militant about "leveling the playing field" of trade with Latin America and enticing it to use its Great Power influence in the region. This attitude was reinforced by the United States's continued importance to Latin America, not only for reasons of tradition but because it had become the most likely OECD trade partner by default. Other potential OECD trade partners have been reluctant to accept open trade in products of special importance to Latin America; exports to Japan have fallen prey to the bewildering obstacles and lack of tradition that limit easy growth in trade to the Far East; and the EEC is unwilling to open its markets further, which is accentuated by anticipation and uncertainty surrounding full market integration in 1992. Shocking as it may seem to Latin American trade observers, the United States as a potential trade partner looks good by comparison.

The Regional Resurgence of the United States

When the debt crisis began in 1982, the United States recognized that exports to the region would suffer and pressures in Latin America to export more to the United States would intensify. As it had in the 1930s, the United States accepted the adjustment burden of Latin American exports. In the end, that role combined with the political behavior of the U.S. trade policy apparatus in multilateral and bilateral negotiations to cause new Latin American worries about bilateral dependence. Congressional protectionism, only partly revealed in trade legislation in 1984 and 1988, underscored those concerns and betrayed U.S. political weaknesses vis-à-vis its own persistent trade deficit and declining global hegemony.

As Table 5.2 shows, Latin American trade with the United States shifted sharply in the wake of the debt crisis. In the first crucial years of the debt crisis, the role of the United States was stark in contrast to the rest of the OECD. The United States became the default OECD trade partner after Canada and the EEC reduced imports from the region radically. From 1981 to 1983, Latin American trade volume with Canada plummeted from U.S.$4.4 billion to a mere U.S.$713 million. During the same period,

European Community trade volume with Latin America dropped from U.S.$24.4 billion to U.S.$9.6 billion. And yet Latin American trade with the United States during the same period declined only from U.S.$75.9 billion to U.S.$62.8 billion.

U.S. exports to Latin America also fell radically after 1982, as high-debt countries (and those in their orbit that suffer collateral effects of the debt crisis) shut down imports as part of a policy package to generate trade surpluses for debt repayment and domestic economic growth. The United States itself adopted a new line of export liberalism and import protectionism, particularly in regard to new competition in manufactures and industrial goods from Latin American countries. Even as the debt crisis enters its second decade, trade, stabilization, and development goals have yet to be combined artfully to suggest a partial solution to the current economic problems of the inter-American system.

The critical role of the United States in Latin American trade adjustment has been attributed to its traditional importance in regional trade, the general openness of the U.S. economy compared to those of the other OECD countries, and the robustness of the U.S. recovery from the recession of 1981–82, as compared with slow and conservative responses in Europe and Canada. An equally important aspect of the trade phenomenon has gone unobserved, however: the political influence gained by the United States from the reorientation of Latin American trade northward, and the corresponding trade vulnerability of Latin American nations in the current period, which may be termed the years of institutionalized debt crisis. Faced with the specter of Fortress Europe in 1992, the great difficulties of opening trade with Japan, and the virtual collapse of intra-regional trade for the foreseeable future, Latin America is subject now as perhaps never before to the vicissitudes of trade with the Colossus of the North—an outcome against which virtually every government of Latin America has struggled for a generation. Moreover, the prospect that the United States might actually address the consumption side of its macroeconomic problems carries with it the prospect that Latin American exports to the United States would be sacrificed in the short term for the sake of longer-term macroeconomic stability, lower interest rates, and stable exchange rates.[29]

These observations lead to another angle on the politics of inter-American trade: the relative importance of trade to the economic growth of different Latin American countries, the importance of the United States to that trade, and the relationship of trade to economic development. For most of this decade, that set of relationships has revolved around stabilization and adjustment. The themes of stabilization and adjustment have been established by the United States with its interests in mind. The degree

TABLE 5-2
Latin American Trade Balances with the United States and the Industrial Countries, Selected Years, 1975–88

	Global			United States			Industrial countries		
	Exports	Imports	Balance	Exports	Imports	Balance	Exports	Imports	Balance
Argentina									
1975	3.0	3.5	-0.5	0.2	0.6	-0.4	1.4	2.6	-1.2
1980	8.0	9.4	-1.4	0.7	2.4	-1.7	3.5	7.2	-3.7
1985	8.4	3.5	4.9	1.1	0.7	0.4	3.5	2.3	1.2
1986	6.9	4.4	2.5	0.9	0.9	0.1	3.1	2.8	0.3
1987	6.4	5.4	1.0	1.1	1.1	0.0	3.1	3.5	0.4
1988	8.9	4.9	4.0	1.4	1.1	0.4	4.9	3.6	1.3
Brazil									
1975	8.5	12.0	-3.5	1.3	3.4	-2.1	5.2	9.1	-3.9
1980	20.1	23.0	-2.9	3.5	4.6	-1.1	11.5	11.6	-0.1
1985	25.5	13.1	12.4	7.5	3.1	4.4	16.3	6.4	9.9
1986	22.5	14.0	8.5	6.8	3.9	3.0	14.8	9.1	5.7
1987	26.2	15.1	11.1	7.9	4.0	3.9	17.0	9.2	7.8
1988	33.8	14.7	19.1	9.3	4.2	5.1	21.7	9.2	12.5
Chile									
1975	1.6	1.7	-0.1	0.1	0.4	-0.3	1.1	0.9	0.2
1980	4.7	5.3	-0.6	0.6	1.6	-1.0	3.1	3.4	-0.3
1985	3.8	3.0	0.8	0.7	0.7	0.1	2.6	1.5	1.1
1986	4.2	3.1	1.1	0.8	0.8	0.0	2.8	1.7	1.1
1987	5.2	4.0	1.2	1.0	0.8	0.2	3.4	2.2	1.2
1988	7.0	4.8	2.2	1.2	1.1	0.1	4.9	2.6	2.3
Colombia									
1975	1.7	1.4	0.3	0.5	0.6	-0.1	1.1	1.3	-0.2
1980	4.1	3.9	0.2	1.2	1.9	-0.7	3.3	3.9	-0.6
1985	3.7	3.7	0.0	1.3	1.5	-0.1	2.8	3.0	-0.2
1986	5.3	3.4	1.9	1.9	1.3	0.6	4.2	2.9	1.3
1987	5.7	3.9	1.8	2.2	1.4	0.8	3.6	3.2	0.4
1988	5.3	4.5	0.8	2.2	1.8	0.4	3.9	3.8	0.1

Ecuador									
1975	1.0	1.0	0.0	0.5	0.4	0.1	0.6	0.8	-0.2
1980	2.5	2.2	0.3	0.7	0.9	-0.2	1.2	1.8	-0.6
1985	2.9	1.6	1.3	1.8	0.6	1.2	1.8	1.3	0.5
1986	2.2	1.6	0.6	1.5	0.6	0.9	1.5	1.3	0.2
1987	2.0	2.1	0.0	1.3	0.6	0.7	1.3	1.4	-0.1
1988	2.2	1.6	0.6	1.2	0.7	0.6	1.2	1.2	0.0
Mexico									
1975	3.0	6.3	-3.3	1.7	4.1	-2.4	2.1	5.9	-3.8
1980	16.3	19.0	-2.7	9.7	12.8	-3.1	12.5	17.9	-5.4
1985	21.7	13.2	8.5	19.1	13.6	5.5	19.5	12.1	7.4
1986	16.0	11.5	4.5	17.3	12.4	4.9	14.6	11.4	3.2
1987	20.7	12.2	8.5	20.3	14.6	5.7	24.4	18.9	5.5
1988	20.7	18.9	1.8	23.3	20.6	2.6	26.6	26.0	0.6
Peru									
1975	1.3	2.4	-1.1	0.3	0.7	-0.4	0.7	1.8	-1.1
1980	3.9	3.1	0.8	1.3	1.3	0.0	2.6	2.7	-0.1
1985	3.0	1.8	1.2	1.1	0.5	0.6	2.1	1.0	1.1
1986	2.5	2.6	-0.1	0.8	0.7	0.1	1.7	1.2	0.5
1987	2.6	3.1	-0.5	0.8	0.8	0.0	1.7	2.0	-0.3
1988	2.7	2.7	0.0	0.7	0.8	-0.1	1.8	1.3	0.5
Venezuela									
1975	8.9	5.5	3.4	3.5	2.6	0.9	5.6	4.8	0.8
1980	19.3	11.3	8.0	5.3	5.3	0.0	11.2	9.6	1.6
1985	14.7	7.5	7.2	6.5	3.2	3.4	10.8	6.0	4.8
1986	9.1	7.9	1.2	5.1	3.1	2.0	5.7	6.5	-0.8
1987	10.6	8.8	1.8	5.6	3.6	2.0	7.5	7.3	0.2
1988	10.4	10.9	-0.5	5.2	4.6	0.7	7.1	8.7	-1.6
Latin America total									
1975	36.2	42.2	-6.0	9.8	14.8	-5.0	21.0	30.8	-9.8
1980	92.7	93.9	-1.2	25.9	34.7	-8.8	54.6	64.8	-10.2
1985	94.3	61.2	33.1	46.9	30.3	16.6	68.8	39.0	29.8
1986	79.2	61.8	17.4	41.9	30.6	11.3	53.4	42.9	10.5
1987	90.1	69.8	20.3	46.8	34.4	12.5	60.8	55.0	5.8
1988	102.6	78.2	22.4	43.1	51.3	8.1	78.6	64.5	14.1

SOURCE: IMF, *Direction of Trade Statistics*, various years.
NOTE: These statistics should be considered indicators of orders of magnitude. They are revised routinely and vary even within the same source.

to which those themes serve the interests of Latin American countries is a function of the depth and efficiency of Latin American reproduction of U.S. technologies and styles of development.[30] As the 1990s begin, it appears that the stabilization and adjustment process has been followed—as liberal economists recommend—by a phase of real trade liberalization, led by Chile, Mexico, and, to a lesser extent, Brazil. The senior partner in this transition to a liberal trading scheme is the United States, both by historical imperative and by its ideological insistence on the virtues of free trade.

It may be observed, as well, that the United States seems uniquely ill-suited to the role of regional hegemon because it defends a GATT that is no longer a product of consensual U.S. trade policy, and because its projection of power in Latin America is muddled by its inconsistent policies regarding trade, national security, drugs, debt, and other major agenda items. Although the putative role of the United States is similar to what it was in the 1930s and 1940s, U.S. regional politics lacks internal consistency, so that trade, security, and development goals often run at cross-purposes, diminishing the political influence gained from trade dominance. U.S. sugar and apparel trade quotas, for example, harm the development prospects of drug-exporting countries at the same time that the United States is pushing them to embrace economic alternatives to marijuana and coca. The United States allows the International Coffee Agreement to collapse, even as one of its main beneficiaries, Colombia, is pushed to substitute cocaine production by supporting legitimate rural incomes, and another, Brazil, is in economic crisis. Trade policies and development assistance programs clash over issues of sustainability and resource conservation, even as the United States's own conservation policies push aside conservation concerns and critiques of agricultural and water resource sustainability. The messages of the United States in Latin America reflect the internal confusion in Congress and the executive branch over the goals of trade policy in general and the virtues of projection of power in Latin America in the 1990s.

The Importance of Latin America for the United States

In a recent book on national security and U.S. policy toward Latin America, Lars Schoultz has raised one of the most persistent questions in the hemispheric agenda: the importance of Latin America for U.S. trade, development, and national security policy, and how that importance should affect U.S. policy toward the region.[31] Schoultz concentrates on the national security side of the matter but at least mentions economic aspects by posing questions about the relationship between economic development and U.S. national security. One of the purposes of this chapter is to assess various trade-based strategies to bolster general economic growth and to raise the equity question in Latin America once again. That assessment took place partly in the treatment of the multilateral system and in a later section on Latin American national strategies toward the United States. But it is also important to assess the value of trade in overall U.S. foreign policy goals with respect to Latin America, to evaluate how important Latin America is to the United States, and to estimate the role of trade policy in responding to that importance.

First, it is essential to recognize that the United States has viewed Latin American trade as an aspect of national security policy and not simply as an economic matter. This argument goes Hirschman one better. It is not simply a question of enhancing national influence over others in an expanding international system, but of connecting foreign economic policy to national security policy in more integral ways. Whereas Hirschman's argument conveys the sense of a power exploiting commerce for the sake of expanded influence, U.S. foreign economic policy toward Latin America—and to a great extent elsewhere—has been delivered to a reluctant Congress on a national security platter.

Certainly, in the U.S. attempt to dominate the Isthmian canal, economic concerns over the expansion of the Pacific trade and the continental consolidation of the American republic conveniently joined the Monroe Doctrine. Likewise, in the interventionist expansionism of the Theodore Roosevelt era, U.S. national interest was linked to opening the world to U.S. commerce. And from Wilsonian pretensions to make Mexico "elect good men and protect the interests of U.S. business," to the dollar diplomacy of the Harding and Coolidge years, commercial relations with Latin America were guided by the expansionary ambitions of the United States. The Good Neighbor policy of the Franklin Roosevelt administration, led by the Pan-American initiatives of Cordell Hull, had in mind the national security of the United States vis-à-vis the rising Axis powers. Trade competition married well with Great Power conflict in the 1930s.

After World War II, national security reflected the Cold War mentality, and U.S. intervention, aid, and overall foreign policy in Latin America have been analyzed in light of the East-West struggle ever since. National security, national interest, and economic interest have blended in subtle and sometimes contradictory ways over the course of the postwar years to confuse the importance of Latin America to the United States.[32] The Alliance for Progress is a monument to the conflation of economic assistance, liberal social reform, and U.S. national security policies in Latin America.

Latin America is generally a trade policy residual of the United States, despite persistent evidence that Latin America is especially interesting as a region, from a trade and financial standpoint. U.S. trade policy toward the region has evolved in the context of U.S. hegemony and is still largely governed by the political norms of postwar power. The nations of Latin America still view the United States as very much the hegemon, even while its influence at the global level is declining. And though in times of crisis in the postwar period the United States has accepted the burden of Latin American adjustment to external shock, Latin America has accepted the burden of adjustment on the side of capital flows from the oil shocks of the 1970s.[33] In a sense, then, the United States is the "trade pole of last resort" in Latin American commercial relations with the OECD, a trade pole to be diversified away from in the best of circumstances, and to be grudgingly accepted as a partner when other alternatives are uncertain.

The evolution of the Bretton Woods system was based on a combination of factors that prejudiced the system against full Latin American participation and consideration. Among those factors were the hostility and insecurity bred by depression and default in the 1930s, Eurocentric paternalism in the creation of the postwar system, the inability of the GATT to attend to the special needs of less developed countries, and the institutionalized hostility of the United States to the U.N. Conference on Trade and Development as a special venue for less developed countries' trade complaints.

Foremost among the shortcomings of the multilateral system, however, was the deep history of institutionalized bilateralism in U.S. economic relations with Latin America resulting from the Great Power conflict over Latin American loyalties in the 1930s, U.S. reaction to Mexican economic nationalism, and a continuing U.S. "fiduciary" role in Central America.

This bilateral tradition, which was consciously overcome in the institutional arrangements of the GATT, has continued in U.S.–Latin American relations. This institutional and "strategic policy" dynamic has ignored or misread several new characteristics of Latin America. At times when the future course of the multilateral system is unclear, or when that course does not appear to be steered by the aging hegemon, the United States retreats to that bilateral tradition, though it often uses more cryptic terms to describe it.[34]

First, Latin America stands apart from the rest of the Third World because of its market size and potential for OECD exports. Historically, it could be expected that the United States would benefit disproportionately (vis-à-vis OECD competitors) from increases in Latin American trade. But a key policy goal shared by virtually all major trade partners of the Latin

American region is to diversify trade away from the United States because of its perceived hostility and instability as a partner.

Second, the large Latin American economies show signs of changing their roles in the international system. Some, perhaps most, in the U.S. trade policy establishment interpret this to mean that Argentina, Brazil, and Mexico have become "newly industrialized countries." That reading, in turn, has led the United States to group leading Latin American traders with the "gang of four" or "four tigers" of East Asia—South Korea, Taiwan, Hong Kong, and Singapore—and to demand that the U.S.–Latin American trade bill be brought into balance, that graduation in the Generalized System of Preferences be effected (by trade category and by a general weaning away from preferences), and that trade liberalization be implemented in the short term.

Third, as the GATT talks showed, Latin America is not only increasingly important to the success of any new multilateral negotiations but is objectively important to the U.S. trade deficit. The U.S. trade deficit with Latin America represents about 10 percent of the global trade deficit. U.S. exports lost to the high-debt Latin American countries since 1982 are important even against the overall U.S. deficit with the EEC. In 1985, the U.S. deficit with Latin America surpassed $16 billion.[35] Yet, how does policy attention given to those countries differ from that to the EEC? When comparing the prospects for opening the EEC to more U.S. exports versus opening Latin American markets, the imbalance in policy attention becomes more obvious.

With regard to U.S. agricultural production and trade, Latin America's importance becomes even clearer. U.S. agricultural trade with Latin America grew in nominal terms from about U.S.$2.9 billion in 1970 to more than $12 billion in 1987. Latin America's share of U.S. agricultural exports during that period grew from 9 to 13 percent,[36] and that share is projected to grow even further as the EEC becomes more and more a competitor rather than a large market for U.S. agricultural products. Even more happily from the U.S. perspective, the share of Latin America in U.S. agricultural imports did not grow in that same period, though the region's share in U.S. imports stayed relatively steady between 35 and 40 percent. When the importance of Latin America in agricultural trade is combined with the realization of the debt-ridden underconsumption rife in the region, the U.S. interest in reviving Latin American trade and economic growth is clear.

Looking at the structure of U.S.–Latin American trade and the relative shares of Latin American countries in regional trade, we find that three-fourths of U.S. trade is with four countries, and two countries—Brazil and

Mexico—account for two-thirds of U.S.–Latin American trade. Overall, then, in strict trade terms, Latin America is neither homogeneous nor important, except for a few large countries. When we introduce larger issues of regional development and the relationship between U.S. trade and Latin American economic stability (and therefore political stability and enhanced U.S. national security, as U.S. policy logic goes), Latin American countries that are the least important in volume and value of trade with the United States are often the most important in U.S. policy attention. Historically, those economies have included Cuba, the Dominican Republic, and all of Central America.

Changing U.S. Domestic Interests and Trade Politics

An old cliché has it that foreign economic policy is domestic economic policy exported.[37] Certainly the multilateral, regional, and bilateral trade agendas are infused with domestic politics, and much of the hemispheric trade agenda is denominated "intermestic," to suggest the combination of international and domestic concerns. OECD agricultural politics at home govern national postures in multilateral negotiations, just as domestic agricultural surpluses in the 1950s gave rise to foreign food aid programs under PL 480, the agricultural surplus disposal program misnamed "Food for Peace." In the twilight of U.S. hegemony worldwide, the political behavior of the United States in trade converges with that of other, less powerful countries. In the Western Hemisphere, both the United States and Latin American nations seek to maximize the gains from trade without sacrificing the insulation of domestic producers from foreign competition. The common denominator of trade politics in the 1980s has been the simultaneous rise in export liberalism and import protectionism.

In the OECD markets, the United States is the leading trade partner, and despite its many barriers to trade, the U.S. trade system is "transparent" relative to those of Europe or Japan.[38] This is evident throughout U.S. trade legislation. The formal policies and procedures governing antidumping, injury, and countervailing duties have been consistent since the Trade Act of 1974. The political force of the recognized leader of the GATT has been behind streamlined dispute settlement procedures, greater transparency, national treatment for foreign investors, and generally reduced barriers to trade. That commitment extends at least in rhetoric to agricultural trade policy, in which the United States has adopted much of the Cairns Group agenda to lead OECD calls for phasing out all agricultural export subsidies by the year 2000.[39]

Even in its power negotiations over the new GATT round, the potential

U.S. reaction to failure is transparent. An automatic triggering device was put into the Omnibus Trade and Competitiveness Act of 1988 so that failure in the GATT agricultural negotiations will produce an additional impetus to the "export expansion" of U.S. agricultural policy (read, sub-sidies). Leading congressmen call for quick retaliation under the so-called Super 301 feature of the new trade bill, which calls for specific and automatic retaliation against countries that employ "unfair trade prac-tices" that damage the United States.[40] And countries singled out for bilateral jawboning by the United States are given a certain amount of time to respond before the threat of sanctions is implemented.

Though the United States has accepted the trade burden of Latin Ameri-can external adjustment during the debt crisis, it sullies its virtue with a number of collateral policies that protect it against certain imports of importance to Latin America, as well as the endless rhetoric in Congress that keeps the fires of neoprotectionism well ventilated. In 1981, for example, the United States reinstated the sugar quota, which it has used on a unilateral basis to favor certain countries' exports over others, to exclude socialist economies (Cuba and Nicaragua) from the U.S. trade system, and to protect a few thousand cane and beet farmers in the United States, as well as the growing corn sweetener industry.

Likewise, the United States has for some years engaged in nasty negotia-tions over Voluntary Restraint Agreements (VRAs) in such key industries as steel and automobiles. Among the "big five" exporters of steel to the United States are Brazil and Mexico (the others are the EEC, Korea, and Japan), and voluntary restraint agreements with them were among the 28 such agreements negotiated by the United States in 1989.[41] Brazil, though it is considered a menace to the U.S. steel industry, has successfully negotiated a "major" increase in exports to the United States under the VRAs. By 1992, when the VRAs expire, Brazil will be permitted a whop-ping 2.1 percent of the U.S. market.[42]

Latin America fears that the reorientation of its trade in the direction of the U.S. orbit will make it increasingly vulnerable to being used as a foil for U.S. multilateral or domestic trade interests, as a weak whipping boy for overall U.S. foreign economic policy frustrations, as an object of special pleading by U.S. industries before the U.S. trade policy apparatus, and as a victim of overt political uses of trade as a part of U.S. national security projection in the hemisphere. As simple examples of the first of these fears, Brazil was chided and threatened for not being willing to go along with a new GATT round that included services, when the OECD trade policy committee itself had not even committed to such a principle. Brazil was named in 1989 a Super 301 unfair trader, while other countries perhaps equally guilty of such offenses received milder treatment. When

Brazil, along with Japan and India, was named for Super 301 attention, it was acknowledged that one reason for Brazil's appearance on the list was to find a country to "keep Japan company."[43] In 1990, in response to a new government in Brazil and new trade concessions by the Japanese, the United States removed both Brazil and Japan from the Super 301 list, leaving benighted India alone as a chronic unfair trader.

The U.S. trade policy process also offers substantial room for industry-specific pleading as a part of bilateral negotiations. This has become especially true in the period since the establishment in the 1970s of the private sectory advisory process by which private sector leaders participate in advisory committees hosted by the U.S. Trade Representative. In several spectacular cases, U.S. industry groups have used the U.S. government as a militant on their behalf in bilateral consultations with Latin American countries.[44] In 1984 and 1985, U.S. pharmaceutical companies successfully rewrote an amended pharmaceutical law in Mexico by pushing the U.S. Trade Representative to argue that the law constituted an unfair barrier to trade and inadequate patent protection. In 1989, the Super 301 decision on Brazil was governed at least to some extent by industry pressures to get favorable treatment for McDonnell Douglas Corporation and Hughes Aircraft Company in a contract for telecommunications equipment in Brazil. According to a leading official of Hughes, the letter designating Brazil as a Super 301 company was meant to convey "that the Brazilian decision [to accept the U.S. bids] could go a long way toward helping to establish better relations [between Brazil and the United States]."[45]

Latin America in general fears the recurrence of U.S. trade sanctions as a national security policy goal, as has been repeated in Allende's Chile (1970–73) and postrevolutionary Cuba (1960–present) and Nicaragua (1979–90). A substantial motivation for Mexican food security policy in the 1970s was to decrease vulnerability to U.S. "food weaponry." Mexican oil policy was steered (unsuccessfully) toward diversification of trade partners because it ran against Mexican national security interests to export the preponderance of its oil to the United States.

Regularly, the nations of Latin America are jawboned by U.S. trade policymakers who use as threats denial or graduation under the Generalized System of Preferences; the application or denial of the "injury test," depending on whether the target nation has signed the GATT subsidies code;[46] reallocation of sugar allotments under the U.S. quota; or the exclusion of certain countries from preferential trade agreements because of membership in OPEC or because they are communist.

The U.S. trade bureaucracy is still committed to free trade and the continuation of the GATT, but increasingly the U.S. Congress plays its neoprotectionist role by reducing the level of discretion available to the president in pursuing "unfair trade practices" actions against trading partners and by insisting on an agricultural policy that emphasizes export promotion through subsidies. The Super 301 provisions of the trade legislation currently in effect are the most obvious trademark of congressional protectionism, but they certainly do not stand alone. In 1989, Senator Max Baucus demanded that the United States undertake a "biplurilateral" approach to future negotiations in the event of GATT failure.[47] That might mean calling for a "super GATT" to include only those parties willing to adopt the U.S. agenda in the multilateral system and leaving such Great Powers as the new EEC "out in the cold," or even designating them as Super 301 unfair traders. At the same time, Baucus called for further bilateral accords by the United States as a hedge against the growing power of the EEC.[48]

Statements such as these from the Congress reveal a traditional tension between the executive and legislative branches in American trade politics. To be fair, it is unclear that a biplurilateral approach or an increased emphasis on bilateral negotiations would be harmful to the multilateral system.[49] It is also far from clear that U.S. threats of "going it alone" are credible policy alternatives, rather than the usual high-toned puffery that accompanies international trade negotiations. The point here is that the primary agenda of the United States and Latin America under such a vision becomes the bilateral consultation or the regional forum for trade negotiations, not the multilateral trade negotiations themselves.

Another aspect of domestic U.S. politics that infuses current hemispheric trade politics involves the agricultural trade agenda. Since the mid-1980s the United States has been both the world's largest debtor and a large agricultural exporter in the midst of a farm crisis. In both aspects, it shares some problems with Latin American countries, but the solution to U.S. farm problems is not necessarily consistent with Latin America's own goals in agricultural policy.

There are many complications in trade versus domestic politics in U.S. farm policy. It appears that a durable solution to the U.S. farm crisis may be found in reviving Latin American agricultural import capacity. But in the absence of a multilateral commitment to abandoning farm subsidies, the United States can compete in Latin American markets only through aggressive farm subsidies of its own. (In fact, as the GATT talks veered toward failure, U.S. secretary of agriculture and former Trade Representative Clayton Yeutter threatened an agricultural subsidy war.)

In 1987 and 1988 those subsidies helped revive the agricultural sector after the crisis of the mid-1980s, but at an annual cost of $25 to $30 billion in farm subsidies, especially the euphemistically named Export

Enhancement Program. It remains to be seen whether the GATT can avert an agricultural subsidy war, and it is unclear whether the United States will be able to commit itself domestically to the drastic shift that removal of subsidies would represent in domestic farm policy. The domestic political implications would include abandonment of traditional congressional pork barrel in the farm belt, resistance by Congress to threats against the mythical yeoman farmer,[50], and acceptance of reduced U.S. farm income just as the agricultural sector is recovering from the mid-1980s crisis and cutting the support structure from under the already failing U.S. savings and loan industry, which relies to some extent on farm land values.

The Debt-Trade Connection Revisited in Bilateral Context

John Maynard Keynes, in his prophetic assessment of post–World War I Europe, asked:

> Will the discontented peoples of Europe be willing for a generation to come so to order their lives that an appreciable part of their daily produce may be available to meet a foreign payment the reason for which . . . does not spring compelling from their sense of justice or duty? . . . I do not believe that any of these tributes will continue to be paid, at the best, for more than a very few years. They do not square with human nature or agree with the spirit of the age.[51]

This acerbic comment on the post-Versailles arrangements in Europe applies as well to the tensions created by debt in Latin America. Debt, along with the U.S.–Latin American trade relationship and the Uruguay Round of multilateral trade negotiations, frames the international setting for Latin American trade and development. Those factors determine, to some extent, national power relations and their relevance for trade, and the "political space" available for nations in Latin America to govern their foreign relations for the sake of external stabilization, structural adjustment, domestic development, and political progress.

The contention that the debt crisis is "mainly political" fits well with the proposition that foreign economic relations create internal political questions about development. Obviously, the debt crisis has its own complicated dynamics, only part of which are represented in trade politics. Some of those were treated in Chapter 2 and do not bear repeating here. But it is important to concentrate on the complicating effects of debt on trade in the 1990s, especially in light of the deep and antagonistic trade relations between the principal debtors (in Latin America) and the principal creditors (in the United States) in the political environment of the late 1980s;

the limited opportunities to export; and the development implications of exporting to pay the debt. Specifically, it is important to analyze the relationship between debt, trade concentration, and the political terms of trade; the impact of long-term trade surpluses from Latin America on U.S. domestic politics when the latter has its own debt problems; the alternative prospects for Latin American trade adjustment; and the role of each of these phenomena in future trade negotiations.

Perhaps the most interesting connection between debt and trade from the standpoint of international economic policy-making is the replacement of simple trade arrangements with structural-adjustment-linked development assistance, even as trade opportunities are reduced or constrained in certain key areas. For example, in the European Community, the emphasis has turned away from opening Lomé in favor of promises of development assistance for high-debt countries. At the same time, the integration of Europe in 1992 brings fear especially to Lomé sugar and banana traders, who will be subject to increasingly competitive trade arrangements. The obligation of the EEC, according to its officers, is to replace some of the exclusiveness of Lomé with greater adjustment aid.[52] The United States and the World Bank are also devotees of tying improved trade relations to structural adjustment lending and debt resolution through orthodox shocks to restore free market dominance in Latin American societies.

Debt, Trade Adjustment, and Inter-American Thinking About Trade

The debt crisis has reoriented thinking about international trade in fundamental ways. Latin American countries are committed intellectually to free trade in ways not seen since the onset of import-substitution industrialization and the emergence of the ECLA "Prebisch thesis" after World War II. Only a decade ago, Latin American specialists and politicians alike were touting "resource power" as the weapon by which Latin America would extract its due from the international system. At that time, it was difficult to find politicians admitting to the necessity of expanded trade relations with the United States or conceding much about the virtue of trade itself. Nationalism meant separation from the international trade system, which, along with multinational capital, was the vehicle by which imperialism expressed itself in the postcolonial world.

Now, even erstwhile advocates of radical nationalism have come around to the position that trade is the flagship of Latin American hopes for economic growth. The entire dialogue of the 1970s, which was dominated by skepticism about the relationship of trade to development in

Latin America, has been dropped in favor of new arguments about how to increase Latin American integration into the international trade system. Sometimes concern is evinced for the conditions of that integration; other times, it seems that Latin American economics has—at least on the export side—become ideologically free-trade-oriented. Expanded trade surpluses are necessary to service the debt. Trade is necessary to modernize industries and to guarantee the flow of key inputs to industrial transformation. Capital generated by trade is more important as a source of domestic savings and investment, because of the contraction of foreign bank lending and the reticence of direct foreign investors in the 1980s. Like it or not, trade is back as a keystone of Latin American economic thinking.

In addition to the phenomenal changes in Latin American economic thinking wrought by the realities of the debt crisis, the new desperation to trade as a central part of economic policy has meant a reorientation of Latin America's external sector toward the United States. After a generation in which Latin America tried to struggle free of U.S. hegemony by diversifying trade, Latin America must see the United States as the default opportunity for increasing exports. In reality, this view is tarnished by U.S. economic policy toward Latin America, which includes a clumsy Generalized System of Preferences policy, repeated attempts to impose its GATT preferences through power politics, and bilateral consultations that reveal the United States as a liberal exporter and protectionist importer.

On the U.S. side, after all, an adjustment process is also under way. In a political climate that does not permit the expansion of huge subsidy programs in favor of domestic industries—remember the failure in Congress of the industrial policy legislation of 1983—the United States is searching for ways to right the trade deficit. The two official mechanisms for that process are the GATT and the quotidian bilateral "consultations" between U.S. officials and key trade partners. Out of the former, the United States hopes to continue conversing about future agreement permitting expanded trade in services with Europe, Japan, and the key economies of the Third World; rights of establishment for service-related industries in other economies; privatization of public monopolies that restrict trade in services; and transparency in trade procedures that would unmask unfair administrative barriers to increased trade penetration from the United States. From the latter, the United States expects to continue pressure on key trade partners to liberalize imports, to reduce subsidies, and to restrict trade in key products that purportedly threaten U.S. industries. Mexico, Brazil, and Argentina figure importantly in those bilateral consultations, though they do not have the same kind of high-level attention or permanent dialogue that the EEC and Japan enjoy (suffer?).

Thus, voluntary export restraints are negotiated on steel from Brazil and Mexico; threats are issued against Brazilian ethanol and Argentine apple juice; pressure is applied successfully to force radical changes in Mexico's pharmaceutical law; and a muscular exchange continues between Brazil and the United States on the market reserve policy in "informatics." Because Latin American nations are only beginning to be considered to be "key players" in the GATT consensus—which became clear in U.S. dealings with Brazil over its opposition to a new round—their position in the U.S. trade adjustment process is as a residual irritant, to be dealt with on an issue-specific basis.

The dialogue is often shrill. U.S. trade policymakers have accused Brazil, Mexico, and Argentina of hiding behind the debt crisis to create artificial advantages for their own industries. Brazil accuses the United States of trying to break the back of its national economy. Authors of the Mexican national austerity program under President Miguel de la Madrid are accused of selling the Mexican economy to the International Monetary Fund. Argentina was seen in the United States as a crass opportunist—by American policymakers apparently unsympathetic to Argentina's worst economic crisis since the Great Depression—for taking advantage of the Carter grain embargo to increase trade with the USSR.

Latin America is seen as a key region to solve the U.S. trade deficit, especially since it is relatively weaker in international organizations than the EEC or Japan. Among Latin American politicians in the 1980s, as was true in the 1970s, debt is preferred in Latin America over direct foreign investment, which is viewed as "selling the country." International economic policy coordination is done without the Latin American nations, or even the other non-Latin newly industrialized countries, who are still the stepchildren of the international economic system.

The renewed insertion of Latin America into the U.S. trade orbit limits the freedom enjoyed by those countries. Trade is forced by the debt crisis but brings little relief domestically and strains already distorted allocations of economic and natural resources. Until Brazil declared a debt moratorium in February 1986, it returned virtually its entire trade surplus of $1 billion per month, much of which was artificially generated by cutting imports, to international banks in debt service payments. Its current macroeconomic policies are weighed down by a growing debt burden and the political difficulty of constructing a new agreement with the IMF and commercial banks until domestic inflation subsides.[53]

From the U.S. standpoint, its trade opportunities are held hostage by the international financial community's stalemate with Brazil. As long as Brazil generates its exaggerated trade surpluses by subsidizing exports and constraining import opportunities, the United States will be unable to exploit fully South America's largest market. Yet the debt crisis and the legacy of the past decade have made it virtually impossible to liberalize successfully without losing the trade surpluses constructed as a short-term response to the external payments crisis. To the United States, the only apparent avenue to opening the Brazilian market is through bilateral threats in the consultative mechanism and through concentrated state-bashing, which is designed to release the grip of the public sector on trade. Surprisingly, this view survives despite the evidence that new leadership in Brazil and Mexico (Fernando Collor de Mello in Brazil and Carlos Salinas de Gortari in Mexico) is more important to changes in foreign economic policy-making than U.S. pressure. (Of course, it must be conceded that this last might be viewed in Washington as a result of persuasive U.S. pressure tactics and the newly rediscovered virtues of the market.)

Perhaps more difficult than Brazil is Mexico, though U.S. trade policy-makers have been more successful there in recent years. In the summer of 1987, because of momentary oil price increases and surges in manufactured exports (partly the result of competitive devaluations over five years), Mexico suddenly found itself with $14 billion in foreign exchange reserves. The government was stymied over how to use it because, despite Mexico's unflinching adherence to IMF- and U.S.-sponsored external stabilization programs, (1) new spending would have been seen by U.S. investors as a return to profligate policies of the past; (2) the economic basis for future surpluses was unclear, as earlier drops in oil prices had shown (Mexican export revenue from oil declined from $14 billion in 1985 to $5.7 billion in 1986); and (3) using the surplus to service debt or to reduce the public sector deficit further had become politically unacceptable at home. Mexico's adherence to the canons of the IMF and the trade liberalization program supported by the United States meant virtual political paralysis. The domestic implications of debt policy continue to be unacceptable; the international implications of treating domestic development needs are equally unacceptable. The relationship between Mexico and the United States governs domestic policies more than it has in recent years, and the long-term consequences for Mexican politics are unknown.

In general, Latin America cannot be counted on as a growth market for U.S. exports unless trade surpluses are generated and debt reform is accomplished. Latin America has to pay now for imports because the key trading partners in the region are not eligible for concessional credit agreements from the United States or the World Bank, and partly because commercial credits are increasingly difficult to obtain without debt reform. Both the debt service burden and the moral opprobrium accompanying moratoria limit the amount of trade financing available to Latin America. Instability of the financial system, itself partly a product of the debt crisis and the U.S. fiscal crisis, makes concessional financing (such as the EXIM bank) more difficult and costly. The Baker Plan did not generate new money upon which its success depended and unwittingly encouraged the increase in overall debt obligations by encouraging capitalization. At its best it would have funneled only about $3 billion a year to the high-debt countries, about one-seventh of expected needs. The Brady Plan is designed to encourage voluntary debt reduction by the private banks, partly by empowering the IMF and the World Bank to initiate programs to lower debt service obligations of countries applying the proper economic reforms. To some extent, this has angered the private bankers, who had led the way in insisting on bank agreement before resources were committed to high-debt countries.[54]

The U.S. Congress says that imports from Latin America will not increase without reciprocity; that is, the equation is turned around to put the burden on Latin America because of the region's import restrictions. And as a further portent of coming difficulties, new trade legislation reduces presidential discretion to forgo trade retaliation. So Latin America treats the United States as the regional hegemon, though the global conditions for U.S. hegemony have disappeared. Therefore, some of the more obvious propositions of Hirschman about the "generous" trade behavior of the hegemon for power purposes do not obtain. That is, the United States does not consider its foreign economic policy a matter of hegemonic projection but a function of domestic adjustment problems, in which it finds itself increasingly afflicted by the policy problems of other countries. In fact, the regional equation is a somewhat dissipated form of traditional hegemony, in which a weakening global power turns its trade policy in a regional direction to satisfy increasingly protectionist sentiment at home, at the same time that it commits itself to a dated multilateral system of its own creation.

This climate of uncertainty and trade pessimism is complicated even further by presidential elections during 1988–90 in key trading states of the region, including the United States, Argentina, Brazil, Chile, Colombia, Mexico, and Peru. Some argue that the political cycle is always present, so that Bush and Salinas are both allegedly hurrying toward a bilateral free trade agreement before the U.S. congressional election campaign of 1992 and before the end of Salinas's term in 1994. In those electoral contests, each of which obviously has its own economic and political environment, trade has loomed large as a political issue. Whatever the commitments to postwar economic internationalism, the constrained economic climate of the inter-American system in this period makes national accommodation to international integration a political liability.

The economic principle that one man's subsidy is another man's tariff certainly applies to the trade problems of the hemisphere. Yet this principle is lost in most debates over liberalization versus protection. Repeatedly, the U.S. Congress has ignored the high cost of the sugar quota to U.S. consumers in its enthusiasm to protect a small coterie of cane and beet producers (and, increasingly, the corn sugar industry as well). Interestingly, small Caribbean sugar producers with little opportunity to change to a different export profile and equally dim prospects to influence the international sugar market are particularly eager to continue participating in a U.S. quota program.

Similarly, the debate in 1985 (and again in 1988) over new restrictions on textile imports would have ignored the economic cost to the United States had it not been for insistent and well-presented economic analysis from the U.S. Trade Representative. Likewise, in Latin America, governments regularly protect superannuated "infant industries" and "industries of transformation" without regard for the tax they represent on consumers and the long-run inefficiencies they seem to guarantee. Mexico's legendary inability to produce competitive consumer durables resulted in permanent protection for import-substituting industries, which sacrificed efficiencies in the short term by restricting imports and undercut long-term competitiveness with imports from other industrial countries. Now, even after thirty years of industrial growth unparalleled in Latin America, topped by a four-year oil boom, it is still not clear that Mexico is able to produce a broad set of manufactured goods for the international market, absent the remarkable devaluations of 1982–90 and the highly peculiar circumstances of U.S.-Mexican ventures and *maquiladora* trade. Ironically, the prospect of a broad bilateral free trade agreement with the United States would make the border industries the leading edge of bilateral integration, with significant domestic adjustment costs in both countries.

By contrast, Brazil's protection of the informatics industry through a limited market reserve for a long time was touted as a policy success (thanks in some measure to the high-tech priorities of the national security regime that ruled for two decades).[55] But that success was built on subsidies for the strongest internationally linked national firms (such as the Itaú Bank and its high-technology affiliate Itaútec) and an extraordinary tax on consumers (the price of an IBM-PC compatible microcomputer in Brazil hovered near U.S.$10,000 in mid-1987). With the performance of the export sector wavering throughout 1987, followed by explosive inflation in 1988 and 1989 and the continuing high local costs of computer production, it is unclear that the logic of the informatics law in Brazil is any more attentive to broad domestic social costs than is the developed countries' restrictive Multi-Fibre Agreement.

The state has been the bulwark against domination by the external sector. *Dependentistas* correctly fault the state for falling into the lap of externally connected dominant elites and thereby serving the interests of dependent economic integration into the international system. But economic nationalism has prevailed to a significant extent in the postwar Latin American states, so that the institutionalization of import-substitution strategies has meant a state-centered development strategy in many countries. This is particularly true of the large economies, which have been more ambitious and relatively successful in import substitution.

To a great extent, the debt crisis has provided the economic forum and the ideological bludgeon that have brought the interventionist Latin American state to heel. External stabilization and structural adjustment have meant massive reductions in the state's economic role, in favor of markets. That stabilization and liberalization process has been accompanied by increasing U.S. insistence on the expansion of the multilateral free trade system and a steadfast demand that the Latin American public sector stand aside. It is clear from case materials and from polemic that the United States envisions this demand to be economically rational, as well as in its own trade interests. U.S. support for such liberalization has been somewhat uneven, though in the case of Mexico, the Brady Plan provisions and recent Generalized System of Preferences concessions both indicate that the rewards of liberalization and destatization are in the United States's favor.

That favor is far from purely concessional, of course. In the case of Mexico, in 1989 the Generalized System of Preferences review subcommittee of the interagency Trade Policy Staff Committee agreed to consider 80 commodity-specific petitions, in contrast to two dozen in 1988. Over half were submitted by Mexico, and favorable consideration was explicitly linked to Mexican trade liberalization favoring the United States. In the case of the beer industry, which had been removed from the Generalized System of Preferences in 1983, Mexican beer producers had petitioned for renewal of GSP status after the government had reduced all tariffs to a maximum of 20 percent and eliminated import licensing requirements. The potential for U.S. beer purveyors in Mexico is great, but the size of the Mexican beer industry and its minuscule export performance suggest marginal benefits to Mexico. Potential increases in beer production in Mexico under liberal trade conditions also may favor U.S. barley and hops producers over their less competitive Mexican counterparts.[56]

Conclusion: Discriminating
Among Latin American Traders

The trick of comparative analysis is to discriminate among the Latin American trade partners of the United States to refine our understanding of U.S. influence and the freedom Latin American countries have to choose alternative trade partners. In many ways, these discriminators will govern the analysis presented in the next chapter. It is sadly apparent that the traditional structuralist literature seems to hold up well. Tropical product exporters are less flexible than their temperate zone neighbors, though less because of the export enclave thesis than the nature of the commodities they produce and the markets they command. Primary commodity producers are at a relative disadvantage, compared with their manufacturing and service-exporting neighbors, but more because of poor economic multipliers, extreme sectoral fragmentation among producer countries, and gross inefficiencies among traditional agricultural enterprises (such as sugar) than because of secular declines in the terms of trade. And, of course, large countries seem to have a great advantage over small countries, to no one's surprise.

These conclusions by themselves are not startling. The result, however, is a highly constrained, hemisphere-bound trade environment in which virtually none of the countries of Latin America has any room to maneuver for domestic development advantage. The United States, embattled hegemon in decline, is unwilling and unable to provide the development assistance leadership even to validate Hirschman's Great Power thesis— that the self-seeking hegemon will make trade concessions to achieve greater power among its lesser trade partners. As the next chapter shows, this setting gravely reduces the strategies available to Latin American traders as they face the development challenges of the 1990s.

National Goals for Latin American Trade Politics: Issues of Insulation and Autonomy

Free Trade: Cause of all business troubles.
—Gustave Flaubert, *The Dictionary of Received Ideas*

The government makes a bad businessman.
—Pedro Fermín de Vargas

THE TRADE PICTURE painted in the previous chapters is a grim one, governed by a hegemon reluctant to accept its role as default trading partner of the weaker countries of the region and populated by countries with little flexibility in a world breaking into regional trading blocs. Despite these many constraints, the necessity of using trade in a national development strategy is historically and economically overdetermined. There is no escape from open-system macroeconomics in the debt crisis. Capital formation and external payments equilibrium depend on trade. The fiscal profligacy of military dictatorship in Brazil or oil boom *triumfalismo* in Mexico and Venezuela are excesses of the past, virtual political and economic impossibilities in the near future. Economic nationalism led by the state has a hollow ring, in light of the failures of state-led capitalism in Latin America. In the early 1990s, the international system is able to exert more pressure on Latin American trade policies than in the heyday of import-substitution industrialization. That pressure is in the direction of freer trade.

The bias toward trade coincides with an ideological reordering in Latin America that stems from the failure of statist development strategies over the past two decades, the (perhaps temporary) exhaustion of traditional populism and its successor bureaucratic authoritarian military regimes, the virtual fiscal collapse of the Latin American state, and the need for external stabilization schemes supervised by the OECD central banks, the IMF, and commercial bankers. So, the successor to Miguel de la Madrid in Mexico does not respect the political pendulum that seemed to govern past presidencies; instead, Salinas deepens the drive toward privatization and liberalization while embracing the logic of the market almost without reservation.[1] Fernando Collor de Mello in Brazil begins his administration by declaring the most radical privatization and destatization scheme in Brazilian memory. President Alberto Fujimori reverses the course of Alan Garcia's Aprista nationalism and declares a "Peruvian perestroika."[2] And the success of Carlos Menem in Argentina or Patricio Aylwin in Chile is measured to some extent by their ability to observe the ideological rigors of the age: international integration and the virtue of market-driven economies.

Despite the positive climate for internationalist liberalism, the desperation of the moment stands as an obstacle to liberalization. Most of the major traders of Latin America—Argentina, Brazil, Mexico, and Peru— are in such bad straits that trade policy seems ridiculously inadequate to meet the demands of domestic development.[3] Argentina came to the brink of economic collapse in 1989 and 1990. Brazil, which only once in the 1980s operated with less than 200 percent annual inflation, closed the decade with new inflation records topping the 1,000 percent range, and even under the radical new Collor Plan has failed to stop inflation or reintroduce a modicum of predictability into the economy. Mexico has been renegotiating its debt since the inauguration of President Salinas, the latest (July 1989) accord coming at the last moment to stave off another "default."[4] And even before its extraordinary 1990 presidential elections, Peru was in such disarray that high trade officials there did not even pretend to a trade policy beyond foreign exchange crisis management. Each of these countries is in the middle of various protracted battles over political legitimacy, in which the presiding governments have little authority to pursue concerted trade and development programs and not much economic space in which to operate. In the Mexican case, it is remarkable—perhaps even revolutionary—that the president would bet his own political future and his nation's economy on a relatively ungoverned economic relationship with the United States.[5]

The small countries of Central America and the Caribbean have even less political mobility to create national strategies for trade and development. Commodity prices have been low for a decade. Alternative markets appear to have dried up, as Europe moves toward 1992 and consolidates the Lomé IV accords with its African, Caribbean, and Pacific preference system.[6] Central American conflict has ruined opportunities for intraregional trade, and the evaporation of the oil boom took with it Mexican and Venezuelan ambitions to combine oil trade with concessional development assistance to the region. The U.S. Caribbean Basin Initiative is so modest as to escape notice in the balance sheets of the U.S. deficit; even so, the initiative and the sugar quota are the main sources of export earnings for the countries included in it.

Such desperate conditions make it difficult to speak of national strategies for trade and development in Latin America. As the integration of Latin American and OECD economies continues to progress in the 1990s, it is reasonable to expect that OECD domestic macroeconomic policy will have an increasing effect on Latin American trade and development prospects. Because of the generally limited impact of Latin America on the OECD, its political economy has a much more modest effect on the rest of the globe. At the same time, as the public sector retreats from its traditional roles in guiding economic development in Latin America, so too will the national steering capacity of Latin American states vis-à-vis the international trade system recede.

The political weakness of the present should not suggest that Latin America has enjoyed a great deal of political space for progressive trade politics in the past, however. The remedies of the 1930s—default and subordinate reintegration or import substitution—were limited options, with their own economic and social costs. Even in the brief heyday of delinking, cartelizing, and southern militance in the 1970s, little scholarship on delinking or decoupling Third World nations from the international economic system offered convincing prospects for national wealth under such a regime. The economic prospects of exile from the hemispheric system seem to shrink in direct function of a country's previous openness and dependence on international markets for its economic activities.[7]

Particularly now, in a time of international economic restructuring, the consolidation of the European Economic Community, the emergence of Japan as a global economic power, the appearance of the East Asian tigers and their much-vaunted export-oriented industrialization model, the decline of American hegemony in the West, and the depth and apparent permanence of the Latin American debt crisis, delinking seems an almost forgotten bit of nationalist fantasy. Like it or not, Latin American nations for the most part are locked into trade expansion for the sake of economic growth, and the virtues of trade are debated less than the proper mix of partners, the size and disposition of trade surplus, and the need for special trade preferences in the next iteration of the GATT or of regional trading blocs.

A fair amount of irony accompanies this picture of trade in the 1980s. Latin American countries embrace trade in economic desperation as they make an uncomfortable political shift toward internationalism, all the while looking over their shoulders at resurgent populist nationalism. Economic nationalists and internationalists alike despair over dependence on the United States, all the while worrying about the next economic slowdown there that will foreshorten their export opportunities. The United States, in equally dramatic fashion, recites the virtues of the post–World War II free trade system, even as the U.S. Congress fulminates about retaliating against "unfair traders" such as Brazil, India, and Japan. Congressional leaders wax poetic about the virtues of Mexican structural adjustment, though the United States has steadfastly refused to acknowledge its own need to adjust in similar ways. After more than a decade of hammering at Mexican nationalism, the Bush administration has included little specific development assistance in the proposed bilateral free trade agreement. The West generally promotes trade expansion for traditional reasons, while the South suspects another round of dependency, new perhaps only for its product mix. As the OECD leadership pushes against neoprotectionist pressures and struggles to overcome the collapse of Latin American imports in the 1980s, the GATT slowly bicycles forward to an uncertain destination, its few remaining pedalers balanced by free trade incantations from the past.

Inherent in the current situation, as in crises earlier in this century, is a countervailing tendency toward trade-averse behavior, even as the international system demands more open trade politics from Latin America.[8] The foreign exchange constraint and the demands of debt service force another wave of import substitution to the forefront of policy-making. The suppression of domestic demand in high-debt countries further constrains the import capacity of Latin American economies. The West's slow growth and its neoprotectionist tendencies limit the prospect of a new round of export optimism. Nationalist critics of trade liberalization have yet to mobilize opposition to the impact of liberalization on domestic adjustment. Domestic adjustment to free trade has yet to show itself fully as costs levied against fragile democratic processes. Thus the political demands of Latin America's economic dilemmas may yet contradict the economic demands of international trade and adjustment.

A pessimistic estimation of national sovereignty over trade politics has led us to examine the origins and limits of individual countries' initiative on trade and to trace some of the structural constraints and opportunities for trade policy. Particularly important is the mix between domestic development objectives and external economic policy goals, now combined in a recipe of external payments equilibrium and economic stabilization versus domestic economic growth, equity, and sustainability.

The argument posed here is twofold: first, that the explicitly political terms of Latin America's insertion into the international division of labor can be clarified by comparing approaches to the trade-development-sustainability problem; second, that the new international division of labor in the 1990s has reduced the difference between alternative political approaches that used to be called nationalist and internationalist. The growing integration of Latin American nations into a restructured international economic order—under the pressure of the debt crisis, the evaporation of state legitimacy as an economic agent, and the push to privatization—has meant that nationalist populism is only a specter and that the resource, development, and trade agendas of the region offer little freedom to the politician short of radical change.[9]

What has yet to be determined, however, is the nature and vehicle for political reaction to domestic trade adjustment problems. Will leading private sector organizations in Latin America stand quietly by as they are outcompeted by foreign providers? Will small firms in Mexico accept being outsourced by transnational suppliers to large manufacturing firms? Will U.S. trade unions remain politically divided if East Asian competitors use Mexican or other Latin American free trade environments to gain more access to the U.S. market? And, most importantly, will political opponents of current administrations in power resist the opportunity to take advantage of the costs of adjustment to take their parties and candidates to electoral success? To what extent will those political voices represent legitimate national alternatives to trade liberalization, as opposed to polemical nationalism lacking an economically viable alternative?

Some Structural and Institutional Determinants of National Strategies

In Chapter 4, we explored some of the theoretical principles underlying the relationship between concentration of trade partners and Latin American vulnerability to U.S. hegemony in the region. It remains now to examine the "policy space" available to Latin American governments seeking escape from the more pernicious effects of that bilateral dependence. I have already raised questions about the reliability of the simple relationship of state presence to economic openness, as well as its relevance for national development in Latin America. Nevertheless, the degree of an economy's openness must be a preliminary indicator of policy space in trade matters. Likewise, the ability of the public sector to manipulate that space—the "stateness" or "governing capacity" factor—is relevant to trade strategy. With all the relevant caveats in mind, then, it is stipulated that the capacity of the state to manipulate variables such as exchange rates affects the potential impact of external shock on domestic economic performance.

Another way of discriminating among country cases on the relationship between state or government presence and economic openness is to assess qualitatively the degree to which governments are "captured" by a commitment to increased trade and integration into the international system versus a commitment to reduce international vulnerability through inward-looking development policies. An obvious example is the Concordancia in Argentina during the 1930s, when the government was committed to internationalist reintegration with Britain, contrasted with the import-substituting economic nationalism during the Perón years. Another likely contrast is Mexico under López Portillo (1976–82) versus Mexico under De la Madrid (1982–88) or Salinas de Gortari (1988–present). Perhaps the most spectacular case today is Chile, where the highly "managed"[10] neoliberal dictatorship of General Augusto Pinochet (1973–90) opened the economy over fifteen years, in stark contrast to the economic nationalism of both Christian Democrat and Popular Unity governments before 1973.

In addition to the historical and political-ideological battles over economic nationalism or internationalism, the debt crisis has affected the political expression of economic nationalism, particularly in light of the "heterodox shocks" of Argentina and Brazil, the unprecedented accommodation by Mexico to IMF orthodoxy (with some unique Mexican heterodoxies), along with a turnaround on Mexican accession to the GATT.

The process of economic modernization—and especially industrialization—under economic nationalism in Latin America has been circuitous. More predictable have been the conflict between new and old domestic and international actors and the durability of old patterns of international relations, particularly U.S. hegemony over the region. Underlying the region's industrial transformation, after all, is a complex struggle within heavily state-intervened economies, with contending parties debating the terms of the nation's insertion into the world economy. In the end, however, the debate has been about the terms of insertion and not about options to refuse deeper integration into the international system.

The Hemispheric Context of Political Strategies

Chapter 5 detailed the fundamental role of the United States in determining the insertion of Latin America into the world economy, both as primary trade partner to the region and as leading free trade ideologue in the GATT system. Today, in the heart of the debt crisis, that role is more vivid than ever, at least partly because new import substitution is such a limited possibility.[11] To some degree, the political space available to Latin American trade managers is defined by movements in the U.S. economy. The importance of the United States to the region's trade and industrialization, of course, is a product of its historical ascendance since the middle of the nineteenth century. The relationship between the United States and Latin America is special enough that the putative decline in U.S. hegemony in the world system does not extend to Latin America, particularly as such hegemony is denominated by potential economic influence.

To understand the United States's political gains from trade does not require a malefic plan by U.S. policymakers to squeeze Latin America economically. That possibility does exist, but it is more likely that trade policymakers are engaged in "small games" of bilateral consultations without a coherent strategic architecture, save improved export performance and continued dominance over Latin American trade partners. The general ideological and macroeconomic pressures from the United States find a convenient home in debt or "free trade" negotiations in both bilateral and multilateral venues. Conceding this, it is still true that the United States benefits from trade-gained political influence by being able to export its domestic trade politics with more modest costs than would be possible for a small power. On the other side of the coin, to Latin American trade policy officials and various Latin American publics, the political language of U.S.–Latin American trade—privatization, liberalization, and the like—makes up a heavy-handed and politically contrary set of goals. In light of historical experience, it must seem impossible in Latin America to think of U.S. trade advantage without imputing hegemonic designs.

In recent Latin American history, conjunctural political victories by economic nationalists have emerged under two different circumstances: economic expansion under conditions of trade pessimism, in which an inward-looking strategy was made possible and defensible; and, conversely, under economic contraction and duress, driven by foreign exchange constraints, low commodity prices, and a failure of the international economic system to find a "progressive" niche for Latin American economies. Broadly conceived, economic nationalism found its best opportunities in the wake of the Great Depression and in the post–World War II wave of import-substitution industrialization, with many other minor occurrences in the century. A possible third wave may be found in the current international reordering, in which economic nationalists have almost come to power by posing mainly traditional platforms of economic nationalism and political populism in Mexico, Brazil, Peru, and Bolivia, all in the face of powerful external crises.

Economic internationalism, in contrast, has found its strongest political position in times of trade expansion and trade optimism, when the development dividends of a more open economy have been obvious at least to the politically dominant elements of national power. The internationalist option had its heyday in 1870–1914, in critical periods between 1958 and 1973, and apparently as the politically victorious response to the crisis of the 1980s. It would be foolish, however, to ignore the attempts after 1929 to resuscitate liberal internationalism via preferential arrangements with ascending and descending hegemons.

The abiding legacy of internationalism has been the attempt by Latin American nations to gain advantage through willful subordination to Great Power traders or to gain from trade through a diversified and not concentrated set of partners. The latter syndrome has been much less in evidence than the former. Such a strategy might be considered progressive economically, were it accompanied by the Great Power attachments analyzed by Hirschman. To the extent that Latin America requires the umbrella of alliance to a Great Power to extract extra-market advantage from the internationalist option, this may be a particularly poor time for untrammeled integration, even in the unique political circumstances of a country such as Mexico.

The Limits of Choice

To argue that international trade or its avoidance somehow offers the allure of a "way out" for Latin America is to acknowledge the region's ideology but to ignore its history. Even the illusion of a trade-based escape from dependence is the exclusive property of the large countries. Most smaller economies in Latin America enjoy little maneuverability on any trade dimension. In the small countries, internationalism has been the order of the day throughout the nineteenth and twentieth centuries. Economic nationalism is an abbreviated public philosophy that has stalled on heretofore failed attempts at regional integration. Domestic markets and resources are too puny for sustained inward development, and the influence on international markets of the small countries is too modest to give much political relief from the market terms of trade. These countries have little hope of passing a "threshold of political autonomy," through which they might exercise some freedom in determining the mix or the degree of their integration with the international economic system.

Even among small countries of South America, the difference between, say, Peru and Ecuador is fundamental. Peru in the late 1960s took the opportunity to combine trade expansion with radical political reform, creating a paternalistic state apparatus designed to force the military's version of equitable development.[12] Although the results of state intervention have been generally disastrous, the size of the Peruvian economy led government officials to undertake industrial transformation and elaborate welfare politics that escape the capacity of the smaller economy. Ecuador, with a GDP less than half that of Peru and a much more limited export bill, faces a much more difficult prospect of creating the fiscal and administrative wherewithal to challenge market-dominated export liberalism. A

TABLE 6.1

Room for Maneuver in Trade Politics:
Latin American Countries
Ranked on the Three Criteria of Size of GDP,
Openness, and Value Added in Manufacturing

Size of GDP	Openness (1988)	Value added in manufacturing
Brazil	Brazil	Brazil
Mexico	Guatemala	Mexico
Argentina	Argentina	Argentina
Venezuela	Mexico	Chile
Colombia	Colombia	Colombia
Peru	Ecuador	Peru
Chile	Nicaragua	
Ecuador		

SOURCE: Elaborated using data from IDB, *Economic and Social Progress in Latin America: Working Women* (Washington, D.C.: IDB, 1990).
    NOTE: In column 2 countries are ranked from least to most (openness); 1 and 3 are largest to smallest (GDP and value added).

cynical interpretation of state intervention might call this an advantage for Ecuador, but in the long run it means less political space in which the country can create its political options. While Ecuador's GDP is less than half that of Peru, the next Latin American country by economic size is Guatemala, about two-thirds the size of Ecuador.

In short, and with very limited precision, by size, openness, and industrial output, few countries have any opportunity historically or economically to maneuver against the structure of international economic relations (see Table 6.1). Few Latin American countries have any leverage in the trade environment or the capacity to turn inward in times of crisis. Most are open and vulnerable to external shocks. And few can substitute exports of manufactured goods for primary commodities. The rest are mainly dependent and powerless, if sometimes noisy, riders on the juggernaut of international commerce. As small powers they are generally limited to trying to maneuver into a position of strategic import (à la Somoza, or the current governments of El Salvador and Honduras, exploiting the national security ideology of the United States).

The simplistic rank ordering shown in Table 6.1 ignores the historicist possibility that the sequence and timing of state presence, economic transformation, political modernization, and other watershed events determine the success or failure of these countries' trade policies. Such an argument would suggest, for example, that the earlier the state became an economic actor on the scene, the greater would be the prospect for successful import substitution (and, therefore, the higher the prospect of domestic insulation from the external sector). Or, the earlier the shift from the "old oligarchy" based on agricultural export to the populists and their new political mission of industrialization, the greater the chance for relative economic independence. These propositions are not an explicit part of the development economics literature of Latin America, but they are part of the general underpinning of development discourse in the twentieth century. The economic historiography of the big countries (Argentina, Brazil, and Mexico), for example, revolves around the ideology of industrialization, the formation of domestic economic elites bent on modernization, the adoption of Keynesian economics, and so on.

Even within this group, Colombia and Mexico are hampered by late industrialization relative to Argentina, Brazil, and even Chile. Peru and Venezuela were even later and less successful in their industrialization efforts. Venezuela is constrained by excessive reliance on petroleum as its most important export commodity and Mexico by its excessive trade dependence on one partner, the United States. So, even among the "winners" in this crude hierarchy, gross structural limits impinge upon their political autonomy. And it is far from obvious that the earlier industrializers are in a better international position today than their less precocious counterparts. These complications confuse further the already formidable conceptual issues posed by the development literature.

This crude schema does allow the obvious conclusion that the gains from trade are more important to countries that are more dependent on trade as a source of economic growth, and more important to a small country than to a large country. Equally, it is more important to a country whose trade is concentrated with a single partner or in a single commodity to attend to the partner or the commodity upon which it depends.

It is reasonable to expect that the greater an economy's openness and the geographic concentration of its trade, the greater will be its vulnerability to external shock. A sort of index of vulnerability to external shock might be calculated by weighting the influence of openness by the terms of trade. Unfortunately, this appealing prospect is ruined by several important distortions of the 1980s. Both the terms of trade and the coefficient of exports were heavily intervened, and Latin American terms of trade in the 1980s jumped all over the board (see Chapter 2), affected grossly by programs of exchange rate stabilization, among other factors. It is absurd to suggest that such indexes, which in the context of state intervention to address external crisis have all the robustness of cotton candy, can tell us much about underlying economic or political values.

That does not invalidate the hypothesis that the degree of openness and the terms of trade vary directly. With those limitations in mind, we can suggest that a loose index of vulnerability to "major partner shock" could be constructed by taking the index of vulnerability to external shock in general and weighting it by the degree of concentration in trade with the United States. This would also provide "in normal times" a rustic indicator of the importance of the United States for the domestic economic performance of a given Latin American country. Because this index is a further derivation of the index of terms of trade weighted by openness, however, its numerical values are equally suspect for the 1980s.

Again, in normal times, these same indexes on the import side might provide a sense of the extent to which an increment of import liberalization in Latin America means an increment of export gain for the United States. This is of critical importance in determining the importance of Latin America for the United States.

Despite the frustration in calculating such indexes for the 1980s in meaningful ways, Hirschman's treatment of the influence of Great Power trade partners is still useful. According to Hirschman, the power of the oligopolist trade partner is a function of the degree to which the smaller country's trade is concentrated with the oligopolist, and the degree to which the remainder of its trade is concentrated with other partners. Here an explicitly political dimension has been added by considering the degree to which trade is negotiated on a bilateral basis for explicitly political purposes.

If we can distinguish among nationalist and internationalist options historically, and between the strong and the weak in regard to ranges of trade policy choice, it is still impossible to explain Brazilian or Mexican trade politics convincingly because they have hung by precarious electoral threads in the late 1980s. Luis Ignacio "Lula" da Silva nearly became the president of Brazil, and Brazil under Lula would certainly have had different trade politics than under Collor. Mexico might have had (and may still have) as president Cuauhtemoc Cárdenas, who espouses an economic nationalism radically different from the internationalism of Salinas de Gortari.[13] Political leadership does make a difference, particularly in the poorly institutionalized societies of postauthoritarian South America. And from José Santos Zelaya in Nicaragua to Juan Perón in Argentina, evidence abounds that short-term economic rationality does not circumscribe politics in strong presidential or authoritarian systems.

National Goals for the Trade System

I have argued that Latin American experience with trade has been uneven and unusually fraught with foreign control over the national economies, imperial disdain for Latin American peoples, and rapacious exploitation of Latin American resources. Particularly since the Great Depression, Latin American states have included varying degrees of nationalist response to unqualified integration into the international trade system, principally to avoid or to insulate the national system against dependence on foreign powers and markets. Part of that perspective is clearly built on notions of resistance against formal empire, the "imperialism of free trade," and the "technological and productive imperialism" of multinational corporations and their national allies. Among countless others, Prebisch criticized the trade basis of the international division of labor in favor of increasing the sense of national autonomy in Latin America.[14] Later, national autonomy was one of the defining characteristics of the prescriptive literature fighting against the conditions of dependency.[15]

Given the current debility of Latin American nations in the international trade system (in the context of their historical weakness vis-à-vis hegemonic powers), the goals of national trade policies remain steadfast, despite the enormous ideological changes in nationalist versus internationalist political leadership. It is ironic, but true, that while Latin America finds itself more deeply integrated into the international system and less able to resist that vortex, it remains attached to national goals for trade policy that run against the grain of integration.

Insulating the National Economy

Enhancing national autonomy of economic decision making allegedly involves, first of all, insulating Latin American economies against external shock. Operationally, that has involved a variety of trade strategies, listed here in descending order of their putative "insulation value": (1) increasing value added in exports; (2) diversifying northern trade partners; (3) diversifying commodity exports; (4) increasing intraregional trade; (5) controlling imports; and (6) manipulating the exchange rate. Reflecting the dependence of the region on trade, even these goals are *mainly* trade-prone strategies; more trade-averse strategies include controlling imports, demanding export performance, and the like. They have been generally unsuccessful, on both insulation and development criteria.

The large industrial economies of Latin America have increased value-added in their domestic economies through industrialization. Industrial transformation has been limited, however, and only the largest economies have substantial intermediate and capital goods sectors. Even fewer countries have a record of success exporting manufactures, especially when measured against the importance of the sector in GDP. Industrial transformation offers only limited success, especially on the export side.

The alternative has been to continue to emphasize the primary sector, but to try to add more value in processing. Critics argue that little increase in value-added has accompanied Chile's recent shift from copper to new agricultural exports. Instead of copper, Chile exports agricultural commodities, and it appears that copper is resurging in importance because of price improvements. The test will be whether future exports will bring forward linkages to agroindustrial exports. The other, smaller and less industrially endowed countries have shown little improvement in their export bills (see Tables 6.2 and 6.3). Even the second largest industrial producer in Latin America, Mexico, shows little success in exporting manufactures at a level reflective of domestic industrialization in general.[16]

An analysis of the role of primary commodity exports in recent Latin American history suggests that the industrial diversification of exports has come at the cost of primary commodities, an argument well-known to Argentines living through the Perón era.[17] In fact, the import-substituting countries of the post–World War II era turned the terms of trade against agriculture in favor of industry. Even though agriculture often continued to garner its share of capital during the period of import substitution, the industrial countries of Latin America clearly moved their trade bill away from commodity exports. It has been argued that Latin America should not have lost its share of primary commodity exports, and that comparative advantage dictates a return to a primary export base in the 1990s. The persistence of agricultural exports even in the industrialized countries of the region and the weakness of exports in manufactures suggests some validity to this notion, considered from the trade standpoint alone. The social implications for development are complicated and country-specific.

As for the second insulator, I have already argued that Latin American nations historically have found it nearly impossible to achieve a secular diversification of northern trade partners. The external shocks of the 1970s and 1980s have reduced those prospects in ways that do not suggest solution in the near future. For most of Latin America, the national goal of diversifying away from the United States clashes with current international economic conditions. Even with the potential for diversification in selected countries (e.g., the African-Caribbean-Pacific countries, which also participate in the Caribbean Basin Initiative), diversification does not diminish the power aspect of trade relations. So, following Hirschman again, for most small countries trade partner concentration with the United States is compounded by the secondary concentration of trade with other OECD partners.[18] We have already seen in Chapter 4 that the Hirschman indexes of concentration do not betray any great success in diversification.

Diversification without subordination to Great Power trade politics is an obvious goal, and intraregional trade is offered frequently as a potential answer, with the severe limits recounted in the previous chapter.

TABLE 6.2

The Share of Agriculture and Manufacturing in GDP and Exports,
Selected Latin American Countries and Years, 1960–88

(*Percent*)

	1960	1970	1980	1984	1985	1986	1987	1988
Argentina								
Agri/GDP	14%	12%	11%	14%	14%	13%	13%	14%
Mfg/GDP	22	24	22	20	20	21	21	2
Agex/export	95	–	71	77	69	69	63	–
Mfgex/export	4	3	23	–	–	24	34	–
Brazil								
Agri/GDP	18	14	10	11	11	10	11	11
Mfg/GDP	26	28	29	26	26	27	26	26
Agex/export	89	–	52	43	41	39	37	–
Mfgex/export	3	2	39	–	–	44	48	–
Chile								
Agri/GDP	11	8	8	9	10	10	10	9
Mfg/GDP	22	25	22	21	20	21	21	2
Agex/export	4	–	25	35	36	39	35	–
Mfgex/export	4	8	20	–	–	9	9	–
Colombia								
Agri/GDP	29	25	23	22	22	21	21	21
Mfg/GDP	20	21	22	21	21	21	21	21
Agex/export	79	–	78	55	63	68	42	–
Mfgex/export	4	4	20	–	–	21	25	–
Ecuador								
Agri/GDP	29	25	14	14	15	16	18	17
Mfg/GDP	13	13	18	18	17	17	18	16
Agex/export	99	–	33	28	30	56	60	–
Mfgex/export	1	–	3	–	–	3	4	–
Mexico								
Agri/GDP	15	11	8	8	8	9	9	8
Mfg/GDP	17	21	22	21	21	21	21	21
Agex/export	64	–	14	9	10	18	13	–
Mfgex/export	12	1	39	–	–	32	49	–
Peru								
Agri/GDP	18	16	10	12	12	12	11	13
Mfg/GDP	25	25	24	22	22	23	24	23
Agex/export	50	–	17	15	18	26	18	–
Mfgex/export	1	5	16	–	–	23	19	–
Venezuela								
Agri/GDP	6	5	5	5	6	6	6	6
Mfg/GDP	14	16	17	19	20	20	20	20
Agex/export	26	–	0	1	2	4	1	–
Mfgex/export	0	–	2	–	–	9	8	–

SOURCE: IDB, *Economic and Social Progress in Latin America,* various volumes.
    NOTE: "Agri/GDP" means "agricultural production as a percent of GDP"; "Mfg/GDP" means "manufacturing as a percent of GDP"; "Agex/export" means "agricultural exports as a percent of total exports"; and "Mfgex/export" means "exports of manufactures as a percent of total exports."

TABLE 6.3

Growth in Value Added by Sectors, Selected Countries, 1960–89

(*Percent*)

Country	Agri-culture	Mining	Manufac-turing	Construc-tion	Utilities	Commerce	Transpor-tation	Finance
Argentina								
1961–70	2.4%	8.7%	5.2%	6.3%	10.6%	3.8%	3.7%	3.1%
1971–80	2.1	3.3	1.6	2.6	6.9	3.2	1.9	4.2
1981–89	1.0	0.7	−2.6	−11.9	3.8	−3.3	0.0	−2.0
Brazil								
1961–70	4.2	13.3	6.8	1.8	7.5	6.6	4.9	5.0
1971–80	4.7	7.2	9.0	10.2	12.4	8.3	13.5	9.1
1981–89	3.0	7.3	0.9	0.9	6.7	1.3	6.1	2.7
Chile								
1961–70	1.9	2.6	5.3	4.0	5.7	3.9	5.7	5.9
1971–80	2.2	3.4	1.1	−0.8	4.9	3.7	3.9	3.9
1981–89	3.9	3.5	2.6	4.0	4.6	2.6	4.6	1.8
Ecuador								
1961–70	3.3	−6.6	5.0	6.7	6.9	4.7	10.3	−0.9
1971–80	3.0	42.7	12.8	5.8	8.9	8.9	10.3	7.3
1981–89	3.9	5.8	1.4	−0.7	14.9	1.0	3.0	1.2
Mexico								
1961–70	3.9	2.4	9.2	8.5	13.8	6.7	6.7	7.2
1971–80	3.4	9.4	7.1	7.0	9.4	6.5	11.4	4.7
1981–89	0.5	2.7	1.4	−1.7	6.3	0.4	1.6	4.0
Peru								
1961–70	4.3	2.9	5.3	3.7	7.9	6.0	7.1	n.a.
1971–80	−0.6	7.4	3.3	4.3	10.0	4.0	6.1	n.a.
1981–89	3.5	−3.1	−1.6	−0.9	2.8	−1.6	0.3	n.a.

SOURCE: IDB, *Economic and Social Progress in Latin America: Working Women* (Washington, D.C.: IDB, 1990).

Intraregional trade has not failed because Latin America has not pursued it over the postwar years, but—apart from the economic weakness of its proponents—because it reflects the same political issues at the regional level as Latin America voices in the global trade system: specialization versus transformation, trade power inequalities, conflicting philosophies of public sector involvement, problems of adjustment, and fears of Great Power imperialism. To Bolivia, the immediate "colossus" is Brazil, not the United States. To Ecuador, historically, Colombia and Peru are equally dangerous trade partners. To Peru, Chile is a nemesis; and so on.

The main success in Latin America has come in the form of commodity diversification and import restriction, neither of which is a very powerful instrument of trade insulation. Commodity diversification has been a successful strategy in Chile in the mid-1980s, as it has been in Brazil over the past two decades. Colombia and Peru have had less success, as have most of the smaller economies of Central America and the Caribbean. The evidence that import restriction has been implemented widely is also less

TABLE 6.4
Coefficients of Exports, Imports, and Total Trade, Latin America, 1970, 1980, and 1988
(Percent of GDP)

	Exports			Imports			Total trade		
	1970	1980	1988	1970	1980	1988	1970	1980	1988
Argentina	9.2	11.2	16.5	9.0	15.0	10.5	18.2	26.2	27.0
Bolivia	20.2	17.0	23.3	20.3	15.4	22.8	40.5	32.4	51.1
Brazil	6.5	5.6	12.9	6.9	6.9	7.2	6.5	12.5	20.1
Chile	12.4	22.8	27.9	20.4	25.8	24.1	12.4	48.6	52.0
Colombia	14.2	15.8	17.8	15.8	17.2	16.6	14.2	32.9	34.5
Costa Rica	34.2	35.6	44.8	39.6	39.2	41.9	34.2	74.8	86.7
Dominican Republic	17.2	18.4	20.0	24.5	29.9	22.9	17.2	48.3	42.9
Ecuador	14.8	20.4	27.4	19.2	32.0	18.1	14.8	52.3	45.5
El Salvador	21.3	23.6	19.5	23.4	25.6	22.6	21.3	49.1	42.1
Guatemala	19.3	21.0	14.1	16.4	14.2	10.6	19.3	35.2	24.6
Guyana	56.5	45.6	53.1	57.0	42.8	51.3	56.5	88.4	109.4
Haiti	12.3	17.7	19.2	14.0	26.1	35.2	12.3	43.7	54.4
Honduras	29.6	30.5	35.9	34.5	44.0	31.7	29.6	74.5	68.6
Jamaica	33.3	31.9	57.2	37.5	37.4	61.1	33.3	69.4	118.3
Mexico	7.7	9.1	17.7	9.7	14.3	9.7	7.7	23.4	27.4
Nicaragua	29.1	41.6	14.1	28.7	63.3	31.7	29.1	104.9	45.8
Panama	36.3	49.2	38.1	44.3	44.9	29.6	36.3	94.4	67.7
Paraguay	13.6	15.4	20.8	15.3	21.0	26.1	13.6	36.4	46.9
Peru	21.6	14.0	17.3	13.8	13.4	15.6	21.6	27.4	32.8
Trinidad and Tobago	38.7	27.4	35.0	47.6	30.5	25.7	38.7	57.9	60.7
Uruguay	14.9	21.6	22.6	16.9	20.9	19.6	14.9	42.5	42.2
Venezuela	26.2	7.7	25.1	18.2	30.5	14.7	26.2	38.3	39.7
All Latin America	12.3%	10.9%	17.8%	12.6%	15.1%	11.9%	12.3%	26.0%	29.7%

SOURCE: IDB, Economic and Social Progress in Latin America: Savings, Investment, and Growth.

clear than expected. Even though the importance of imports to general economic activity declined from 15 percent to 12 percent regionally over the course of the 1980s,[19] Table 6.4 shows that many countries of the region have not been able to suppress imports even with great political effort, sharp disincentives in exchange rates, and internal reductions in overall consumption. It may be that exchange rate policies have reduced the importance of luxury consumer goods in imports (in some limited cases), but that hardly insulates an economy from the international system. Successful insulation on the import side would also imply success in an area most often mentioned as one of the great failures of import-substitution industrialization: the continuing need to import heavy industrial goods and intermediate goods necessary to production.

More important than these empirical indicators of insulation, however, is the mistaken assumption that insulation and autonomy necessarily go together. That assumption seems to derive from the historical role of the public sector in guaranteeing or enhancing insulation values in Latin American society, and from the national security element in economic policy thinking over the period since 1930.

Sovereignty, Economic Security, and the External Sector

The ambitious state manager has always had a taste for acquiring public sector control over commerce as a matter of political power. At times, that power might be turned to enhance national sovereignty in the international system. Alexander Hamilton argued that domestic manufacturing would "tend to render the United States independent of foreign nations for military and other essential supplies."[20] Later, Friedrich List, in his study of industrial policy and its relation to European commerce, stressed the connection between a highly developed industrial system and military power.[21] After World War II, the Eisenhower administration used its trade and finance policies toward Latin America to guarantee future access to strategic materials,[22] a policy that continued through the Carter years with the strategic stockpiles programs.[23] The United States still considers natural resource trade issues to be a matter of national independence, at least rhetorically. And, of course, food security has been a much-publicized goal of many Third World countries in the years since the grain crisis of the early 1970s.

Latin American military governments similarly have stressed self-sufficiency in the production of manufactured goods because of a linkage to the military power of the state (e.g., state promotion of an indigenous steel industry).[24] Brazil is perhaps the most obvious modern case in which national security significance has been attached to the "national patrimony." Such an attachment was not simply the fetish of the "national security state" in 1964–85 but antedated that military government by nearly a century, with the national security ambitions expressed in the first republican constitution. That sentiment was invoked by Getulio Vargas in 1946 in his famous speech on the Amazon[25] and again by senator and former naval engineer Renato Archer in 1954, when he declaimed on the necessity of Brazil's nationalizing the nuclear industry to save uranium resources for the nation.[26] Since the return to civilian government in 1985, the relatively unchallenged national security ideologues in the military have updated that long-standing penchant in resource politics by tightening regulations on scientific expeditions and demarcating huge national security areas that include the entire northern watershed of the Amazon basin and all of the Amazon frontier municipalities. Though Brazil is a particularly vivid example, its history is not qualitatively different from those of Argentina or Mexico.

In trade terms, national security seems to have a single, reasonable goal: to insulate national economic growth from external instability and to guarantee protection of the national patrimony through an ambitious and active public sector. A nationalist might interpret that to mean movement toward a more closed economy, particularly in strategic industries and resources. It would mean more control over national production of previously imported strategic items and tighter management of the export of strategic national resources. Clearly, national policies of nationalizing key export industries—the Mexican petroleum decision of 1938,[27] the Peruvian IPC decision of 1968, and the Chileanization program for copper in the 1960s—all fit loosely together. Brazilian aircraft and computer development programs under military aegis, as well as the national energy program, fall under this rubric. Mexican food security certainly has had a national security aspect, defined by self-reliance in basic grains against the United States.

A national security aspect to trade policy is not the exclusive domain of so-called national security states. The Mexican government has included national security in its trade goals over the years, even though it little resembles the Brazilian national security state. Once again, the first requirement is size. To have a national security strategy with a trade base, there presumably must be some expectation that trade will bring greater national autonomy (or national insulation). As Table 6.4 shows, Latin America as a region is more open (i.e., trades more as a share of overall economic activity) in 1988 than it was in 1970. None of the smaller economies of Latin America has shown a secular reduction in its openness since 1970. And none of the economies outside war-torn Central America has reduced the share of exports in GDP.

If overall trade (imports plus exports) is calculated, the findings are even more contrary to expectations. The argument suggested by the law of declining trade is that the larger economies, notably Brazil, would have lowered the share of foreign trade in national production significantly over time.[28] The overall political goals of Brazilian or Mexican industrial development and trade plans over the past three decades certainly pushed toward those goals. The trade pessimists' alternative of import substitution centered on reducing dependence on trade. The principal focus of "deepening" the industrialization experience after the purported exhaustion of the easy phase of import-substitution industrialization was to insulate the economy from disappointingly expensive and persistent intermediate and capital goods imports. From sugar to nuclear power, the grandiose energy plans of the Brazilian generals were nationalist inventions of the national security state. Through the entire postwar period, the veer inward among the industrialized nations of Latin America clearly has reflected the national strategy of the larger Latin American economies to avoid the unreliable fluctuations of the external sector.

So much more striking, then, is the finding that none of the larger countries was able to insulate itself effectively from the international market, at least measured by indicators of openness or overall measures of the importance of the external sector to national economic activity. The modest gains achieved in a few countries occurred surprisingly in the smaller economies as well, especially in Central America. Given the extraordinary measures taken by the high-debt countries to reduce imports, it must be conceded that even these minor achievements are overstated. Under free market conditions, higher levels of trade overall would be expected.

There are two flaws in the connection between economic insulation and national security/national autonomy of economic decision-making. First, it is wrong to argue that Latin America has the capacity to insulate economic activity by controlling trade, and second, it is not necessarily true that the benefits of economic nationalism accrue to the nation. Let us examine these briefly one at a time.

The connection between economic insulation through trade and national autonomy depends on the presumption that national actors can positively affect the accumulation of capital and create nationally self-contained systems of production, exchange, distribution, and consumption. It is the argument of early twentieth-century economic nationalism, which, for a variety of reasons already treated, opted for modernization via creation of national industries of transformation. In the post–World War II period, however, the trend toward the standardization of productive processes and the globalization of productive capital[29] superseded this "closed system" model of Latin American political economy in favor of a transnational model of growth, depending on international flows of financial and productive capital, free transfer of technology, production of goods and services that conform to international standards, and a relatively complete standardization of techniques of production. The world car (or computer, or small aircraft, or pharmochemical) makes obsolete the pretensions of national states to productive autonomy. The success of Brazilian industrial strategy demands higher levels of national self-sufficiency in key areas, but the economic viability of those industries depends on their openness to new technologies that enhance comparative advantage, both domestically and internationally. The success of Brazilian or Mexican steel resides in part on the modernness of their—imported—production techniques. The export value of Argentine or Brazilian soya depends on internationally exchanged agricultural technologies, as well as the production policies of the OECD countries. And the international viability of Chilean wine, Mexican beer, Brazilian citrus, or any number of other exports depends less on their identifiable national origin than their ability to appeal to international standards of quality, which are dictated primarily by the wealthy consumer countries of the North. Any disheartened champion of Mexican beer, for example, can attest to its "acculturation" to the export market.

One might argue that insulation is the most highly prized political value and that competitiveness, international acceptability, and technological modernity are lesser qualities. This is a sort of distorted version of the logic of "appropriate technology" in a nationalist context. In India and China, as well as Cuba, this argument has become an economic way of life in some sectors. So the modernization of spinning mills or agricultural practices is forsworn in favor of nationally appropriate technologies that spin necessity into virtue.

On some ecological grounds, some of these technologies are more appropriate, especially compared with the wasteful practices of Western industry, and in the absence of foreign technologies and capital, they exploit abundant factors of production more readily. But they do not treat the question of the external sector adequately (India is hardly a model of Third World trade policy) and are certainly against the grain politically and historically in Latin America. The logic is one of delinking the nation from the international system altogether, or of accepting a productive role reminiscent of the nineteenth-century international division of labor. The choice of the 1990s seems to be integration or obsolescence, in the context of the globalization of trade and production.

Short of radical delinking, control of trade does not offer autonomy of economic decision-making because it merely establishes limited qualitative or quantitative boundaries on imports or exports. As the data show convincingly, even those limits are extremely circumscribed by the import-connectedness of production, the political complications of trade restrictions, and the technological demands of modern production. The inescapable conclusion is that the creation of national systems of industrial or agricultural production does not provide insulation from international influences.

The ultimate disappointment for nationalists stems not from the interconnectedness of trade and production, however. It is the mistaken idea that greater national autonomy would accrue from greater trade insulation. That is, even if greater national insulation from the international trade system were possible as a political choice, it is not clear that the nation benefits, as Brazilian informatics policy shows. Because that policy was not accompanied by aggressive fiscal controls or a progressive policy of national development with public controls, the benefits of nationalism accrued to the grand purveyors of computer technology in the private sector, not to the public sector. As many have remarked in their analyses of economic nationalism in Latin America, the benefits accruing to Latin American nationals from traditional nationalism are far more modest and concentrated than was the hope of progressive populism.

Using Trade for Political Power

Aside from turning national economic growth toward greater internal insulation from the external sector, E. H. Carr and Hirschman, among others, suggest that economic power is pressed into the service of national politics through national influence over others.[30] Through the export of capital and the control of foreign markets, powerful countries strengthen their ability to influence events outside their national boundaries. Formal empire is not required. This is the essence of "business imperialism," discussed in Chapter 1. This approach has been of limited use to weak Latin American nations, perhaps extending only to the momentary euphoria over OPEC price policy in the 1970s, which spawned ambitious but unsuccessful cartels from bananas and bauxite to copper. The United States traditionally has cited the potential control of foreign markets in strategic minerals as one of its chief national security concerns in Latin America, but those worries generally do not withstand careful examination.[31] Power politics based on resources may encourage populism, but rarely with good results, as Jamaican Prime Minister Michael Manley found in the case of bauxite in the 1970s.

This does not mean that Latin America does not consider economic power as a source of political power. But economic power in the region has been viewed most often as a means of resisting external influence rather

than influencing others, a characteristic of weaker nations. On the "positive policy" side, such logic also extends obviously to the food security
policies of Mexico,[32] the notorious "market reserve" policy of Brazil in
informatics, and the "Chileanization" of the "commanding heights" of
that country's economy during the period 1964–73.[33] In a more defensive
mode, and more obviously reactive to the international system, were the
strategic moves away from copper in Chile since 1982 and the drastic
Bolivian response to the collapse of tin prices after 1985.[34]

Carr paid less attention than Hirschman to the purchasing power of advanced industrial societies as a mechanism of control via import policy, although he acknowledged it as a potential "international asset."[35] Hirschman argued that industrial nations have considerable leverage to shape the
trading system to their own advantage, which he called "power policy."
The dependence of underdeveloped economies on a few markets for their
exports (e.g., sending raw materials to specific industrial societies) has
become an important advantage for industrial nations in implementing
their "purchasing power" to influence events in the Third World. Therefore, weak countries are susceptible not only to commodity concentration
but also to geographic concentration. As a result, in the process of increasing a nation's economic power through industrialization, state managers
also have to worry about diversifying their markets to avoid falling under
the influence of a powerful buyer.

It goes without saying that the primary-commodity-dependent exporters of Latin America have little mobility in these matters, except during
times when international demand is high, and then only with serious
limiting stipulations. But as the presentation of coefficients of concentration showed, certain Latin American countries have managed to diversify
at certain periods in recent history, only to be brought back to focus on
the United States as their principal partner. In this regard, the African-
Caribbean-Pacific countries of Lomé, because of their preferential access
to the EEC, and the countries of the Southern Cone, because of their
tradition of trade with Europe, are more diverse in their trade partners.
Porfirio Díaz's lament that Mexico was too far from God and too close to
the United States is more than a refrain.

A common power policy threat is for a nation to close its market as a
way of increasing its bargaining power in particular issues. The United
States, for instance, in 1987 successfully changed Brazil's policy of not
allowing U.S. software to enter the Brazilian market by threatening to
close its own market to specific Brazilian products. In 1989, with the same
issues on the agenda, the Bush administration cited Brazil, along with
Japan and India, as unfair traders to be subjected to unilateral retaliation.
In less spectacular but perhaps more effective fashion, the United States

has used its countervailing duty and other trade policies to close or limit exports from Latin American countries it considers to be trading unfairly.

Characterizing Latin American Trade and Development Strategies

Export-Led Growth as an Element of Strategy

The large economies of Latin America have tried to promote exports of manufactures so as to change their roles in the international division of labor. Industrialization plays an equally important role in trade and development, in view of the quest to use industry to insulate Latin American economies from the dependence of the old international division of labor, in which the southern countries were the "hewers of wood and the drawers of water" for the developed capitalist world. Beyond the symbolic role of industrialization in diversifying their countries' development and export base, early Latin American industrializers have fared generally better in export performance, returned value of exports to the domestic economy, and generation of employment. Moreover, industrialization enabled Latin America to turn inward in the Depression, first escaping "the tyranny of the external" at the moment of its collapse. Import-substitution industrialization succeeded in shifting employment away from agriculture and speeding the modernization and urbanization of Latin American life before it foundered on the problems of payments imbalances, domestic inflation, and industrial deepening.[36]

The importance of an export-led development strategy as opposed to import-substitution industrialization in recent years in Latin America has been a mixed blessing. Two of the largest players in the export promotion strategy, Brazil and Mexico, undertook export promotion as a coherent strategy after the oil shocks of the 1970s, for very different reasons. Brazil was rightly concerned with reacting to its overwhelming import requirement for energy, and the foreign exchange necessary to pay for it. Mexico has promoted exports, albeit with mixed success, since its first attempts to *sembrar el petróleo* (sow the oil), instead of relying on petroleum exports alone. In both cases, Brazil and Mexico turned outward as a way of easing their balance-of-payments burdens as well as developing the industrial bases of their national economies. The success of Mexican *maquiladoras* in the wake of the debt crisis is almost an embarrassment to the Mexican government because it is an indirect confession of the weakness of domestic business compared with the twin-plant in-bond border industries.[37]

Oil exports after 1977 allowed Mexico to relax its import policy some-

TABLE 6.5
Latin American Trade Balances, 1980–89
(Millions of dollars)

Country	1980	1981	1982	1983	1984	1985	1986	1987	1988	1989
Argentina	−1,378	755	2,742	3,711	3,940	4,897	2,460	975	4,254	5,765
Bolivia	368	85	332	259	312	161	−51	−128	−50	202
Brazil	1,242	789	6,486	13,114	13,114	12,411	8,396	11,106	19,184	16,111
Chile	−764	−2,677	63	987	363	851	1,099	1,230	2,219	1,578
Colombia	−297	−1,572	−2,245	−1,495	246	−23	1,922	1,869	648	1,301
Costa Rica	−373	−87	63	−42	4	−60	40	−137	−71	−272
Dominican Republic	−558	−264	−490	−494	−389	−548	−630	−880	−715	−1,026
Ecuador	278	174	140	927	1,055	1,294	555	−33	589	669
El Salvador	178	−100	−100	−74	−189	−216	−124	−334	−368	−49
Guatemala	47	−262	−117	34	−52	−12	173	−351	−340	−357
Honduras	−104	−115	−14	−58	−148	−90	17	−50	−24	3
Mexico	−3,388	−3,905	6,941	13,764	12,897	8,450	4,577	8,450	1,703	−645
Nicaragua	−353	−414	−317	−349	−414	−499	−479	−533	−483	−341
Panama	−816	−974	−1,008	−928	−905	−925	−768	−798	−432	−612
Paraguay	−275	−374	−315	−225	−288	−192	−162	−97	−208	−74
Peru	823	−555	−427	295	1,008	1,169	−53	−517	−56	1,517
Uruguay	−610	−362	218	417	192	178	273	102	292	463
Venezuela	8,174	7,840	2,748	8,162	8,580	7,131	1,260	1,735	−1,347	4,549
All Latin America	−2,122	−2,377	7,248	29,566	38,408	33,122	17,323	20,289	23,481	26,769

SOURCE: IDB, *Economic and Social Progress in Latin America: Working Women* (Washington, D.C.: IDB, 1990).

what, after the stifling stabilization of the first year of López Portillo's government. Energized by the new oil finds, the Mexican government dramatically increased foreign borrowing for development purposes. López Portillo apparently viewed oil as the "wonder drug for Mexico's ills," whose exports should be used as "a lever for economic and social development by channeling the funds deriving from this source into development policy priorities."[38] The articles on this subject seem endless and are now mainly interesting as period pieces.

The debt crisis in the 1980s, however, further increased both Mexico's and Brazil's need to export. Coupled with sharp cuts in imports and an aggressive export promotion policy by the state, the two countries experienced impressive trade surpluses, as Table 6.5 indicates. Other countries were unable to produce such remarkable surpluses, for various reasons. Bolivia has been unable to cut imports; Peru has been unable either to increase exports or to cut imports; Argentina has been able to cut imports but has had little success increasing exports. Predictably, Chile is the only country other than Brazil and Mexico able to increase exports substantially while cutting imports sharply. As Table 6.2 showed, except in the large industrial powers of Latin America, exports of manufactures have not performed in keeping with their importance to the economy in general.

All of the principal trading economies of the region have sought to increase exports, but the reasons and mechanisms are as diverse as the countries themselves. Chile led the ideological fight for liberal internationalism, in great part to form a national coalition among capitalist supporters of the Pinochet government and to eliminate the public sector, which the government considered a haven for socialist engineering. Argentina, Mexico, and Brazil sought new exports as a way to offset the import costs of industrialization and to diversify their exports. All three saw manufactured exports as a major test of their ambitions as newly industrializing countries in a new international division of labor.

In the 1990s, it would appear that the large economies have the best opportunity to promote a new phase of export-oriented industrialization, but much of the potential success for exports of manufactures rides on direct foreign investment by transnational corporations and the establishment of transnational economic linkages.[39] It has also been contended that Latin American countries that depend on foreign investment and transnational linkages suffer a trade deficit in those activities, so the net trade impact of exports of manufactures depends to some extent on intrafirm trade and the like.[40] Whatever the case, it is a mistaken notion to assume that an East Asian model applies to Latin American manufactured exports.[41]

The Primary Commodity Trap

For all but the select, large, early-industrializing countries of Latin America, trade focuses on primary commodities, especially agricultural products. The relationship between increased trade and domestic development for those producers is highly individual and complicated. We have seen some of those complications in discussing the International Coffee Agreement, and all of them are applicable to tin or other commodities. In agricultural trade, the impact on Latin America of total trade liberalization in grain, livestock, and sugar in the industrial market economies in 1985 was estimated to be a loss of U.S.$4 per capita. Nevertheless, Argentina realized a gain of $12 per capita, the lion's share of which went to producers. Consumers in all countries suffered, even though foreign exchange earnings increased. Trade liberalization in the developing economies shows similar results in the aggregate, but the Mexican consumer comes out as the beneficiary, largely at the expense of the Mexican producer. Total liberalization of all markets means overall losses to Latin American consumers, some gains for producers in the large exporting countries, and wide variation by country.[42]

Arthur Lewis argued that the agricultural option is really two options: to export or to produce for domestic consumption. Bulmer-Thomas, among others, has shown that export agriculture is intimately connected to domestic use agriculture in ways that complicate Lewis's earlier assertion. Lewis also contended that the way to improve the factoral terms of trade is to modernize agriculture, which will increase the price of export crops.[43] But agricultural modernization in Latin America has produced extremely negative social consequences by skewing credit, natural resources, inputs, technical assistance, and land assets in favor of an export and agroindustrial elite. Because much of poor Latin America is still rural, agricultural modernization (sometimes called agricultural development) has contravened redistributive policy. As the resource implications of agricultural growth become clearer, the costs of using agriculture to lead development rise.

Nevertheless, as a recent study pointed out, both export promotion and import substitution under the duress of debt favor sectors that are large and can absorb incentives. Agriculture invariably figures among the leading sectors in which trade is expected to solve external payments problems.[44] Traditional literature on agricultural trade argues that export agriculture and domestic use agriculture compete with each other; often they are treated practically as separate sectors of activity.[45]

In any event, three primary values of national strategy in agriculture include (1) achieving a proper mix between self-sufficiency and export, or between domestic use agriculture and export agriculture; (2) strengthening the association between agricultural property and incomes policy, or land assets with rural poverty;[46] and (3) achieving the first two values without sacrificing resource sustainability over the long term. From the standpoint of agriculture, the primary commodity trap is that none of these criteria is satisfied by the expansion of agricultural trade. The tension between producers' and consumers' interests is clear, with perhaps only Mexico as a case in which producers' interests also represent a significant part of progressive incomes policies. And agricultural trade, because of the role of the large developed countries in consumption and pricing policies in key commodities (basic grains, coffee, cocoa, and most industrial minerals), is less controllable at home than manufactures.

More than ever, the imperative in agriculture is to trade, as the international system swings slowly toward agricultural trade liberalization. The large industrial exporters will find that this will prejudice their overall wage policies by attenuating cheap food policies to industrial workers. The welfare of consumers in Latin America becomes a function of international agricultural trade negotiations. And as Dale Hathaway correctly observes, "in most trade negotiations, consumer interests are not the overwhelming issue that drives national negotiations."[47]

The Atrophy of the Public Sector in Trade

The growing importance of trade in the economy after World War II enhanced the state's role in a variety of ways. In Brazil, market reserve legislation, import licenses, and broad intervention through subsidies in new industries marked the Brazilian government as the most *dirigiste* of the development-minded governments of Latin America. Even among the state-led development experiences of Latin America, however, the recipes for increasing trade output and domestic development without sacrificing too much national economic autonomy were remarkably similar.

The discussion of industrial and trade policies in Latin America suggests the differing strategies the countries have taken in the process of seeking autonomy and the implications of these choices over time. Clearly, state participation in the market is a key variable. State participation in the economy can also be an important (although not necessary) component of an industrial policy. State intervention can guide imports, in both kind and volume. Parastate enterprises can lead national development policy and overall domestic investment.

Unfortunately, there is no satisfactory data base to examine the role of the state in Latin American economies. Parastate enterprises are often "off-budget," decentralized units, for which aggregate time-series data are

TABLE 6.6

Value Added by Government, Latin America, 1980–89
(Millions of 1988 dollars)

	1980	1981	1982	1983	1984	1985	1986	1987	1988	1989	Ave. annual growth rates (percent)		
											1961–70	1971–80	1981–89
Barbados	188	192	186	187	188	197	206	214	216	219	8.5%	1.7%	1.7%
Bolivia	270	275	286	309	316	326	305	316	313	317	7.5	7.0	1.8
Brazil	19,672	20,103	20,557	21,010	21,489	21,697	22,421	22,874	23,353	23,836	n.a.	n.a.	2.2
Chile	1,135	1,114	1,082	1,105	1,092	1,099	1,087	1,082	1,132	1,226	2.5	1.9	.9
Colombia	2,372	2,510	2,570	2,519	2,744	2,861	3,037	3,252	3,495	3,652	4.9	6.8	4.9
Costa Rica	562	572	555	546	555	557	568	583	597	612	6.9	5.8	1.0
Dominican Republic	364	389	405	416	429	433	431	408	440	454	6.3	6.3	2.5
Ecuador	773	790	803	818	834	835	841	846	852	762	9.8	8.6	-.2
El Salvador	351	356	366	377	395	423	442	460	476	489	5.0	6.5	3.7
Guatemala	394	411	427	447	456	464	482	508	526	543	3.2	6.5	3.6
Guyana	80	80	73	72	72	72	72	72	71	71	6.0	6.1	-1.3
Haiti	65	73	62	70	82	85	88	88	87	86	2.2	-.6	3.2
Honduras	172	191	177	171	184	198	208	229	236	240	2.9	15.2	3.8
Jamaica	296	303	310	312	298	281	271	273	282	272	2.1	6.9	-.9
Mexico	3,080	3,222	3,441	3,607	3,820	3,752	3,726	3,697	3,692	3,655	8.9	8.3	1.9
Nicaragua	76	80	84	96	102	104	106	105	105	98	4.2	5.9	2.8
Panama	618	685	713	739	763	795	815	837	811	801	7.5	5.5	2.9
Paraguay	153	188	195	191	196	202	206	212	213	242	7.9	4.3	5.2
Peru	1,826	1,876	1,891	2,018	2,171	2,182	2,366	2,479	2,323	1,893	9.4	4.9	.4
Suriname	166	203	219	236	237	243	258	273	287	301	4.9	5.2	6.9
Trinidad and Tobago	659	736	705	704	746	737	743	754	724	715	4.9	4.9	.9
Venezuela	4,450	4,487	4,490	4,408	4,360	4,336	4,512	4,623	4,837	5,060	4.1	7.5	1.4
All Latin America	37,721	38,833	39,597	40,357	41,527	41,148	43,190	44,184	45,069	45,542	5.8%	6.4%[a]	2.1%

SOURCE: Same as Table 6.5.
NOTE: Figures on Argentina, the Bahamas, and Uruguay are not available. Figures for Guyana include electricity, gas, and water.
[a] Average calculated on the period 1971–79.

not available publicly. Even defining the public or private character of the firm is difficult, as studies of the subject have shown.[48] Much of the work on public enterprises in Latin America is descriptive and data-poor.[49] And the leading comparative study, conducted under the IMF's aegis, despairs of producing time-series data.[50] Data that do exist on public investment are miserably inadequate and in no sense comparable. Even in large countries such as Colombia, separate data are not kept on investment in public enterprises before 1980. Elsewhere, confusion exists between budgeted and nonbudgeted public enterprises and therefore the budgetary burden of the sector as a whole. Some countries have significant public enterprises at the local level, which are not included in aggregate data.

There are some rough indicators of the role of the public sector in trade and development, particularly on the trade side. Public budget, international taxation, and public investment as a proportion of GDP are flawed but available surrogates for measuring the degree of government activity in the economy. Table 6.6 shows the levels of one such indicator in Latin America over the past decade, though this does not equal state presence in any satisfying way.

The role of the state in promoting industrialization has long been a part of the development literature dealing with late industrializers. The move toward industrialization takes place amid the growing participation of "state managers" in establishing an economic development strategy. Weaknesses of the domestic class structure (particularly of an infant industrialist bourgeoisie) further give rise to what mistakenly has been characterized as "state capitalism."[51] Here I will refer more simply to the question of a proper role for the public sector.

For Latin American countries, a central question is how much of trade can be managed by government to good effect. That question, in turn, revolves around the role of trade in economic development, the predisposition of the private sector to regulate itself, and the legitimacy of domestic demands for protection. All of these considerations are sketched against a historical background of Latin American state intervention in traded goods. In Brazil, for example, at the turn of the twentieth century coffee trade was conducted under a valorization scheme that continued to evolve into a complex subsidy. Even in rubber, a proposal was forwarded in the Brazilian Chamber of Deputies in 1906 to create a government monopoly to control rubber exports.[52] Capitalists in both cases greeted public sector intervention with glee. More modern examples include the Mexican oil monopoly PEMEX, a broad range of Latin American grain marketing boards, and majority-owned firms in the "commanding heights" of the economy: transportation, communication, and other "natural monopolies."

The U.S. predisposition to "destatize" trade in favor of the market has found favor at the World Bank and other international institutions as part of a more general privatization campaign to reduce public sector deficits, enhance economic efficiencies by reducing market distortions, and increase investor confidence in Third World economies. Even though the profitability of public sector firms is difficult to calculate, it has been argued in general that the public sector is economically inefficient and that dismantling its enterprises will enhance overall economic welfare. The United States, the IMF, the World Bank, and business specialists in general assume that a link exists between public sector management and inefficiency, and between public involvement and market-distorting regulation.[53] Unfortunately, public entities in both the United States and Latin America have provided ample evidence of such inefficiencies.[54]

The debt-induced wave of IMF-supervised stabilization agreements in Latin America during the early 1980s encouraged or forced many Latin American countries to rethink the role of the state in trade and development. Ironically, the same dynamic resulted in endorsements of public sector intervention in the economy by erstwhile critics of the state. With an IMF agreement (Mexico) or without (Brazil), governments are required by the size and persistence of public sector deficits to address the question of state enterprises, their effect on trade, the extent of general government regulation of trade, and the like.

Managing investment is an even broader trade-related question in Latin America, thanks to doleful experiences with uncontrolled multinational corporations throughout the region in the 1950s and 1960s.[55] Typically, stronger economies and more sophisticated governments exercise more management leverage. Brazil legislated a broad market reserve for informatics in 1984, and Mexico a new pharmaceutical law, both of which resulted in tensions over investment and patent protection and threats of retaliation by the United States. The Brazilian law ratified and extended a market reserve for microcomputers that has been in effect since 1981, with the explicit intention of "Brazilianizing" the microcomputer industry. The Mexican pharmaceutical decree had a similar intention but a greater public sector component, given the high state demand for pharmaceuticals for distribution in the social security program.[56] By mid-1985, Mexico had succumbed to U.S. pressure to soften the decree, acceding to virtually all of the demands of U.S.-based transnationals. It appears now that Brazil is softening its stand on informatics, with an eye toward eliminating the market reserve under the new Collor government.[57]

What is for the United States a straightforward question of efficiencies is for Latin America a more complex development question. The United States views managed trade and investment as an obstacle to structural adjustment, for example, which in the context of U.S.–Latin American trade means unrestricted access to domestic markets of Latin American countries. The argument assumes the virtue of international resource allocation according to comparative advantage and resource efficiencies.[58]

Latin American countries are unwilling to resume the free trade dependency that is associated historically with the pre-Depression international division of labor. They are also loath to disassemble state enterprises that spurred their growth under import substitution, especially after disastrous attempts to do so in authoritarian Chile and Argentina. The role of the public sector in employment and income generation combines with the government's vulnerability in the current economic crisis to make a serious blow against public enterprises and state management of investment politically dangerous. And the payoffs from loosening the public sector's grip on trade and investment are unclear. Certainly, there is no direct relationship between destatization and economic recovery in the short term. And evidence that the market is an *equitable* allocator of goods and services is hard to come by. In Mexico, "market forces" favored by government over thirty years have decapitalized the country through capital flight.[59] In Brazil, the national campaigns to control inflation in 1986 and again in 1990 were met by rampant hoarding and gouging by entrepreneurs at all levels.

To reduce the argument for the sake of clarity, no country has a clear monopoly on virtue regarding the role of the public sector in trade-related activities. The United States tends to value the market excessively and is inattentive to the "social calculus" that is the putative source of Latin American *dirigiste* trade regimes, whereas Latin America is generally lax in asking who are the beneficiaries of such trade regimes and inattentive to the continual need to reexamine the social benefits of statist restrictions. The question on both sides boils down to who benefits from protection and who is asked to pay the economic and social costs. Often, the negative social aspects of trade promotion (e.g., commercial fishing eliminating artisan fishermen and displacing local fish consumption) are ignored by both Latin American and U.S. policies.

If we choose value added by government as a surrogate indicator of state activity in the economy, Table 6.6 shows the involvement of the public sector for Latin American countries for comparative purposes. Mexico, Peru, and Brazil show themselves to be "active" states, and with the exception of Chile, Latin America shows high levels of growth in the public sector during the 1970s. Appropriately, the region showed a uniformly reduced rate of growth of the state in the 1980s.

If we plot the growth of this proxy of public sector involvement against openness over time (Figure 6.1), there is a general slowdown in public

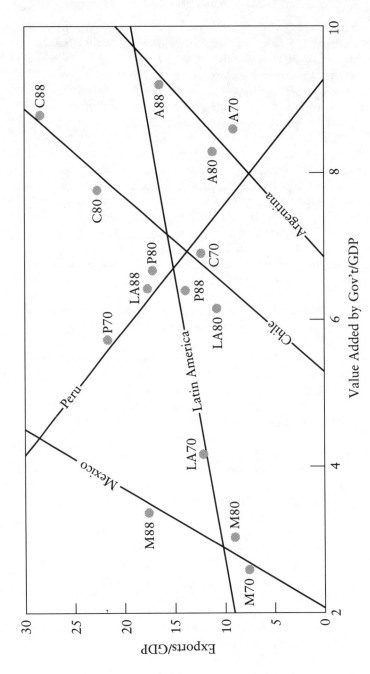

Figure 6.1. Change in Openness and Public Sector Activity, Selected Countries of Latin America, 1970, 1980, and 1988. Countries are Argentina (A), Chile (C), Mexico (M), and Peru (P). Latin America as a whole is shown as LA. Source: International Development Bank, *Economic and Social Progress in Latin America: Savings, Investment, and Growth.* Based on 1988 dollars.

involvement and a sharp shift upward toward an outward orientation of the economy. Although the typology of development strategies suggested in Chapter 4 still holds in general (with Mexico occupying the imaginary Cell I, Peru Cell II, the United States clearly Cell III, and Chile IV), one also notices an increase in the importance of exports in the strategies of all Latin American countries, as shown by the regional curve in Figure 6.1. Chile, which occupied Cell III in the early 1970s, has moved dramatically to Cell IV. Peru, which occupied Cell II during most of the "reformist" period, moved down to Cell IV as part of the new free market capitalist policies (though its export performance has been poor, resulting in a sharply downward sloped curve in Figure 6.1). Brazil's and Argentina's state participation is moderate when compared to the Mexican case— standing in the borderline between Cells I and III. Brazil is particularly difficult to plot because of national accounts data reporting problems. The current episodes of Mexican destatization stand out more clearly as radical public policy in this context.

The general patterns for all countries, with the exception of the United States, is a significant shift indicating a growing outward orientation of the economy, and the impact both the oil and the debt crises have had in further tying the local economy to the international market. The only factor identifying differences in strategies at this aggregate level has been the degree of public sector involvement, in a range between Mexico and Chile since 1973.[60]

The significance of this shift in productive orientation in Figure 6.1 lies in the pattern of external dependence that the economic crisis has created for many Latin American countries. This returns us to U.S. hegemony in the 1980s. Faced with the need to export, Latin America falls into Hirschman's "purchasing power" trap. The Latin American economic crisis came at a time of growing U.S. prosperity and historically low domestic savings, which resulted in growing U.S. import capacity. Latin American countries were thereby more vulnerable to U.S. bargaining power.

Such a shift is crucial in understanding the structure of economic domination in international politics today. The growing prominence of trade, even in traditionally inward-oriented economies such as Brazil and Mexico, points us away from the law of declining trade explanation (or perhaps to the later phase of the curve, where a decline in trade as a share in GDP is reversed as the economy becomes more competitive internationally) and toward a more critical look at the role of international dynamics shaping domestic events. Hirschman's geographic trade concentration index is particularly helpful in assessing the Latin American experience during the last three decades. In the late 1960s and early 1970s, as many Latin American countries reaped the benefits of industrialization and trade diversification, geographic trade concentration tended to decline. As markets closed for their exports in the late 1970s, trade reconcentrated. As a result, the United States emerged again as a powerful partner in desperate times. Although continuing U.S. openness offered a safety valve to Latin American exporters, the prospect that such openness was contingent upon certain kinds of "appropriate behavior" became a powerful political threat. As the 1980s progressed, that threat rose in importance as a direct function of the U.S. trade deficit.

Although prosperity in the United States has meant greater imports from Latin America, the region's growing dependence on the U.S. market also challenges the general notion that U.S. hegemony is on the decline.[61] Although such a decline may be occurring at the global level, the evidence for such an argument is absent from U.S. relations with Latin America. In addition to the military arguments usually made in support of continuing U.S. hegemony in the region, a simple U.S. threat of retaliation against "unfair" trade practices by a Latin American country is often enough to make a significant impact on the exporter's domestic policy process. Such a power capability has often been exploited to assure U.S. business opportunities in those countries, regardless of their position vis-à-vis foreign investors.[62]

The argument of U.S. hegemonic decline may be most evident in the defensive quality of U.S. power policy in hemispheric trade. The United States hardly uses its trade power advantages to good effect in Latin America, and Congress finds itself in a neoprotectionist mood, parried repeatedly by a chief executive committed to free trade ideology. Insofar as U.S. policy is linked to some kind of development strategy for Latin American nations, it is disconnected from the bilateral realities of U.S.–Latin American trade and confused by a multilateralism that holds little promise for Latin American traders.

The development strategies Latin American nations have adopted since the end of World War II have made significant changes in the sophistication of their local economies. Although small economies such as Chile and Peru still continue to depend on exports of primary products for their survival, there is no doubt that larger economies such as Mexico, Brazil, and Argentina have experienced a drastic restructuring of capital toward the manufacturing sector. The rise of these latter countries as newly industrializing states also points toward the increasing difficulty of studying Latin America as a homogeneous region.

Viewing the development experiences of these countries suggests four possibilities. The linkage between industrial policy (illustrated by the pervasiveness of state-led capitalism) and trade policy (the participation of peripheral nations in the world economy) suggests the importance of international politics in shaping domestic processes. After all, industrialization programs have often come as a response to international economic dependence. The state may take the lead in promoting industrialization, but the past orientation of the economy (outward or inward) also helps shape the pattern of development a country undergoes. Small economies dependent on the exports of a few primary products are particularly vulnerable to international politics. Large economies, however, often have the advantage of concentrating on import substitution by closing themselves and turning inward in their industrialization strategy. This policy choice, nevertheless, does not relieve the country from international pressure, particularly from countries such as the United States that are interested in investing in the local economy or further protecting previous investments.

This latter point leads to another observation about the nature of international relations in the 1980s. Although many have argued about U.S. hegemonic decline, Latin America would be the first to dispute this common wisdom. Development has meant greater independence from basic imports, but the Latin American countries' heightened need to penetrate the U.S. market has given the United States greater bargaining power to manipulate the domestic policy debate about industrialization. Further, the need to export has made Latin America even more cognizant of its competitiveness in the international market. As the state becomes less and less able to supply the resources needed for research and development, the economy turns to international capital as a way of ensuring technological transfer. The growing dependence on foreign technology and the irrelevance of much indigenous technology result in an additional source of foreign bargaining power. As the economy turns outward, the old criticisms of Latin American internationalism surface, as integration becomes equated with the deficiencies of past Latin American development.

Conclusion

THE RIGORS OF inter-American diplomacy test the human spirit. Nearly six decades ago in Montevideo, the Uruguayan chief of protocol, while laying place cards for a dinner in celebration of the 1933 Inter-American Conference, fell ill from anxiety and swooned.[1] One could easily imagine more casualties of vertigo, syncope, and apnea among participants in current negotiations on tropical products trade, the future of the GATT, and the resolution of bilateral trade conflicts in U.S.–Latin American relations.

Under better conditions, Latin America would be the prime growth area for U.S. exports in the 1990s, especially with the difficulties of penetrating the EEC and the fragility of intraregional trade in Latin America itself. To the extent that investment by multinational corporations is integrated with trade—and it is in Latin America—a positive Latin American investment climate means greater U.S. trade for the region. That may be the clearest message emanating from the U.S.-Mexican bilateral talks. And, more clearly, intraregional trade, which depends on righting the external imbalances of Latin American nations, benefits the economic growth and reduces the external vulnerability of the region.[2]

It is also true that the United States is absolutely essential for Latin American prosperity, though it is as much a problem as an asset. Growing U.S. agricultural exports to Mexico hurt rural producers, though they benefit urban consumers. Slow U.S. growth hurts Mexican exports and further lowers the price of oil, which represented three-quarters of total export value in 1984, two-thirds in 1985, and even after six years of declining prices and public policies to diminish its importance was still Mexico's largest merchandise export in 1988.[3] In Colombia, half of export value is in coffee, dependent on the U.S. market and sensitive to U.S. growth. Even Brazil, a closed economy with only one-fifth to one-fourth of its trade with the United States, depends on a high trade surplus with the United States and the future conciliatory attitude of U.S. policymakers.

In Latin America today, trade for growth is necessary; trade growth leading to development is unlikely; the United States as a long-term partner by default for Latin American adjustment is as necessary as U.S. tolerance for high regional trade deficits is improbable. The great contradiction in Latin American trade politics today is that the United States is perceived both as the enemy of Latin America autonomy and the most likely partner for future Latin American trade growth. As Europe 1992 becomes a reality and the irony of Spain and Portugal's accession to the Common Market sinks in, OECD openness depends on U.S. trade policy. And the signals from Washington become ever more important for Latin America.

The unfortunate venue for this complicated situation has been the GATT, with the disputatious Uruguay Round setting the multilateral agenda for the near future. Despite attention to Third World issues such as agricultural trade, the Uruguay Round has been another OECD tea party, insofar as the issue areas most attended are set in terms of OECD interests. Nothing that has appeared in the Uruguay Round could be considered a concession to a new North-South dialogue. Among the leaders of the GATT, the United States is little interested in a new North-South agenda. The EEC is already burdened and divided over its Third World preferences system, concentrated in the Lomé agreements. The EEC Stabex fund for countries suffering from commodity price drops has been shaken by repeated declines in commodity prices in Lomé countries. And Japan is neither a traditional nor a likely prospect for shifting the trade costs of Latin American adjustment.

The failure of the GATT to end successfully in 1990 presages more pressure among U.S. free traders for expanded regional initiatives, which fits smoothly with the Bush administration's Latin American pronouncements and the ideological predisposition of many Latin American presidents. But the pressure generated by the GATT failure is unlikely to create a positive environment for U.S.–Latin American trade, especially as the United States labors under its first recession in a decade.

It appears that the United States is unaware (perhaps blinded by its own fiscal problems) that a bilateral or regional approach to the "new multilateralism" necessarily implies Great Powers' substituting more development assistance for free markets in commodities. Otherwise, any claim the United States might make about fostering a development agenda will surely be revealed as empty bluster. But at a time when the United States should be supporting commodity prices in the South, it has no intention of doing so. As a Washington insider bluntly put it in reference to commodity agreements, "commodity pacts are an endangered species . . . [and] it doesn't look like there will be any new agreements springing up."[4] Nearly two centuries after Latin America first fell into the free trade embrace, the language of dominance sounds the same.

All of this is compounded by the intractability of the U.S. trade deficit, congressional elections, and the eventual debate over whatever GATT agreements emerge after 1990. The political outcome is always difficult to predict in the United States, but the stage is practically set for a new rise in protectionist sentiment. Presidential elections in Argentina, Brazil, Chile, Mexico, and Peru further contribute to the political uncertainty.

On the Latin American side, it seems likely that import constraints will sharpen, to the point of affecting domestic growth. This will export responsibility for new domestic austerity programs and add fuel to new populism in the region,[5] reducing the prospect for progressive trade initiatives and new thinking on the relationship of trade to development. Small open economies do not enjoy even these limited degrees of freedom, instead having to slump along slowly, vulnerable to U.S. growth rates. Lost in this rather depressing scenario are the purposes of trade as a stimulus for development, not to mention the once engaging (if incomplete) polemic about the difference between growth and development. Likewise, there seems to be little reexamination of the empirical or political basis for trade policies in the countries of the region, as those policies become more stylized and rigid under the purview of professional foreign policy bureaucracies.

The purpose of this book has been, in part, to resuscitate these latter issues in order to provoke a political analysis of inter-American trade that goes beyond the debt stalemate currently preoccupying the hemisphere. It also has been important to rethink traditional trade politics to include long-term issues of ecological and producer sustainability, in which the incentive to trade is tempered by the need to husband resources for the sake of rural development and environmental conservation.

The case is only partly made that trade does not offer an avenue of escape from Latin America's durable economic woes. But as Latin American countries close the "American century," the record is one of deeper integration into the international system, worsening distribution of wealth, continuing external payments problems, and accelerating resource depletion. As the twenty-first century nears, it may be that Latin America has little option but to trade, but little hope for the results of trade.

Such a dismal prospect leads in several suggestive directions. Rather than retracing the obvious and prescribing incremental improvements in the trade system that will likely obtain in any case, I will concentrate in this conclusion on less-attended corners of thinking on the trade system.

First, it is difficult to see the gains from obstructing the newly departed

GATT round or future multilateral negotiations. Brazil can show little for its years of resistance against the U.S. services agenda, except for its inclusion in the list of Super 301 countries. According to the analysis in this book, no country in Latin America has the potential to move the international trade system in the manner of a hegemon or "great player." And a regional coalition able to make a more persuasive Third World trade case than UNCTAD is nowhere in evidence. Practically, this suggests that Latin American nations should stay in the multilateral system and count on it for little in the way of concession or sensitivity. It may be that Europe 1992 will be the vivisectionist of multilateralism and that it will become more an icon than a reality of future trade relations. Latin America in its current external sector straits is in an excellent position to opt for reciprocity, with an escape: a sort of "best efforts" submission to new multilateralism.

It also seems clear that all Latin American countries should put more energy into their bilateral consultations with the United States and make those consultations a matter of high profile, in the manner of Mexican President Salinas. That does not commend the Mexican approach to free trade integration but does suggest that certain shortcomings and development connections of trade can be pointed out as a direct product of bilateral talks, and not more general polemics disconnected from policy questions. It seems inappropriate, to say the least, that alternatives to free trade are rarely encountered in current political literature on Latin America, and that few Mexicans (Brazilians, Ecuadoreans, and others) are studying the prospective domestic impact of bilateral free trade.

One of those often-dismissed connections that might be raised in bilateral meetings is the matter of resource conservation and trade. Latin America is in an excellent position to beat the environmental drum, asking not only the United States but the international system in general for import concessions in environmentally sensitive areas such as lumber, fuel, and foodstuffs; rewards for conservation; funds for "environmental adjustment" that address the styles of development issues brought up in Chapter 3; and so on. It is doubtful, given the U.S. reluctance on the World Climate Trust Fund, its frankly destructive role in the recent 1990 World Climate Conference, and its concerns over other important environmental finance issues of its own, that the results will be epochal. But by avoiding the environmental connection to trade and development, Latin American leaders are putting ammunition in the hands of the OECD countries, when they should be explaining their own roles in trade-related environmental degradation instead. Once again, the U.S.-Mexican free trade agreement may be the first battleground in which the environmental consequences of trade are fought out on a bilateral basis.

It is also worthwhile for Latin American governments to resist the blanket demands of the North for privatization. One of the arguments of this book is that the public sector plays an important role in trade and development. If that is the case, the Latin American state is the most likely defender of public prerogatives against the forces of privatization in the World Bank, the IMF, and the U.S. government. Certainly there is a balance-of-payments escape rationale for managing imports through the public sector, revealed in part by the disappearing trade surpluses accompanying Mexican liberalization and privatization. There are at least two defensible arguments on behalf of continued public involvement, however. The first involves the expanded sense of economic rationality and clear sense of public purpose that the state can bring to macroeconomic life. The second has to do with the necessary role of the state as a potential interlocutor in deepening democratic processes and public accountability. It goes without saying that the state's case is damaged endlessly by the bad use to which trade-related welfare is put. Latin America has a chance to change the "fiscal responsibility" agenda by arguing for state reform, not budgetary liquidation.

What does all this mean for Latin American trade policy in the future? The argument presented in this volume comes to an analytically useful but politically dismal conclusion: that there is a new epoch facing Latin America in its integration with the international community; that the signature of the forthcoming epoch is bilaterally dominated regionalism, led once again by the newly demure United States; and that the traditional strategies of economic nationalism, led by the state, or "export-optimistic" internationalism based on Great Power preference, are useless.

It may be that in the historiography of the twenty-first century, this period will turn out to be transitional, in the way that the 1930s were an interwar transition from the old international division of labor to the new. But even transitional periods have their important dynamics, and it may be worthwhile to mention some of those that seem apparent now, if only in schematic form.

A set of guiding propositions limits alternative trade and development strategies. Because full-fledged national and regional empirical research is necessary to validate each of these propositions, they are offered here mainly as a prolegomenon to future research and as part of the ten concluding hypotheses to this study about Latin American trade and development.

1. *The Brazilian Model is dead.* By this it is meant that the high-state developmentalist option of the 1960s and 1970s is fiscally and politically bankrupt, and that the closed-economy, high-state quadrant described in Chapter 2 is historically and financially impossible to replicate in the

foreseeable future. The expected course of Figure 6.1 continues downward and to the right.

2. *The prospects for nationally governed trade and development adjustment are limited to the early industrializers.* This means that, for the most part, Latin American nations are left without alternatives, other than prostrating themselves before the international trade system and adopting domestic political strategies that afford them preferential treatment by large trading partners.

3. *The Big State, Eventual Liberalization Model (the Neo-Brazilian model?) is crippled by the weakness of the states and imperiled by the hazards of liberalization.* The large states are distinguishable on several economic grounds from small states and are not as vulnerable, but the suggestion that even the most privileged states in Latin America have trade leverage seems mistaken.

4. *Integration by trade will redound to the environmental detriment of Latin America, as the "styles of development" generated in the North are adopted with even fewer constraints in the South.* Indicative of this trend is a prophecy of a California farmer: "You're going to see more movement in agriculture southwards from California as water becomes scarcer, and as issues of fertilizer use, high land costs, and potential labor shortages loom larger."[6] Whether by physical or technological reorganization, Latin America has the potential to become the environmental dumping ground of the Western Hemisphere through trade and investment.

5. *The styles of development constraint on environmentally and developmentally sound economic change cannot be addressed as long as the public sector is in retreat.* No matter the ascendance of civil society in postauthoritarian politics, the public sector has an ineluctable role in the protection of public goods and the generation of ecologically responsible politics and poverty policies. The retreat of the public sector is politically equivalent to removing the rudder from the public policy of sustainable development, and certainly minimizes the chances of changing industrial process and labor organization in the directions required for that purpose.

6. *The success of Latin American nations in export competition with other traders will vary inversely with social policy.* The premises of export competitiveness in Latin America are competitively devalued exchange rates, extremely low tax rates on investment, and retrogressive wage policies that reduce to a minimum the cost of labor in production. Trade

may lead to growth in some circumstances, but little suggests that it is the foundation for socially progressive politics in Latin America.

7. *The developed countries have turned away completely from the North-South agenda of "managing" international trade, while refusing to eliminate their own internal trade and production management.* This means that producers of primary commodities have been set adrift without commodity agreements, and that the OECD has determined that "free markets" should determine the production of primary goods. At the same time, OECD agricultural subsidies continue to manage the international agricultural system without regard to the consequences for Latin America.

8. *The developed countries have returned to the foreign policy of the 1950s and 1960s, concentrating on official development assistance and the multilateral development system to substitute for trade preference.* The great difference is the absence of commodity agreements and trends downward in commodity prices (especially nonfuel commodities), heightening the needs of commodity exporters, when the commitment to official development assistance is lowered. Given the controversial nature of foreign aid, a reduced menu of aid based on developed-country strategies is not an inspiring option for the future.

9. *There is little credible difference between internationalism and nationalism in the debt-laden trade and development policies of Latin America.* The internationalization of productive processes and the transnationalization of trade and investment, as well as the standardization of commodities and manufactures, diminish the difference between economic nationalism and internationalist integration. With the current foreshortening of the trade-development debate, the distinction between nationalism and internationalism is even narrower.

10. *Trade's connection to development is undone when trade's domestic impact is considered a "given" benefit to society. In the new international division of labor this means nothing less than the disarticulation of economic growth from progressive social policy.* This is the last and most important proposition.

In the end, to conceive of trade in Latin America as a progressive economic stimulus, rather than being fettered by international domination, a new politics of sustainability, a new multilateral equity, and a new posthegemonic responsibility by the United States to Latin America must appear. In 1990, such prospects seem a century away.

Reference Matter

Notes

For full forms of citations shortened in the Notes, see the Bibliography following.

Introduction

1. Maier, *In Search of Stability.*
2. Streeten, "Development Dichotomies," pp. 360–61.
3. These volumes include Abel and Lewis, eds., *Latin America, Economic Imperialism and the State*; Thorp, ed., *Latin America in the 1930s*; Cortes Conde and Hunt, eds., *Latin American Economies*; Cortes Conde and Stein, eds., *Latin America*; and Love and Jacobsen, eds., *Guiding the Invisible Hand.*
4. Of course, thanks to Raul Prebisch and Arthur Lewis, Latin America and the Caribbean were always well represented in development economics.
5. Lal, *Poverty of "Development Economics."*
6. Lewis, *Growth and Fluctuations*, p. 167.
7. De Janvry, *The Agrarian Question and Reformism in Latin America*, p. 173.
8. Maier, "Politics of Productivity," p. 129.
9. For good examples, see the 1989 report of the Inter-American Dialogue, *The Americas in 1989.*

Chapter 1

1. Entry points to the vast literature covering historical antecedents to the current debt crisis can be found in Fishlow, "Lessons from the Past," Marichal, *Century of Debt Crises*, and Stallings, *Banker to the Third World.* The most obvious and devastating case of trade collapse is in the period of the Great Depression. Admirable accounts of the consequences of the Depression for Latin America may be found in Bulmer-Thomas, *Political Economy of Central America*, and Thorp, ed., *Latin America in the 1930s.*
2. Of the most persuasive *dependencia* literature, see Cardoso and Faletto, *Dependency and Development in Latin America.* One of the most articulate spokesmen of the "structuralist" position is Furtado, especially in *Obstacles to Development in Latin America.*
3. This refers to the expansion of an informal British empire through commerce

in the period dating roughly from 1880, and in the literature is distinguished from the general economic liberalism that characterized the nineteenth century. It is interesting to this analysis because its empirical base focuses on Latin America, not the British colonies, and because it dovetails with other monographic research on the British influence in Latin America during the past century. For a convenient and controversial entry point to the literature on free trade imperialism, see Gallagher and Robinson, "Imperialism of Free Trade," the argument of which is elaborated most fully in an edited volume dedicated to the controversy: Louis, ed., *Imperialism*. Previous critical perspectives on this literature come from Platt, "Imperialism of Free Trade," and Platt, "Further Objections to an 'Imperialism of Free Trade.' "

4. W. Arthur Lewis, a prominent development economist, made his own nod in the direction of historiographical dispute, when he averred that "history . . . consists not of facts but of historians' opinions of what happened, and of why it happened" (*Theory of Economic Growth*, p. 15).

5. Barman, *Brazil*, pp. 43–50; *New York Times Magazine*, Nov. 5, 1989.

6. The quote is from the writings of the Brazilian minister in London in 1862, cited in Graham, *Britain and the Onset of Modernization in Brazil*, p. 108.

7. Predictably, the Prebisch thesis has been oversimplified through use and time. For a clear exposition of the thesis, see Fishlow, "The State of Latin American Economics."

8. Halperin Donghi, "Economy and Society," p. 28; Deas, "Venezuela, Colombia, and Ecuador," p. 213; Woodward, "Central America," p. 185; Bertram and Thorp, *Peru*, p. 127.

9. Hirschman, *National Power*, p. 20.

10. Halperin Donghi, "Economy and Society," p. 2.

11. Gootenberg, "Beleaguered Liberals," p. 64.

12. Behrman, *Foreign Trade Regimes and Economic Development*, p. 5.

13. Perhaps the most vivid such opposition came in Colombia, where the nationalists and liberals fought the "War of the Thousand Days" over issues of national foreign and fiscal policy, including paper money and tariffs. See Bergquist, *Coffee and Conflict in Colombia*, especially Part II. The inherent conflict between liberalism and nationalism probably is related to the differentiation of political issues over time. Initially, nationalism meant to a great extent nation building and freedom from external empire, so it went well with the secularizing vision of nineteenth-century Britain and the new commercial potential of Anglo–Latin American relations. Later, as laissez-faire economic liberalism differentiated itself from economic nationalism, the friction began to show.

14. Graham, *Britain and the Onset of Modernization in Brazil*, p. 106.

15. In the Brazilian case, the opposition arose because of the already heavy-handed involvement of Britain in Brazilian trade. That increasingly dominant position may be traced to treaties with Portugal in 1810, as well as other conventions signed a century earlier. See Barman, *Brazil*, pp. 146–47.

16. Lynch, "The River Plate Republics," p. 323.

17. McGreevey, *Economic History of Colombia*, pp. 78–80.

18. Haber, *Industry and Underdevelopment*, p. 38; Cardoso de Mello and Tavares, "Capitalist Export Economy in Brazil," p. 96.

19. Bertram and Thorp, *Peru*, chap. 3.

20. For a good example of those reforms in the Brazilian context, which was the least interrupted by independence struggles in the early nineteenth century, see Barman, *Brazil*, pp. 10–11, 47–48. A capsule version of the Bourbon reforms may be found in Brading, "Bourbon Spain and Its American Empire."

21. In the words of Aureliano Candido Tavares Bastos of Brazil, liberalism was the tonic for the many deficiencies of Brazilian character, including the "spirit of timidity—Chinese, lazy, late, inimical to newness, passive, and accommodating." The Brazilian liberal insisted that "we must change our customs. . . . And I know of no better way than to open freely the doors of the Empire to the foreigner" (quoted in Graham, *Britain and the Onset of Modernization in Brazil*, p. 35).

22. This was certainly true in Central America, where liberal and conservative were mainly personalistic labels. See Bulmer-Thomas, *Political Economy of Central America*, p. 17.

23. For the comparison of the old and new international division of labor, see Sanderson, ed., *The Americas in the New International Division of Labor*. The idea is conveyed succinctly in a recent volume as the process by which "Europe as a whole came to specialize in the production of manufactures, [while] the tropical areas . . . would be induced to supply the needed raw materials and agricultural products while serving as a market for manufactured goods" (Ruggie, "Introduction," p. 7). Halperin Donghi characterized Latin American economic dependence in the nineteenth century as "above all the acceptance of a place in the international division of labor as defined by the new economic metropolis" ("Economy and Society," p. 29). The dates of this period are intended as a conceptual convenience and are somewhat arbitrary. They are broadly consistent with the economic history of the region. Among the countries of the global "periphery," only Brazil and Argentina grew by 10 percent in real per capita income over the two decades before 1870. With the growth of world trade in the 1870s and the rise in British informal empire after 1880, the rest of Latin America began to grow more quickly in response (Lewis, *Growth and Fluctuations*, p. 29). Some histories close the period of British domination in 1930. Here, 1914 is chosen because of the economic impact of the outbreak of World War I.

24. The classics on this evolution of Buenos Aires are Scobie, *Argentina, a City and a Nation* and *Revolution on the Pampas*, and Smith, *Politics and Beef in Argentina*. For a thorough bibliography of both Spanish and English literature, see Rock, *Argentina, 1516–1987*.

25. For the rise of Santiago, see Loveman, *Chile*. For the information in the remainder of the paragraph, see Love, *São Paulo in the Brazilian Federation*, p. 26; Bergquist, *Coffee and Conflict in Colombia*, p. 35; Halperin Donghi, "Economy and Society," p. 45; Deas, "Venezuela, Colombia, and Ecuador," p. 213.

26. Marichal, *Century of Debt Crisis*, p. 17.

27. Cariola and Sunkel, "Growth of the Nitrate Industry and Socioeconomic Change in Chile," p. 201; Hunt, "Growth and Guano in Nineteenth-Century

Peru," p. 299; Cortes Conde, "Export Economy of Argentina," p. 320; Greenhill, "Brazilian Coffee Trade," p. 198; Deas, "Venezuela, Colombia, and Ecuador," p. 219; Marichal, *Century of Debt Crises*, p. 17.

28. Bulmer-Thomas, *Political Economy of Central America*, pp. 18–19.

29. Stallings, *Banker to the Third World*, p. 63.

30. See Calder, *Impact of Intervention*, and Healy, *Gunboat Diplomacy in the Wilson Era*. Calder's bibliography offers a full comparative treatment of U.S. intervention in the Caribbean.

31. Bulmer-Thomas, *Political Economy of Central America*, chap. 2. For the lurid details, see also Schlesinger and Kinzer, *Bitter Fruit*, and Immerman, *CIA in Guatemala*.

32. The Brazil and River Plate Conference was the largest; Caribbean and West Coast conferences followed suit. Most large carriers were involved in shipping conferences, and nonmembers tended to follow conference guidelines. See Greenhill, "Shipping," pp. 129–30, 119. This treatment, along with several other essays in Platt, ed., *Business Imperialism*, assigns no political purpose to such dominance and urges the reader to avoid exaggerating the importance of "neutral" business concerns in local politics.

33. This does not mean that the Porfirian rail network was unambitious, and, in fact, a relatively well-integrated rail system did exist by 1910. There is a difference, however, between felicitous economic spin-offs and the core objectives of foreign concessions. For the Mexican case, see Haber, *Industry and Underdevelopment*, chap. 2; Coatsworth, "Railroads, Landholding and Agrarian Protest"; and Sanderson, *Agrarian Populism and the Mexican State*, chap. 3.

34. This was not true across all commodities. Coffee in Central America, for example, contrasts remarkably with bananas, though its role as an economic catalyst elsewhere is mixed. See esp. Bulmer-Thomas, *Political Economy of Central America*, chap. 1.

35. Wright, *British-Owned Railways in Argentina*, chap. 2; Scobie, *Revolution on the Pampas*, p. 40.

36. Graham, *Britain and the Onset of Modernization in Brazil*, pp. 68–69; McGreevey, *Economic History of Colombia*, p. 30; Bonilla, *Guano y burguesia en el Perú*, p. 58, translated in Marichal, *Century of Debt Crises*, p. 88.

37. Quoted in Greenhill, "Merchants and the Latin American Trades," p. 161.

38. Behrman, *Foreign Trade Regimes and Economic Development*, pp. 10–12; Cariola and Sunkel, "Growth of the Nitrate Industry and Socioeconomic Change in Chile," table 17.

39. Abreu, "Anglo-Brazilian Economic Relations," pp. 379–93; Haber, *Industry and Underdevelopment*, pp. 40–42; Meyer, *Mexico and the United States in the Oil Controversy*; Diaz-Alejandro, "The Argentine Economy Before 1930," table 1.18. See also Lewis, "Railways and Industrialization"; Rock, ed., *Argentina in the Twentieth Century*; Ferns, *Britain and Argentina in the Nineteenth Century*.

40. Matthew, "Imperialism of Free Trade." The characterization is by Platt, in *Business Imperialism*, p. 9. See also Matthew, "Antony Gibbs and Sons, the Guano Trade and the Peruvian Government."

41. Greenhill, "Nitrate and Iodine Trades," pp. 231–32.

42. For specifics, see the excellent contributions in Thorp, ed., *Latin America in the 1930s.*

43. Palma, "From an Export-Led to an Import-Substituting Economy," table 3.2.

44. There is some irony in this, especially since the administration of banana prices and the responsiveness of the foreign enclaves helped terms of trade in bananas outdo coffee and other commodities. See Bulmer-Thomas, "Central America in the Inter-War Period," figure 11.2.

45. Hull, *Memoirs*, vol. 1, pp. 323–24.

46. Topik, in *The Political Economy of the Brazilian State*, disagrees with the argument that the Great Depression fathered a new kind of interventionist state, asserting instead that the state was already quite developed by that time. His argument rests on an unfortunate premise that a state based on coffee valorization and a rudimentary national financial system is equivalent to the post-Keynesian interventionist state, which other economic historians mark as the significant break of the 1930s. It is less the extent than the nature of intervention that should be the focus of the old order–new order historiographical debate about the role of the state.

47. Haber, *Industry and Underdevelopment*, chaps. 9 and 10; Mosk, *Industrial Revolution in Mexico.*

48. For a recent definition of Latin American populism, see Perruci and Sanderson, "Presidential Succession, Economic Crisis and the Resurgence of Populism in Brazil."

49. For a classic exposition of the political goals of such entrepreneurial classes, see Mosk, *Industrial Revolution in Mexico.*

50. A particularly welcome addition to this literature is Marichal, *Century of Debt Crises*, which also contains a convenient guide to the historical bibliography on Latin American debt.

51. Graham, *Britain and the Onset of Modernization in Brazil*, chap. 3.

52. Ibid., p. 49.

53. Furtado, in *The Economic Development of Latin America*, discriminates among three economic models of Latin American growth, based on specialization in temperate zone agricultural commodities, tropical zone agricultural commodities, and mineral extraction. He argues that the former economies are more likely to develop forward linkages enhancing domestic industrialization and employment.

54. See particularly Spalding, *Organized Labor in Latin America*; Rock, *Argentina, 1516–1987*; Bergquist, *Labor in Latin America.*

55. Bergquist, *Labor in Latin America.*

56. Especially Bertram and Thorp, *Peru.*

57. See Bulmer-Thomas's critical remarks about Furtado in Thorp, ed., *Latin America in the 1930s.*

58. Sonnichsen, *Colonel Green and the Copper Skyrocket.*

59. Hull, *Memoirs*, vol. 1, p. 308.

60. The literature is relatively well-known. A convenient and entertaining review of premises and critique can be found in Platt, "Dependency and the Historian: Further Objections," pp. 29–39, and O'Brien, "Dependency Revisited," pp. 40–69, both in Abel and Lewis, eds., *Latin America, Economic Imperialism and the State*. Platt's argument also connects well to the Robinson-Gallagher controversy over free trade imperialism, though Platt represents to both debates what P. T. Bauer offers to development economics.

61. Platt, "Introduction," in Platt, ed., *Business Imperialism*, p. 14.

62. A particularly clear example of this stereotype is found in the description of the 1930s Pan American system by a biographer of Cordell Hull. He says about Latin Americans that "in the main they supported themselves by growing coffee, wheat, beef, mutton, wool and mahogany, and by mining silver, gold, copper, and semiprecious stones, selling these in Europe and in the United States and spending the proceeds on automobiles, travel, suits from Savile Row, champagne, and the amenities of life for the top economic strata. While their system was not wholly desirable or praiseworthy, since it operated through extreme concentration of wealth resting on widespread and abject poverty, it had been in effect ever since the Conquistadores had brought the so-called blessings of Spanish civilization to the New World, and it had the merit of being a going concern" (Hinton, *Cordell Hull*, p. 242).

63. Tucker, *Inequality of Nations*; Rothstein, *The Weak in the World of the Strong* and *Global Bargaining*.

64. See Hansen, *Beyond the North-South Stalemate*; Fishlow, Fagen, Diaz-Alejandro, and Hansen, *Rich and Poor Nations*.

65. Wolf, *Europe and the People Without History*, chap. 6.

66. Williams, *Contours of American History*, pp. 91–93.

67. Thoreau and George Emerson, quoted in Worster, *Nature's Economy*, pp. 66–67, 69.

68. Meier, "Formative Period," p. 9.

69. Interestingly, this is very similar to Gardner's definition of multilateralism (*Sterling-Dollar Diplomacy*, p. 13).

70. Hirschman, *National Power*, p. 5.

71. The role of economic ideas is critical in the evolution of Latin American economic nationalism. For further reference to the importance of Raul Prebisch and developmentalist nationalism, see Prebisch, "Five Stages," and Fishlow, "State of Latin American Economics."

72. For advocacy of a new approach to the role of the state in Latin America, see Fishlow, "Latin American State," pp. 61–74.

73. For a convenient treatment of the export optimists and pessimists through the years, see Athukorala, "Export Performance of 'New Exporting Countries.'"

74. This infelicitous characterization of the development economics tradition, built in a climate of policy optimism, is from Lal, *Poverty of "Development Economics"*, chap. 1.

75. Nurkse, "International Trade Theory and Development Policy," pp. 234–35.

76. A production function is the maximum output of a system with a given technology.

77. Myrdal, *Rich Lands and Poor*, p. 154.

78. This "primitive accumulation," by which land and capital were concentrated in proportions sufficient for a capitalist transition, was a standard part of the liberal reforms of the Latin American national period. The disentailment of the clergy also meant the elimination of indigenous "primitive communism" for the sake of a universal system of private tenure. See Sanderson, *Agrarian Populism and the Mexican State*, chap. 2; Bushnell and Macaulay, *Emergence of Latin America*.

79. Viz., Berger, *Capitalist Revolution*.

80. Rosecrance, *Rise of the Trading State*, p. 62.

81. McCullough, *Path Between the Seas*; LaFeber, *Panama Canal*.

82. Quoted in Louis Pérez, *Cuba Between Empires*, p. 361.

83. The classic case study of this period is Hilton, *Brazil and the Great Powers*.

84. Classic evidence of this is found in Charles Kindleberger's *Foreign Trade and the National Economy*, which has a perfunctory last chapter on the effect of trade on social and political life. Notable recent exceptions include John Sheahan's *Patterns of Development*.

85. See esp. Furtado, *Economic Development of Latin America*.

86. Bergquist, *Coffee and Conflict*, p. 85.

87. Hunt, "Growth and Guano in Nineteenth-Century Peru"; Matthew, "Imperialism of Free Trade"; the original study of guano as an enclave is found in Levin, *Export Economies*. See also Bonilla, *Guano y burguesia en el Perú*.

88. Halperin Donghi, "Economy and Society," pp. 8–9.

89. From the Spanish and Portuguese verbs *entregar*, to surrender or give up. *Entreguismo* is the polemical denunciation of the politics of surrender, used to describe internationalist elites from Cuba to Nicaragua to South America. Nationalist backlash is the natural response to such policies; even such a great nationalist icon as Augusto Cesar Sandino is said to have rankled at being denounced as a "sell-out" because of Nicaragua's prostration before the United States and Britain. See Hodges, *Intellectual Foundations of the Nicaraguan Revolution*, p. 9.

90. Ibid., p. 90.

91. Topik, *Political Economy of the Brazilian State*. In the end, this argument is not convincing because it ignores the tremendous watershed represented by the embrace of Keynesian economics after 1930 and understates the importance of parastate enterprises and state-led development after World War II versus regulatory control, subsidies, and the creation of a national system of development finance before 1930.

92. Dean, *Brazil and the Struggle for Rubber*, p. 22.

Chapter 2

1. Especially Waisman, *Reversal of Development in Argentina*, and Sheahan, *Patterns of Development in Latin America*.

2. In *Growth and Fluctuations* (pp. 161–62), Lewis uses Argentina as an example of trade as the engine of growth; Britain and the United States (cotton) and Germany (chemicals) are used as examples of trade resulting from growth, with comparative advantage in one sector leading to rapid export expansion. As to the balance-of-payments example, Lewis notes that a number of countries have suffered export deficiencies as "lubricating oil" but that the literature sometimes treats the phenomenon as if it were confined to Latin America.

3. Bertram and Thorp, *Peru*, p. 18.

4. A leading example of this literature is Balassa et al., *Toward Renewed Economic Growth in Latin America*. Many of the assumptions are also found in broader trade policy literature, including the contributions to Cline, ed., *Trade Policy in the 1980s*, and Hufbauer and Schott, *Trading for Growth*. For a critical review of trade as an engine of growth, see Streeten, "Trade as the Engine, Handmaiden, Brake or Offspring of Growth?"

5. For various meanings of adjustment over the past three decades, see Feinberg, "Open Letter to the World Bank's New President," pp. 11–14.

6. For examples of such work by prominent economists, see various authors' case studies in the National Bureau of Economic Research Special Conference Series on Foreign Trade Regimes and Economic Development. Latin American cases include Brazil, Chile, and Colombia and can be found in the bibliography under entries for Jere Behrman, Carlos Díaz-Alejandro, and Albert Fishlow.

7. For example, Mexico previously imported much greater volumes and variety of U.S. goods under an illiberal, controlled trade regime than it does now under a liberal trading order plagued by suppressed domestic demand and a foreign exchange constraint. Presumably, free traders are thinking of a liberal regime with high domestic demand and plenty of foreign exchange. These circumstances are hard to come by.

8. Helleiner, "Policy-Based Program Lending."

9. Jacques de Larosière, "The Debt Problem and the Challenges Facing the World Economy," p. 358, cited in Helleiner, "Policy-Based Program Lending," p. 47.

10. The marvel is that this concession that growth is necessary as part of the adjustment process is itself considered progress in the IMF thinking. As Latin American stabilization experiences show, the track record of traditional IMF-led "shock treatments" was not good from any vantage point. See esp. Thorp and Whitehead, eds., *Latin American Debt*.

11. Hufbauer and Erb, *Subsidies in International Trade*.

12. Furtado, *Economic Development of Latin America*, pp. 47–57.

13. Lewis, *Growth and Fluctuations*, p. 192.

14. Diaz-Alejandro, "Latin America in the 1930s," pp. 20, 38.

15. Barter terms of trade refer to the ratio of exchange between commodities. Factoral terms of trade involve the exchange between productive resources (land, labor, and capital).

16. Lewis attributes this in great part to the infinite elasticity of Latin American

supply owing to unlimited supplies of low-cost labor and land (*Growth and Fluctuations*, p. 190).

17. Ibid., chap. 7.

18. Diaz-Alejandro, *Foreign Trade Regimes and Economic Development*, p. 236.

19. Berhman, *Foreign Trade Regimes and Economic Development: Chile*, pp. 308–11.

20. This statement must be qualified by criticisms of Lewis's argument that the marginal product of rural labor is zero and that traditional land use is nonuse.

21. Donkin, *Spanish Red*.

22. Sanderson, *Transformation of Mexican Agriculture*, pp. 158–63.

23. For a convenient summary and beginning bibliography, see Spero, *Politics of International Economic Relations*, chap. 9.

24. Mexico is not a member of OPEC and may be considered a "free rider" on cartel policies.

25. Girvan, *Corporate Imperialism*.

26. Morawetz, *Why the Emperor's New Clothes Are Not Made in Colombia*.

27. Lewis, *Growth and Fluctuations*, p. 190.

28. Prebisch, "Five Stages," p. 178. Perhaps the most stunning example comes from Asia, not Latin America. Demand for Bangladesh's jute and tea exports is highly inelastic, but it is so important in the world jute supply that its revenue declines when it increases exports. Its tea exports are not significant in the world market, but increases in exports mean decreases in revenue for competitors, all developing countries (Lipton, "Comment," p. 49n).

29. Kindleberger, *Foreign Trade and the National Economy*, chap. 7.

30. See Corden, "Booming Sector and Dutch Disease."

31. This kind of income redistribution is partly what made the postwar Mexican economic boom socially progressive, at least at first. The classic account is still Reynolds, *Mexican Economy*. The current Salinas government hopes to derive such a redistribution from a new free trade relationship with the United States.

32. Lewis, *Growth and Fluctuations*, pp. 160–63.

33. Seers, "The Birth, Life and Death of Development Economics," p. 714.

34. This shortcoming is an implicit critique of policy-based Latin American economic literature. It is so tied up with current scenarios of debt, trade, and winning the momentary affections of the Washington policy establishment that it ignores rafts of academic literature on subjects of great concern to economic growth in the future.

35. Hufbauer and Schott, *Trading for Growth*.

36. Keesing, *Trade Policy for Developing Countries*.

37. Sheahan, *Patterns of Development in Latin America*, p. 15.

38. Ibid., chap. 4.

39. Meier, "Formative Period," p. 8.

40. For convenience, Latin America is referred to in general at times in the book. This is not to suggest that Latin American trade policies or conditions are

homogeneous; quite the contrary. Individual country differences will be shown in the empirical materials.

41. Streeten, "Development Dichotomies," p. 337.

42. This also serves as acknowledgment of Hirschman's paternity in the case of a new index, avoiding the difficulties of the Gini coefficient and the Herfindahl index. See Hirschman, "Paternity of an Index."

43. Lewis, *Development Process*, p. 12.

44. These artifices are suggested in Hirschman, "Dissenter's Confession," and Lewis, "Development Economics in the 1950s." Hirschman calls these two tests the monoeconomics claim and the mutual benefits claim and describes them both in "The Rise and Decline of Development Economics."

45. These are obviously gross characterizations, which do not include everyone. "Orthodoxy" is a particularly vexing term. Orthodox Marxists who focus on the role of imperialism in the transformation of Third World economies, for example, are unenthused by structural implications of delinking. The leading example is Warren, *Imperialism*.

46. Lewis, "Development Economics in the 1950s," p. 123.

47. In the ideological battle over the proper role for the public sector, it is often contended that the state is a force against the market. Actually, with the exception of socialist transitions in Latin America, the state represents a political influence in, rather than a substitute for, the market.

48. Diaz-Alejandro called development economics a "School for Scandal" ("Comment," p. 114).

49. For a convenient summary of some thinking on these questions, see Adelman, "Development Economics"; Arndt, "Development Economics Before 1945"; Morawetz, *Twenty-five Years of Economic Development*; and Sheahan, "The Elusive Balance Between Stimulation and Constraint in Analysis of Development."

50. The standard basic needs treatment is International Labour Office, *Employment, Growth and Basic Needs*. A later contribution is Streeten et al., *First Things First*. The post-debt-crisis literature is led by Cornia, Jolly, and Stewart, eds., *Adjustment with a Human Face*. Griffin, *Land Concentration and Rural Poverty*, and Lipton, *Land Assets and Rural Poverty*, operate from distinct perspectives but link the question of poverty alleviation to a redistribution of economic assets.

51. For an excellent discussion of the radical implications of even small changes of this kind, see Fagen, "Equity in the South in the Context of North-South Relations."

52. The leading representative is perhaps Chenery et al., *Redistribution with Growth*.

53. Sheahan, *Patterns of Development*.

54. Barbier, "Concept of Sustainable Economic Development," p. 102. I offer a more complete bibliography of the growing literature on sustainability in Chapter 3 below.

55. See particularly, Williams, *Export Agriculture and Political Instability in*

Central America. Barkin, *El fin de autosuficiencia alimentaria*; Bulmer-Thomas, *Political Economy of Central America*; De Janvry, *Agrarian Question and Reformism in Latin America*; and Sanderson, *Transformation of Mexican Agriculture* also have criticized the connection between agricultural modernization, agro-industrialization, and the sacrifice of traditional domestic agriculture.

56. Maier quotes Thomas Schelling's definition of political economy as "economics in a context of policy, where the policy is more than the economics but the 'more' cannot be separated from the economics" and reverses the emphasis to define political economy as "economics in a context of politics, where the economics is less than the politics but the 'less' cannot be separated from the political" (*In Search of Stability*, p. 3n). The Schelling quote is from his *Choice and Consequence*, p. vii.

57. Actually, there are two distinct "new" traditions in political economy: one deriving from individualist perspectives on political choice and rationality, the other from a more structuralist, often statist perspective emanating from European Marxism. For some distinctions, see Maier, *In Search of Stability*, pp. 2–16, and Staniland, *What Is Political Economy?*

58. This is manifestly not the case with the public choice literature, which stems from an individualist "choice-based" set of premises emphasizing rationality. See Staniland, *What Is Political Economy?*

59. Meier, *International Trade and Development*, p. 125; Myrdal, *International Economy*.

60. The export multiplier is a concept that tries to account for the domestic impact of additional exports. It is, according to Lewis, the reciprocal of the marginal propensity to import. An economy is thus able to use its exports for domestic growth in inverse function of the "leakage" of export revenues in the form of imports. Ergo, it will impose import restrictions.

61. For this observation, I am obliged to Clark Reynolds, who made this argument in a conference on industrial policy toward high-technology industries, co-sponsored by Stanford University and the Instituto Universitario de Pesquisa do Rio de Janeiro (IUPERJ), Rio de Janeiro, Jan. 1987.

62. Cited in Griffith-Jones and Sunkel, *Debt and Development Crises*, p. 117.

63. Feinberg and Kallab, eds., *Adjustment Crisis in the Third World*; Thorp and Whitehead, eds., *Latin American Debt and the Adjustment Crisis*.

64. Feinberg et al., *Between Two Worlds*.

65. Cornia, Jolly, and Stewart, eds., *Adjustment with a Human Face*, vol. 1.

66. Kahler, ed., *Politics of International Debt*; Weintraub, ed., *Economic Stabilization in Developing Countries*; Griffith-Jones and Sunkel, *Debt and Development Crises*; Stallings and Kaufman, *Debt and Democracy in Latin America*.

67. For some sources on the "heterodox shocks" brought into momentary vogue by the Argentine Austral Plan (mid-1985) and the Brazilian Cruzado Plan (February 1986), see Arida, ed., *Inflação zero*; and Lopes, *Choque heterodoxo*.

68. These questions are important, but they are not the concerns of this study. For an example of the best in this rich literature, see Thorp and Whitehead, *Latin American Debt and the Adjustment Crisis*.

69. From a more conventional international economics viewpoint, the workshop on international economic policies of the high-debt countries organized by John Whalley of the University of Western Ontario is helpful. Contributions by economists from Brazil, Chile, and Argentina to that project help frame the economic policy side of the Latin American debate. See Whalley, ed., *Dealing with the North.*

70. Marichal, *Century of Debt Crisis*, pp. 6, 27.

71. Deas, "Venezuela, Colombia, and Ecuador," p. 219.

72. Brazil went through all of these variations at different times. Because of its unique transition to independence, trade with the center was not interrupted in the 1820s. The diversity of its exports and the coincidence of independence with a decline in the very sugar producers that had pushed Brazil to the side in the eighteenth century meant that Brazil was able to finance its debt through trade and to grow on the basis of expanded trade (Alden, "Late Colonial Brazil," pp. 310–11). In contrast to the rest of Latin America, Brazil was able to avoid the collapse of trade that led to insolvency in the region. In turn, its prospects for borrowing later in the century were much better than those of countries that had defaulted. A century later, the onset of World War I severed economic relationships between agricultural exporters and the European market. Brazilian coffee proceeds were able to soften the collapse of the European market in World War I because by then Brazil had shifted its coffee exports almost entirely to the United States, which did not suffer the ravages of the Continental conflict. Financial crisis did not ensue. Chile thrived, not on agricultural exports but on nitrate, imported to Europe as war matériel (Palma, "External Disequilibrium and Internal Industrialization in Chile," pp. 319–21). In the 1920s and 1930s, however, the Brazilian trade-finance problem was different. The "defense of coffee" through valorization required great sums of public money because of the secular decline in coffee prices in the 1920s. The Brazilian fiscal system could not support coffee prices through its stock purchasing scheme without foreign borrowing. But because of Brazil's poor financial record after World War I, the general climate of caution among international bondholders, and the disinclination (or inability) of the Brazilian system to engage in systemic fiscal reform loans for the coffee defense were not forthcoming. The result was a trade crisis, predicated on a financial crisis, which left Brazil in an extremely vulnerable position at the onset of the crash of 1929 (Topik, *Political Economy of the Brazilian State*, chap. 3).

73. Arthur Lewis shows that the terms of trade for this period did not deteriorate from 1870 to 1913, but passed through a Kondratiev cycle, beginning with a deterioration in merchandise terms of trade in the 1880s and 1890s, then turning upward in the first decade of the twentieth century (*Growth and Fluctuations*, pp. 170–71).

74. Chapter 5 will show the problems associated with diversification. Chapter 6 will examine the importance of the state in such strategies.

75. Helleiner, "Policy-Based Program Lending," pp. 47–66.

76. Stallings, *Banker to the Third World*, p. 28.

77. Diaz-Alejandro, "Some Aspects of the Development Crisis in Latin America."

78. See Stallings, *Banker to the Third World*, pp. 29–30.

79. For a narrative but theoretically unsatisfying treatment, see Blakemore, *British Nitrates and Chilean Politics.* Stallings, *Banker to the Third World,* pp. 244–46, treats the British background in Peru and follows with a much more detailed historical interpretation of U.S. investment in Peru. For more detail on the Peruvian case, see Bertram and Thorp, *Peru;* Levin, *Export Economies;* and Bonilla, *Guano y burguesia en el Perú.* Diaz-Alejandro suggests that Argentina is an excellent example because "the real transfer of foreign savings into Argentina presented no serious difficulties, while the relaxed balance-of-payments situation of most years also facilitated the transformation of domestic savings into imported capital goods" ("Argentine Economy Before 1930," p. 28).

80. This is the sense of Frenkel and O'Donnell's critique of the Argentine stabilization plan in the mid-1970s, in "Stabilization Programs."

81. The depth of the resonance of this slogan is indicated by the fact that it originated in the mayoral campaign in Rio de Janeiro in 1985. Needless to say, the impact of the mayor's disposition on the international debt is modest. It is also worth noting that the somewhat anachronistic target for populist resentment of the adjustment process is the IMF, not the commercial banks.

82. See esp. Thorp and Whitehead, eds., *Latin American Debt and the Adjustment Crisis,* pp. 318–54.

83. On the less coherent side, see the critique of Argentina in Frenkel and O'Donnell, " 'Stabilization Programs.' " In contrast, Chile under Pinochet is extremely coherent in its programmatic and ideological intentions, if not its performance. See Whitehead, "Adjustment Process in Chile."

84. "Hands Off the IMF."

85. These documents include "Recent Economic Events" reports that the IMF routinely prepares on those countries with ongoing IMF agreements. Needless to say, the competition with the U.S. Treasury, commercial banks, and the World Bank should not be seen as defining the leading edge of compassion for social dislocation under adjustment.

86. This is the case, at least, in Chile. See Behrman, *Foreign Trade Regimes and Economic Development,* p. 5.

87. Sanderson, "Mexican Agricultural Politics in the Shadow of the U.S. Farm Crisis."

88. See esp. Barkin, *Distorted Development,* and Adelman and Taylor, "Is Structural Adjustment with a Human Face Possible?"

89. The range is based on the estimate of the percentage of the population protected from the adjustment process by being able to insulate their personal economic well-being from external shocks. See Bulmer-Thomas, "The Balance of Payments Crisis and Adjustment Programmes in Central America," pp. 302–6.

Chapter 3

1. See Aníbal Pinto's lament in "Comments on 'The Interaction Between Styles of Development and the Environment in Latin America.' "

2. See World Bank, *Striking a Balance.*

3. This measure, not surprisingly, promises to end international tropical timber trade for the short-term future, because the ITTO estimates that only 0.15 percent

of tropical timber enterprises are sustainable. For details of the European Community's position, see reports of the November meeting of the EEC Environment Directorate, esp. Reuters, Nov. 19, 1989.

4. The meeting came only one month after the Toronto Economic Summit proclaimed the danger of debt, environmental destruction, and poverty to the world community. Norwegian Prime Minister Gro Harlem Brundtland, chair of the World Commission on Environment and Development, was the host.

5. For a characteristic statement, see Carlson, "Monetary Talks End with Call for Freer Trade to Ease Poverty," or Conable's speech to the GATT midterm review in Montreal, Dec. 6, 1988, reported in the *International Trade Reporter* of that date.

6. A framework accord was announced at the Montreal midterm review in December 1988. By mid-1989, however, less developed countries were again voicing their unhappiness at lack of progress on a tropical products accord. See "With Exception of U.S., GATT Nations Approve Tropical Products Trade Accord," and "Third World Accuses Developed Nations of Delaying Action on Tropical Products."

7. MacNeill, "Strategies for Sustainable Economic Development," p. 159. This article appeared in an issue of *Scientific American* devoted humbly to "managing planet earth."

8. I am now beginning work on a separate project to develop a consistent data set discriminating among individual Latin American countries' responses to external shocks and the implications for domestic resource use.

9. This argument often focuses on export crops, viz., Bramble, "Debt Crisis"; for a summary and critique, see Repetto, *Economic Policy Reform for Natural Resource Conservation*, p. 6. The classic exposition of the connection between debt and resource degradation is found in the World Commission on Environment and Development, *Our Common Future*, p. 74.

10. McNeely, *Economics and Biological Diversity*, pp. 44–56.

11. For an example of the best the policy approach has to offer, see Ascher and Healy, *Natural Resource Policymaking*.

12. For an empirical exposition, see Ana Doris Capistrano and Steven Sanderson, "Tyranny of the External."

13. For a useful history with ample treatment of this conflict, see Worster, *Nature's Economy*. A provocative recent essay is McKibben, *The End of Nature*.

14. Craig, "Logwood as a Factor in the Settlement of British Honduras."

15. Naylor, *Penny Ante Imperialism*, p. 37.

16. Naylor, "The Mahogany Trade as a Factor in the British Return to the Mosquito Shore."

17. Woodward, "Central America," pp. 195–96.

18. Donkin, *Spanish Red*, p. 25.

19. The rubber tappers of the western Amazon are one likely example, as are communities engaged in chicle extraction in Mesoamerica. For an introduction to the former, see Hecht and Cockburn, *Fate of the Forest*. Perhaps the most vivid recent case involves the Yanomami of the northern Amazonian watershed, who

are facing annihilation because of the intrusion of Brazilian military and gold prospectors. This case is detailed in Ramos, "Economy of Waste."

20. Hemming, *Red Gold* and *Amazon Frontier*.

21. Wolf, *Europe and the People Without History*, p. 150; Cortesão, "Angola e a formação do bandeirismo," p. 24.

22. Elliott, "Spanish Conquest," p. 13.

23. For a ready guide to the anthropological bibliography, see Larson, *Colonial Rule and Agrarian Transformation in Bolivia*.

24. Lynch, "River Plate Republics," p. 315; Loveman, *Chile*.

25. Rosecrance, *Rise of the Trading State*.

26. Wolf, *Sons of the Shaking Earth*; Bulmer-Thomas, *The Political Economy of Central America Since 1920*, pp. 21–22; Hu-DeHart, *Yaqui Resistance and Survival*; Sanderson, *Agrarian Populism*, chap. 3; Spicer, *Cycles of Conquest*; Bergquist, *Coffee and Conflict in Colombia*, p. 27; Halperin Donghi, "Economy and Society," p. 40.

27. Dean, "Deforestation in Southeastern Brazil," pp. 50–67; McNeill, "Deforestation in the Araucaria Zone of Southern Brazil"; Dean, *Brazil and the Struggle for Rubber*, p. 131.

28. Crosby, *Columbian Exchange* and *Ecological Imperialism*.

29. For relevant cites, see Sunkel, "The Interaction Between Styles of Development and the Environment in Latin America."

30. It is perhaps too generous to characterize these moves as mistakes, because a great deal of deception and unconcern for available knowledge has been documented in government policies for development in fragile areas.

31. For a sample of these errors, see National Research Council, Panel on Common Property Resource Management, *Proceedings*.

32. Fearnside, "Charcoal of Carajás." See also Fearnside and Rankin, "Jari and Carajás."

33. For provocative surveys of some of these issues, see United States, Library of Congress, Science and Technology Division, "Draft Environmental Report on Peru"; Freeman et al., *Bolivia*. The Agency for International Development (USAID) has contracted a number of these studies for AID countries in Latin America; the studies provide survey material on questions of environment and development.

34. See Carter and Alvarez, "Changing Paths." Neither the environmental nor the labor market consequences of *parcelación* are clear at this point.

35. On CITES, see, for example, Nietschmann, "Cultural Context of Sea Turtle Subsistence Hunting." See also Iversen and Jory, "Shrimp Culture in Ecuador"; Terchunian et al., "Mangrove Mapping in Ecuador"; Siddall, Atchue, and Murray, "Mariculture Development in Mangroves"; and various issues of the *Marine Fisheries Review*. The trend toward more intensive resource exploitation has generated a controversial Brazilian government agreement with the International Tropical Timber Organization. The agreement emphasizes "sustainable" production in tropical rain forests and is financed by Japan, the largest timber importer in the world. The Japanese are hardly known for conserving Asian rain forests. See

Brazil, Agency for Cooperation, ITTO project document, "Integration of Forest-Based Development in the Western Amazon."

36. As an example, one recent treatment of the interaction of economic development models and natural systems does not even treat the international system as a consideration in development planning. See Hufschmidt et al., *Environment, Natural Systems, and Development.*

37. These arguments are treated elegantly in Abbott and Haley, "International Trade Theory and Natural Resource Concepts."

38. The literature on such conservation has expanded tremendously in recent years. The original Hotelling article is "The Economics of Exhaustible Resources." A convenient guide to the recent literature may be found in Sutton, ed., *Agricultural Trade and Natural Resources.* A more complete, critical view of discounting can be found in Markandya and Pearce, *Environmental Considerations and the Choice of the Discount Rate in Developing Countries.*

39. Clark, *Mathematical Bioeconomics.*

40. An argument often made in general is that land values do not increase as rapidly as they would otherwise in Latin America because of policies turning the internal terms of trade against agriculture (Repetto, *Economic Policy Reform,* p. 5). This generalization is virtually useless because of the limitless range of crop prices, land values, population pressures, and other factors that must be considered. And a leading specialist in Brazilian land policies argues that land prices are forced up artificially by government policy because subsidies are part of the capitalized value of land (Binswanger, *Brazilian Policies,* pp. 3–4). But even if Repetto's assertions are true, they only make the arguments that follow here more severe without government intervention.

41. For a welcome exception, see Browder, "Social Costs of Rain Forest Destruction."

42. Binswanger, "Fiscal and Legal Incentives with Environmental Effects on the Brazilian Amazon"; Mahar, *Government Policies.* For a more general theoretical and empirical treatment across continents, see Repetto and Gillis, *Public Policies and the Misuse of Forest Resources.*

43. The government creates a rent on domestic production by restricting competition, creating extraordinary profits that would not exist under conditions of free competition and unrestricted imports. The difference in import restrictions of this kind versus tariffs is that the rent accrues to the private sector producer instead of the government, which presumably could reallocate it to social purposes.

44. This argument has been used to suggest that environmental controls chase corporations offshore. The evidence of studies to date, according to Segerson ("Natural Resource Concepts in Trade Analysis"), is that such costs are insufficient to scare away domestic production. It is not clear that this is true in Latin America, but, given the multiple reasons for foreign direct investment in a country, an argument can be made that increased environmental costs at the margin will not dissuade investors. A stronger argument could be made that once costs are sunk in production, greater environmental restrictions could be imposed without inordinate fear of losing investment.

45. Trade retaliation against countries offering "upstream subsidies" to production was narrowly averted in the 1985 Trade Act. The U.S. Congress especially favored such retaliation as a protectionist measure against Mexican exports to the United States. Brazilian subsidies in steel were also the target of this proposed legislation.

46. For a useful and thorough summary of definitions in the literature, see Barbier, "Concept of Sustainable Economic Development"; Pezzey, *Economic Analysis of Sustainable Growth and Sustainable Development*, pp. 63–71; and Simon, "Sustainable Development." A particularly telling critique may be found in O'Riordan, "The Politics of Sustainability." His argument is that sustainable resource use allows developers to tag whatever activity they want to pursue with the sustainable descriptor to absolve themselves of environmental criticism. The lack of clear definition of the concept allows that liberty.

47. A good survey of the sustainability literature can be found in Batie, "Sustainable Development." See also Redclift, *Sustainable Development*.

48. This definition is not without controversy. See Tisdell, "Sustainable Development."

49. According to a consulting report prepared for Forestry Canada by Woodbridge, Reed and Associates, Brazil will see 1985's industrial hardwood timber supply of 35 million metric tons soar to 76 million by the year 2000 (about 32.2 billion board feet). Brazilian plantation hardwood, along with Chilean softwood, will dominate Latin American exports to the world. See "Sun Will Not 'Set' on Forest Industry in Next 20 Years." This conclusion is highly speculative, given the state of the Brazilian economy and the controversy surrounding both pig iron and timber exports. But there is little reason to assume that Brazil will categorically reject such a future, or control it, for that matter.

50. A 1989 proposal in the European Parliament, backed by the Friends of the Earth, among others, recommends an import tax on all tropical timber arriving in the EEC from countries that do not extract the timber in sustainable ways. The International Tropical Timber Organization suggested that virtually no tropical timber is extracted on a sustainable basis. At a meeting of the EEC Environmental Directorate in November 1989, it was suggested that such a tax would be used for tropical forest conservation and for energy conservation in the EEC.

51. Cardoso, "Development and the Environment," p. 127.

52. Two examples of such deals are the oil component of the U.S.-Mexican bailout program of 1983, in which the United States bought more oil than it would have ordinarily and used it to fill the strategic oil stockpile; and recent Japanese-Mexican negotiations, in which Mexico is encouraged to provide more low-cost oil to Japan, ironically in return for Japanese contributions to pollution control programs in Mexico City.

53. This does not intend to suggest that civil society in general does not have an important role. In fact, in Latin America, nongovernmental organizations of various stripes have been principals in the evolution of such concerns as sustainability and biological diversity.

54. See, for example, Spears, *Containing Tropical Deforestation*.

55. Ayres, "Debt-for-Equity Swaps and the Conservation of Tropical Rain Forests."

56. Stabilization is a multifaceted concept, but in the Latin American context it generally refers to policies geared to balancing external accounts or attacking the rate of inflation.

57. See, for example, Corbo and de Melo, "Lessons from the Southern Cone Policy Reforms."

58. As has been observed, "getting prices right is not the end of development, but getting them wrong often is" (Streeten, "Development Dichotomies," p. 346).

59. MacNeill, "Strategies for Sustainable Economic Development," p. 162.

60. See Gerardo Otero's thesis of the "disappearing middle" in his "Agrarian Reform in Mexico." The implications of increased pressures on steep-slope agriculture are alarming. In some countries of Latin America (Colombia, El Salvador, Guatemala, Haiti, and Peru), half or more of the agricultural population already works the steep slopes. In Mexico the estimate is 45 percent of the agricultural population. The environmental and productive contributions of these farmers are complex. See Posner and McPherson, "Agriculture on the Steep Slopes of Tropical America."

61. Laarman, Schreuder, and Anderson, *Overview of Forest Products Trade.*

62. The vehicle for Japanese involvement is the International Tropical Timber Organization, a new international organization funded heavily by the Japanese. Recently, the ITTO concluded an agreement with the Brazilian government that headlined a pilot program for sustainable tropical forest production in Acre, Brazil. See Brazil, Agency for International Cooperation, ITTO project document, "Integration of Forest-Based Development in the Western Amazon." McNeely (*Economics and Biological Diversity*, pp. 189–90), along with many other ecologists, apparently accepts the good-faith claims of ITTO, though the emphasis of the Brazilian agreement is production, not conservation.

63. An evocative portrayal of this "hamburger connection" can be found in the documentary film *Jungleburger*, as well as in articles such as Matteucci, "Is the Rain Forest Worth Seven Hundred Million Hamburgers?"; Nations and Komer, "Rainforests and the Hamburger Society"; and Uhl and Parker, "Is a Quarter-Pound Hamburger Worth a Half-Ton of Rain Forest?" For a strong critique, see Browder, "Social Costs of Rain Forest Destruction." For a more complete treatment of U.S. markets for manufacture-quality beef, see Sanderson, *Transformation of Mexican Agriculture.* This was brought to absurd heights recently, when the U.S. Congress investigated Brazil's role in the Iraqi military buildup. Senator Albert Gore, apparently inventing as he went along, asserted that "the biggest single customer for beef coming out of the Amazon is—has been Iraq" (U.S. Congress, Joint Economic Committee, Subcommittee on Science and Technology, Hearings, "U.S. Policy on High Technology Exports"). The Brazilian Amazon is a net importer of beef.

64. This demand has been reduced somewhat by domestic breeding programs for experimental animals in the United States.

65. The emphasis here is on *relative* factor abundance. For most of the re-

gion, little is abundant, except in relation to the general scarcity of capital and technology.

66. IDB, *Economic and Social Progress in Latin America* (1989), p. 294.

67. Ayres, "Debt-for-Equity Swaps and the Conservation of Tropical Rain Forests," p. 332.

68. This simple correlation does not control for such possible intervening variables as a combination of declining prices and currency adjustment, which might be masking an underlying positive relationship between debt and trade in resource-based products. That level of discrimination is currently being undertaken in separate research with Ana Doris N. Capistrano. The point here is that there is no straightforward relationship between debt and resource exports and that individual countries' responses vary widely, despite the common condition of debt.

69. Capistrano and Sanderson, "Tyranny of the External."

70. IDB, *Economic and Social Progress in Latin America* (1989), p. 27.

71. That does not mean that similar levels of investment and consumption would necessarily generate the same kind of performance now as occurred in the 1970s.

72. For further details, see Goodman and Redclift, eds., *International Farm Crisis*, and Austin and Esteva, eds., *Food Policy in Mexico*.

73. This is hardly a new observation. For the classic exposition of these and other ecological themes, see Geertz, *Agricultural Involution*.

74. Repetto and Gillis, *Public Policies and the Misuse of Forest Resources*; McNeely, *Economics and Biological Diversity*; Mahar, *Government Policies*; Binswanger, *Brazilian Policies*.

75. Hecht and Cockburn, *Fate of the Forest*.

76. See Sanderson, *Agrarian Populism and the Mexican State* and *Transformation of Mexican Agriculture*. Exploitation of the Texas high plains generated a policy debate under the Carter administration on the "structure of agriculture." For an illuminating document from that debate, see USDA, *A Time to Choose*. The durability of the breadbasket myth is remarkable. For a recent academic example, see Hall, "Agrarian Crisis in Brazilian Amazonia." Even though Hall provides a cogent critique of Brazilian government plans for agricultural development, he concludes by advocating appropriate technologies to exploit the floodplains of Amazonia, a long-standing ambition of the government which has been roundly criticized in the central Amazon.

77. Because internationalism has been identified with liberalization, privatization, and reliance on markets, it is assumed here that redistribution is not a major priority. The benefits of trickle-down don't trickle down.

Chapter 4

1. O'Neill, "HICs, MICs, NICs, and LICs."

2. Figures are for 1988, taken from IDB, *Economic and Social Progress in Latin America: Savings, Investment, and Growth*.

3. These averages are for 1983–87, from ibid.

4. The IDB, for example, sets Brazil apart from the region in characterizing its unusually low vulnerability to trade shock (IDB, *Economic and Social Progress in Latin America: The External Sector*, Table 2).

5. A convenient summary of the literature can be found in Mommsen, *Theories of Imperialism*, pp. 86–93. Also see Chapter 1 above for citations of the literature on free trade imperialism.

6. Pieterse, *Empire and Emancipation*, p. 12.

7. Lake, *Power, Protection, and Free Trade*; Katzenstein, *Small States in World Markets*; and Keohane, *After Hegemony*.

8. This does not mean that the analysis here is entwined in public choice theory, which does not fit the focus of this work. The purpose in saying that a country *chooses* one path or another is to locate the structural and historical conditions for that choice, not the rationality (or the theorizing) about particular political choices. If we accept the divisions of Staniland in *What Is Political Economy?* the analysis in this research comes from an entirely different tradition than the public choice literature.

9. One is reminded of Juan Perón in this connection, as he is alleged to have ignored the advice of economists in favor of his own populist political goals.

10. Semmel, *Rise of Free Trade Imperialism*, p. 4; Platt, "Imperialism of Free Trade," p. 305n.

11. Embedded in this contention is a critique of simplistic notions of public choice, which are crippled by the lack of alternatives available to make choice a meaningful concept.

12. The literature on Anglo-Argentine economic relations in the later nineteenth and early twentieth centuries is extraordinarily rich. For beginning guides, see Ferns, *Britain and Argentina in the Nineteenth Century*; Chiaramonte, *Nacionalismo y liberalismo económico en la Argentina*; Rock, *Argentina in the Twentieth Century* and *Argentina*; Diaz-Alejandro, *Essays on the Economic History of the Argentine Republic*; Platt, *Latin America and British Trade*; and Rippy, *British Investments in Latin America*.

13. For an excellent synthesis of Argentina's condition before 1930, see Diaz-Alejandro, "Argentine Economy Before 1930"; for agriculture in third place, ibid., p. 10.

14. Hirschman, *National Power and the Structure of Foreign Trade*, p. 27; Haberler, *Prosperity and Depression*, pp. 461–73. The calculus of this is rather difficult. As Halperin Donghi points out in the Latin American case, import liberalization in the nineteenth century is generally thought to have resulted in the pauperization of urban artisans who were outcompeted by the British. Perhaps, however, even before the British onslaught the urban craft industries were on the decline and the expansion of trade opened new opportunities for those artisans based on a growing internal market. This kind of historiographical question cannot be resolved here, but is worth noting. See Halperin Donghi, "Economy and Society," pp. 28–29. Bertram and Thorp, *Peru*, develop a more sophisticated notion of "returned value," which attempts to assess the developmental gains from trade based on the flows of foreign exchange and domestic investment.

15. Lynch, "River Plate Republics," p. 314.

16. Ibid., p. 320.

17. The general validity of this observation—that import dependence is a development deficiency, not an asset—is theoretical and relies here on anecdotal evidence, without full proof that alternative uses of capital would have been superior for national development. Given the possibility of alternative misuse of capital, however, it is still generally the case that excessive imports are related to low domestic savings and investment rates, from the rubber boom in Manaus to the U.S. trade deficit in the 1980s. For the more general point, see Halperin Donghi, "Economy and Society," p. 6. For more thorough treatment of the economic arguments, see World Bank, *World Development Report, 1989*.

18. This evocative term has been appropriated unfortunately as a trademark of the "stages of growth" literature, thanks to Rostow's *Stages of Economic Growth*. It is used here for its evocative connotation of growth and should not be associated with Rostow. See Lynch, "River Plate Republics," p. 348.

19. Diaz-Alejandro, "Stages in the Industrialization of Argentina." Imports were substituted in foodstuffs and some other light industries, but the bulk of agricultural machinery and consumer durables was imported. Likewise, the bulk of the expanding industrial base was exported.

20. Diaz-Alejandro, "Argentine Economy Before 1930," p. 30.

21. Ibid., p. 20.

22. Smith, *Authoritarianism*, chap. 2. See also Murmis and Portantiero, *Estudios sobre los orígenes del peronismo/1*; and Llach, "Dependencia" and "El Plan Pinedo."

23. In the presentation of data that follows, total value of exports as a percentage of gross domestic product has been used. Obviously, total trade would include imports as well. And one could certainly fashion an openness index to reflect debt service payments, because they are so important to trading nations of Latin America. Exports are used for their sensitivity to movement in the international system and for their consistency with convention. Imports, especially since the onset of the debt crisis in 1982, have been artificially reduced in almost all high-debt countries at some time in the past several years and reflect other phenomena than structural openness. The Inter-American Development Bank uses both imports and exports as its measure of openness.

24. Unfortunately, as the next chapter shows, this index is not viable in the current climate of state-led adjustment crisis and response because of the wild swings in terms of trade and coefficients of exports.

25. As late as 1981, Mexico's exports of manufactures was small considering its size and industrial diversity. In 1979, Brazil exported three times Mexico's value in manufactures. In that year, Mexico exported about one-eighth of the region's manufactures, despite attracting 29 percent of total foreign investment. Manufacturing exports in 1978 represented less than 3 percent of GDP, compared with 5.5 percent for Brazil and 9 percent for Argentina (IDB, *Economic and Social Progress in Latin America: The External Sector*, chap. 5).

26. For reasons of parsimony, dependence here is used in its most modest

conception, connoting reliance on a more powerful partner for trade. To keep to the core of the argument, dependence is shaped after the conceptualization outlined by Caporaso, "Dependence, Dependency, and Power in the Global System," rather than its more full-fledged relative from the dependency literature. The argument regarding trade diversification is related to, but not the same as, the argument in favor of agricultural or industrial diversification.

27. This literature is accessible through Robinson, ed., *Economic Consequences of the Size of Nations*, and is questioned in Khalaf, "Country Size and Trade Concentration." See also Lloyd, *International Trade Problems of Small Nations*.

28. See Chapter 2 in this volume; also Prebisch, *Economic Development*, and O'Donnell and Linck, *Dependencia y autonomía*. See also Bertram and Thorp, *Peru*, pp. 11–12.

29. Prebisch, "Five Stages," p. 178; IDB, *Economic and Social Progress in Latin America: Economic Integration*.

30. Mahler, "Controlling International Commodity Prices and Supplies," p. 160.

31. The exhaustion of the easy phase of import-substitution industrialization is a hotly debated question. It has been asserted, particularly in the literature on associated dependent development, that import-substitution industrialization ran into a structural problem in the mid-1950s: the inability to "deepen" the domestic industrial base to overcome one of the primary obstacles to autonomous development—dependence on imports of intermediate and capital goods. Because one of the primary objectives of import-substitution industrialization was import relief, this obstacle spelled a limit to it based on light consumer goods. For a clear definition of the "easy phase" and its origins in economic thinking, see Diaz-Alejandro, "Stages in the Industrialization of Argentina," p. 208n. See also, Albert O. Hirschman, *The Strategy of Economic Development* (New Haven, Conn.: Yale University Press, 1958). For critical analysis of the exhaustion thesis, see the contributions of Serra, Hirschman, and O'Donnell, in Collier, ed., *New Authoritarianism in Latin America*. An article taking issue with the historicity of that exhaustion and its relationship to populism is Perruci and Sanderson, "Presidential Succession, Economic Crisis and the Resurgence of Populism in Brazil."

32. U.S. Department of Commerce, *Latin America Trade Review 1988*, p. 26.

33. IDB, *Economic and Social Progress in Latin America: Savings, Investment, and Growth*, p. 294 and Table F-2.

34. See Teitel, "The Nature, Costs and Benefits."

35. Reciprocity is one of the key terms debated in international trade negotiations. It is contrasted with preference, especially under the Generalized System of Preferences approved as the most serious concession of the GATT to Third World trade partners.

36. For a critique of this principle and a description of unease about it in developed countries, see Rothstein, *Global Bargaining*, chap. 7.

37. Cline, "Reciprocity."

38. Prebisch, "Five Stages," p. 180.

39. Hudec, *Developing Countries in the GATT Legal System.*

40. Gootenberg, "Beleaguered Liberals," p. 68.

41. Barman, *Brazil,* p. 18.

42. Albert Fishlow, "Comment" on Prebisch, "Five Stages," p. 193.

43. This is far from our trail in this book, but part of the international element of the "Great Debate" about value and incentive in socialist Cuba revolved around whether Cuba could assign values to labor and products without regard to the law of value dominating capitalist society. That is, to some extent the question of delinking depends on the ability of the delinking society to depart from the determination of a commodity's value according to its "bourgeois mercantile" character. If this debate seemed strained in the 1960s in tiny Cuba, it seems utopian in the 1990s, when the very socialist bloc on which it depends for noncapitalist circulation is dissolving. For an instructive period piece, see Mora, "On the Operation of the Law of Value."

44. Cuba argued that a socialist economy, even one as open as its own, did not have to "obey the laws of value" in commerce. Politically, this meant that Cuba enjoyed the freedom to price its output according to administrative criteria (consistent with principles of socialist economics) and to ignore international markets in its decisions to allocate economic values for national production. Cuba's vulnerability to hegemonic influence in the East-West context and the poor performance of sugar as an export commodity made this theoretical position optimistic in the extreme. The apparent surrender of the Eastern European members of the Council of Mutual Economic Assistance to the international law of value puts Cuba in an even more compromised position.

45. For a clear exposition of this "law," see Kindleberger, *Foreign Trade and the National Economy,* p. 179.

46. One might argue that insulation can also be measured by a sustainable reduction of imports.

47. Diaz-Alejandro, "Latin America in the 1930s."

48. William C. Smith (personal communication), with typical acuity, has suggested a very inviting way to extend this analysis by comparing Latin American states with East Asian developmental states. Although doing so is well beyond the scope and empirical refinement of the current analysis, it is suggested that the reader consult Gereffi, "Rethinking Development Theory," and Evans, "Predatory, Developmental, and Other Apparatuses."

49. This is a political term to describe what economists would call the structural adjustment process. Under the Argentine dictatorship from 1976 to 1983, political authoritarianism was more important to the process than was economically sound adjustment.

50. The reason it is unfortunate has to do with the broader responsibility of economists both at the University of Chicago and in Santiago for the policies of the Pinochet regime. For illuminating remarks on the political insensitivity of Chicago economists treating the Chilean "success story," see Garcia and Wells, "Chile"; Ffrench-Davis, "The Monetarist Experiment in Chile"; and Lehmann, "The Political Economy of Armageddon."

51. Sheahan, *Patterns of Development*, p. 8 and Part II.

52. Cavarozzi, "Political Cycles in Argentina"; Wynia, *Argentina in the Postwar Era*; and William C. Smith, *Authoritarianism*.

53. Luciano Martins, "The 'Liberalization' of Authoritarian Rule"; Skidmore, *The Politics of Military Rule*.

54. See Foxley, "Towards a Free Market Economy."

55. For a clear exposition of this and other theoretical propositions regarding trade liberalization, see Whalley, *Trade Liberalization Among Major World Trading Areas*, esp. chap. 2. The quote is on p. 23.

56. This observation is not strictly confined to small countries of Latin America. In the famous case of voluntary export restraints on Japanese automobile exports to the United States, the U.S. consumer bore the additional cost of imported vehicles, which were scarcity rents. An artificial scarcity rent also accrued to U.S. producers, who raised their own prices to match Japanese imports. One of the strongest criticisms of such arrangements (versus a formal tariff or free trade) is that they permit the rent to accrue to the producer, rather than to the government imposing the restraint or to the consumer (in the form of tax relief, for example).

57. IDB, *Economic and Social Progress in Latin America: Savings, Investment, and Growth*, p. 136.

58. In this connection, it is interesting to wonder whether Sheahan or others now would consider Mexico moving toward or already among the "market authoritarian" models of development.

59. For a current survey of Brazilian agricultural policy, see USDA, "Amid Turmoil, Brazil's Agricultural Growth to Slow." For a more comprehensive policy statement, see World Bank, *Brazil*.

60. The association between economic growth and U.S. national security concerns in Latin America is treated well in Schoultz, *National Security and U.S. Policy Toward Latin America*, chap. 2. The inherent paradox in that posture is not criticized there, however. If economic growth and structural transformation create the conditions for reducing poverty (a dubious but prevalent argument for much of the postwar period in Washington), the initial arc of the Kuznets curve graphs the concentration of income, the dispossession of noncapitalist landowners, and a general reorientation of national economic imperatives that certainly do not enhance political stability in the short and medium term. Given the short political horizons of the hegemon, it seems unlikely that the economic transformation of traditional society in Latin America enhances political stability in ways to assuage intervention-minded national security analysts in the United States.

61. This is the argument of the Colombian government in regard to recent disputes over the breakup of the International Coffee Agreement, in which the United States has opposed discounted sales of coffee to nonmember countries. Brazil and Colombia are the two largest coffee producers in the world, and the United States and other consuming nation members of the ICA are demanding a radical new agreement to supplant the now-expired 1983 agreement. There is some empirical literature to support the U.S. claim that "free riders" on the

international agreement (nonmember consuming countries) benefit from the ICA, as do large producers, while small producers and member-country consumers suffer from price regulation through quotas. See especially Herrmann, "International Allocation of Trade-tied Aid," "Free Riders and the Redistributive Effects of International Commodity Agreements," and "Measuring National Interests in the International Coffee Agreement." For general analysis of the allocation of quotas, see Bates and Lien, "On the Operations of the International Coffee Agreement."

62. One recent exception can be found in Hakkert and Goza, "Demographic Consequences of Austerity in Latin America."

63. One recent critique can be found in Fishlow, "Latin American State."

Chapter 5

1. See, for example, Hayes, "The U.S. and Latin America," p. 180; and "Trends."

2. See particularly Keohane, *After Hegemony* and "Hegemonic Leadership and U.S. Foreign Economic Policy"; Russett, "The Mysterious Case of Vanishing Hegemony"; and Strange, "Management of Surplus Capacity" and "Persistent Myth of Lost Hegemony." A good critical treatment of different approaches to this question as they pertain to trade is Cowhey and Long, "Testing Theories of Regime Change."

3. The most likely venue for this reticence will be the U.S.-Mexico bilateral free trade negotiations, as the real costs of adjustment to North American integration become apparent to the Congress. The U.S.-Mexico talks may offer nationalists on both sides of the border the opportunity to create momentary alliances to defeat free traders.

4. For convenient access to the massive literature on Bretton Woods, see Gilpin, *Political Economy of International Relations.* Key revisionist interpretations of the Bretton Woods system include Block, *Origins of International Economic Disorder;* Kolko and Kolko, *Limits of Power;* and Yergin, *Shattered Peace.* The monetary classic is Bergsten, *Dilemmas of the Dollar;* for the GATT system, see Dam, *GATT.* More specific literature will be cited below.

5. Gardner, *Sterling-Dollar Diplomacy,* pp. 13–14.

6. There is no doubt that the GATT round collapsed at the end of 1990, but many countries, including the United States, were interested in keeping the round alive into 1991. Of the two fundamental obstacles to the Uruguay Round's survival, the U.S. presidential negotiating authority was extended in May 1991. But the EEC has yet to propose a meaningful negotiating position in agriculture.

7. The date 1992 is partly symbolic. The single market concept will be phased in over several years, and the ambitions of European unification that are implied in the idea still require much work beyond 1992. A convenient entry point into the potential for 1992 is Colchester and Buchan, *Europower.*

8. This prospect, of course, is denied consistently by officials of the EEC, who argue that the principle of European integration and the idea of Fortress Europe are contradictory. Nevertheless, the integration plan contains components that bode ill for those outside the new EEC. A characteristic denial of Fortress Europe

is the statement of EEC President Jacques Delors, who said that the EEC is "founded on the principle of an open trading system" and that "it would be illogical to employ a different philosophy vis-à-vis the outside" ("OECD Ministers Upbeat on Economic Outlook but Divisive on Agricultural Subsidy Issues"). Of course, since that statement was made, the agricultural subsidy issue brought down the GATT talks and showed Europe's inclination to defy a growing consensus on freer trade in agricultural products.

9. On growing international regionalism, see Ludlow, "Future of the International Trading System."

10. Helmut Kohl's reluctance to support more aggressive liberalization of agriculture in the GATT was a function of his electoral strategy in newly unified Germany, and his overarching need to placate domestic farm interests.

11. Jordan, "In Brazil, the Coffee King, Soy Takes Pride of Place."

12. OECD, *National Policies and Agricultural Trade*, p. 314.

13. For an entry point into the literature about the Sistema Alimentario Mexicano, see Austin and Esteva, eds., *Food Policy in Mexico*.

14. The distinction between export agriculture and domestic use agriculture, traditionally cited as the culprit in the failure of nationalist food strategies, is overdrawn. As Bulmer-Thomas has shown in the Central American context and I have argued in the case of Mexican basic grains, domestic use agriculture and export agriculture are deeply intertwined. Nevertheless, the distinction is important for the bias it portrays in market destination, as well as allocation of credit and other inputs.

15. Very different views of the virtue of such competition are expressed in the statements of EEC and African-Caribbean-Pacific leaders after a meeting between the two in January 1989. EEC officials insisted that preferential treatment "has got to go" in favor of "a single market for bananas." Barbados's ambassador to Europe worried about the "real" threat from Central American bananas, which have price and quality advantages. These concerns are echoed throughout Latin America in relations with the EEC after 1992. See "Caribbean Leaders Weigh Impact of EC 1992 Single Market Plan on Banana, Sugar Trade."

16. See "Yeutter Increases Sugar Import Quotas, Extends Period Through September 1990."

17. For formal treatment of the "gamesmanship" of the International Coffee Agreement, see Bates and Lien, "On the Operation of the International Coffee Agreement."

18. Merriman, "Colombia Blames Producers and U.S. for Coffee Pact Failure."

19. Percentages are estimates for the period 1983–87 from IDB, *Economic and Social Progress in Latin America: Savings, Investment, and Growth*, Table F-2. As the head of the Brazilian Coffee Institute said in 1989, "Brazil can do whatever it wants in coffee and in whatever volume . . . Brazil is in a position to leap to the top again" (quoted in Merriman, "Coffee Falls to Eight-Year Low as Price War Looms").

20. IDB, *Economic and Social Progress in Latin America: Economic Integration*, p. 108.

21. IDB, *Economic and Social Progress in Latin America: Savings, Investment, and Growth*, p. 77.

22. Ibid., p. 74.

23. Ibid., p. 71.

24. This effort has just begun and was discussed during the OAS meetings in June 1990. See UPI, June 1, 1990.

25. *International Trade Reporter*, May 4, 1988.

26. See Drake, *Money Doctor*; Smith, "Morrow Mission"; Meyer, *Mexico and the United States in the Oil Controversy*; Bertram and Thorp, *Peru*, pp. 95–111. One of the theoretically most interesting treatments of foreign involvement in Chilean copper is Moran, *Multinational Corporations and the Politics of Dependence*.

27. The GATT allows regional agreements, with some restrictions, under Article XXIV. An excellent treatment of the origins, weaknesses, and ultimate failure of the constraints in that article may be found in Dam, *GATT*, chap. 16. The United States has encouraged some regional integration efforts, including the Caribbean and Central American common markets. It has also undertaken modest regional preference arrangements of its own, of which the Caribbean Basin Initiative is the most ambitious. A prospective U.S.-Mexico bilateral free trade agreement as the second (Canada being the first) bilateral element in a hemispheric free trade area would obviously eclipse previous initiatives.

28. An excellent recent treatment of the Central American economies is Bulmer-Thomas, *Political Economy of Central America*; see also Robert Williams, *Export Agriculture and the Crisis in Central America*.

29. This is not to say that such outcomes would not be preferable in the abstract, but the character of international economics is so complex that it is reasonable to assume that such U.S. policy adjustments on private or public savings, for example, would have a negative impact on trade politics between ever-desperate Latin American countries and their single most important trade partner, the United States.

30. This is consistent with the general argument of the new international division of labor, which is based on the globalization of competitive international capital, the standardization of labor processes, and the coincidence of national politics of industrial development and trade.

31. Schoultz, *National Security and United States Policy Toward Latin America*.

32. One of the clearest cases of that confusion is the overthrow of the Guatemalan government in 1954, which is generally seen as a combination of narrow defense of United Fruit interests against agrarian and labor reform, as well as the anticommunist foreign policy of the Dulles brothers in the Eisenhower administration. For the former, see Immerman, *CIA in Guatemala*, and Schlesinger and Kinzer, *Bitter Fruit*; for a more interesting interpretation, see Rabe, *Eisenhower and Latin America*.

33. The former will be demonstrated in this chapter. The latter argument is made in Stallings, *Banker to the Third World*.

34. One of the priceless examples of this wordsmith's talent is the concept of "biplurilateralism," a concept forwarded by the U.S. Trade Representative when it appeared that the new GATT round might not be endorsed in the OECD. The United States threatened to negotiate on a bilateral basis with whoever came to the table. It would be a multilateral negotiation, but based on the bilateral tradition.

35. High-debt countries include Argentina, Brazil, Chile, Mexico, Peru, and Venezuela.

36. Drabenstott, Barkema, and Henneberry, "The Latin American Debt Problem and U.S. Agriculture," Tables 3 and 4.

37. The source of this cliché in academic writing may be Schattschneider, *Politics, Pressures and the Tariff*. For a good introduction and critique of that literature, see Lake, "The State and American Trade Strategy in the Pre-Hegemonic Era" and *Power, Protection, and Free Trade*. This premise is the point of departure for the recent volume, Nau, ed., *Domestic Trade Politics and the Uruguay Round*. In that volume, see especially Kennedy and Fonseca, "Brazilian Trade Policy and the Uruguay Round," and Rubio, Rodriguez, and Blum, "The Making of Mexico's Trade Policy and the Uruguay Round."

38. "Transparency" is one of the principal trade policy goals of the United States in the current round of GATT negotiations. It means, simply, that rules governing the import and export of goods and services should be clear and explicit, rather than hidden administrative or other obstacles that cannot be dealt with in the multilateral system.

39. The Cairns Group, named after the city in Australia where it convened, is made up of Australia, Argentina, Brazil, Canada, and New Zealand. Initially, the group proposed an end to all agricultural subsidies by the year 2000, in addition to a freeze on subsidies in 1988 and 10 percent cuts in 1989 and 1990. The United States called for elimination of subsidies by the end of the century as well but did not agree to any short-term measures. The EEC has refused steadfastly to consider eliminating agricultural subsidies altogether. Although the United States has been critical of the Cairns Group, the group has been important in agricultural trade in general and for this analysis because of the participation of Argentina and Brazil.

40. The so-called Super 301 requires the U.S. Trade Representative to initiate some Section 301 investigations autonomously, based on the controversial annual National Trade Estimates Report, which identifies foreign barriers to trade and investment. Before 1985, Section 301 investigations responded to industry complaints and did not emanate from the executive branch without such initiation from the private sector. There is also a "special 301," which refers strictly to intellectual property disputes. Super 301 permits investigation of "bundled practices," rather than individual responses to specific commodity-based complaints. For an extremely generous interpretation of the 1988 trade act with focus on Section 301, see Holmer and Bello, "The 1988 Trade Bill." Holmer was Deputy U.S. Trade Representative and Bello General Counsel for the Trade Representative at the time of the legislation.

41. "U.S. Negotiators Conclude Second Round of VRA Talks with Big Five Suppliers."

42. "U.S., Brazil Agree to Renew Brazil's Share of Steel VRA."

43. Weil, " 'Super 301' Will Do Little to Trim Trade Gap."

44. This is not exclusive to Latin America, of course, as can be seen in the many cases brought before Japan in televisions, telephone equipment, cargo transport, and so on.

45. "U.S. Message to Brazil Seen Linking 301 to Sale of U.S. Telecommunications Equipment."

46. This action was widely considered to be a violation of the Tokyo Accords because it denied equal treatment to all nations under the GATT umbrella, depending on whether they had signed a voluntary code not incorporated into the main body of the GATT. The United States could deny the second, and most important, step in countervailing duties cases, which requires an investigation into the injury caused by trade subsidies by partner countries. This unilateral practice was used most seriously in the case of Mexico in the mid-1980s, when the injury test was promised as a reward for Mexico's accession to the GATT.

47. Characterizing Baucus's approach as biplurilateral stems from the U.S. Trade Representative's own definition of that concept. Biplurilateralism is a multilateral approach centered in the United States but dealing with only those members of the multilateral system willing to come to the bargaining table under specific conditions committing them to transparency, the most-favored nation principle, reciprocity, and so on.

48. "Baucus Urges Bush to Seek Talks on 1992 Plan."

49. For an argument that bilateralism fortifies the GATT, see Ludlow, "Future of the International Trading System."

50. I am obliged to Richard Hofstader's essay "The Myth of the Happy Yeoman" for this characterization.

51. Keynes, *Economic Consequences of the Peace*, p. 179.

52. This has become a rather hollow cry as the EEC falls short of the development assistance needs of the Lomé countries facing trade adjustment and the collapse of commodity agreements. To the small banana, cocoa, coffee, or sugar producer, "becoming more competitive" in international markets has little charm when competitiveness is not accompanied by market power.

53. The new Collor government has had some momentary successes in both: reducing inflation in 1990 and signing an accord with the IMF in September 1990. But the Mideast conflict sent oil prices and domestic energy costs soaring. Brazil still has not managed to placate the large commercial banks, led by Citibank, and the short-term prospects for the national economy are still uncertain.

54. Sachs, "Making the Brady Plan Work." Some critics argued that the Brady Plan was mainly a foil for U.S. plans for Mexico because the Bush administration is full of Texans with great interest in the future economic health of its southern neighbor. See Fidler, "Bankers Face Down Brady Plan in Mexico Debt Talks." This criticism ignores the targeting of 39 different countries under the Brady Plan, and special emphasis on Venezuela, as well as Mexico.

55. Adler, *Power of Ideology*; Evans, "State, Capital, and the Transformation of Dependence"; Schwartzman, "High Technology and Self-Reliance."

56. See "Products from Mexico Occupy Center Stage at GSP Subcommittee Annual Review Hearings."

Chapter 6

1. The logic of this policy is spelled out to some extent in a treatment of the structural constraints on the Mexican presidential succession of 1982. See Sanderson, "Presidential Succession and Political Rationality in Mexico."

2. *New York Times*, July 1, 1990.

3. This is not to say that trade policies are irrelevant to general macroeconomic concerns. Their role is described in Ardito Barletta, Blejer, and Landau, eds., *Economic Liberalization and Stabilization Policies in Argentina, Chile and Uruguay.*

4. Though Mexico's momentary economic health is rated improved by many international economic observers, its trade and development agendas are full of problems familiar to countries in much worse economic condition. The impact of Mexico's stabilization on domestic development is not positive from the standpoint of distribution of domestic resources, though it may be from the standpoint of the private sector.

5. At this writing, the bilateral trade negotiations between the United States and Mexico are just beginning. It is interesting that on both sides of the border, concerns are being voiced about the labor force adjustment costs of bilateral free trade. But the natural resource costs—in petroleum shifted to an expanding integrated industrial sector instead of exported for U.S. use, or dry lands shifted away from domestic food consumption, or semiarid lands turned to export agriculture—have not been considered fully. And one of the biggest questions to be answered in bilateral free trade—the consequences for migrant labor entering the United States—has been rejected by the latter as an inappropriate issue for the talks.

6. This generalization obviously must be qualified by the agreement at the end of 1989 to include the Dominican Republic and Haiti in the new Lomé IV accord. Still, while African-Caribbean-Pacific country leaders are concerned with Central American competition in bananas in a unified European market, Central Americans are concerned with being shut out of a "Fortress Europe."

7. Diaz-Alejandro, "Delinking." Several authors join this question at a less global level as "the self-reliance problematic," in Ruggie, ed., *Antinomies of Interdependence*, Part II.

8. The U.S. version of this trade-averse behavior is manifest in congressional (and private sector) reluctance to negotiate new free trade agreements. At the moment the GATT talks broke down in Brussels in early December 1990, U.S. senators were drafting a resolution to withdraw fast-track authorization from the president to conclude the negotiations.

9. These two arguments offer another concluding line of inquiry, which is too broad to fit into this study and more properly derives from Sheahan's work on comparative state-market relations in Latin America. An analytical pattern of state-market relations must be derived from the history of Latin American politi-

cal economy to enhance our preliminary understanding of current state strategies toward trade. The fit of regional strategies with U.S. trade policy could be examined as an optic for assessing the prospects of Latin American trade politics in the 1990s.

10. The term is Sheahan's, from *Patterns of Development*.

11. Thorp and Whitehead, eds., *Latin American Debt and the Adjustment Crisis*, p. 3.

12. Opinion varies on the post-1968 Peruvian government, and this is only one interpretation. For contending approaches, see Stepan, *State and Society*; Bertram and Thorp, *Peru*; Fitzgerald, *The State and Economic Development*; Lowenthal, ed., *Peruvian Experiment*; and McClintock and Lowenthal, eds., *Peruvian Experiment Reconsidered*. An early but ultimately unsatisfying anti-imperialist interpretation is found in Quijano, *Nationalism and Capitalism in Peru*.

13. Economic nationalism is increasingly taking on the bilateral free trade negotiations as a target building toward the elections of 1994.

14. Prebisch, "Five Stages in My Thinking," p. 179.

15. O'Donnell and Linck, *Dependencia y autonomía*.

16. This statement must be qualified by the incredible growth of the *maquiladoras*, which now encompass 1,700 firms employing nearly 500,000 people and which promise to ensure manufacturing exports under a bilateral free trade agreement. For now, they are a special category under separate tariff rules, and their success in the 1980s follows fifteen years of modest growth and accomplishment.

17. Tironi, "Reappraisal of the Role of Primary Exports in Latin America."

18. Khalaf, "Country Size and Trade Concentration," argues that the relationship between country size and trade concentration "is not as strong as *a priori* reasoning suggests." The treatment is overly simplistic, however, and is based on a statistical association of a sample of 80 countries, irrespective of region, rather than country and regional analysis that might take historical development and politics more seriously.

19. IDB, *Economic and Social Progress in Latin America: Savings, Investment, and Growth*.

20. Quoted in Carr, *Twenty Years' Crisis*, p. 122.

21. List, *National System of Political Economy*.

22. Rabe, *Eisenhower and Latin America*, chap. 4.

23. Schoultz, *National Security and United States Policy Toward Latin America*; Krasner, *Defending the National Interest*.

24. Gill and Law, *Global Political Economy*, esp. pp. 103–24.

25. Vargas, "Discurso do Rio Amazonas," pp. 3–6.

26. Interestingly, thirty years later Archer was responsible for the implementation and expansion of the market reserve in informatics as minister of science and technology in the Sarney government.

27. The Mexican petroleum decision was but the culmination of a series of national policy decisions dating from the constitution of 1917, in which the subsoil resources of the Mexican nation were made part of the national patrimony. See Meyer, *Mexico and the United States in the Oil Controversy*, pp. 54–172.

28. This does not ignore the long-term trend toward more trade after a period of decline. There is little to suggest that Latin America historically or developmentally has passed through the trough and should expect increases in trade as a natural product of a new phase of economic development.

29. For fuller theoretical treatment, see Sanderson, "Critical Approach to the New International Division of Labor," which also provides a bibliography behind these arguments.

30. Carr, *Twenty Years' Crisis.*

31. Schoultz, *National Security and United States Policy Toward Latin America*; Krasner, *Defending the National Interest.*

32. For fuller treatment of this strategy and its international context, see Austin and Esteva, eds., *Food Policy in Mexico*; Sanderson, *Transformation of Mexican Agriculture.*

33. Stallings, *Class Conflict and Economic Change in Chile.*

34. Latin America Bureau, *Great Tin Crash.*

35. Carr, *Twenty Years' Crisis*, p. 129.

36. For a discussion of the exhaustion of the easy phase of import-substitution industrialization and the deepening thesis, see Hirschman and Serra in Collier, ed., *New Authoritarianism in Latin America.*

37. The concerns over domestic sourcing for *maquiladoras* have led the Mexican government to enact domestic content provisions in the law governing border industries. Both the United States and Mexico will have to negotiate domestic content in the event that the bilateral talks go forward. Domestic content is likely to be the political wedge of nationalist business interests against foreign competition and a U.S. strategy to avoid Japanese intrusion in the Mexican market to gain preferential access to the United States.

38. Statement from Mexico's 1980 Global Development Plan, as quoted in Velasco-S., *Impacts of Mexican Oil Policy on Economic and Political Development*, p. 30.

39. Gereffi, "Rethinking Development Theory," pp. 519–23.

40. Lahera, "Transnational Corporations and Latin America's International Trade."

41. Again, see Gereffi's excellent synthesis of the conceptual flaws in "Rethinking Development Theory."

42. Hathaway, *Agriculture and the GATT*, Tables 4.4, 4.6, 4.7.

43. Bulmer-Thomas, *Political Economy of Central America*; Lewis, "Development Economics in the 1950s," pp. 122, 124, citing his "Economic Development with Unlimited Supplies of Labour."

44. Arnade, Shane, and Stallings, *Foreign Debt, Capital Formation, and Debtor Behavior*, p. 13.

45. For two different alternative approaches that point up the fallacy of this assumption in Mexico and Central America, see Bulmer-Thomas, *Political Economy of Central America*, and Sanderson, *Transformation of Mexican Agriculture.* Bulmer-Thomas emphasizes more than previous authors the interconnections of domestic use agriculture and export agriculture in small economies of Central

America. The argument found in Sanderson emphasizes the integration of domestic and international agriculture through the new international division of labor.

46. For an excellent discussion of the relationship, see Lipton, *Land Assets and Rural Poverty*, which differs radically from such authors as Keith Griffin, in *Land Concentration and Rural Poverty*, regarding the relationship between property and poverty.

47. Hathaway, *Agriculture and the GATT*, p. 101.

48. See, for example, Saulniers, *Public Enterprises in Peru*.

49. Saulniers, ed., *Economic and Political Roles of the State in Latin America*.

50. Floyd, Gray, and Short, *Public Enterprise in Mixed Economies*.

51. Baer, Newfarmer, and Trebat, *On State Capitalism in Brazil*. See also, Topik, *Political Economy of the Brazilian State*. Others from a neo-Marxist perspective might have called this phenomenon monopoly capitalism led by the state. The misnomer "state capitalism" is either a great disservice to Lenin or a startling characterization of the Brazilian economy as a socialist transition.

52. Dean, *Brazil and the Struggle for Rubber*, p. 44.

53. The best recent critique can be found in Fishlow, "Latin American State."

54. Rohatyn, "World Bank."

55. See, for examples, Bennett and Sharpe, *Transnational Corporations vs. the State*; Gereffi, *The Pharmaceutical Industry and Dependency in the Third World*; Girvan, *Corporate Imperialism*; Moran, *Multinational Corporations and the Politics of Dependence*.

56. Gereffi, "Transnational Corporations and the Pharmaceutical Industry in Mexico"; Sanderson, "Trends in Mexican Investment Policy and the Forces That Shape Them."

57. New questions were raised about the commitment of the Collor government to technological and market liberalization when it announced that facsimile machines would continue to be reserved for domestic producers for the time being.

58. United States, Office of the United States Trade Representative, *Annual Report of the President of the United States on the Trade Agreements Program, 1984–1985*.

59. Lessard and Williamson, *Capital Flight and Third World Debt*.

60. For an insightful discussion about neoconservative experiments in Latin America, see Foxley, *Latin American Experiments*.

61. For an instructive summary of the hegemonic-stability literature, see Gill and Law, *Global Political Economy*, pp. 335–59. Among the several criticisms found in the literature, the following stand out: Kugler and Organski, "End of Hegemony?"; Strange, "Persistent Myth of Lost Hegemony"; and Russett, "Mysterious Case of Vanishing Hegemony." While much of the criticism has centered on the "security regime," this analysis looks at how premature this decline has proven. The "hegemonic stability" model often focuses on the economic processes of the hegemon, ignoring events at the periphery. After all, the hegemon's power is enhanced when other nations' economies collapse—as long as such a collapse does not disturb its domestic economy. Such is the case of U.S.–Latin American relations in the 1980s.

62. One of the more telling recent cases has been the 1985 changes in the Mexican pharmaceutical law in response to threats from U.S.-based multinationals and bilateral consultations with the U.S. Trade Representative. As a result, the Mexican government changed the pharmaceutical law virtually word for word in accordance with the demands of the U.S. private sector. See Gereffi, "Transnational Corporations and the Pharmaceutical Industry in Mexico"; Sanderson, "Trends in Mexican Investment Policy and the Forces That Shape Them."

Conclusion

1. Hull, *Memoirs*, vol. 1, p. 339.
2. IDB, *Economic and Social Progress in Latin America: Economic Integration.*
3. The future of oil exports in the context of U.S.-Mexican free trade is unclear. How long Mexico will take to respond to current price stimuli from the Mideast crisis of 1990, how much oil in future years will go to domestic use, and how much foreign capital will be permitted in the sector all have yet to be determined.
4. Merriman, "Outlook Bleak for Commodity Stabilisation Pacts."
5. Perruci and Sanderson, "Presidential Succession, Economic Crisis, and the Resurgence of Populism in Brazil."
6. Tony Ramirez, California business consultant, "Made in Mexico," quoted in Douglas Bartholomew, "A Continent in Flux: Mexico Opens the Door," *Euromoney* (Sept. 1989), p. 231.

Bibliography

The bulk of the citations here are in English, for two reasons: first, an increasing amount of seminal material is being written by Latin Americans in English, and second, I wanted to make the sources behind this book as accessible as possible to a U.S. audience. In the country literature, I have tried to include "gateway" literature, which will lead the interested reader to Spanish- and Portuguese-language sources.

Abbott, Philip C., and Stephen L. Haley. "International Trade Theory and Natural Resource Concepts." In John D. Sutton, ed., *Agricultural Trade and Natural Resources: Discovering the Critical Linkages*, pp. 35–62. Boulder, Colo.: Lynne Rienner, 1988.

Abel, Christopher, and Colin Lewis, eds. *Latin America, Economic Imperialism and the State: The Political Economy of the External Connection from Independence to the Present.* London: Athlone Press, 1985.

Abreu, Marcelo de Paiva. "Anglo-Brazilian Economic Relations and the Consolidation of American Pre-Eminence in Brazil, 1930–1945." In Christopher Abel and Colin Lewis, eds. *Latin America, Economic Imperialism and the State: The Political Economy of the External Connection from Independence to the Present,* pp. 379–93. London: Athlone Press, 1985.

———. "Developing Countries and the Uruguay Round of Trade Negotiations." *Proceedings of the World Bank Annual Conference on Development Economics,* pp. 21–46. Washington, D.C.: World Bank, 1989.

Abreu, Marcelo de Paiva, and Winston Fritsch. "Lessons of History: 1929–33 and 1979–8?" *International Journal of Political Economy* (Spring 1987): 45–63.

Adelman, Irma. "Development Economics—a Reassessment of Goals." *American Economic Review* 65 (May 1975): 302–9.

Adelman, Irma, and Cynthia Taft Morris. *Economic Growth and Social Equity in Developing Countries.* Stanford, Calif.: Stanford University Press, 1973.

Adelman, Irma, and J. Edward Taylor. "Is Structural Adjustment with a Human Face Possible? The Case of Mexico." Giannini Foundation Working Paper No. 500. University of California, Berkeley, July 1989.

Adler, Emanuel. *The Power of Ideology: The Quest for Technological Autonomy in Argentina and Brazil.* Berkeley: University of California Press, 1987.

Ahearn, Raymond J., and Alan Reifman. "Trade Policymaking in the Congress." In National Bureau of Economic Research, Conference Report, *Recent Issues and Initiatives in U.S. Trade Policy,* pp. 37–41. Cambridge, Mass.: National Bureau of Economic Research, 1984.

Aho, Michael, and Jonathan Aronson. *Trade Talks: America Better Listen!* New York: Council on Foreign Relations, 1985.

Alden, Dauril. "Late Colonial Brazil, 1750–1808." In Leslie Bethell, ed., *Colonial Brazil,* pp. 284–343. Cambridge: Cambridge University Press, 1987.

Ardito Barletta, Nicolas, Mario I. Blejer, and Luis Landau, eds. *Economic Liberalization and Stabilization Policies in Argentina, Chile and Uruguay: Applications of the Monetary Approach to the Balance of Payments.* Washington, D.C.: World Bank, 1983.

Arida, Persio, ed. *Inflação zero: Brasil, Argentina, Israel.* Rio de Janeiro: Paz e Terra, 1986. Published in English as *Inflation and Indexation: Argentina, Brazil and Israel.* Cambridge, Mass.: MIT Press, 1985.

Arnade, Carlos, Matthew Shane, and David Stallings. *Foreign Debt, Capital Formation, and Debtor Behavior.* Washington, D.C.: U.S. Department of Agriculture, Economic Research Service, 1989.

Arndt, H. W. "Development Economics Before 1945." In Jagdish Bhagwati and Richard Eckaus, eds., *Development and Planning: Essays in Honour of Paul Rosenstein-Rodan,* pp. 13–29. Amsterdam: North-Holland Press, 1972.

Ascher, William, and Robert Healy. *Natural Resource Policymaking in Developing Countries: Environment, Economic Growth, and Income Distribution.* Durham, N.C.: Duke University Press, 1990.

Athukorala, Premachandra. "Export Performance of 'New Exporting Countries': How Valid Is the Optimism?" *Development and Change* 20 (1989): 89–120.

Austin, James E., and Gustavo Esteva, eds. *Food Policy in Mexico: The Search for Self-Sufficiency.* Ithaca, N.Y.: Cornell University Press, 1987.

Avery, William P., and David P. Rapkin, eds. *America in a Changing World Political Economy.* New York: Longman, 1982.

Ayres, José Márcio. "Debt-for-Equity Swaps and the Conservation of Tropical Rain Forests." *Tree* 4, no. 11 (Nov. 1989): 331–35.

Baer, Werner, and Malcolm Gillis, eds. *Export Diversification and the New Protectionism: The Experiences of Latin America.* Champaign: University of Illinois, Bureau of Economic and Business Research, 1981.

Baer, Werner, Richard Newfarmer, and Thomas Trebat. *On State Capitalism in Brazil: Some New Issues and Questions.* Technical Papers Series No. 1. Austin: Institute of Latin American Studies at the University of Texas at Austin, 1976.

Balassa, Bela, Gerardo M. Bueno, Pedro-Pablo Kuczynski, and Mario Henrique Simonsen. *Toward Renewed Economic Growth in Latin America.* Washington, D.C.: Institute for International Economics, 1986.

Barbier, Edward B. "The Concept of Sustainable Economic Development." *Environmental Conservation* 14, no. 2 (Summer 1987): 101–10.

Barkin, David. *Distorted Development: Mexico in the World Economy.* Boulder, Colo.: Westview Press, 1990.

——. *El fin de autosuficiencia alimentaria.* Mexico City: Nueva Imagen, 1982.

Barman, Roderick J. *Brazil: The Forging of a Nation, 1798–1852.* Stanford, Calif.: Stanford University Press, 1989.

Bates, Robert H., and D. H. D. Lien. "On the Operations of the International Coffee Agreement." *International Organization* 39 (1985): 553–59.

Batie, Sandra S. "Sustainable Development: Challenges to the Profession of Agricultural Economics." Presidential Address, American Agricultural Economics Association National Meeting, July 30–Aug. 2, 1989. Typescript.

"Baucus Urges Bush to Seek Talks on 1992 Plan, Use Trade Law's New 'Super 301' Provisions." *International Trade Reporter* 5, no. 49 (Dec. 14, 1988): 1631.

Bauer, P. T. "Remembrance of Studies Past: Retracing First Steps." In Gerald Meier and Dudley Seers, eds., *Pioneers in Development*, pp. 27–43. New York: Oxford University Press and the World Bank, 1984.

Behrman, Jere R. *Foreign Trade Regimes and Economic Development: Chile.* New York: National Bureau of Economic Research and Columbia University Press, 1976.

Bennett, Douglas, and Kenneth Sharpe. *Transnational Corporations vs. the State: The Political Economy of the Mexican Automobile Industry.* Princeton, N.J.: Princeton University Press, 1985.

Berger, Peter. *The Capitalist Revolution: Fifty Propositions About Prosperity, Equality and Liberty.* New York: Basic Books, 1986.

Bergquist, Charles. *Coffee and Conflict in Colombia, 1886–1910.* Durham, N.C.: Duke University Press, 1986 (orig. ed. 1978).

——. *Labor in Latin America.* Stanford, Calif.: Stanford University Press, 1987.

Bergsten, C. Fred. *America in the World Economy: A Strategy for the 1990s.* Washington, D.C.: Institute for International Economics, 1989.

——. *The Dilemmas of the Dollar.* New York: NYU Press and the Council on Foreign Relations, 1975.

Bertram, Geoffrey, and Rosemary Thorp. *Peru, 1890–1977: Growth and Policy in an Open Economy.* New York: Columbia University Press, 1978.

Bethell, Leslie, ed. *Colonial Spanish America.* Cambridge: Cambridge University Press, 1987.

——. *Spanish America After Independence, c. 1820–c. 1870.* Cambridge: Cambridge University Press, 1987.

Bhagwati, Jagdish, and Richard Eckaus, eds. *Development and Planning: Essays in Honour of Paul Rosenstein-Rodan.* Amsterdam: North-Holland Press, 1972.

Binswanger, Hans. *Brazilian Policies That Encourage Deforestation in the Amazon.* World Bank Environment Department Working Paper No. 16. Washington, D.C.: World Bank, 1989.

——. "Fiscal and Legal Incentives with Environmental Effects on the Brazilian Amazon." Manuscript, 1987.

Bjorndal, Karen A., ed. *Biology and Conservation of Sea Turtles: Proceedings of the World Conference on Sea Turtle Conservation.* Washington, D.C.: Smithsonian Institution Press, 1981.

Blakemore, Harold. *British Nitrates and Chilean Politics, 1886–1896: Balmaceda and North.* London: Athlone Press, 1974.

Block, Fred. *Origins of International Economic Disorder: A Study of United States International Monetary Policy from World War II to the Present.* Berkeley: University of California Press, 1977.

Bonilla, Heraclio. *Guano y burguesía en el Perú.* Lima: Instituto de Estudios Peruanos, 1974.

Bradford, Colin I., Jr. "The NICs: Confronting US 'Autonomy.'" In Richard Feinberg and Valeriana Kallab, eds., *Adjustment Crisis in the Third World*, pp. 119–38. Washington, D.C.: Overseas Development Council, 1984.

Brading, D.A. "Bourbon Spain and Its American Empire." In Leslie Bethell, ed., *Colonial Spanish America*, pp. 112–62. Cambridge: Cambridge University Press, 1987.

Bramble, Barbara. "The Debt Crisis: The Opportunities." *The Ecologist* 17, nos. 4–5 (1987): 192–99.

Brazil. Agency for Cooperation. ITTO project document. "Integration of Forest-Based Development in the Western Amazon—Phase I—Forest Management to Promote Policies for Sustainable Production." 1988. Typescript.

Browder, John O. "The Social Costs of Rain Forest Destruction: A Critique and Economic Analysis of the 'Hamburger Debate.'" *Interciencia* 13, no. 3 (June 1988): 115–20.

Bulmer-Thomas, Victor. "The Balance of Payments Crisis and Adjustment Programmes in Central America." In Rosemary Thorp and Laurence Whitehead, eds., *Latin American Debt and the Adjustment Crisis*, pp. 271–317 Cambridge: Cambridge University Press, 1987.

———. "Central America in the Inter-War Period." In Rosemary Thorp, ed., *Latin America in the 1930s*, pp. 279–314. Cambridge: Cambridge University Press, 1984.

———. *The Political Economy of Central America Since 1920.* Cambridge: Cambridge University Press, 1988.

Bushnell, David, and Neill Macaulay. *The Emergence of Latin America in the Nineteenth Century.* New York: Oxford University Press, 1988.

Calder, Bruce J. *The Impact of Intervention: The Dominican Republic During the U.S. Occupation of 1916–1924.* Austin: University of Texas Press, 1984.

Canak, William L., ed. *Lost Promises: Debt, Austerity, and Development in Latin America.* Boulder, Colo.: Westview, 1989.

Capistrano, Ana Doris, and Steven Sanderson. "Tyranny of the External: Links Between International Economic Change and Natural Resource Use in Latin America." Paper presented at the Latin American Studies Association conference, Apr. 1991.

Caporaso, James. "Dependence, Dependency, and Power in the Global System: A Structural and Behavioral Analysis." *International Organization* 32, no. 1 (Winter 1978): 13–44.

Cardoso, Eliana, and Rudiger Dornbusch. "Brazil's Tropical Plan." *American Economic Review* 77, no. 2 (May 1987): 288–92.

Cardoso, Fernando Henrique. "Development and the Environment: The Brazilian Case." *CEPAL Review* 12 (Dec. 1980): 111–27.

Cardoso, Fernando Henrique, and Enzo Faletto. *Dependencia y desarrollo en America Latina.* Mexico City: Siglo XXI, 1969. Translated as *Dependency and Development in Latin America.* Berkeley: University of California Press, 1979.

Cardoso de Mello, João Manoel, and Maria de Conceição Tavares. "The Capitalist Export Economy in Brazil, 1884–1930." In Roberto Cortes Conde and Shane Hunt, eds., *The Latin American Economies: Growth and the Export Sector, 1880–1930*, pp. 82–136. New York: Holmes and Meier, 1985.

"Caribbean Leaders Weigh Impact of EC 1992 Single Market Plan on Banana, Sugar Trade." *International Trade Reporter* 6, no. 7 (Feb. 15, 1989).

Cariola, Carmen, and Osvaldo Sunkel. "The Growth of the Nitrate Industry and Socioeconomic Change in Chile, 1880–1930." In Roberto Cortes Conde and Shane Hunt, eds., *The Latin American Economies: Growth and the Export Sector, 1880–1930*, pp. 137–254. New York: Holmes and Meier, 1985.

Carlson, Alver. "Monetary Talks End with Call for Freer Trade to Ease Poverty." *Reuter Business Report*, Sept. 29, 1988.

Carr, E. H. *The Twenty Years' Crisis.* New York: Harper & Row, 1964.

Carter, Michael R., and Elena Alvarez. "Changing Paths: The Decollectivization of Agrarian Reform Agriculture in Coastal Peru." In William C. Thiesenhusen, ed., *Searching for Agrarian Reform in Latin America*, pp. 156–87. Boston: Unwin and Hyman, 1989.

Cavarozzi, Marcelo. "Political Cycles in Argentina since 1955." In Guillermo O'Donnell, Philippe C. Schmitter, and Laurence Whitehead, eds., *Transitions from Authoritarian Rule: Prospects for Democracy*, pp. 19–48. Baltimore: Johns Hopkins University Press, 1986.

Chenery, Hollis, Montek S. Ahluwalia, C. L. G. Bell, John H. Duloy, and Richard Jolly. *Redistribution with Growth.* New York: World Bank and Oxford University Press, 1974, 1976.

Chiaramonte, Jose Carlos. *Nacionalismo y liberalismo económico en la Argentina, 1860–1880.* Buenos Aires: Solar/Hachette, 1971.

Clark, Colin W. *Mathematical Bioeconomics: The Optimal Management of Renewable Resources.* New York: Wiley, 1976.

Clarke, Michael. "Evaluating Lomé." *Journal of Common Market Studies* 20, no. 3 (Mar. 1982): 288–92.

Cline, William R. *Exports of Manufactures from Developing Countries.* Washington, D.C.: Brookings Institution, 1984.

———. "'Reciprocity': A New Approach to World Trade Policy?" In William R. Cline, ed., *Trade Policy in the 1980s*, pp. 121–58. Washington, D.C.: Institute for International Economics, 1983.

———, ed. *Trade Policy in the 1980s.* Washington, D.C.: Institute for International Economics, 1983.

Coatsworth, John. "Railroads, Landholding, and Agrarian Protest in the Early Porfiriato." *Hispanic American Historical Review* 27, no. 1 (Feb. 1974): 48–71.

Cockcroft, James D. *Neighbors in Turmoil: Latin America.* New York: Harper & Row, 1989.

Colchester, Nicholas, and David Buchan. *Europower: The Essential Guide to Europe's Economic Transformation in 1992.* London: Economist Books, 1990.

Collier, David, ed. *The New Authoritarianism in Latin America.* Princeton, N.J.: Princeton University Press, 1979.

Corbo, Vittorio, and Jaime de Melo. "Lessons from the Southern Cone Policy Reforms." *The World Bank Research Observer* 2, no. 2 (July 1987): 111–42.

Corden, W. M. "Booming Sector and Dutch Disease. Economics: Survey and Consolidation." *Oxford Economic Papers* 36 (1984): 359–80.

Cornia, Giovanni Andrea, Richard Jolly, and Frances Stewart, eds. *Adjustment with a Human Face: Protecting the Vulnerable and Promoting Growth.* New York: Oxford University Press, 1987.

Cortes Conde, Roberto. "The Export Economy of Argentina, 1880–1920." In Roberto Cortes Conde and Shane Hunt, eds., *The Latin American Economies: Growth and the Export Sector, 1880–1930,* pp. 319–81. New York: Holmes and Meier, 1985.

Cortes Conde, Roberto, and Shane Hunt, eds. *The Latin American Economies: Growth and the Export Sector, 1880–1930.* New York: Holmes and Meier, 1985.

Cortes Conde, Roberto, and Stanley Stein, eds. *Latin America: A Guide to Economic History, 1830–1930.* Berkeley: University of California Press, 1977.

Cortesão, Jaime. "Angola e a formação do bandeirismo." *A Manhã,* Aug. 15, 1948. Quoted in José Honório Rodrigues, *Brazil and Africa.* Translated by Richard A. Mazzara and Sam Hileman. Berkeley: University of California Press, 1965.

Cowhey, Peter F., and Edward Long. "Testing Theories of Regime Change: Hegemonic Decline or Surplus Capacity?" *International Organization* 37, no. 2 (Spring 1983): 157–88.

Craig, Alan K. "Logwood as a Factor in the Settlement of British Honduras." *Caribbean Studies* 9, no. 1 (1969): 53–62.

Crosby, Alfred W. *The Columbian Exchange: Biological and Cultural Consequences of 1492.* Westport, Conn.: Greenwood Press, 1972.

———. *Ecological Imperialism: The Biological Expansion of Europe, 900–1900.* Cambridge: Cambridge University Press, 1986.

Dam, Kenneth W. *The GATT: Law and the International Economic Organization.* Chicago: University of Chicago Press, 1970.

Dean, Warren. *Brazil and the Struggle for Rubber: A Study in Environmental History.* Cambridge: Cambridge University Press, 1987.

———. "Deforestation in Southern Brazil." In Richard P. Tucker and J. F. Richards, eds., *Global Deforestation and the Nineteenth-Century World Economy,* pp. 50–67. Durham, N.C.: Duke University Press, 1983.

Deas, Malcolm. "Venezuela, Colombia, and Ecuador." In Leslie Bethell, ed.,

Spanish America After Independence, c. 1820–c. 1870, pp. 207–38. Cambridge: Cambridge University Press, 1987.

De Janvry, Alain. *The Agrarian Question and Reformism in Latin America.* Baltimore: Johns Hopkins University Press, 1981.

de Larosière, Jacques. "The Debt Problem and the Challenges Facing the World Economy." *IMF Survey*, Nov. 25, 1985, pp. 354–58.

de Melo, Jaime, and Sherman Robinson. *Trade Adjustment Policies and Income Distribution in Three Archetype Developing Economies.* Staff Working Paper No. 442. Washington, D.C.: World Bank, 1980.

Diaz-Alejandro, Carlos. "The Argentine Economy Before 1930." In Carlos Diaz-Alejandro, *Essays on the Economic History of the Argentine Republic*, pp. 1–66. New Haven, Conn.: Yale University Press, 1970.

———. "Comment" on Albert O. Hirschman, "A Dissenter's Confession." In Gerald Meier and Dudley Seers, eds., *Pioneers in Development*, pp. 112–14. New York: Oxford University Press and the World Bank, 1984.

———. "Delinking: Unshackled or Unhinged?" In Albert Fishlow, Richard Fagen, Carlos Diaz-Alejandro, and Roger Hansen, *Rich and Poor Nations in the Global Economy*, pp. 87–162. New York: McGraw-Hill, 1978.

———. *Essays on the Economic History of the Argentine Republic.* New Haven, Conn.: Yale University Press, 1970.

———. *Foreign Trade Regimes and Economic Development: Colombia.* New York: National Bureau of Economic Research and Columbia University Press, 1976.

———. "Latin America in the 1930s." In Rosemary Thorp, ed., *Latin America in the 1930s: The Role of the Periphery in World Crisis*, pp. 17–49. Cambridge: Cambridge University Press, 1984.

———. "Some Aspects of the Development Crisis in Latin America." In Rosemary Thorp and Laurence Whitehead, eds., *Latin American Debt and the Adjustment Crisis*, pp. 9–27. Cambridge: Cambridge University Press, 1987.

———. "Stages in the Industrialization of Argentina." In Carlos Diaz-Alejandro, *Essays on the Economic History of the Argentine Republic*, pp. 208–76. New Haven, Conn.: Yale University Press, 1970.

Donkin, R. A. "Spanish Red: An Ethnogeographical Study of Cochineal and the Opuntia Cactus." *Transactions of the American Philosophical Society*, vol. 67, pt. 5. Philadelphia: American Philosophical Society, 1977.

Dornbusch, Rudiger. "Comment on 'Exports and Policy in Latin American Countries.'" In Werner Baer and Malcolm Gillis, eds., *Export Diversification and the New Protectionism: The Experiences of Latin America*, pp. 43–47. Champaign: University of Illinois, Bureau of Economic and Business Research, 1981.

Drabenstott, Mark, Alan Barkema, and David Henneberry. "The Latin American Debt Problem and U.S. Agriculture." *Economic Review* (Federal Reserve Bank of Kansas City), 73, no. 7 (July–Aug. 1988), pp. 21–38.

Drake, Paul. *Money Doctor in the Andes: The Kemmerer Missions, 1923–1933.* Durham, N.C.: Duke University Press, 1989.

Elliott, J. H. "The Spanish Conquest." In Leslie Bethell, ed., *Colonial Spanish America*, pp. 1–58. Cambridge: Cambridge University Press, 1987.

Epstein, Edward C. "Antiinflation Policies in Argentina and Chile: Or, Who Pays the Cost." *Comparative Political Studies* 11, no. 2 (July 1978): 211–30.

Evans, Peter. *Dependent Development: The Alliance of Multinational, State, and Local Capital in Brazil*. Princeton, N.J.: Princeton University Press, 1979.

———. "Predatory, Developmental, and Other Apparatuses: A Comparative Political Economy Perspective on the Third World State." *Sociological Forum* 4, no. 4 (1989): 561–87.

———. "State, Capital, and the Transformation of Dependence: The Brazilian Computer Case." *World Development* 14, no. 7 (1986): 791–808.

Fagen, Richard. "Equity in the South in the Context of North-South Relations." In Albert Fishlow, Richard Fagen, Carlos Diaz-Alejandro, and Roger Hansen, *Rich and Poor Nations in the Global Economy*, pp. 163–214. New York: McGraw-Hill, 1978.

———, ed. *Capitalism and the State in U.S.–Latin American Relations*. Stanford, Calif.: Stanford University Press, 1979.

Fearnside, Philip M. "The Charcoal of Carajás: A Threat to the Forests of Brazil's Eastern Amazon Region." *Ambio* 18, no. 2 (1989): 141–43.

Fearnside, Philip M., and J. R. Rankin. "Jari and Carajás: The Uncertain Future of Large Silvicultural Plantations in the Amazon." *Interciencia* 7 (1982): 326–28.

Feinberg, Richard E. "An Open Letter to the World Bank's New President." In Richard Feinberg et al., *Between Two Worlds: The World Bank's Next Decade*, pp. 3–30. Washington, D.C.: Overseas Development Council, 1986.

Feinberg, Richard E., and Valeriana Kallab, eds. *Adjustment Crisis in the Third World*. Washington, D.C.: Overseas Development Council, 1984.

Feinberg, Richard E., et al. *Between Two Worlds: The World Bank's Next Decade*. Washington, D.C.: Overseas Development Council, 1986.

Ferns, H. S. *Britain and Argentina in the Nineteenth Century*. Oxford: Oxford University Press, 1960.

Ffrench-Davis, Ricardo. "The Monetarist Experiment in Chile: A Critical Survey." *World Development* 11, no. 11 (Nov. 1983): 905–26.

Fidler, Stephen. "Bankers Face Down Brady Plan in Mexico Debt Talks." *Financial Times*, June 7, 1989, p. 9.

Fishlow, Albert. "Comment," on Raul Prebisch, "Five Stages in My Thinking." In Gerald M. Meier and Dudley Seers, eds., *Pioneers in Development*, pp. 192–96. New York: Oxford University Press, 1984.

———. *Foreign Trade Regimes and Economic Development: Brazil*. New York: NBER, 1976.

———. "The Latin American State." *Journal of Economic Perspectives* 4, no. 3 (Summer 1990): 61–74.

———. "Lessons from the Past: Capital Markets During the 19th Century and the Interwar Period." In Miles Kahler, ed., *The Politics of International Debt*, pp. 37–93. Ithaca, N.Y.: Cornell University Press, 1986.

———. "The State of Latin American Economics." In Inter-American Development Bank, *Economic and Social Progress in Latin America: External Debt: Crisis and Adjustment*, pp. 123–148. Washington, D.C.: IDB, 1985.

Fishlow, Albert, Richard Fagen, Carlos Diaz-Alejandro, and Roger Hansen, *Rich and Poor Nations in the World Economy*. New York: McGraw-Hill, 1978.

Fitzgerald, E. V. K. *The State and Economic Development: Peru Since 1968*. Cambridge: Cambridge University Press, 1976.

Floyd, Robert H., Clive S. Gray, and R. P. Short. *Public Enterprise in Mixed Economies: Some Macroeconomic Aspects*. Washington, D.C.: International Monetary Fund, 1985.

Foxley, Alexandro. *Latin American Experiments in Neoconservative Economics*. Berkeley: University of California Press, 1983.

————. "Towards a Free Market Economy." *Journal of Development Economics* 10, no. 1 (1982), 3–29.

Foxley, Alexandro, Michael S. McPherson, and Guillermo O'Donnell, eds. *Development, Democracy, and the Art of Trespassing: Essays in Honor of Albert O. Hirschman*. Notre Dame, Ind.: University of Notre Dame Press, 1986.

Freeman, Peter H., et al. *Bolivia: State of the Environment and Natural Resources*. McClean, Va.: JRB Associates, 1980.

Frenkel, Roberto, and Guillermo O'Donnell. "The 'Stabilization Programs' of the International Monetary Fund and Their Internal Impacts." In Richard Fagen, ed., *Capitalism and the State in U.S.–Latin American Relations*, pp. 171–216. Stanford, Calif.: Stanford University Press, 1979.

Friedman, Milton. *Milton Friedman en Chile: Bases para un desarrollo economico*. Santiago: Fundación de Estudios Económicos BHC, 1975.

Furtado, Celso. *The Economic Development of Latin America*. 2d ed. Cambridge: Cambridge University Press, 1976.

————. *Obstacles to Development in Latin America*. New York: Anchor Books, 1970.

Gallagher, John, and Ronald Robinson. "The Imperialism of Free Trade." *The Economic History Review* 2d series, 6, no. 1 (Aug. 1953): 1–15.

García H., Alvaro, and John Wells. "Chile: A Laboratory for Failed Experiments in Capitalist Political Economy." *Cambridge Journal of Economics* 7, no. 3/4 (Sept.–Dec. 1983): 287–304.

Gardner, Richard N. *Sterling-Dollar Diplomacy in Current Perspective: The Origins and the Prospects of Our International Economic Order*. New expanded ed. New York: Columbia University Press, 1980.

Geertz, Clifford. *Agricultural Involution: The Processes of Ecological Change in Indonesia*. Berkeley: University of California Press, 1963.

Gereffi, Gary. *The Pharmaceutical Industry and Dependency in the Third World*. Princeton, N.J.: Princeton University Press, 1983.

————. "Rethinking Development Theory: Insights from East Asia and Latin America." *Sociological Forum* 4, no. 4 (1989): 505–33.

————. "Transnational Corporations and the Pharmaceutical Industry in Mexico." Paper prepared for the United Nations Centre on Transnational Corporations, 1982. Typescript.

Gerschenkron, Alexander. *Economic Backwardness in Historical Perspective.* Cambridge: Cambridge University Press, 1962.

──────. *War and Change in World Politics.* Cambridge: Cambridge University Press, 1981.

Gill, Stephen, and David Law. *The Global Political Economy: Perspectives, Problems, and Policies.* Baltimore: Johns Hopkins University Press, 1988.

Gilpin, Robert. *The Political Economy of International Economic Relations.* Princeton, N.J.: Princeton University Press, 1987.

Girvan, Norman. *Corporate Imperialism: Conflict and Expropriation.* New York: M. E. Sharpe, 1976.

Gomes, Gustavo Maia. *The Roots of State Intervention in the Brazilian Economy.* New York: Praeger, 1986.

Goodman, David, and Michael Redclift, eds. *The International Farm Crisis.* London: Macmillan, 1989.

Gootenberg, Paul. "Beleaguered Liberals: The Failed First Generation of Free Traders in Peru." In Joseph Love and Nils Jacobsen, eds., *Guiding the Invisible Hand: Economic Liberalism and the State in Latin American History,* pp. 63–97. New York: Praeger, 1988.

Graham, Richard. *Britain and the Onset of Modernization in Brazil, 1850–1914.* Cambridge: Cambridge University Press, 1968.

Greenhill, Robert. "The Brazilian Coffee Trade." In D. C. M. Platt, ed., *Business Imperialism, 1840–1930: An Inquiry Based on British Experience in Latin America,* pp. 198–230. Oxford: Clarendon Press, 1977.

──────. "Merchants and the Latin American Trades: An Introduction," in Platt, ed., *Business Imperialism,* pp. 159–97.

──────. "The Nitrate and Iodine Trades, 1880–1914." In Platt, ed., *Business Imperialism,* pp. 231–83.

──────. "Shipping, 1850–1914." In Platt, ed., *Business Imperialism,* pp. 119–55.

Griffin, Keith. *Land Concentration and Rural Poverty.* New York: Holmes and Meier, 1986.

Griffith-Jones, Stephany, and Osvaldo Sunkel. *Debt and Development Crises in Latin America: The End of an Illusion.* Oxford: Clarendon Press, 1986.

Haber, Stephen. *Industry and Underdevelopment: The Industrialization of Mexico, 1890–1940.* Stanford, Calif.: Stanford University Press, 1989.

Haberler, Gottfried. *Prosperity and Depression.* Geneva: League of Nations, 1942.

Hakkert, Ralph, and Franklin W. Goza. "The Demographic Consequences of Austerity in Latin America." In William Canak, ed., *Lost Promises: Debt, Austerity, and Development in Latin America,* pp. 69–97. Boulder, Colo.: Westview, 1989.

Hall, Anthony. "Agrarian Crisis in Brazilian Amazonia: The Grande Carajás Programme." *Journal of Development Studies* 23 (July 1987): 522–52.

Halperin Donghi, Tulio. "Argentina: Liberalism in a Country Born Liberal." In Joseph Love and Nils Jacobsen, eds., *Guiding the Invisible Hand: Economic Liberalism and the State in Latin American History,* pp. 99–116. New York: Praeger, 1988.

————. "Economy and Society." In Leslie Bethell, ed., *Spanish America After Independence, c. 1820–c. 1870*, pp. 1–47. Cambridge: Cambridge University Press, 1987.

"Hands Off the IMF." *The Economist* 284, no. 7253 (Sept. 1982): 15–16.

Hansen, Roger. *Beyond the North-South Stalemate.* New York: McGraw-Hill, 1979.

Hathaway, Dale E. *Agriculture and the GATT: Rewriting the Rules.* Washington, D.C.: Institute for International Economics, 1987.

Hayes, Margaret Daly. "The U.S. and Latin America: A Lost Decade?" *Foreign Affairs: America and the World* 68, no. 1 (1989): 180–98.

Healy, David F. *Gunboat Diplomacy in the Wilson Era: The U.S. Navy in Haiti, 1915–1916.* Madison: University of Wisconsin Press, 1976.

Hecht, Susanna, and Alexander Cockburn. *The Fate of the Forest: Developers, Destroyers and Defenders of the Amazon.* London: Verso, 1989.

Helleiner, Gerald K. "Policy-Based Program Lending: A Look at the Bank's New Role." In Richard Feinberg et al., *Between Two Worlds: The World Bank's Next Decade*, pp. 47–66. Washington, D.C.: Overseas Development Council, 1986.

Hemming, John. *Amazon Frontier: The Defeat of the Brazilian Indians.* Cambridge, Mass.: Harvard University Press, 1987.

————. *Red Gold: The Conquest of the Brazilian Indians.* Cambridge, Mass.: Harvard University Press, 1978.

Herrmann, Roland. "Free Riders and the Redistributive Effects of International Commodity Agreements: The Case of Coffee." *Journal of Policy Modeling* 8, no. 4 (1986): 597–621.

————. "The International Allocation of Trade-tied Aid: A Quantitative Analysis for the Export Quota Scheme in Coffee." *Weltwirtschaftliches Archiv* 124, no. 4 (1988): 675–700.

————. "Measuring National Interests in the International Coffee Agreement." *Kieler Arbeitspapiere*, no. 288 (May 1987).

Hilton, Stanley. "The Argentine Factor in Twentieth-Century Brazilian Foreign Policy Strategy." *Political Science Quarterly* 100, no. 1 (Spring 1985): 37–51.

————. *Brazil and the Great Powers, 1930–1939.* Stanford, Calif.: Stanford University Press, 1975.

Hinton, Harold B. *Cordell Hull: A Biography.* Garden City, N.Y.: Doubleday, 1942.

Hirschman, Albert O. *A Bias for Hope: Essays on Development and Latin America.* New Haven, Conn.: Yale University Press, 1971.

————. "A Dissenter's Confession: The Strategy of Economic Development Revisited." In Gerald M. Meier and Dudley Seers, eds., *Pioneers in Development*, pp. 87–111. New York: World Bank and Oxford University Press, 1984.

————. *Essays in Trespassing: Economics to Politics and Beyond.* Cambridge: Cambridge University Press, 1981.

————. *National Power and the Structure of Foreign Trade.* Berkeley: University of California Press, 1980. Original ed. 1945.

———. "The Paternity of an Index." *American Economic Review* 54 (Sept. 1964): 761–62.

———. "The Rise and Decline of Development Economics." In *Essays in Trespassing: Economics to Politics and Beyond*, pp. 1–24. Cambridge: Cambridge University Press, 1981.

———. "The Turn to Authoritarianism in Latin America and the Search for Its Economic Determinants." In David Collier, ed., *The New Authoritarianism in Latin America*, pp. 61–98. Princeton, N.J.: Princeton University Press, 1979.

Hodges, Donald. *Intellectual Foundations of the Nicaraguan Revolution.* Austin: University of Texas Press, 1986.

Hofstader, Richard. "The Myth of the Happy Yeoman." In Lawrence W. Levine and Robert Middlekauff, eds. *The National Temper: Readings in American History*, pp. 223–32. New York: Harcourt Brace, 1968.

Hojman, David E. "The Andean Pact: Failure of a Model of Economic Integration?" *Journal of Common Market Studies* 20, no. 2 (Dec. 1981): 139–60.

Holmer, Alan F., and Judith Hippler Bello. "The 1988 Trade Bill: Is It Protectionist?" *International Trade Reporter* 5, no. 39 (Oct. 5, 1988): 1347.

Hotelling, Harold. "The Economics of Exhaustible Resources." *Journal of Political Economy* 39 (1931): 137–75.

Hudec, Robert. *Developing Countries in the GATT Legal System.* Brookfield, Vt.: Gower Publishers, for the Trade Policy Research Centre, London, 1987.

———. "The Participation of Developing Countries in the GATT Legal System." Paper prepared for the Trade Policy Research Centre, Mar. 1986. Manuscript.

Hu-DeHart, Evelyn. *Yaqui Resistance and Survival: The Struggle for Land and Autonomy, 1821–1910.* Madison: University of Wisconsin Press, 1984.

Hufbauer, Gary Clyde, Diane T. Berliner, and Kimberley Ann Elliott. *Trade Protection in the United States: 31 Case Studies.* Washington, D.C.: Institute for International Economics, 1985.

Hufbauer, Gary Clyde, and Joanna Shelton Erb. *Subsidies in International Trade.* Washington, D.C.: Institute for International Economics, 1984.

Hufbauer, Gary Clyde, and Jeffrey J. Schott. *Trading for Growth: The Next Round of Trade Negotiations.* Washington, D.C.: Institute for International Economics, 1985.

Hufschmidt, Maynard M., et al. *Environment, Natural Systems, and Development: An Economic Valuation Guide.* Baltimore: Johns Hopkins University Press, 1983.

Hull, Cordell. *The Memoirs of Cordell Hull.* 2 vols. New York: Macmillan, 1948.

Hunt, Shane. "Growth and Guano in Nineteenth-Century Peru." In Roberto Cortes Conde and Shane Hunt, eds., *The Latin American Economies: Growth and the Export Sector, 1880–1930*, pp. 255–318. New York: Holmes and Meier, 1985.

Imaz, José Luis de. *La "Revolucion Argentina."* Buenos Aires: Ediciones Depalma, 1966.

Immerman, Richard. *The CIA in Guatemala: The Foreign Policy of Intervention.* Austin: University of Texas Press, 1982.

Inter-American Development Bank (IDB). *Economic and Social Progress in Latin America: The External Sector.* Washington, D.C.: IDB, 1982.

———. *Economic and Social Progress in Latin America: Economic Integration.* Washington, D.C.: IDB, 1984.

———. *Economic and Social Progress in Latin America: External Debt: Crisis and Adjustment.* Washington, D.C.: IDB, 1985.

———. *Economic and Social Progress in Latin America: Savings, Investment, and Growth.* Washington, D.C.: IDB, 1989.

Inter-American Dialogue. *The Americas in 1989: Consensus for Action.* Washington, D.C.: Aspen Institute, 1989.

International Labour Office. *Employment, Growth and Basic Needs: A One-World Problem.* Geneva: International Labour Office, 1978.

Iversen, Edwin S., and Darryl E. Jory. "Shrimp Culture in Ecuador: Farmers Without Seed." *Sea Frontiers, Sea Secrets* 32, no. 6 (Nov.–Dec. 1986): 442–53.

Johnson, Jay A., and W. Ramsay Smith, eds. *Forest Products Trade: Market Trends and Technical Developments.* Seattle: University of Washington Press, 1988.

Jordan, Miriam. "In Brazil, the Coffee King, Soy Takes Pride of Place," *Reuter Library Report,* July 1, 1988.

Kahler, Miles, ed. *The Politics of International Debt.* Ithaca, N.Y.: Cornell University Press, 1986.

Katzenstein, Peter. *Small States in World Markets: Industrial Policy in Europe.* Ithaca, N.Y.: Cornell University Press, 1985.

Keesing, Donald B. *Trade Policy for Developing Countries.* World Bank Staff Working Paper No. 353. Washington, D.C.: World Bank, 1979.

Kennedy, J. Ray, and Roberto Giannetti da Fonseca. "Brazilian Trade Policy and the Uruguay Round." In Henry R. Nau, ed., *Domestic Politics and the Uruguay Round,* pp. 29–50. New York: Columbia University Press, 1989.

Keohane, Robert. *After Hegemony: Cooperation and Discord in the World Political Economy.* Princeton, N.J.: Princeton University Press, 1984.

———. "Hegemonic Leadership and U.S. Foreign Economic Policy." In William P. Avery and David P. Rapkin, eds., *America in a Changing World Political Economy,* pp. 49–76. New York: Longman, 1982.

Keynes, John Maynard. *Economic Consequences of the Peace.* London: Macmillan, 1919.

Khalaf, Nadim G. "Country Size and Trade Concentration." *Journal of Development Studies* 11, no. 1 (Oct. 1974): 81–85.

Kindleberger, Charles. *Foreign Trade and the National Economy.* New Haven, Conn.: Yale University Press, 1962.

———. *The Terms of Trade.* New York: Wiley, 1956.

———. *The World in Depression, 1929–1939.* Berkeley: University of California Press, 1973.

Kolko, Gabriel, and Joyce Kolko. *The Limits of Power: The World and United States Foreign Policy, 1945–54.* New York: Harper & Row, 1972.

Krasner, Stephen. *Defending the National Interest: Raw Materials Investments and U.S. Foreign Policy.* Princeton, N.J.: Princeton University Press, 1978.

Kuczynski, Pedro-Pablo. *Latin American Debt.* Baltimore: Johns Hopkins University Press, 1988.

Kugler, Jacek, and A. F. K. Organski. "The End of Hegemony?" *International Interactions* 15, no. 2 (1989): 113–28.

Laarman, Jan G., Gerard F. Schreuder, and Erick T. Anderson. *An Overview of Forest Products Trade in Latin America and the Caribbean Basin.* Forestry Private Enterprise Initiative (FPEI) Working Paper No. 21. Durham, N.C., FPEI, June 1987.

LaFeber, Walter. *The Panama Canal: The Crisis in Historical Perspective.* New York: Oxford University Press, 1978.

Lahera, Eugenio. "The Transnational Corporations and Latin America's International Trade." *CEPAL Review* 25 (Apr. 1985): 45–65.

Laird, Sam, and Julio Nogues. "Trade Policies and the Highly Indebted Countries." *The World Bank Economic Review* 3, no. 2 (1989): 241–61.

Lake, David. *Power, Protection, and Free Trade: International Sources of U.S. Commercial Strategy, 1887–1939.* Ithaca, N.Y.: Cornell University Press, 1988.

———. "The State and American Trade Strategy in the Pre-Hegemonic Era." *International Organization* 41, no. 4 (Autumn 1987): 33–58.

Lal, Deepak. *The Poverty of "Development Economics."* Cambridge, Mass.: Harvard University Press, 1985.

Larson, Brooke. *Colonial Rule and Agrarian Transformation in Bolivia.* Princeton, N.J.: Princeton University Press, 1988.

Latin America Bureau. *The Great Tin Crash: Bolivia and the World Tin Market.* London: Latin America Bureau, 1987.

Lehmann, David. "The Political Economy of Armageddon: Chile, 1970–1973." *Journal of Development Economics* 5, no. 2 (June 1978): 107–23.

Lessard, Donald R., and John Williamson. *Capital Flight and Third World Debt.* Washington, D.C.: Institute for International Economics, 1987.

Levin, Jonathan V. *The Export Economies: Their Pattern of Development in Historical Perspective.* Cambridge, Mass.: Harvard University Press, 1960.

Levine, Lawrence W., and Robert Middlekauff, eds. *The National Temper: Readings in American History.* New York: Harcourt Brace, 1968.

Lewis, Colin M. "Railways and Industrialization: Argentina and Brazil." In Christopher Abel and Colin Lewis, eds., *Latin America, Economic Imperialism and the State: The Political Economy of the External Connection from Independence to the Present,* pp. 199–230. London: Athlone Press, 1985.

Lewis, W. Arthur. "Development Economics in the 1950s." In Gerald M. Meier and Dudley Seers, eds., *Pioneers in Development,* pp. 121–37. New York: World Bank and Oxford University Press, 1984.

———. *The Development Process.* United Nations Executive Briefing Paper No. 2. New York: United Nations. 1970.

———. "Economic Development with Unlimited Supplies of Labour." *Manchester School of Economic and Social Studies* (May 1954): 139–91.

———. *Growth and Fluctuations, 1870–1913.* New York: Allen & Unwin, 1978.

———. *The Theory of Economic Growth.* Homewood, Ill.: Richard D. Irwin, 1955.

Linder, Staffan B. *Trade and Trade Policy for Development.* New York: Praeger, 1967.

Lipton, Michael. "Comment" on P. T. Bauer, "Remembrance of Studies Past: Retracing First Steps." In Gerald M. Meier and Dudley Seers, eds., *Pioneers in Development*, pp. 44–50. New York: Oxford University Press and the World Bank, 1984.

———. *Land Assets and Rural Poverty.* Washington, D.C.: World Bank Working Paper No. 744, 1985.

List, Friedrich. *The National System of Political Economy.* Trans. Sampson S. Lloyd. New York: Longmans, Green, 1909.

Llach, Juan José. "Dependencia, procesos sociales y control del estado en la década del treinta." *Desarrollo Económico* 12 (Apr.–June 1972): 172–83.

———. "El Plan Pinedo de 1940, su significado histórico y los orígenes de la economía política del peronismo." *Desarrollo Económico* 23 (Jan.—Mar. 1984): 515–58.

Lloyd, Peter J. *International Trade Problems of Small Nations.* Durham, N.C.: Duke University Press, 1968.

Lopes, Francisco. *Choque heterodoxo: Combate à inflação e reforma monetária.* Rio de Janeiro: Editora Campus, 1986.

Louis, William Roger, ed. *Imperialism: The Robinson and Gallagher Controversy.* New York: Franklin Watts, 1976.

Love, Joseph L. *São Paulo in the Brazilian Federation, 1889–1937.* Stanford, Calif.: Stanford University Press, 1980.

Love, Joseph L., and Nils Jacobsen, eds. *Guiding the Invisible Hand: Economic Liberalism and the State in Latin American History.* New York: Praeger, 1988.

Loveman, Brian. *Chile: The Legacy of Hispanic Capitalism.* 2d ed. New York: Oxford University Press, 1988.

Lowenthal, Abraham, ed. *The Peruvian Experiment: Continuity and Change Under Military Rule.* Princeton, N.J.: Princeton University Press, 1975.

Ludlow, Peter M. "The Future of the International Trading System." *Washington Quarterly* 12, no. 4 (Autumn 1989): 157–69.

Lynch, John. "The River Plate Republics." In Leslie Bethell, ed., *Spanish America After Independence, c. 1820–c. 1870*, pp. 314–75. Cambridge: Cambridge University Press, 1987.

McClintock, Cynthia, and Abraham Lowenthal, eds. *The Peruvian Experiment Reconsidered.* Princeton, N.J.: Princeton University Press, 1983.

McCullough, David. *The Path Between the Seas: The Creation of the Panama Canal, 1870–1914.* New York: Simon and Schuster, 1977.

McGreevey, William Paul. *An Economic History of Colombia, 1845–1930.* Cambridge: Cambridge University Press, 1971.

McKibben, Bill. *The End of Nature.* New York: Anchor Books, 1989.

McNeely, Jeffrey A. *Economics and Biological Diversity: Developing and Using Economic Incentives to Conserve Biological Resources.* Gland, Switzerland: International Union for Conservation of Nature and Natural Resources, 1988.

MacNeill, Jim. "Strategies for Sustainable Economic Development." *Scientific American* 261:3 (Sept. 1989): 154–65.

McNeill, John R. "Deforestation in the Araucaria Zone of Southern Brazil, 1900–1983." In John F. Richards and Richard P. Tucker, eds., *World Deforestation in the Twentieth Century*, pp. 15–32. Durham, N.C.: Duke University Press, 1988.

Mahar, Dennis J. *Government Policies and Deforestation in Brazil's Amazon Region*. Washington, D.C.: World Bank, 1989.

Mahler, Vincent A. "Controlling International Commodity Prices and Supplies: The Evolution of United States Sugar Policy." In LaMond Tullis and Ladd Hollist, eds., *Food, the State, and International Political Economy: Dilemmas of Developing Countries*, pp. 149–79. Lincoln: University of Nebraska Press, 1986.

Maier, Charles S. "The Politics of Productivity: Foundations of American International Economic Policy After World War II." In Charles S. Maier, *In Search of Stability: Explorations in Historical Political Economy*, pp. 121–52. Cambridge: Cambridge University Press, 1987.

———. *Recasting Bourgeois Europe: Stabilization in France, Germany, and Italy in the Decade After World War I*. Princeton, N.J.: Princeton University Press, 1988. Orig. ed. 1975.

———. *In Search of Stability: Explorations in Historical Political Economy*. Cambridge: Cambridge University Press, 1987.

Marichal, Carlos. *A Century of Debt Crises in Latin America: From Independence to the Great Depression, 1820–1930*. Princeton, N.J.: Princeton University Press, 1989.

Markandya, Anil, and David Pearce. *Environmental Considerations and the Choice of the Discount Rate in Developing Countries*. Environment Department Working Paper No. 3. Washington, D.C.: World Bank, 1988.

Martins, Carlos Estevam, ed. *Estado e capitalismo no Brasil*. Sao Paulo: Hucitec, 1977.

Martins, Luciano. "The 'Liberalization' of Authoritarian Rule in Brazil." In Guillermo O'Donnell, Philippe C. Schmitter, and Laurence Whitehead, eds., *Transitions from Authoritarian Rule: Prospects for Democracy*, pp. 72–94. Baltimore: Johns Hopkins University Press, 1986.

Matteucci, Silvia Diana. "Is the Rain Forest Worth Seven Hundred Million Hamburgers?" *Interciencia* 12, no. 1 (1987): 5.

Matthew, W. M. "Antony Gibbs and Sons, the Guano Trade and the Peruvian Government, 1842–1861." In D. C. M. Platt, ed., *Business Imperialism, 1840–1930: An Inquiry Based on British Experience in Latin America*, pp. 337–70. Oxford: Clarendon Press, 1977.

———. "The Imperialism of Free Trade: Peru, 1820–1870." *Economic History Review* 2d series, 21 (1968): 562–79.

Meier, Gerald M. "The Formative Period." In Gerald Meier and Dudley Seers, eds., *Pioneers in Development*, pp. 3–22. New York: Oxford University Press and the World Bank, 1984.

———. *International Trade and Development*. New York: Harper & Row, 1963.

———. *Pioneers in Development: Second Series*. New York: Oxford University Press and the World Bank, 1987.

Meier, Gerald M., and Dudley Seers, eds. *Pioneers in Development.* New York: Oxford University Press and the World Bank, 1984.

Merriman, Jane. "Coffee Falls to Eight-Year Low as Price War Looms." *Reuter Business Report,* July 7, 1989.

———. "Colombia Blames Producers and U.S. for Coffee Pact Failure." *Reuter Library Report* June 13, 1989.

———. "Outlook Bleak for Commodity Stabilisation Pacts." *Reuter Library Report,* Mar. 21, 1989.

Meyer, Lorenzo. *Mexico and the United States in the Oil Controversy, 1917–1942.* Translated by Muriel Vasconcellos. Austin: University of Texas Press, 1977. First published as *México y los Estados Unidos en el conflicto petrolero (1917–1942).* Mexico City: El Colegio de México, 1972.

Mikklelsen, Vagn. *State Economic Intervention in Brazil.* Stockholm: Institute of Latin American Studies, 1978.

Mommsen, Wolfgang J. *Theories of Imperialism.* New York: Random House, 1977.

Mora, Alberto. "On the Operation of the Law of Value in the Cuban Economy." In Bertram Silverman, ed., *Man and Socialism in Cuba: The Great Debate,* pp. 219–30. New York: Atheneum, 1971.

Moran, Theodore H. *Multinational Corporations and the Politics of Dependence: Copper in Chile.* Princeton, N.J.: Princeton University Press, 1974.

Morawetz, David. *Twenty-five Years of Economic Development, 1950 to 1975.* Washington, D.C.: World Bank and Johns Hopkins University Press, 1977.

———. *Why the Emperor's New Clothes Are Not Made in Colombia.* Washington, D.C.: World Bank and Oxford University Press, 1981.

Mosk, Sanford A. *Industrial Revolution in Mexico.* Berkeley: University of California Press, 1950.

Moss, Joanna, and John Ravenhill. "Trade Developments During the First Lomé Convention." *World Development* 10, no. 10 (1982): 841–56.

Murmis, Miguel, and Juan Carlos Portantiero. *Estudios sobre los orígenes del peronismo/1.* Buenos Aires: Siglo XXI, 1972.

Myint, Hla. "An Interpretation of Economic Backwardness." *Oxford Economic Papers* 6, no. 2 (June 1954): 132–63.

Myrdal, Gunnar. *An International Economy.* New York: Harper & Row, 1956.

———. *Rich Lands and Poor.* New York: Harper & Brothers, 1957.

National Research Council. Board on Science and Technology for International Development. Office of International Affairs. Panel on Common Property Resource Management. *Proceedings of the Conference on Common Property Resource Management.* Washington, D.C.: National Academy Press, 1986.

Nations, James D., and Daniel I. Komer. "Rainforests and the Hamburger Society." *The Ecologist* 17, nos. 4–5 (1987): 161–67.

Nau, Henry R., ed. *Domestic Trade Politics and the Uruguay Round.* New York: Columbia University Press, 1989.

Naylor, Robert A. "The Mahogany Trade as a Factor in the British Return to the Mosquito Shore in the Second Quarter of the 19th Century." *Jamaican Historical Review* 7 (1967): 40–67.

————. *Penny Ante Imperialism: The Mosquito Shore and the Bay of Honduras, 1600–1914.* Cranbury, N.J.: Fairleigh Dickinson Press, 1989.

Nederveen Pieterse, Jan P. *Empire and Emancipation: Power and Liberation on a World Scale.* New York: Praeger, 1989.

Nietschmann, Bernard. "The Cultural Context of Sea Turtle Subsistence Hunting in the Caribbean and Problems Caused by Commercial Exploitation." In Karen A. Bjorndal, ed., *Biology and Conservation of Sea Turtles: Proceedings of the World Conference on Sea Turtle Conservation*, pp. 439–45. Washington, D.C.: Smithsonian Institution Press, 1981.

Nurkse, Ragnar. "International Trade Theory and Development Policy." In H. S. Ellis, ed., *Economic Development for Latin America*, pp. 234–74. New York: St. Martin's Press, 1961.

O'Brien, Phil, and Jackie Roddick. *Chile: The Pinochet Decade; The Rise and Fall of the Chicago Boys.* London: Latin American Bureau, 1983.

Odell, John. "Latin American Trade Negotiations with the United States." *International Organization* 34, no. 2 (Spring 1980): 207–28.

O'Donnell, Guillermo. *Modernization and Bureaucratic Authoritarianism.* Berkeley: University of California Institute of International Studies, 1973.

O'Donnell, Guillermo, and Delfina Linck. *Dependencia y autonomía.* Buenos Aires: Amorrortu, 1979.

O'Donnell, Guillermo, Philippe C. Schmitter, and Laurence Whitehead, eds. *Transitions from Authoritarian Rule: Prospects for Democracy.* Baltimore: Johns Hopkins University Press, 1986.

"OECD Ministers Upbeat on Economic Outlook but Divisive on Agricultural Subsidy Issues." *International Trade Reporter* 5:21 (May 25, 1989): 749.

O'Neill, Helen. "HICs, MICs, NICs, and LICs: Some Elements in the Political Economy of Graduation and Differentiation." *World Development* 12, no. 7 (1984): 693–712.

Organization for Economic Cooperation and Development (OECD). *National Policies and Agricultural Trade.* Paris: OECD, 1987.

O'Riordan, Timothy. "The Politics of Sustainability." In R. Kerry Turner, ed., *Sustainable Environmental Management: Principles and Practice*, pp. 29–50. Boulder, Colo.: Westview Press, 1988.

Otero, Gerardo. "Agrarian Reform in Mexico: Capitalism and the State." In William C. Thiesenhusen, ed., *Searching for Agrarian Reform in Latin America*, pp. 276–304. New York: Unwin Hyman, 1990.

Palma, Gabriel. "External Disequilibrium and Internal Industrialization in Chile, 1914–1935." In Christopher Abel and Colin Lewis, eds., *Latin America, Economic Imperialism and the State: The Political Economy of the External Connection from Independence to the Present*, pp. 318–38. London: Athlone Press, 1985.

————. "From an Export-led to an Import-substituting Economy: Chile, 1914–1939." In Rosemary Thorp, ed., *Latin America in the 1930s*, pp. 50–80. Cambridge: Cambridge University Press, 1984.

Parkin, Vincent. "Economic Liberalism in Chile, 1973–82: A Model for Growth and Development or a Recipe for Stagnation and Impoverishment?" *Cambridge Journal of Economics* 7 (June 1983): 101–24.

Patterson, Gardner, and Eliza Patterson. "Importance of a GATT Review in the New Negotiations." *World Economy* 9 (June 1986): 153–69.

Pérez, Louis. *Cuba Between Empires, 1878–1902.* Pittsburgh: University of Pittsburgh Press, 1983.

Perruci, Gamaliel, and Steven E. Sanderson. "Presidential Succession, Economic Crisis, and the Resurgence of Populism in Brazil." *Studies in Comparative International Development* 24, no. 3 (Fall 1989): 34–51.

Pezzey, John. *Economic Analysis of Sustainable Growth and Sustainable Development.* World Bank Environment Department Working Paper No. 15, Mar. 1989.

Pinto, Aníbal. "Comments on 'The Interaction Between Styles of Development and the Environment in Latin America.'" *CEPAL Review* 12 (1980): 51–54.

Platt, D. C. M. "Further Objections to an 'Imperialism of Free Trade,' 1830–1860." *Economic History Review* 2d series, 26, no. 1 (Feb. 1973): 77–91.

———. "The Imperialism of Free Trade: Some Reservations." *Economic History Review* 2d series, 21, no. 2 (Aug. 1968): 296–306.

———. *Latin America and British Trade, 1806–1914.* London: Adam and Charles Black, 1972.

———, ed. *Business Imperialism, 1840–1930: An Inquiry Based on British Experience in Latin America.* Oxford: Clarendon Press, 1977.

Posner, Joshua L., and Malcolm F. McPherson. "Agriculture on the Steep Slopes of Tropical America: Current Situation and Prospects for the Year 2000." *World Development* 10, no. 5 (1982): 341–53.

Prebisch, Raul. *The Economic Development of Latin America and Its Principal Problems.* New York: United Nations, 1950.

———. "Five Stages in My Thinking." In Gerald M. Meier and Dudley Seers, eds., *Pioneers in Development*, pp. 175–91. New York: Oxford University Press and the World Bank, 1984.

Preeg, Ernest H., ed. *Hard Bargaining Ahead: U.S. Trade Policy and Developing Countries.* Washington, D.C.: Overseas Development Council, 1985.

"Products from Mexico Occupy Center Stage at GSP Subcommittee Annual Review Hearings." *International Trade Reporter* 6:39 (Oct. 4, 1989): 1258.

Quijano, Aníbal. *Nationalism and Capitalism in Peru: A Study in Neo-Imperialism.* New York: Monthly Review Press, 1971.

Rabe, Stephen. *Eisenhower and Latin America: The Foreign Policy of Anti-Communism.* Durham, N.C.: Duke University Press, 1988.

Ramos, Alcida Rita. "An Economy of Waste: Amazon Frontier Development and the Livelihood of Brazilian Indians." *Working Papers*, Tropical Conservation and Development Program, Center for Latin American Studies, University of Florida, 1990.

Redclift, Michael. *Sustainable Development: Exploring the Contradictions.* London: Methuen, 1987.

Repetto, Robert. *Economic Policy Reform for Natural Resource Conservation.*

World Bank Environment Department Working Paper No. 4. Washington, D.C.: World Bank, 1988.

Repetto, Robert, and Malcolm Gillis. *Public Policies and the Misuse of Forest Resources.* Cambridge: Cambridge University Press, 1988.

Reynolds, Clark W. *The Mexican Economy: Twentieth-Century Structure and Growth.* New Haven, Conn.: Yale University Press, 1970.

Richards, John F., and Richard P. Tucker, eds. *World Deforestation in the Twentieth Century.* Durham, N.C.: Duke University Press, 1988.

Rippy, J. Fred. *British Investments in Latin America, 1822–1949.* Minneapolis: Univ. of Minnesota Press, 1949.

Robinson, E. A. G., ed. *Economic Consequences of the Size of Nations.* London: Macmillan, 1960.

Rock, David. *Argentina, 1516–1987: From Spanish Colonization to Alfonsín.* Berkeley: University of California Press, 1987. Orig. ed. 1985.

———, ed. *Argentina in the Twentieth Century.* Pittsburgh: University of Pittsburgh Press, 1975.

Roddick, Jackie. *The Dance of the Millions: Latin America and the Debt Crisis.* London: Latin America Bureau, 1988.

Rohatyn, Felix. "The World Bank: A View from the Private Sector." In Overseas Development Council, *The Future of the World Bank,* pp. 12–17. Washington, D.C.: Overseas Development Council, 1986.

Rosecrance, Richard. *The Rise of the Trading State: Commerce and Conquest in the Modern World.* New York: Basic Books, 1986.

Rostow, W. W. *The Stages of Economic Growth, A Non-Communist Manifesto.* Cambridge: Cambridge University Press, 1960.

Rothstein, Robert L. *Global Bargaining: UNCTAD and the Quest for a New International Economic Order.* Princeton, N.J.: Princeton University Press, 1979.

———. *The Weak in the World of the Strong: The Developing Countries in the International System.* New York: Columbia University Press, 1977.

Rubio, F., Luis, Cristina Rodriguez D., and Roberto Blum V. "The Making of Mexico's Trade Policy and the Uruguay Round." In Henry R. Nau, ed., *Domestic Politics in the Uruguay Round.* pp. 167–90. New York: Columbia University Press, 1989.

Ruggie, John Gerard. "Introduction: International Interdependence and National Welfare." In John Gerard Ruggie, ed., *The Antinomies of Interdependence: National Welfare and the International Division of Labor,* pp. 1–39. New York: Columbia University Press, 1983.

Russett, Bruce. "The Mysterious Care of Vanishing Hegemony: Or Is Mark Twain Really Dead?" *International Organization* 39, no. 2 (Spring 1985): 207–31.

Sachs, Jeffrey. "Making the Brady Plan Work." *Foreign Affairs* (Summer 1989): 87–104.

Safford, Frank. "The Emergence of Economic Liberalism in Colombia." In Joseph Love and Nils Jacobsen, eds., *Guiding the Invisible Hand: Economic Liberalism and the State in Latin American History,* pp. 35–62. New York: Praeger, 1988.

Sanderson, Steven E. *Agrarian Populism and the Mexican State: The Struggle for Land in Sonora.* Berkeley: University of California Press, 1981.

———. "A Critical Approach to the New International Division of Labor." In Steven E. Sanderson, ed., *The Americas in the New International Division of Labor,* pp. 3–25. New York: Holmes and Meier, 1985.

———. "Mexican Agricultural Politics in the Shadow of the U.S. Farm Crisis." In David Goodman and Michael Redclift, eds., *The International Farm Crisis,* pp. 205–33. London: Macmillan, 1989.

———. "Presidential Succession and Political Rationality in Mexico." *World Politics* 35 (April 1983), pp. 315–34.

———. "Recasting the Politics of Inter-American Trade." *Journal of Inter-American Studies and World Affairs* 28, no. 3 (Fall 1986), pp. 87–124.

———. *The Transformation of Mexican Agriculture: International Structure and the Politics of Rural Change.* Princeton, N.J.: Princeton University Press, 1986.

———. "Trends in Mexican Investment Policy and the Forces That Shape Them." Report prepared for the office of the U.S. Trade Representative, May 1985. Typescript.

———, ed. *The Americas in the New International Division of Labor.* New York: Holmes and Meier, 1985.

Saulniers, Alfred H. *Public Enterprises in Peru: Public Sector Growth and Reform.* Boulder, Colo.: Westview, 1988.

———, ed. *Economic and Political Roles of the State in Latin America.* Austin, Texas: Office for Public Sector Studies and Institute of Latin American Studies, 1985.

Schattschneider, E. E. *Politics, Pressures, and the Tariff.* New York: Prentice-Hall, 1935.

Schelling, Thomas. *Choice and Consequence.* Cambridge, Mass.: Harvard University Press, 1984.

Schlesinger, Stephen, and Stephen Kinzer. *Bitter Fruit: The Untold Story of the American Coup in Guatemala.* New York: Anchor, 1982.

Schoultz, Lars. *National Security and United States Policy Toward Latin America.* Princeton, N.J.: Princeton University Press, 1987.

Schwartzman, Simon. "High Technology and Self-Reliance: Brazil Enters the Computer Age." Serie Estudos No. 36. Rio de Janeiro: IUPERJ, 1985. Mimeo.

Scobie, James. *Argentina, a City and a Nation.* New York: Oxford University Press, 1964.

———. *Revolution on the Pampas: A Social History of Argentine Wheat, 1860–1910.* Austin: University of Texas Press, 1964.

Seers, Dudley. "The Birth, Life, and Death of Development Economics." *Development and Change* 10, no. 4 (1979), pp. 707–19.

Segerson, Kathleen. "Natural Resource Concepts in Trade Analysis." In John D. Sutton, ed., *Agricultural Trade and Natural Resources: Discovering the Critical Linkages,* pp. 9–34. Boulder, Colo.: Lynne Rienner, 1988.

Semmel, Bernard. *The Rise of Free Trade Imperialism.* Cambridge: Cambridge University Press, 1970.

Sen, Guatam. *The Military Origins of Industrialization and International Trade Rivalry.* New York: St. Martin's Press, 1984.

Serra, Jose. "Three Mistaken Theses Regarding the Connection Between Industrialization and Authoritarian Regimes." In David Collier, ed., *The New Authoritarianism in Latin America*, pp. 99–164. Princeton, N.J.: Princeton University Press, 1979.

Sheahan, John. "The Elusive Balance Between Stimulation and Constraint in Analysis of Development." In Alejandro Foxley, Michael S. McPherson, and Guillermo O'Donnell, eds., *Development, Democracy, and the Art of Trespassing: Essays in Honor of Albert O. Hirschman*, pp. 169–90. Notre Dame, Ind.: University of Notre Dame Press, 1986.

———. *Patterns of Development in Latin America: Poverty, Repression and Economic Strategy.* Princeton, N.J.: Princeton University Press, 1987.

Siddall, Scott E., Joseph A. Atchue, III, and Robert L. Murray, Jr. "Mariculture Development in Mangroves: A Case Study of the Philippines, Ecuador, and Panama." In John R. Clark, ed., *Coastal Resources Management: Development Case Studies*, pp. 2–53. Washington, D.C.: Research Planning Institute, Inc., for National Park Service and USAID, 1985.

Sigmund, Paul E., ed. *Models of Political Change in Latin America.* New York: Praeger, 1970.

Silverman, Bertram, ed. *Man and Socialism in Cuba: The Great Debate.* New York: Atheneum, 1971.

Simon, David. "Sustainable Development: Theoretical Construct or Attainable Goal?" *Environmental Conservation* 16, no. 1 (Spring 1989): 41–48.

Smith, Peter. *Politics and Beef in Argentina: Patterns of Conflict and Change.* New York: Columbia University Press, 1969.

Smith, Robert Freeman. "The Morrow Mission and the International Committee of Bankers on Mexico: The Interaction of Finance Diplomacy and the New Mexican Elite." *Journal of Latin American Studies* 1, no. 2 (1969): 149–66.

———. *The United States and Revolutionary Nationalism in Mexico, 1916–1932.* Chicago: University of Chicago Press, 1972.

Smith, William C. *Authoritarianism and the Crisis of the Argentine Political Economy.* Stanford, Calif.: Stanford University Press, 1989.

———. "Democracy, Distributional Conflicts and Macroeconomic Policymaking in Argentina, 1983–1989." *Journal of Interamerican Studies and World Affairs* 32, no. 2 (Summer 1990): 1–42.

Sonnichsen, C. L. *Colonel Green and the Copper Skyrocket.* Tucson: University of Arizona Press, 1974.

Spalding, Hobart. *Organized Labor in Latin America: Historical Case Studies of Workers in Dependent Societies.* New York: NYU Press, 1977.

Spears, John. *Containing Tropical Deforestation: A Review of Priority Areas for Technological and Policy Research.* Environment Department Working Paper No. 10. Washington, D.C.: World Bank, Oct. 1988.

Spero, Joan Edelman. *The Politics of International Economic Relations.* 3d ed. New York: St. Martin's Press, 1985.

Spicer, Edward. *Cycles of Conquest: The Impact of Spain, Mexico and the United States on the Indians of the Southwest, 1533–1960.* Tucson: University of Arizona Press, 1962.

Stallings, Barbara. *Banker to the Third World: U.S. Portfolio Investment in Latin America, 1900–1986.* Berkeley: University of California Press, 1987.

———. *Class Conflict and Economic Change in Chile, 1958–1973.* Stanford, Calif.: Stanford University Press, 1975.

Stallings, Barbara, and Robert Kaufman. *Debt and Democracy in Latin America.* Boulder, Colo.: Westview Press, 1989.

Staniland, Martin. *What Is Political Economy? A Study of Social Theory and Underdevelopment.* New Haven, Conn.: Yale University Press, 1985.

Stepan, Alfred. *State and Society: Peru in Comparative Perspective.* Princeton, N.J.: Princeton University Press, 1978.

Strange, Susan. "The Management of Surplus Capacity: Or How Does Theory Stand up to Protectionism 1970s Style?" *International Organization* 33 (Summer 1979): 303–34.

———. "The Persistent Myth of Lost Hegemony." *International Organization* 41, no. 4 (Autumn 1987): 551–74.

Streeten, Paul. "Development Dichotomies." In Gerald M. Meier and Dudley Seers, eds., *Pioneers in Development*, pp. 337–61. New York: Oxford University Press and the World Bank, 1984.

———. "Trade as the Engine, Handmaiden, Brake or Offspring of Growth?" *The World Economy* 5, no. 4 (Dec. 1982): 415–17.

Streeten, Paul, with Shahid Javed Burki, Mahbub Ul Haq, Norman Hicks, and Frances Stewart. *First Things First: Meeting Basic Needs in Developing Countries.* New York: Oxford University Press, 1981.

"Sun Will Not 'Set' on Forest Industry in Next 20 Years." *Forest Industries* 116, no. 10 (Oct. 1989): 23.

Sunkel, Osvaldo. "The Interaction Between Styles of Development and the Environment in Latin America." *CEPAL Review* 12 (1980): 15–49.

Sutton, John D., ed. *Agricultural Trade and Natural Resources: Discovering the Critical Linkages.* Boulder, Colo.: Lynne Rienner, 1988.

Teitel, Simón. "The Nature, Costs, and Benefits of Economic Stabilization-Liberalization Programs in the Southern Cone." In Nicolás Ardito Barletta, Mario I. Blejer, and Luis Landau, eds., *Economic Liberalization and Stabilization Policies in Argentina, Chile, and Uruguay*, pp. 104–8. Washington, D.C.: World Bank, 1983.

Teitel, Simón, and Francisco E. Thoumi. "From Import Substitution to Exports: The Manufacturing Exports Experience of Argentina and Brazil." *Economic Development and Cultural Change* 34 (1986): 455–90.

Terchunian, Aram, et al. "Mangrove Mapping in Ecuador: The Impact of Shrimp Pond Construction." *Environmental Management* 10, no. 3 (1986): 345–50.

Thiesenhusen, William C. *Searching for Agrarian Reform in Latin America.* New York: Unwin and Hyman, 1989.

"Third World Accuses Developed Nations of Delaying Action on Tropical Products." *International Trade Reporter* 6:25 (June 21, 1989): 813.

Thorp, Rosemary, ed. *Latin America in the 1930s: The Role of the Periphery in World Crisis.* Cambridge: Cambridge University Press, 1984.

Thorp, Rosemary, and Laurence Whitehead, eds. *Latin American Debt and the Adjustment Crisis.* Cambridge: Cambridge University Press, 1987.

Tironi, Ernesto. "A Reappraisal of the Role of Primary Exports in Latin America." In Christopher Abel and Colin Lewis, eds., *Latin America, Economic Imperialism and the State: The Political Economy of the External Connection from Independence to the Present*, pp. 472–81. London: Athlone Press, 1985.

Tisdell, C. A. "Sustainable Development: Differing Perspectives of Ecologists and Economists and Relevance to LDCs." *World Development* 16, no. 3 (1988): 373–84.

Topik, Steven. "The Economic Role of the State in Liberal Regimes: Brazil and Mexico Compared, 1888–1910." In Joseph Love and Nils Jacobsen, eds., *Guiding the Invisible Hand: Economic Liberalism and the State in Latin American History*, pp. 117–44. New York: Praeger, 1988.

——. *The Political Economy of the Brazilian State, 1889–1930.* Austin: University of Texas Press, 1987.

"Trends: Has It Been a Lost Decade? Latin America Looks to the 1990s." *The IDB* (Sept.–Oct. 1989), pp. 8–9.

Tucker, Richard P., and J. F. Richards, eds. *Global Deforestation and the Nineteenth-Century World Economy.* Durham, N.C.: Duke University Press, 1983.

Tucker, Robert. *The Inequality of Nations.* New York: Basic Books, 1977.

Tullis, F. LaMond, and W. Ladd Hollist, eds. *Food, the State, and International Political Economy: Dilemmas of Developing Countries.* Lincoln: University of Nebraska Press, 1986.

Uhl, Christopher, and Geoffrey Parker. "Is a Quarter-Pound Hamburger Worth a Half-Ton of Rain Forest?" *Interciencia* 11:5 (1986): 210.

United States. Congress. Joint Economic Committee. Subcommittee on Science and Technology. Hearings. "U.S. Policy on High Technology Exports to Developing Countries and Whether They Effectively Serve U.S. Foreign Policy, National Security, and Economic Objectives." Sept. 21, 1990. Transcript.

——. Department of Agriculture (USDA). "Amid Turmoil, Brazil's Agricultural Growth to Slow." *Agricultural Outlook.* Washington, D.C.: USDA, Aug. 24, 1989.

——. ——. *A Time to Choose: Summary Report on the Structure of Agriculture.* Washington, D.C.: USDA, 1981.

——. Department of Commerce. *Latin America Trade Review 1988: A U.S. Perspective.* Washington, D.C.: U.S. Government Printing Office, 1989.

——. Library of Congress, Science and Technology Division. "Draft Environmental Report on Peru." Washington, D.C.: Department of State, Oct. 1979. Typescript.

——. Office of the United States Trade Representative. *Annual Report of the President of the United States on the Trade Agreements Program, 1984–1985.* Washington, D.C.: USTR, 1985.

"U.S., Brazil Agree to Renew Brazil's Share of Steel VRA, Sources Confirm." *International Trade Reporter* 6:48 (Dec. 6, 1989): 1587.

"U.S. Message to Brazil Seen Linking 301 to Sale of U.S. Telecommunications Equipment." *International Trade Reporter* 6:34 (Aug. 23, 1989): 1085.

"U.S. Negotiators Conclude Second Round of VRA Talks with Big Five Suppliers." *International Trade Reporter* 6:36 (Sept. 13, 1989): 1139.

Vargas, Getúlio. "Discurso do Rio Amazonas." *Revista Brasileira de Geografia* 4 (Apr.–June 1942): 3–6.

Velasco-S., Jésus-Agustin. *Impacts of Mexican Oil Policy on Economic and Political Development.* Lexington, Mass.: D.C. Heath, 1983.

Waisman, Carlos H. *Reversal of Development in Argentina: Postwar Counter-revolutionary Policies and Their Structural Consequences.* Princeton, N.J.: Princeton University Press, 1987.

Warren, Bill. *Imperialism: Pioneer of Capitalism.* London: Verso, 1980.

Weil, Dan. "'Super 301' Will Do Little to Trim Trade Gap, Economists Say." *Reuter Business Report,* June 9, 1989.

Weintraub, Sidney. *Free Trade Between Mexico and the United States?* Washington, D.C.: Brookings Institution, 1984.

———, ed. *Economic Stabilization in Developing Countries.* Washington, D.C.: Brookings Institution, 1981.

Whalley, John. *Trade Liberalization Among Major World Trading Areas.* Cambridge, Mass.: MIT Press, 1985.

———, ed. *Dealing with the North.* London, Ont.: University of Western Ontario, 1987.

Whitehead, Laurence. "The Adjustment Process in Chile: A Comparative Perspective." In Rosemary Thorp and Laurence Whitehead, eds., *Latin American Debt and the Adjustment Crisis,* pp. 117–61. Cambridge: Cambridge University Press, 1987.

Williams, Robert. *Export Agriculture and the Crisis in Central America.* Chapel Hill: University of North Carolina Press, 1986.

Williams, William Appleman. *The Contours of American History.* New York: Franklin Watts, 1973.

Wirth, John. *The Politics of Brazilian Development.* Stanford, Calif.: Stanford University Press, 1970.

"With Exception of U.S., GATT Nations Approve Tropical Products Trade Accord." *International Trade Reporter* 5:48 (Dec. 7, 1988): 1586.

Wolf, Eric. *Europe and the People Without History.* Berkeley: University of California Press, 1982.

———. *Sons of the Shaking Earth.* Chicago: University of Chicago Press, 1959.

Wolf, Martin. "Fiddling While the GATT Burns." *World Economy* 9 (Mar. 1986): 1–18.

Woodward, R. L., Jr. "Central America." In Leslie Bethell, ed., *Spanish America After Independence, c. 1820–c. 1870,* pp. 171–206. Cambridge: Cambridge University Press, 1987.

World Bank. *Brazil: Review of Agricultural Policies.* Washington, D.C.: World Bank, 1981.

———. *Striking a Balance: The Environmental Challenge of Development*. Washington, D.C.: World Bank, 1989.

———. *World Development Report, 1989*. Washington, D.C.: World Bank, 1989.

World Commission on Environment and Development. *Our Common Future*. New York: Oxford University Press, 1987.

Worster, Donald. *Nature's Economy: A History of Ecological Ideas*. Cambridge: Cambridge University Press, 1977.

Wright, Winthrop R. *British-Owned Railways in Argentina: Their Effect on the Growth of Economic Nationalism, 1854–1948*. Austin: University of Texas Press, 1974.

Wynia, Gary W. *Argentina in the Postwar Era*. Albuquerque: University of New Mexico Press, 1978.

Yergin, Daniel. *Shattered Peace: The Origins of the Cold War and the National Security State*. Boston: Houghton Mifflin, 1978.

"Yeutter Increases Sugar Import Quotas, Extends Period Through September 1990." *International Trade Reporter* 6:36 (Sept. 13, 1989): 1146.

Index

In this index an "f" after a number indicates a separate reference on the next page, and an "ff" indicates separate references on the next two pages. A continuous discussion over two or more pages is indicated by a span of page numbers, e.g., "pp. 57–58." *Passim* is used for a cluster of references in close but not consecutive sequence.

Acre (Braz. terr.), 80, 238n62
Adelman, Irma, 58
Adjustment: balance-of-pament problems and, 66; public sector and structural, 137
Africa, 76, 189, 198
Agency for International Development, U.S. (USAID), 235n33
Agrarian reform: in Latin America, 23, 79, 82; United Fruit vs. Guatemalan, 247n32
Agriculture, 59–60, 70, 95, 97, 202–3; deforestation and, 14; modernization of, 36, 91, 102–3, 106; subsidization of, 71, 73, 80, 88, 146, 167–68; steepslope, 79, 89, 238n60; natural resources and, 81; substitution in, 101–3; domestic-use vs. export, 202–3, 246n14, 252–53n45. *See also* Exports, agricultural; Swidden agriculture
Agroindustrialization, 25, 231n55
Aircraft, 108, 116, 155, 194
Alcohol, as Brazilian export, 108, 135
Allende, Salvador, 124, 166
Alliance for Progress, 124, 161
Aluminum, 47. *See also* Bauxite
Amazonia, 80, 82, 91, 194, 239n76. *See also* Rain forests, Brazilian
Andean Pact, 123, 152

Anticommunism, U.S., 166, 247n32
Apparel, 47, 155; U.S. quotas on, 160
Apple juice, 155, 171
Archer, Renato, 194, 251n26
Argentina, 8, 45, 75, 113, 132; economic patterns in, 4, 45, 59, 63, 65, 88, 100, 171, 178, 209f, 223n23, 233n79, 248n35; trade patterns in, 17, 25, 155, 189, 202, 207, 228n2, 233n80; railroads of, 20–21; foreign influences on, 21, 112–15, 154, 170, 182; political patterns in, 23f, 132f, 173, 182, 243n50; industrialization in, 24f, 49, 113–14f, 163, 186; Brazil and, 31, 113; "Infamous Decade" in, 37; as province, 68; exports of, 99, 112ff, 115, 152, 201, 241n19; agriculture in, 103, 112ff, 155; imports of, 113ff, 147, 201, 241n19; "merinization" of, 113. *See also* Buenos Aires; Pampas; Perón, Juan
Artisans, 14, 240n14
Asia, 4, 97, 122, 179, 201. *See also* India
Austerity programs, 66
Australia, 148
Automobiles, 155, 165, 244n56
Autonomy, 131, 193, 197
Axis Powers, 37, 161
Aylwin, Patricio, 133, 178
Ayres, José Márcio, 89

Baker Plan, 173
Bananas: Central American, 20, 77, 107, 148, 224n34, 246n15, 250n6; "foreign," 22; Latin American, 30, 34f, 46f, 197, 225n44; Caribbean, 148, 246n15
Bandeirante, 76
Bangladesh, 229n28
Banker to the Third World (Stallings), 63
Barbados, 246n15
Baring Crisis, 37
Barkin, David, 231n55
Barley, 175
Basic needs, 57f
Baucus, Max, 167, 249n47
Bauer, P. T., 226n60
Bauxite, 30, 46f, 197
Beans, Mexican, 136
Beef, Latin American, 39, 46, 82, 112f, 125, 226n62, 238n63; U.S. fast food from, 79, 91, 238n63
Beer, Mexican, 175, 196
Beets, U.S., 165, 174
Behrman, Jere, 228n6
Belize, 75
Bello, Judith Hippler, 248n40
Bergquist, Charles, 25
Bertram, Geoffrey, 41, 50, 240n14
Bias for Hope, A (Hirschman), 6
Binswanger, Hans, 102
Biplurilateralism, 167, 248n34, 249n47
Bogotá, Col., 19
Bolivia, 31, 36, 152, 191; economic patterns in, 79, 99; trade patterns in, 79, 104–5, 117, 140, 152, 201; populism in, 183. *See also* Tin
Bourgeoisie, industrialist, 205
Brady Plan, 173, 175, 249n54
Brazil, 5, 21, 45, 68, 152; independence of, 13, 223n20, 232n72; Portugal and, 13, 68, 76, 112, 127; trade patterns in, 17, 107–8, 120, 155, 160, 191, 199, 203, 212–13, 240n4; economic patterns in, 19, 63, 67, 80, 93, 100, 104, 115, 160, 171–72, 178, 207, 209f, 223n23, 232n72, 248n35, 253n51; growth of, 19, 23, 25, 39, 100; industrialization of, 24f, 49, 163, 186, 195f; political patterns in, 24, 26, 127, 133, 143, 173, 177, 183, 187; and Argen-

tina, 31, 113; Britain and, 39, 222n15; deforestation in, 75, 77, 80, 82, 87–88, 91, 95, 236n40; U.S. and, 90, 108, 124, 154, 163, 166, 170–72, 180, 198, 212–13, 215; agriculture in, 95, 100, 103, 155; exports of, 99, 124, 152, 172, 174, 199, 201, 205, 232n72, 241n25; population pressures in, 104; currency of, 108; imports of, 147, 152, 172, 199, 201; and International Coffee Agreement, 148–51; as Super 301 culprit, 165–66. *See also* Amazonia; Collor de Mello, Fernando; Estado Nôvo; Rio de Janeiro; São Paulo; Vargas, Getúlio
Brazil and River Plate Conference, 224n32
Brazil and the Great Powers (Hilton), 6
Brazilwood, 75f
Bretton Woods Conference, 30
Bretton Woods trade system, 1f, 4f, 8, 13, 27, 53, 55, 128, 135, 140, 143f, 162. *See also* GATT
Britain: New World trade dominated by, 16, 18, 20, 222n15, 223n23; and Latin America, 27–28, 32, 36–37, 68, 112, 222n3; and Brazil, 29, 222n15; vs. Spain, 75; and Argentina, 112–15, 154, 182; growth-related trade in, 228n2; and Peru, 233n79. *See also* British Imperial Preference System
Britain and the Onset of Modernization in Brazil (Graham), 6
British Imperial Preference System, 25, 126, 154
Brundtland, Gro Harlem, 234n4
Brundtland Commission, *see* World Commission on Environment and Development
Buenos Aires, 18f, 21
Bulmer-Thomas, Victor, 22, 202, 231n55, 246n14, 252n45
Burger King, 91
Bush, George, 1, 8, 128, 173, 180, 198, 213, 249n54

Cacao, 14, 19, 35, 38, 46, 125
Cairns Group, 146, 164, 248n39
Calder, Bruce J., 224n30
Calderón, Rafael, 37

Canada, 156, 247n27
CAPEMI, 86
Capistrano, Ana Doris N., 239n68
Capital, trade and flow of, 64–65
Capitalism, 130, 205, 253n51
Caporaso, James, 242n26
Carajás, Braz., 79
Cárdenas, Cuauhtemoc, 187
Cárdenas, Lazaro, 24
Cardenismo, 23
Cardoso, Fernando Henrique, 85
Caribbean, 55, 189, 198; trade patterns
    in, 4–5, 148, 178, 191; U.S. and, 153,
    155
Caribbean Basin Initiative, 123, 178–79,
    189, 247n47
Caribbean Common Market, 123,
    247n27
Caribbean Conference, 224n32
Carr, E. H., 197f
Cartels, 21, 30, 46f, 179, 197
Carter, Jimmy, 171, 193, 239n76
Cattle, *see* Beef, Latin American
Cayenne, Fr. Guiana, 39
Central America, 38, 55, 69, 75, 91, 223;
    trade patterns in, 4–5, 148, 155, 178,
    191, 194f; U.S. and, 155, 162, 164
Central American Common Market,
    123, 152, 247n27
*Century of Debt Crises in Latin America,
    A* (Marichal), 63, 225n50
Cereals, 136, 146f. *See also* Grain(s)
Charcoal, 79, 90
Chemicals, 83, 228
Chicago, University of, 132, 243n50
Chicle, 46, 234n19
Chile, 8, 21, 45, 233n83; economic pat-
    terns in, 19, 22f, 36, 45–46, 65, 88,
    115, 198, 207, 209f, 248n35; growth
    of, 23, 25, 232n72; industrialization
    in, 24f, 49, 186; Bolivia and, 31, 36;
    Peru and, 31, 36, 127, 191; imports of,
    38, 201; political patterns in, 45–46,
    132f, 173, 182, 201; agriculture in,
    77, 99, 104; exports of, 99, 125, 201,
    210; U.S. and, 124, 154, 166; trade
    patterns in, 140, 155, 160, 189, 191,
    207, 233n86. *See also* Allende, Sal-
    vador; Pinochet, Augusto; Santiago,
    Chile

China, 54, 163, 196
Christian Democrats (Chile), 182
Cinchona, 38
Cinnamon, 39
CIPEC (Conseil Intergouvernemental des
    Pays Exportateurs de Cuivre), 46
CITES (Convention on International
    Trade in Endangered Species), 80, 103
Citibank, 249n53
Citrus, 100, 107–8, 155, 196
Clothing, *see* Apparel; Footwear; Hats
Cloves, 39
Coca, 76, 160
Cocaine, 160
Cochineal, 46, 75–76
Cockburn, Alexander, 102
Cocoa, 151, 203
Coffee: Brazilian, 19ff, 23, 46–48, 77,
    107, 148, 151, 205, 232n72, 244n61,
    246n19; Central American, 20, 77,
    107, 151, 224n34; Colombian, 21, 38,
    45, 77, 151, 212, 244n61; Latin Amer-
    ican, 35, 46, 94, 125, 148–52, 203,
    225n44, 226n62; African, 39, 151;
    arabica, 151. *See also* International
    Coffee Agreement
Cold War, 53
Collor de Mello, Fernando, 172, 178,
    187, 206, 249n53, 253n57
Collor Plan, 178
Colombia, 14, 21, 47, 77, 97, 152, 160,
    238n60; economic patterns in, 4, 19,
    45, 186; trade patterns in, 17, 38, 191;
    political patterns in, 23, 38, 173,
    222n13; exports of, 38, 99, 212; and
    International Coffee Agreement, 151,
    244n61; U.S. and, 154
Colonialism, 15f, 31, 112. *See also* Impe-
    rialism
Commerce, U.S. Dept. of, 3
Common Market, *see* EEC
Common markets, 123, 247n27. *See also*
    Caribbean Common Market; Central
    American Common Market; EEC
Communications industry, 205
Communism, 227n78
Compradores, Central American, 38
Computers, Brazilian, 62, 174–75, 194,
    206
Conable, Barber, 71

Concordancia (Arg.), 39, 182
Conquistadores, 226n62
Conservation, 70, 72, 74, 81, 85, 87f, 160, 214, 237n50. *See also* Environmentalism; Natural resources
Consumption, investment and, 100–101, 239n71
Coolidge, Calvin, 161
Cooperatives, 79, 135
Copper: Chilean, 18, 20, 46, 94f, 104, 125, 154, 189, 194, 198; Latin American, 30, 35ff, 46f, 140, 197, 226n62; Mexican, 36
CORFO (Corporación del Fomento), 23
Corn, 76, 114, 136, 165, 174
Corporations, multinational, 206, 212
Costa Rica, 20, 69, 117, 155
Cotton, 21, 35f, 38, 125, 228n2
Council of Mutual Economic Assistance, 243n44
Coyotes (labor contractors), 77
Cruzado Plan, 93, 99
Cuba, 26, 36, 54, 75, 123, 127f, 196, 243nn43,44; U.S. and, 36, 121, 164ff. *See also* Sugar
Customs unions, 27, 123

Dairy products, Argentine, 113
Da Silva, Luis Ignacio ("Lula"), 87
Day laborers, 82
Dean, Warren, 39, 77
Debt crisis: trade and, 37, 42, 51, 70, 88–100 *passim*, 117, 120, 125, 135–43 *passim*, 139, 141, 143, 156–57, 165–80 *passim*, 201, 209, 214, 239n68; economic nationalism and, 62–69, 182
Declining trade, law of, 90, 128–29, 195, 209
Default, debt, 63f, 232n72
Deforestation, 29, 34, 79, 87–91 *passim*, 95, 102
Deindustrialization, exchange rate and, 67
De Janvry, Alain, 231n55
De la Madrid, Miguel, 102, 171, 177, 182
Delors, Jacques, 246n8
Democracy, debt and, 63

Dependence, bilateral trade, 121–25, 241–42n26
Dependency: politics of economic, 109; international trade, 110–38, 241n17. *See also* Hirschman, Albert O.
Depression, *see* Great Depression
Desertification, 79
Destatization, *see* Privatization
Devaluation, currency, 82, 101
Development, 40–42; economic aspects of, 41, 57–59; growth and, 51–52, 54, 214; political aspects of, 60–62; trade and, 218
Development economics, 6–8, 10, 52–53f, 57–62, 221n4
Díaz, Porfirio, 77, 198
Diaz-Alejandro, Carlos, 45, 54, 131, 228n6, 233n79
Dispossession, of land-holding poor, 33, 81, 89
Diversification, commodity, 189, 191, 198, 210
Dominican Republic, 20, 75, 164, 224n30, 250n6
Donghi, Tulio Halperin, 223n23, 240n14
Dornbusch, Rudiger, 62
Drake, Paul, 6
Dulles, Allen, 247n32
Dulles, John Foster, 247n32
"Dumping," 164
"Dutch Disease," 48, 80
Duties, countervailing, 164, 199, 249n46
Dyewood, 75

Echeverria, Luis, 124
ECLA (Economic Commission for Latin America), U.N., 24, 31, 78, 122, 169
Economic and Social Progress in Latin America (IDB), 139
Economic Growth and Social Equity in Developing Countries (Adelman/Morris), 58
Economic internationalism, 55, 183–85
Economic liberalism, 17–18, 33, 222n13, 223n21
Economic nationalism, 9, 14, 25, 55, 62, 226n71, 251n13; economic liberalism vs., 17, 222n13

Economics: Keynesian, 227n91; "trickle-down," 239n77
Economics and Biological Diversity (McNeely), 87
"Economics of Exhaustible Resources, The" (Hotelling), 236n38
Economies: tropical vs. temperate, 45; open vs. closed, 125–29
Ecuador, 14, 46, 83, 132, 191; economic patterns in, 63, 80, 99, 185; trade patterns in, 120, 125, 184–85
EEC (European Economic Community), 103, 145, 156, 171, 179, 213, 245–46n8; philosophy of, 44, 103, 248n39; and Lomé countries, 144, 169, 198, 249n51; U.S. and, 156, 163, 165, 171; and Latin America, 157, 212, 237n50, 246n15
Efficiency: economic, 32–33; trade-related, 61–62
Eisenhower, Dwight D., 193, 247n32
Electronic appliances, 155
El Salvador, 155, 185, 238n60
Employment, in Latin America, 57
Empreiteiros, 77
Energy, 100, 194, 237n50; subsidization of, 71, 88, 104. *See also* Hydroelectric energy; Nuclear power
Enganchamiento, 77
England, *see* Britain
Enterprise for the Americas, 1, 8
Entreguismo, 22, 38, 227n89
Environmentalism, 83f, 91, 234n4, 236n44, 237n46; Latin America and, 70–74, 80, 83, 89ff, 104ff, 215, 217, 236n44. *See also* Conservation
Environmental Program, U.N., 78
Equity, economic growth and, 58
Estado Nôvo, 23, 26
Ethanol, Brazilian production of, 135, 155, 171
Europe, trade between Latin America and, 91, 97, 155, 164, 198, 223n23. *See also* EEC
European Community, *see* EEC
European Economic Community, *see* EEC
European Parliament, 71, 237n50
Exchange rate, devaluation of, 66
EXIM bank, 173
Expansionism, U.S., 161

Export Enhancement Program, U.S., 167–68
Export multiplier, 61, 231n60
Exports: development and, 40f; devaluation and, 66; imports vs., 112; and economic vulnerability, 116; subsidization of agricultural, 164, 248n39; trade regulation and, 196–97; agricultural modernization and, 202; as gross domestic product unit, 241n23; coefficients of, 241n24

Facsimile machines, Brazilian, 253n57
Farms, crisis of U.S., 167–68. *See also* Agriculture
Fishing, 73, 91, 95, 97, 106, 135, 207
Fishlow, Albert, 228n6
Fish meal, Peruvian, 36, 124
Fixando o homem no campo, 82
"Food for Peace," 164
Footwear, 108, 155
Foreign Trade and the National Economy (Kindleberger), 227n84
Forests, Latin American, 71, 73, 77–84 *passim,* 90f, 95, 97, 102, 106, 233–34n3, 235n35, 237n49, 238n62
"Fortress Europe," 145, 157, 245–46n8, 250n6
France, 16
Franklin, Benjamin, 12, 29
Free trade, 13–14, 51; U.S. and, 3, 6, 62, 77, 97, 142, 166, 180, 213, 250n8; Argentina and, 8, 38–39; Brazil and, 8, 13, 17, 222n15; Chile and, 8, 17; Latin America and, 8, 17, 26f, 35, 48–50, 142, 169; Britain and, 13, 15, 24–25, 31f, 77, 221–22n3; Peru and, 13; Mexico and, 17, 215; defense of, 60–61; purpose of, 85. *See also* Reciprocity; Transparency, trade.
Frenkel, Roberto, 233n80
Friedman, Milton, 132
Friends of the Earth, 237n50
Fujimori, Alberto, 178
Furs, *see* Hides
Furtado, Celso, 6, 25, 44–45, 48, 221n2, 225n53

Gallagher, John, 226n60
Garcia, Alan, 124, 178

Gardner, Richard, 2, 143–44
Gatos (labor contractors), 77
GATT (General Agreement on Tariffs and Trade), 3ff, 51, 140, 144, 162, 179f, 212–15, 247n27, 250n8; and Latin America, 8, 30, 108, 142, 154, 165, 171, 182; U.S. as orchestrator of, 10, 160, 164, 170; and Third World, 27, 71, 126, 242n35; and balance-of-payments problems, 66; accomplishments of, 145; subsidies code of, 145–46f, 166ff, 246nn8,10, 249n46; vs. bilateralism, 162, 248n34. *See also* Generalized System of Preferences; Uruguay Round
Geertz, Clifford, 102
General Agreement on Tariffs and Trade, *see* GATT
Generalized System of Preferences (GSP), 126, 144, 148, 153, 163, 166, 170, 175, 242n35
Germany, 37, 111, 114, 246n10
Gillis, Malcolm, 102
Global warming, deforestation and, 90
Gold, 77, 125, 226n62, 235n19
Good Neighbor policy, 27, 161
Gore, Albert, 238n63
Government, *see* State
Graham, Richard, 6, 17
Grain(s), 100, 103, 108, 113, 146f, 171, 193f, 202f, 205, 246
Gran Colombia, 68
Grande Carajás, 79
Great Britain, *see* Britain
Great Depression, 22–26, 29–30, 34, 37f, 49–50, 55, 59, 112, 114, 129, 199, 221n1, 225n46
"Green Revolution" (Mexico), 102
Griffin, Keith, 230n50, 253n46
Growth and Fluctuations (Lewis), 6
GSP, *see* Generalized System of Preferences
Guano, Peruvian, 19, 21, 36, 38, 46, 65
Guatemala, 14, 20, 26, 35, 68f, 75, 155, 185, 238n60, 247n32
Guayaquil, Ecuador, 19
Guyana, 47

Haiti, 20, 75, 120, 224n30, 238n60, 250n6

Hall, Anthony, 239n76
Hamilton, Alexander, 193
Harding, Warren G., 161
Hardwoods, 91, 237n49
Hathaway, Dale, 203
Hats (Ecuadoran export), 19, 125
Havana, Charter of, 27, 30
Hecht, Susanna, 102
Hegemonic stability thesis, 140
Helleiner, Gerald K., 64
Herfindahl index, 230n42
Hides, 29, 38, 91, 112f
Hilton, Stanley, 6
Hinton, Harold B., 226n62
Hirschman, Albert O., 6f, 31, 52, 57, 109, 127, 140ff, 161, 173, 176, 184, 187, 189, 197f, 209, 230n44; on international trade dependency, 110–12, 115, 120, 122, 135, 137
Hirschman test, 54
Hispaniola, *see* Dominican Republic; Haiti
Hofstader, Richard, 249n50
Holmer, Alan F., 248n40
Honduras, 20, 107, 117f, 155, 185
Hong Kong, 163
Hops, 175
Hotelling rule, 81
Hughes Aircraft Company, 166
Hull, Cordell, 23, 27, 161
Hunting, 80, 97
Hydroelectric energy, Brazil and, 100

ICA, *see* International Coffee Agreement
IDB (Inter-American Development Bank), 54–55, 122–23, 134, 139, 240n4, 241n23
IMF (International Monetary Fund), 7f, 44, 66, 73, 173, 206, 216, 228n10; and Brazil, 67, 171, 233n81, 249n53; and social issues, 67, 71, 233n85; and Latin America, 134, 171f, 177, 182
Imperialism, 108–9, 111, 169, 188, 191, 197. *See also* Colonialism
Imports, 40f, 59, 66, 116, 136, 196–97, 237n50, 241n23
Income redistribution, in Latin America, 57f, 230n50
India, 166, 180, 196
Indians, 21, 29, 31, 36, 38, 76f

Indigo, 38
Industrialization, 186; trade and, 7, 90; in Latin America, 49–50, 188, 198f; and development, 59; import-substitution, 123–24f, 177, 183, 193, 195, 199, 242n31; export-oriented, 179, 201; economic nationalism and, 182; state impetus to, 205, 211
Inflation, 64; in Latin America, 88, 105, 199, 238n56; in Brazil, 171, 174, 178, 207, 249n53
Informatics, Brazilian, 5, 171, 174–75, 197f, 206, 251n26
Inter-American Development Bank, *see* IDB
International Bank for Reconstruction and Development, *see* World Bank
International Bauxite Association, 46f
International Coffee Agreement (ICA), 94, 103, 148–51, 160, 202; and U.S. "war on drugs," 136, 244–45n61
International Coffee Organization, 46
Internationalism, 179–81f, 218, 239n77
International Labour Organization, 58
International Monetary Fund, *see* IMF
International Sugar Agreement, 94, 103
International Trade Commission, 3
International Trade Organization, 27, 30
International Tropical Timber Organization, *see* ITTO
Interventionism, state, 23, 225n46
Iraq, 238n63
Iron, 79, 83f, 90, 237n50. *See also* Steel
Irrigation, 81
Itáu Bank, 174
Itáutec, 174
ITTO (International Tropical Timber Organization), 71, 79, 233n3, 235n35, 237n50, 238n62

Jamaica, 47, 75, 120, 197
Japan, 164–66, 171, 179, 213; Latin American trade with, 37, 79, 91, 122, 155ff, 237n52, 238n62, 252n37; and Third World timber exploitation, 90, 235n35; U.S. and, 165, 170f, 180, 198; exports of, 244n56

Kemmerer, Edwin Walter, 154
Kennedy Round (GATT), 51

Keynes, John Maynard, 30, 168
Kindleberger, Charles, 48, 128, 227n84
Kohl, Helmut, 246n10
Kondratiev cycle, 232n73
Korea, Republic of, 163, 165
Kuczynski, Pedro-Pablo, 63
Kuznets curve, 34

Labor, international division of, 18–19, 23f, 30f, 45f, 56, 65, 91, 94, 113, 127, 143–44, 180, 188, 196, 199, 201, 207, 216, 218, 223n23, 247n30, 253n45
Labor unions, 22, 24ff, 181
LAIA (Latin American Integration Association), 152
Latex, 36
Latin America: exports of, 13f, 43–50, 55, 94f, 101, 120, 124ff, 127, 129, 135, 139ff, 147, 152f, 155, 165, 185, 188f, 194–203 *passim*, 209ff, 217, 231n60; imports of, 44, 50, 55, 59, 62, 64, 101f, 120, 123, 125f, 129, 135f, 139f, 147, 156f, 163, 167, 173, 180, 187ff, 191–93, 195, 201, 203, 211, 214, 231n60, 240n14; intraregional trade in, 68; economic patterns in, 93–94, 207; in international trade picture, 107–38; diversity of, 229–30n40
Latin American Debt (Kuczynski), 63
Latin American Integration Association (LAIA), 152
LDCs (less developed countries), 54, 126
Lenin, V.I., 253n51
Lewis, W. Arthur, 6f, 46f, 49, 55, 127, 202, 221n4, 228n2, 228n16, 229n20, 231n60, 232n73
Liberalism, *see* Economic liberalism
Licenses, trade-related, 61
LICs (low-income countries), 107
Lima, Peru, 18
Linseed, 114
Lipton, Michael, 230n50
List, Friedrich, 193
Livestock, *see* Beef, Latin American; Poultry
Lomé accords, 123, 144, 152, 169, 178, 198, 213, 249n52, 250n6
López Portillo, José, 124, 182, 201
Lumber, *see* Forests, Latin American

Luxuries, as Latin American imports, 113, 193, 226n62

MacDonald's restaurants, 91
McDonnell Douglas Corporation, 166
McNeeley, Jeffrey A., 86, 102, 238n62
Mahar, Dennis, 102
Mahogany, 75, 226n62
Maier, Charles, 2, 6, 52, 60, 231n56
Maize, *see* Corn
Manatees, 75
Manaus, 19
Mango, 39
Mangroves, 80
Manley, Michael, 197
Manufactures, Latin American, 188f, 201, 203, 241n25; Mexican, 121, 155, 172, 189, 241n25
Mapuche, 77
Maquiladoras, 47, 174, 199, 251n16, 252n37
Maranhão, state of, 90
Marichal, Carlos, 63, 225n50
Marijuana, as export crop, 160
Marshall Plan, 154
Marx, Karl, 34
Marxism, 54, 230n45, 231n57
Meat Trusts, Argentinian, 22
Meier, Gerald M., 53
Menem, Carlos, 178
Mercury, 76, 116
Mesoamerica, *see* Central America
Mexico, 20f, 25, 45, 224n33, 250n1; economic patterns in, 4, 19, 23, 69, 80, 93, 100–102, 104, 115, 207, 210, 229n31, 248n35, 250n4; internal problems of, 5, 104f, 174; U.S. pharmaceuticals industry and, 5, 166, 171, 206, 254n62; U.S. and, 5, 31, 36, 103, 121, 124, 152ff, 162, 164, 170–80 *passim*, 186, 198, 212, 215, 228n7, 229n31, 237nn45,52, 245n3, 247n27, 249n54, 250n5, 252n37, 254nn62,63; trade patterns in, 17, 120, 155, 160, 181f, 189, 199, 202f, 228n7, 244n58, 252n37; foreign influences on, 21, 229n24, 249n46; political patterns in, 23f, 143, 173, 183f, 187; food security in, 34, 147, 198; industrialization of, 49, 163, 186, 195; imports of, 68, 146f, 152, 174, 199, 201, 212; deforestation in, 77–78, 91; exports of, 80, 99, 121, 172, 199–201, 212, 237n45, 241n25; agriculture in, 95, 102, 135, 155, 238n60; privatization in, 134–35, 209. *See also* De la Madrid, Miguel; López Portillo, José; Salinas de Gortari, Carlos
Mexico and the United States in the Oil Controversy (Meyer), 6
Meyer, Lorenzo, 6
Michoacán, state of, 78
Militarism, 193–94
Minerals, 124, 197, 203. *See also* Mining
Mining, 17f, 70, 78f, 95. *See also individual ores by name*
Mita, 76
Money Doctor in the Andes (Drake), 6
Monopolies, 21f. *See also* Cartels
Monroe Doctrine, 161
Morawetz, David, 47, 52f
Morris, Cynthia Taft, 58
Morrow, Dwight, 154
Mosquito Coast, 39, 75
Mosquito Indians, 75
Multi-Fibre Agreement, 175
Multilateralism, 143–54
Mutton, 113, 226n62
Myrdal, Gunnar, 33, 57
"Myth of the Happy Yeoman, The" (Hofstader), 249n50

Nationalism, *see* Economic nationalism
Nationalization, 23, 194, 251n27
National Power and the Structure of Foreign Trade (Hirschman), 6f, 52, 109f
National security, 166, 193f; U.S. focus on, 135–36, 160–61, 164ff, 185, 193, 197, 244n60; Brazil and, 174, 193–94f; trade and, 193–95
Natural resources, 194, 215; exploitation of Latin American, 70–106 *passim*, 135–37, 188, 214; public policy and, 84–87, 103–5. *See also* Conservation; Environmentalism
New Deal, 8
Nicaragua, 20, 38, 69, 133, 155, 165f, 227n89. *See also* Zelaya, José Santos
NICs (newly industrialized countries), 107
Nitrates, 18ff, 21, 35f, 65, 232n72

Nuclear power, Brazil and, 100, 194f
Nurkse, Ragnar, 32
Nutmeg, 39

OAS (Organization of American States), 247n24
O'Donnell, Guillermo, 233n80
OECD (Organization for Economic Cooperation and Development), 1, 12, 14, 26f, 71f, 74, 94, 126, 139f, 148, 156; agricultural policies of, 84, 146f, 164; and Latin America, 91, 162, 177, 179f, 189, 196f, 213, 215, 218; and regionalism, 142, 145; and GATT, 165, 248n34
Oil: Mexican, 8, 21, 34, 83, 104, 120, 124, 135, 147, 154, 166, 172, 174, 177f, 194, 199–201, 205, 212, 237n52, 250n5, 251n27, 254n3; Arab, 30, 249n53; Peruvian, 36, 154; Latin American, 47, 70, 80f, 86, 93, 100, 117, 125, 139f, 199; Brazilian, 83, 104; Ecuadoran, 85, 99, 120, 125; Venezuelan, 120, 152, 177f, 186
Oilseeds, 108
Omnibus Trade and Competitiveness Act of 1988, U.S., 165, 248n40
Onganía, Juan Carlos, 133
OPEC (Organization of Petroleum Exporting Countries), 46, 166, 229n24
Organization for Economic Cooperation and Development, *see* OECD
Organization of American States (OAS), 247n24
Organization of Petroleum Exporting Countries (OPEC), 46, 166, 229n24
O'riordan, Timothy, 237n46

Pampas, 18, 21
Panama, 120
Panama Canal, 36, 161
Panic of 1873, 37
Paper, manufacture of, 90f
Paraguay, 113, 117, 120
Parcelación, 235n34
Patents, protection of, 8
Patronage, political, 66
Patterns of Development in Latin America (Sheahan), 52, 227n84
PEMEX, 86, 205

Pepper, Cayenne, 39
Perón, Isabel, 132
Perón, Juan, 23f, 182, 187, 189, 240n9
Peru, 5, 8, 14, 21, 76, 79, 135, 178, 233n79, 238n60; trade patterns in, 17, 120, 127, 184, 191, 201; neighbors of, 18, 31, 36, 191; economic patterns in, 19, 65, 178, 185, 207, 209f, 248n35; political patterns in, 24, 75, 133, 173, 183f, 251n12; Chile and, 31, 36, 127, 191; exports of, 36, 99, 201, 209f; industrialization of, 49, 186; and U.S., 124, 154. *See also* Lima
Petroleum, *see* Oil
Pharmaceuticals industry, 5, 166, 171, 206, 254n62
Philippines, 90
Pinochet, Augusto, 125, 132f, 182, 201, 233n83, 243n50
Pioneers in Development (Meier/Seers [eds.]), 6, 52
Platt, D. C. M., 226n60
Political economy, 60, 231n57; defined, 2, 231n56
Politics of Brazilian Development (Wirth), 6
Pollution, 86, 90
Popular Unity Party (Chile), 182
Populism, 24, 26, 197; in Latin America, 25, 177, 179, 181, 183, 186, 197, 214; vs. free trade, 30; economic nationalism and, 62
Portugal, 16, 36, 213, 222n15; Brazil and, 13, 68, 76, 112, 127
Poultry, 100, 108, 155
Poverty, 66, 85, 107, 127; in Latin America, 7, 10, 28, 51f, 57f, 69, 71ff, 82, 106, 136f, 217, 226n62, 230n50; resources and, 73, 81, 89, 102, 105f; food subsidies and, 147–48; property and, 203, 253n46
Prebisch, Raul, 14, 48, 57, 188, 221n4, 222n7, 226n71; thesis of, 24, 31–32, 169
Privatization: in Latin America, 7, 84, 134–35, 178, 181, 183, 216; ideological zeal for, 42, 134, 137, 170; in Mexico, 105, 177, 216; and resource exploitation, 106; economic recovery and, 207

Production: functions of, 32–33, 227n76; import-connectedness of, 197

Programa Nacional de Alimentación, 102

Protectionism: in Latin America, 14, 17, 62, 64, 129; U.S., 135, 156f, 165–67, 170, 173f, 210, 214. *See also* Rents; Tariffs

Public choice theory, 240nn8,11

Puerto Rico, 36, 123

Quito, 19

Quotas: U.S. sugar, 123, 148, 160, 165f, 174, 179; U.S. apparel, 160; on coffee, 245n61

Railroads, Latin American, 20–21, 78

Rain forests, Brazilian, 80, 82f, 90f, 238n63. *See also* Natural resources

Reagan, Ronald, 3, 15, 125, 156

Recasting Bourgeois Europe (Maier), 2, 6

Recession, 64, 67, 93, 125, 139f, 157, 213

Reciprocity, 125–26, 173, 215, 242n35, 249n47

Redclift, Michael, 58

Regionalism, global, 140, 142

Rents: domestic-production-related, 83, 126, 236n43; scarcity, 244n56

Repetto, Robert, 102, 236n40

Revolutionary War, American, 16, 29

Revolution on the Pampas (Scobie), 6

Reynolds, Clark, 231n61

Rio de Janeiro, 19, 233n81

Rio de la Plata, 75

Robinson, Ronald, 226n60

Roca-Runciman pact, 114

Roosevelt, Franklin D., 26, 161

Roosevelt, Theodore, 153, 161

Rosas, Juan Manuel de, 17

Rosecrance, Richard, 35

Rostow, W. W., 241n18

Rubber, 19, 35–39 *passim*, 46, 205, 234n19, 241n17

Salinas de Gortari, Carlos 102, 172f, 177f, 182, 187, 215, 229n31

Sanctions, U.S. trade, 165f

Sandino, Augusto Cesar, 227n89

Santiago, Chile, 18–19

São Paulo, 19, 21, 25

Sarney, José, 251n26

Savings and loan industry, U.S., 168

Schelling, Thomas, 231n56

Schoultz, Lars, 160

Scientific American, 234n7

Scobie, James, 6

Sea turtles, 75

Security, *see* National security

Seers, Dudley, 51

Segerson, Kathleen, 236n44

Sheahan, John, 52, 133, 227n84, 244n58, 250n9

Sheridan, Philip, 82

Shoes, *see* Footwear

Shrimp, 80, 93, 135

Silver, 38, 75f, 116, 226n62

Singapore, 163

Singer, Hans, 57

Sistema Alimentario Mexicano, 147

Skins, *see* Hides

Slaves, Portuguese, 76

Smith, William C., 114, 243n48

Smoot-Hawley Tariff, 25

Smuggling, 75, 79

Socialism, 165, 230n47, 243n43. *See also* Marxism

Somoza, Anastasio, 185

Sorghum, 155

South Korea, *see* Korea, Republic of

Soya, 84, 146, 155, 196

Spain, 16, 27, 36, 68, 75, 112, 123, 213

Stabilization, economic, 238n56; and the poor, 6; IMF-supervised, 67, 206; in Latin America, 88, 105, 201, 238n56; and resource use, 88, 89; income and, 101; adjustment and, 157–60, 175; exchange-rate, 186

Stages of Economic Growth (Rostow), 241n18

Stallings, Barbara, 63–65, 122, 233n79

Staniland, Martin, 240n8

State: trade and the, 14, 43–44, 56, 62, 185–86, 203–11, 216, 230n47, 250–51n9; "high" vs. "low," 131–33

Steel, 62, 155, 165, 193; Brazilian, 83, 108, 165, 171, 196, 237n45; Mexican, 165, 171, 196

Sterling-Dollar Diplomacy (Gardner), 2

Stewart, Frances, 58
Strange, Susan, 140–41
Streeten, Paul, 6, 53–54
Subsidization, 66, 104, 237n45
Sugar: Latin American, 19, 21, 35, 38, 78, 94, 125, 135, 148, 176, 202; Cuban, 36, 123, 128, 143n44; Brazilian, 76f, 100, 107–8, 135, 148, 195, 232n72; Caribbean, 99, 108, 174; U.S. quotas on, 123, 148, 160, 165f, 174, 179
Super 301, 165–66f, 215, 248n40
Supply, inelasticity of, 44–48
Suriname, 47
Surplus capacity thesis, 140
Sustainability, of economic growth/development, 58, 67, 83, 88, 160, 180, 230n54, 237nn46,53; environmental, 83, 137; politics of, 87, 218; nationalism and, 106
Swidden agriculture, 77, 103

Taft, William Howard, 153
Taiwan, *see* China
Tariffs, 24, 60f, 126, 133–34, 236n43. *See also* Duties, countervailing; Protectionism
Tavares Bastos, Aureliano Candido, 223n21
Tax reform, in Latin America, 63
Tercermundismo, 26
Terms of trade, 14–15, 45, 48, 50, 52, 55, 64f, 169, 184, 228n15, 232n73; openness and, 115, 186–87, 241n24; export vulnerability and, 116
Texas, 102, 239n76
Textiles, 14, 113, 174
Third World, 53, 57, 89, 127, 179; Latin America as, 32, 47, 95, 122, 162; environmental abuses in, 71, 90; pressures on, 126, 179, 206, 213, 230n45, 242n35; food sufficiency in, 146–47, 193; EEC and, 213
Thoreau, Henry, 29
Thorp, Rosemary, 41, 50, 240n14
Tin, 94, 202; Bolivian, 95, 99, 105, 198
Tobacco, 38, 46
Tokyo Accords, 249n46
Tokyo Round (GATT), 51, 145
Tomatoes, 77

Topik, Steven, 225n46
Toronto Economic Summit, 234n4
Trade, 1–2; growth/development and, 2, 6–52 *passim*; benefits of, 5, 50, 56, 141; political terms of, 9, 60–62, 177–211; debt and, 63–67; international aspects of Latin American, 107–38; national power and international, 109–12, 115–38; economic openness and, 115–16; diversification of, 121–25, 242n26; U.S.–Latin American, 139–76; intraregional, 148–53, 189–91. *See also* Exports; Imports; Terms of trade
Trade Act of 1974, U.S., 164
Trade Act of 1985, U.S. 237n45
Trade and Development, U.N. Conference on, 71
Trade politics, 2–5
Trade Representative, Office of U.S., *see* UNCTAD
Trade unions, *see* Labor unions
Transparency, trade, 164, 170, 248n38, 249n47
Treasury, U.S. Dept. of, 67, 233n85
Trees, *see* Forests, Latin American
Twenty-Five Years of Economic Development (Morawetz), 52

Ubico, Jorge, 26, 37
UNCTAD (U.N. Conference on Trade and Development), 71, 142, 215; and trade preference agreements, 153; U.S. vs., 162
Unemployment, in Latin America, 66, 82, 105
Union of Banana Exporting Countries (UPEB), 46
Unions, *see* Labor unions
United Alkali Company, 22
United Fruit Company, 20, 47, 77, 247n32
United Nations, 71. *See also* ECLA
United Nations Conference on Trade and Development, *see* UNCTAD
United States, 29, 56, 166, 173, 206, 216; Europe and, 5, 170; and Mexico, 5, 31, 36, 103, 121, 124, 152ff, 162, 164, 170–80 *passim*, 186, 198, 212, 215, 228n7, 229n31, 237nn45,52,

United States (*cont.*)
  245n3, 247n27, 249n54, 250n5,
  252n37, 254nn62,63; and Latin
  America, 10, 18, 23–37 *passim*, 68,
  87, 97, 103, 110ff, 120–28 *passim*,
  135–38, 153–56, 160–64, 176, 181–
  83, 187, 189, 198–99, 207, 210–16,
  218, 244n60, 253n61; and Dominican
  Republic, 20, 164, 224n30; and
  Guatemala, 20, 155, 247n32; gunboat
  diplomacy of, 20, 153; and Nicaragua,
  20, 133, 155, 165f, 227n89; and
  Cuba, 36, 121, 164ff; trade considerations of, 73, 94, 111, 135, 170,
  241n17; agricultural policy of, 84,
  103, 146, 167–68; and Brazil, 90,
  108, 124, 154, 163, 166, 170–72,
  180, 198, 212–13, 215; and Argentina, 114, 154; and Chile, 124, 154,
  166; and Peru, 124, 154, 233n79; decline of, 141ff, 156, 162, 173, 176,
  179, 183, 210f, 253n61; and Colombia, 154; and Central America, 155,
  162, 164; and EEC, 156, 163, 165,
  171; and OECD, 156; exports of, 157,
  163, 170ff, 174, 187, 212; imports of,
  157, 163, 170, 172f, 209f
UPEB (Union of Banana Exporting
  Countries), 46
Upper Peru, *see* Bolivia
Uranium, Brazilian, 194
Uruguay, 24, 45, 88, 120, 146
Uruguay Round (GATT), 1, 44, 71, 142,
  145–46f, 152, 168, 213, 245n6
USAID (Agency for International Development, U.S.), 235n33
U.S. Steel, 21

Valdivia, Pedro de, 77
Valorization, Brazilian coffee and, 19, 46,
  205, 225n46, 232n72
Vargas, Getúlio, 24, 26, 37, 194

Vargas Llosa, Mario, 13, 16
Venezuela, 46, 186, 249n54; economic
  patterns in, 63, 248n35; trade patterns
  in, 120, 152
Versailles, Treaty of, 168
Videla, Jorge, 133
Viola, Roberto, 133
Voluntary restraint agreements (VRAs),
  165, 171

Wages: under austerity programs, 66; in
  Mexico, 68
"War of the Thousand Days," 222n13
Water: misuse of, 89, 102; user competi-
  tion for, 90
Wendy's restaurants, 91
West Coast Conference, 224n32
Whalley, John, 232n69
Wheat, 68, 112, 114, 155, 226n62
Wilson, Woodrow, 153, 161
Wine, Chilean, 196
Wirth, John, 6
Wolf, Eric, 29
Wool, 112ff, 226n62
World Bank, 7, 44, 54, 134, 169, 172f;
  and social issues, 67, 233n85; environ-
  mental concerns of, 71, 73, 102; and
  privatization, 206, 216
World Climate Conference, 215
World Climate Trust Fund, 215
World Commission on Environment and
  Development, 71f, 234n4
World War, I, 37, 49, 223n23, 232n72
World War II, 23, 25–26, 34–35, 59,
  154

Yanomami, 77, 234–35n19
Yeutter, Clayton, 167
Yrigoyen, Hipólito, 114
Yucatán Peninsula, 75, 77

Zelaya, José Santos, 20, 38, 187

Library of Congress Cataloging-in-Publication Data

Sanderson, Steven E.
  The politics of trade in Latin American development / Steven E.
Sanderson.
    p.   cm.
Includes bibliographical references (p.   ) and index.
ISBN 0-8047-1983-7 (cloth : alk. paper) :
ISBN 0-8047-2021-5 (paper : alk. paper) :
1. Latin America—Commercial policy.   2. Latin America—Economic
policy.   I. Title.
HF1480.5.S33   1992
382'.3'098—dc20
91-39863
    CIP

⊗ This book is printed on acid-free paper. It has been typeset
in 10/12 Sabon by Keystone Typesetting, Inc.